NASHVILLE RADIO

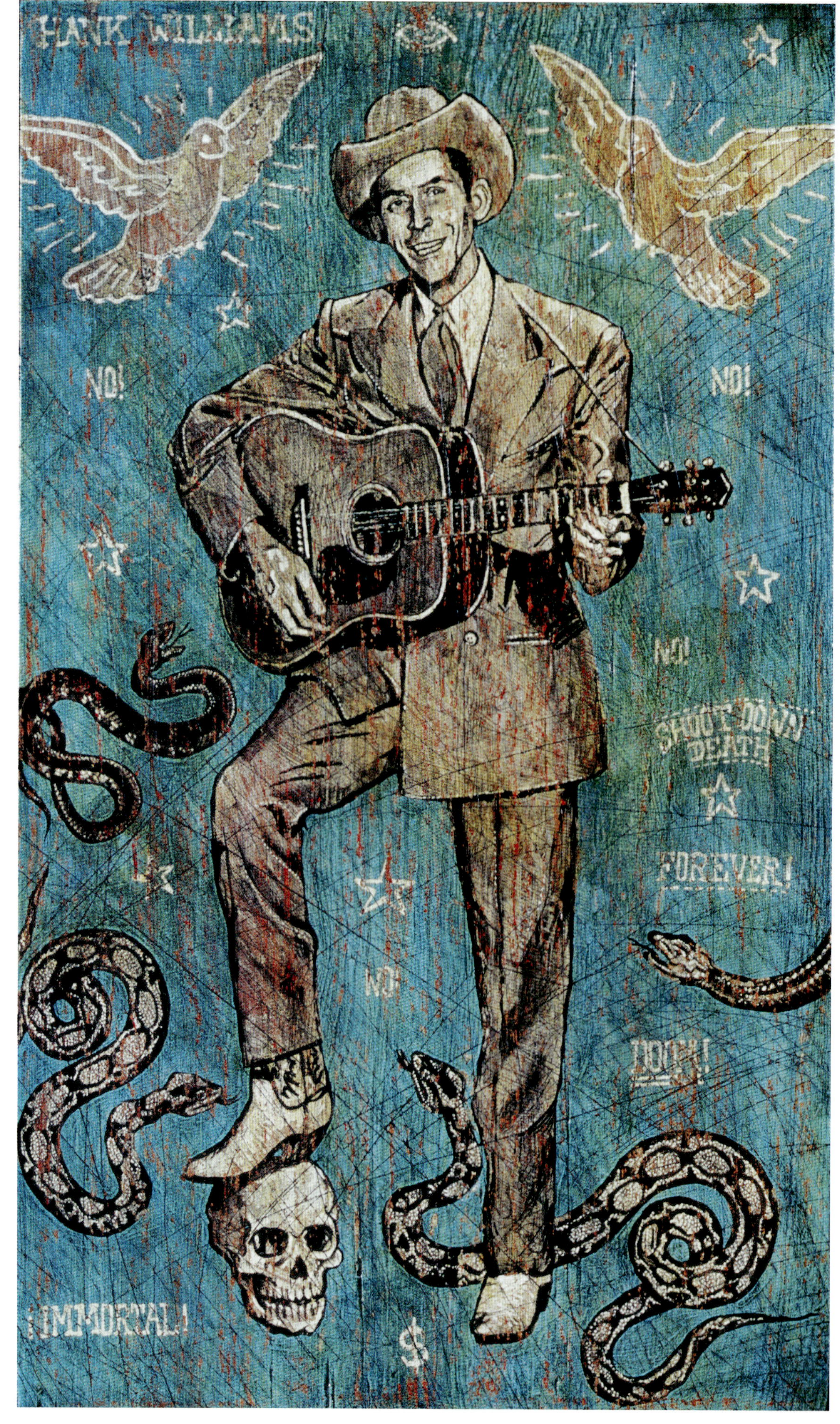

HANK WILLIAMS
$
NO!
NO!
NO!
SHOOT DOWN DEATH
FOREVER!
NO!
NO!!!
¡IMMORTAL!
$

Nashville Radio
Jon Langford

Verse Chorus Press ➡ Portland London Melbourne

For Kevin Coyne

For information please write to:
Verse Chorus Press
PO Box 14806, Portland OR 97293
info@versechorus.com

Editing & design: Steve Connell, Kathryn Juergens
Color guy: Scott Nasburg

Printed in China by C&C Offset Printing Co., Ltd.
CD manufactured in China.

ISBN: 1-891241-19-2

Library of Congress Control Number: 2005937011

FIRST EDITION

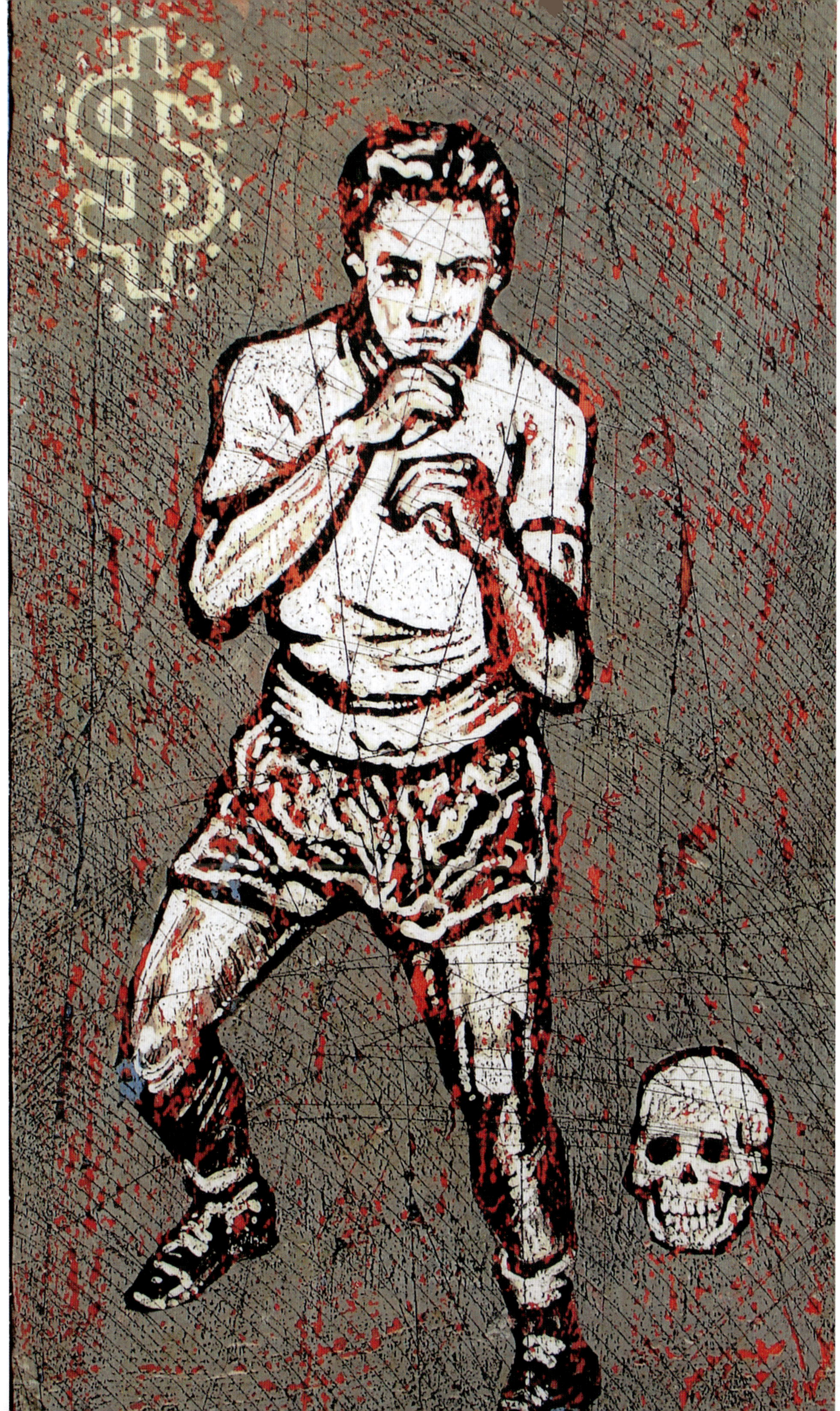

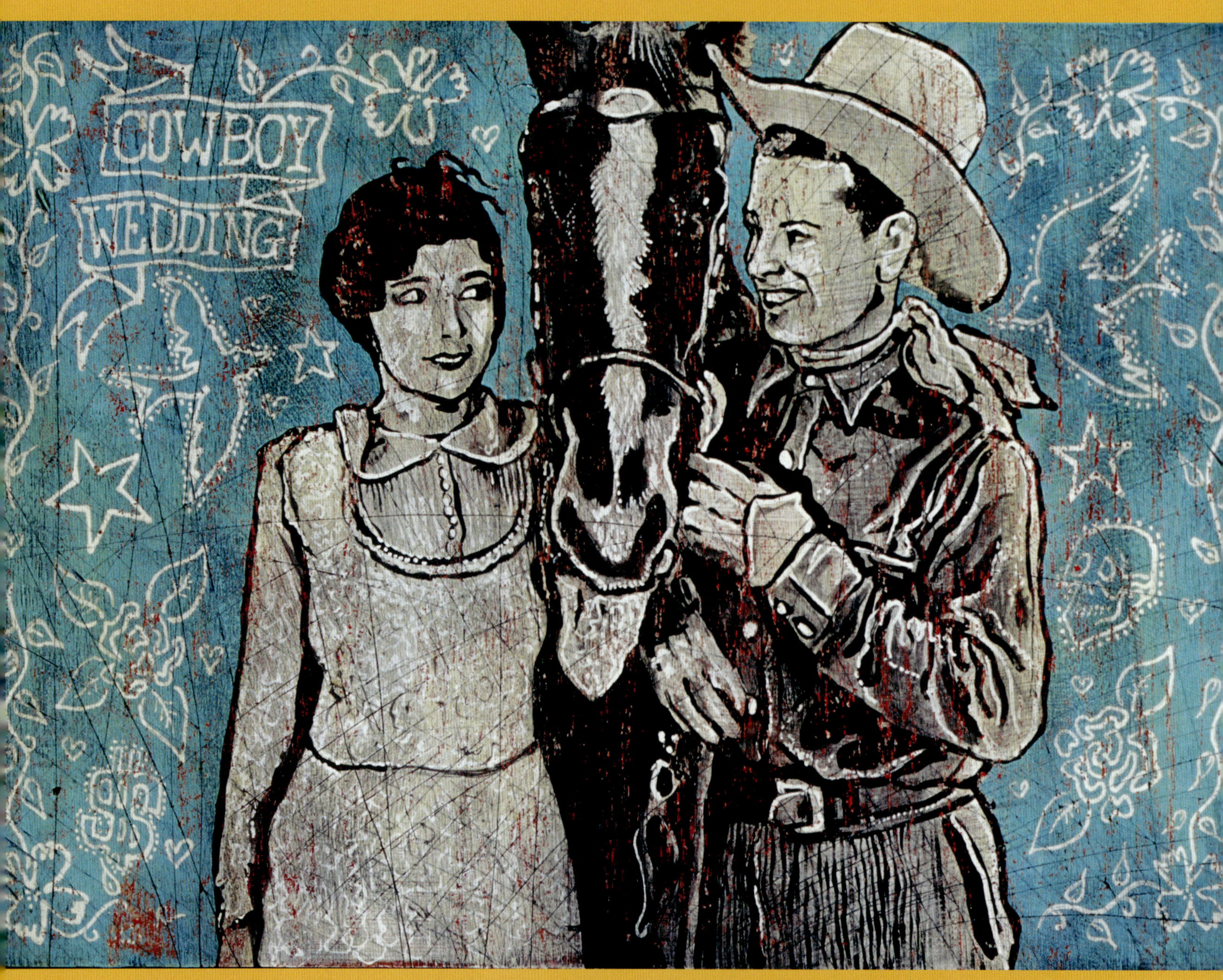
COWBOY
WEDDING

WE KNOW THAT FOR MANY YEARS THERE'S BEEN NO COUNTRY HERE

In August of 1998, the indefatigable Welsh painter, punk-rocker, activist, cartoonist and raconteur Jon Langford braved the belly of the beast by bringing a traveling exhibit of his work called THE DEATH OF COUNTRY MUSIC to Nashville. However daunting it might have been, scheduling a stop in the Country Music Capital of the World—and at a time when the "Hot New Country" of Garth and Shania was still very much in the ascendant—could hardly have been more apt, or prophetic. The location of the show—a midtown gallery just three blocks off Music Row, the epicenter of the country music industry since the 1950s—was equally fitting.

Much of the art consisted of Jon's sullied, scratched-up portraits of Patsy Cline, Johnny Cash, Tammy Wynette, and other Nashville legends—most of them dead. Jon had shown work in this vein before, but not the tombstones that formed the backbone of the exhibit, a dozen or so 135-pound slabs of cold chiseled granite mourning the death of country music. One of the stones, monolithically titled *Country Music*, portrayed Hank Williams as the 3rd century martyr Saint Sebastian. Engraved alongside the image of the singer, his protruding ribcage pierced with arrows, was an epitaph taken from the opening lines of one of Jon's songs: "The bones of country music / Lie there in their casket / Beneath the towers of Nashville / In a deep black pool of neglect." Another headstone, *Hank Williams Signs His Contract*, cast the honky-tonker, pen in hand, seated at a desk strewn with whiskey and pill bottles. A skull loomed ominously in the foreground.

The point of Jon's exhibit, as heavy-handed and incisive as the pieces themselves—and as full of the humor and humanity that galvanize everything he does—was that Nashville had buried its past. That the country music industry had forsaken its roots

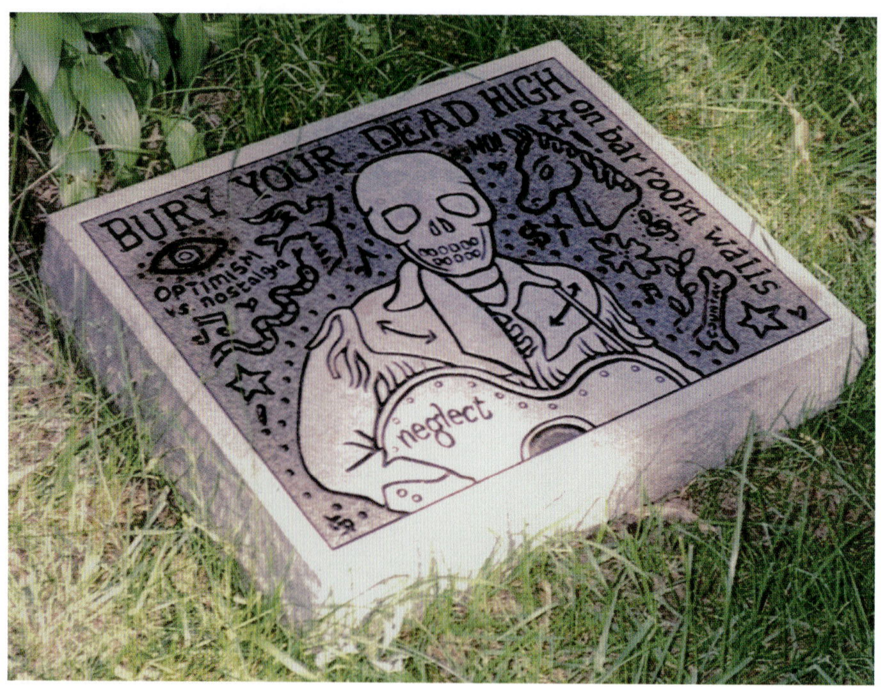

for what Jon, alluding to the likes of Tim McGraw and Kenny Chesney, called "suburban rock music with a cowboy hat on." It certainly gave new meaning to the line, "We know that for many years there's been no country here" from *Country*, the fiddle-charged roar about feeling like an exile in one's homeland that opens 1985's FEAR AND WHISKEY, the epochal country-punk salvo from Jon's longstanding band the Mekons.

Jon originally considered placing his tombstones outside the record company offices along Music Row, then sponsoring a bus tour and making a film about the installation as a piece of guerilla art. In the end he figured that the fact that the monuments existed was enough. He also released an EP called GRAVESTONE to amplify the exhibit. The disc's centerpiece, a lament titled *Nashville Radio*, is a reggae-inflected adaptation of the tune to *Rocky Top* in which Jon inhabits the ghost of Hank Williams: "I gave my life to country music / I took my pills and lost / Now they don't play my songs on the radio / It's like I never was."

This sense of spiritual and moral abandonment pervades all of Jon's gravestones. One of them, inscribed "Bury your dead high on bar room walls," depicts a wraith-like figure in a fringed Western shirt. His head is a skull, which stares blankly forward, and he holds a guitar etched with the word NEGLECT. The inspiration for this stone, as for many of Jon's paintings of musicians, comes from the accidental collages of defaced publicity stills of country singers that cover the walls of Tootsie's Orchid Lounge on Nashville's Lower Broad. Time was that Tootsie's, whose backdoor is just across the alley from the Ryman Auditorium, functioned as the de facto backstage for the Grand Ole Opry; its cast members used to duck into the bar for a snort or two between sets. That was before the venerable radio show headed for the suburbs in 1973, and right about the time that country music itself went suburban.

Jon didn't see the walls of Tootsie's until 1988, when he came to town to promote 'TIL THINGS ARE BRIGHTER, the Johnny Cash tribute/AIDS benefit LP that he produced with Marc Riley. "I went to Tootsie's and saw all those pictures—photos of singers I knew of and singers I'd never heard of staring out from layers of historical snot and dripping with nicotine juice," he told me a decade later. "They were all torn, but they were smiling out hopefully." Jon subsequently began scuffing up his portraits of country singers in homage to the disfigured photos at Tootsie's. "After I finish them," he said, "they have to be scratched up. Sometimes I'll actually throw an etching plate across the floor so that rather than being this pure blank sheet I'm working on, it'll have interference and noise on it. And that's what kind of happens with my paintings. They're not really old, but they do look distressed."

None of Jon's pieces glibly romanticizes the darker side of country music or comes off as kitsch the way that so many dispatches from the alt-country margins do. His sense of humor certainly helps (Hank Williams a martyr?). Just as crucially—and in sharp contrast to today's country music industry, whose big award shows ignored the terrific album Loretta Lynn recently made with Jack White of the White Stripes just because it didn't receive mainstream airplay—Jon doesn't treat the likes of Johnny Cash and George Jones as museum pieces. It's a sensibility, at least as far as his country subjects go, that harks back to the mid-1980s, when the Mekons, the visionary, first-generation punk band that Jon co-founded, reconstituted themselves as a post-apocalyptic hillbilly band.

"We're listening to the country boys and dancing on their graves," Jon exults in *Ugly Band*, an implosive two-step from the Mekons' 1986 album THE EDGE OF THE WORLD. In the album's helter-skelter deconstruction of Hank Williams' *Alone and Forsaken*, fiddle player Suzie Honeyman takes the ethic of *Ugly Band* to the extreme, superimposing her version of the sinister viola ostinato from the Velvet Underground's *Black Angel's*

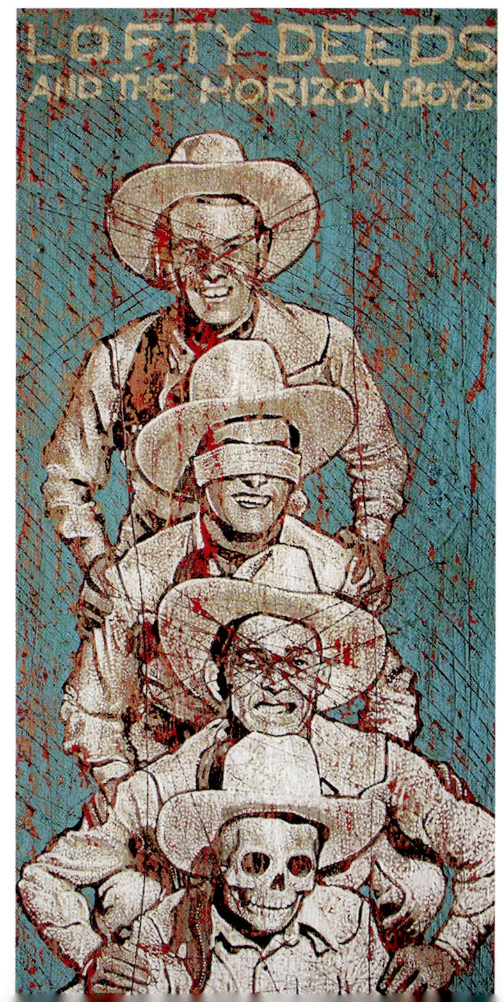

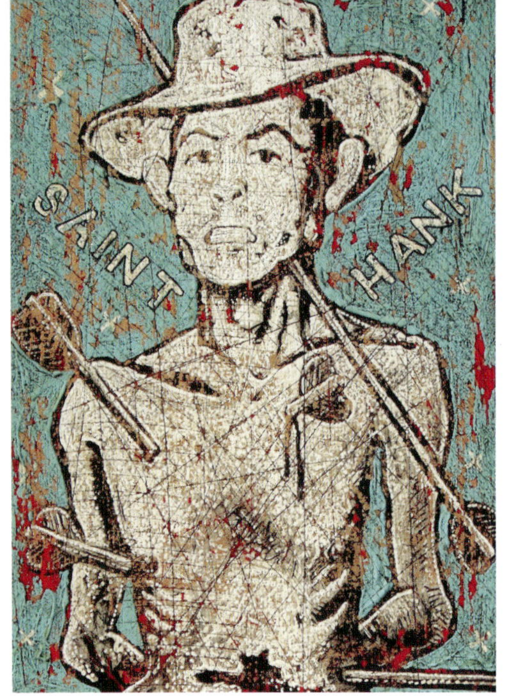

Death Song over a lurching waltz-time cadence. The Mekons were bent on having their way with their beloved honky-tonk, even if they had to raise it from the dead. Not only that—by coming to the music from outside its native culture, they played much the same role that de Tocqueville did with respect to democracy, shining a light on an American treasure that its caretakers had let fall into disrepair. And where the U.S. is concerned, both Jon's artwork and his recordings with his barnstorming alt-country detachment the Waco Brothers borrow a page from de Tocqueville's notebook—or at least from that of some dream combination of H.L. Mencken and Thomas Pynchon—steadfastly taking his adopted homeland to task for all manner of hypocrisy and bad faith. Maybe nowhere are these indictments more persistent than in Jon's ubiquitous portraits of cowboys who, in image after image, appear blindfolded, brandishing big irons and vacant smiles as they blithely wage wars hot and cold, almost always as a death's head looks knowingly on.

Jon's renderings of astronauts are but an extension of his heedless gunslingers—imperialist space cowboys riding roughshod over the wide open spaces of the galaxy. "I saw a brighter future coming / The winners of the human race / Floating weightless up in space / Above the poor and the heavy and the doomed," he sings in *Sputnik 57*. A solo recording from 2004, *Sputnik 57* (the 57 is an allusion to the year Jon was born and the first Sputnik was launched) conveys the hope and subsequent betrayal that Jon felt as a boy when he pinned his dreams for a better world on the exploration of space. The image that he painted for the cover of 2002's MAYORS OF THE MOON, a collaboration with the Toronto surf-tonk band the Sadies, depicts Jon's head as the moon, with a missile or spacecraft piercing the crater of his right eye. "Not too big on the sharing, the gentle or the caring," Jon bemoans in a later solo recording, dolefully rolling his r's as he likens the U.S. and its quest for dominion over everything, even the heavens, to a spoiled child. "So big and so clumsy," he goes on sardonically. "You'd better wipe its fat ass & buy it some toys . . . / It's gonna . . . feed on itself to set us all free / Not too big on the caring, the gentle or the sharing / But still so much fun—the country is young."

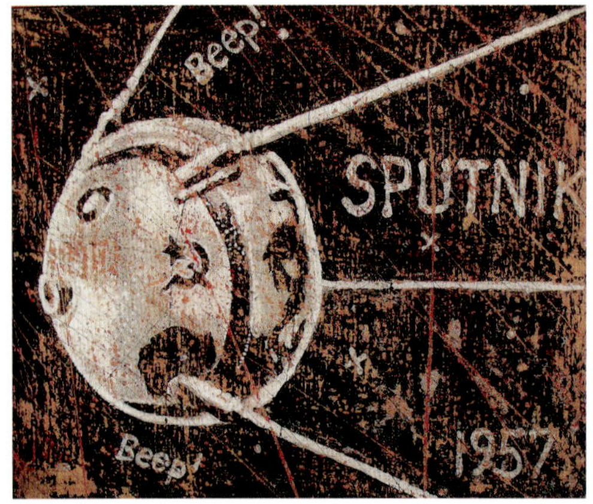

All of which is to say that the Mekons' rebirth as a slantwise country band made abundant sense (as has Jon's ongoing revivification of honky-tonk, rockabilly and Western swing with the Wacos and with his paintings, writings and cartoons). Never the garden variety épater les bourgeois of your average Sex Pistols clone, the Mekons' ethic of resistance and that of Jon's other undertakings has always displayed the resiliency inherent in the best country music. Though often dismissed as fatalistic, country music's plainspoken exhortations to walk the line and to keep the circle unbroken are steeped in a hard-won and class-conscious realism that prides itself on not giving in to what one might be up against. These values might be veiled, or conveyed between the lines, and their links to a conservative-leaning populism might be worlds away from the Mekons' leftist radicalism, but an overriding commitment to struggle and resistance remains. To their considerable credit, Jon and the Mekons were farsighted enough, and averse enough to elitism, to embrace country music and re-make it in their own anarchic image. That they would do so with much the same amateurist verve with which they blurted out their impossibly crude late-'70s singles *Never Been in a Riot* and *Where Were You?* just made it that much more enthralling.

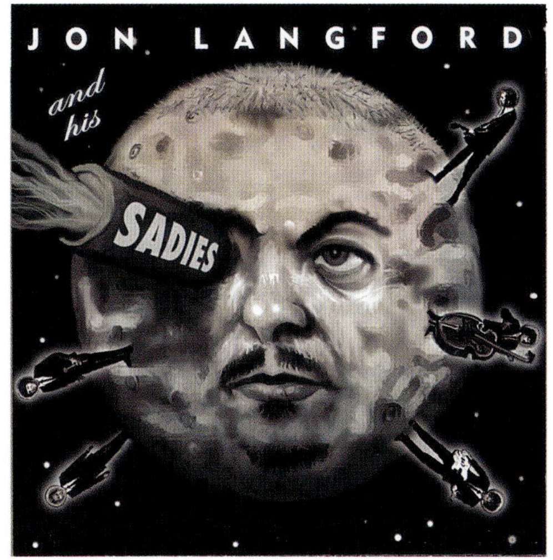

No doubt country music's frequent witness to people driven to drink by their circumstances also resonated with the famously snake-bitten—and sodden—Mekons. Given the class war being waged by the right-wing Thatcher governments of the 1980s, as well as the then not-so-covert Third World treachery of the U.S. military and C.I.A., sometimes, as Mekon Tom Greenhalgh coarsely croons in *Chivalry*, only fear and whiskey keep you going. Or cat food, as Jon howls, interpolating Raymond Chandler, in *Big Zombie* (a.k.a. *I'm Just Not Human Tonight*). Yet whether fortified by Bushmill's or Friskies, Jon and the Mekons always seem to find ways to keep going, and the resolution that they tap from country music fuels that drive as much as fear and whiskey. "Zip your suits, take your pills, secure full masks," one of them barks into a walkie-talkie in *Trouble Down South* as tom-toms burst like anti-aircraft fire and shards of guitar noise go off like air-raid sirens in the background. Even after walking through barbed wire, stepping over broken bodies and sinking in the mud, Greenhalgh still manages to issue the challenge, "Come on, cruel world / Show me what you've got." Likewise Jon's cover art for MAYORS OF THE MOON. As much a self-portrait as a portrayal of our imperiled planet, the image not only has Jon withstanding a rocket as it flames out in his eye socket, it shows his globular mug holding up the rest of the world, including his collaborators the Sadies, who are perched precariously (as the Mekons so frequently have been) on the edge of the world.

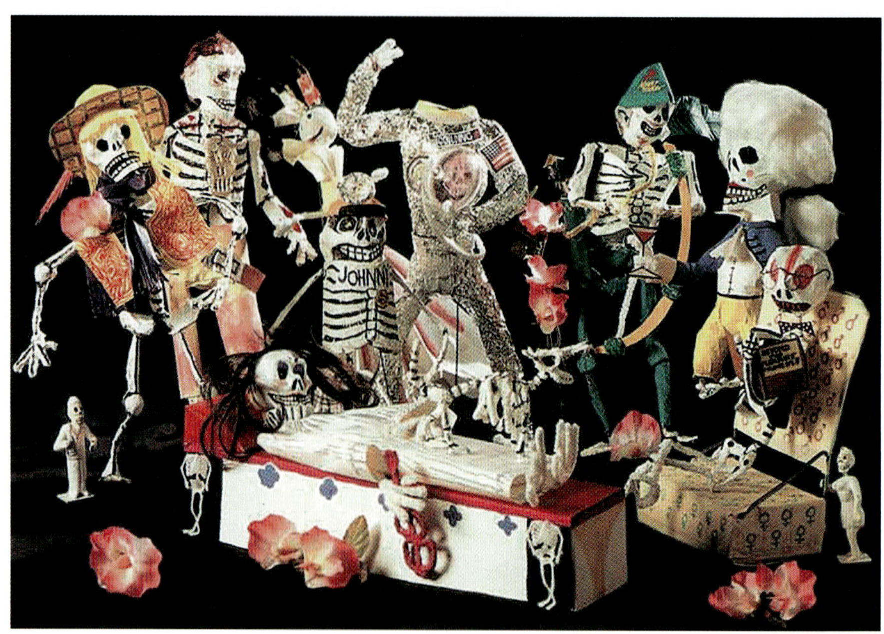

These scenes from the front are more than just vivid backdrops for heady artwork and music. They document, in often surreal fashion, actual wars being fought on the underside of history, whether from under the oppressive heels of Reagan and Thatcher or, as is now the case, from under those of Bush and Blair. In *Ugly Band* a "dance band on the edge of time" that cannily resembles the Mekons is holed up in a bunker beneath the surface of a world "distorted by greed." Bracing for Armageddon, they are "tired of their music and licking their teeth." They aren't weary of the song that they are playing, though. They are sick of the bitter music of the "vile child freedom," the brat who was weaned on social policies that fill homeless shelters and prisons and who grows up to be a global bully. They are sick of the freedom, as the Mekons sang in their early single *32 Weeks*, to work seven-and-a-half months at a drudge's wage to be able to afford a refrigerator. They are sick of the freedom that gives some nations the license to invade or bomb other countries and to see it as something other than terrorism. They are sick, as Jon's three musical installments of THE EXECUTIONER'S LAST SONGS so vehemently protest, of the freedom that some states exercise by executing people who kill people to prove that killing people is wrong.

This recent effort is an outgrowth of Jon's work on behalf of the Illinois Death Penalty Moratorium Project. The death-song compilations he masterminded bring together his art and his extended musical family to support the abolition of capital punishment in his adopted home state—but they go on to unmask how becoming accustomed to death erodes the human spirit and is ultimately as deadly as state-sanctioned killing. Jon even asserts that death has become "sown into the fabric of our lives" in *Dollar Dress*, a recording that he made with the Wacos in 1997. In the artwork inspired by the song (or maybe vice versa), a woman dances gaily as her partner swings her around the dance floor. Superimposed just below the couple's knees, as if cutting their feet out from under them, is the question, "Can you prove you're alive?" In this case Jon needed neither blindfolds nor smirking death's heads to drive home his point.

With the Mekons and his innumerable other collaborations, and now increasingly as a solo singer and painter, Jon has spent the better part of the last three decades resisting anything—intolerance, imperialism, commodification—that habituates people to death or destroys the human spirit. That he would apply this ethic of resistance to the death of country music is hardly surprising, a struggle that through the years has increasingly been represented by the Carter Family's *Will the Circle Be Unbroken*. Outwardly, the song conveys a mix of hope and doubt about the persistence of the human community beyond the grave. Yet at least figuratively, it also speaks to each successive generation's anxiety over whether the links that they forge in the chain of country music—an often misunderstood idiom that emerged, like much of Jon's art, from the underside of history—will extend that tradition or bring it to an end.

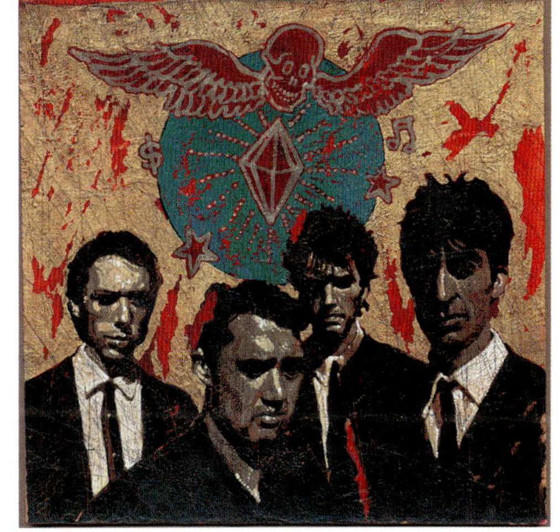

In the Carters' 1935 recording of *Will the Circle Be Unbroken*, Sara Carter grieves for her dead mother, but the body in the horse-drawn wagon that she mourns also serves as a metaphor for the music of the Carter Family and of the country musicians who have carried on in their wake. The circle that Sara, Maybelle and A.P. Carter contemplate on the record's chorus symbolizes the larger country tradition, just as the trio's faith in a "better home a-waiting" suggests that tradition will endure if its adherents build on the past to create something new, a future of their own making. Jon's paintings and tombstones, as well as the rollicking din that he makes with the Mekons, the Wacos, and his myriad side projects, engage this struggle with more force and empathy than seem possible, infusing not just the country tradition, but the larger human community, with sorely needed vigor and goodwill.

—Bill Friskics-Warren
Nashville 2005

Over the years I had picked up some ideas about how art was
not a solitary activity removed from the world, how you had to
be able to talk, explain, and justify your work. How it should
be about your immediate situation and politics, your place in
the food chain, your relationship to the powers that be . . . And
really, it was never a problem for the Mekons to write songs
about those things, given all the music biz crap we'd dealt
with day in and day out for years.

So what was the big difference between a song and a painting
or even a gig and an art show (or, as I was to discover later, a
big label and a big gallery)? Obviously my fine-art insider bag-
gage couldn't just be ditched for some desire to make pretty
pictures. I'd have to step around it, poke it with a long pointy
stick, and find out exactly which bits of it were crippling me.
Or maybe a painting could be like a song? Maybe there is no
difference.

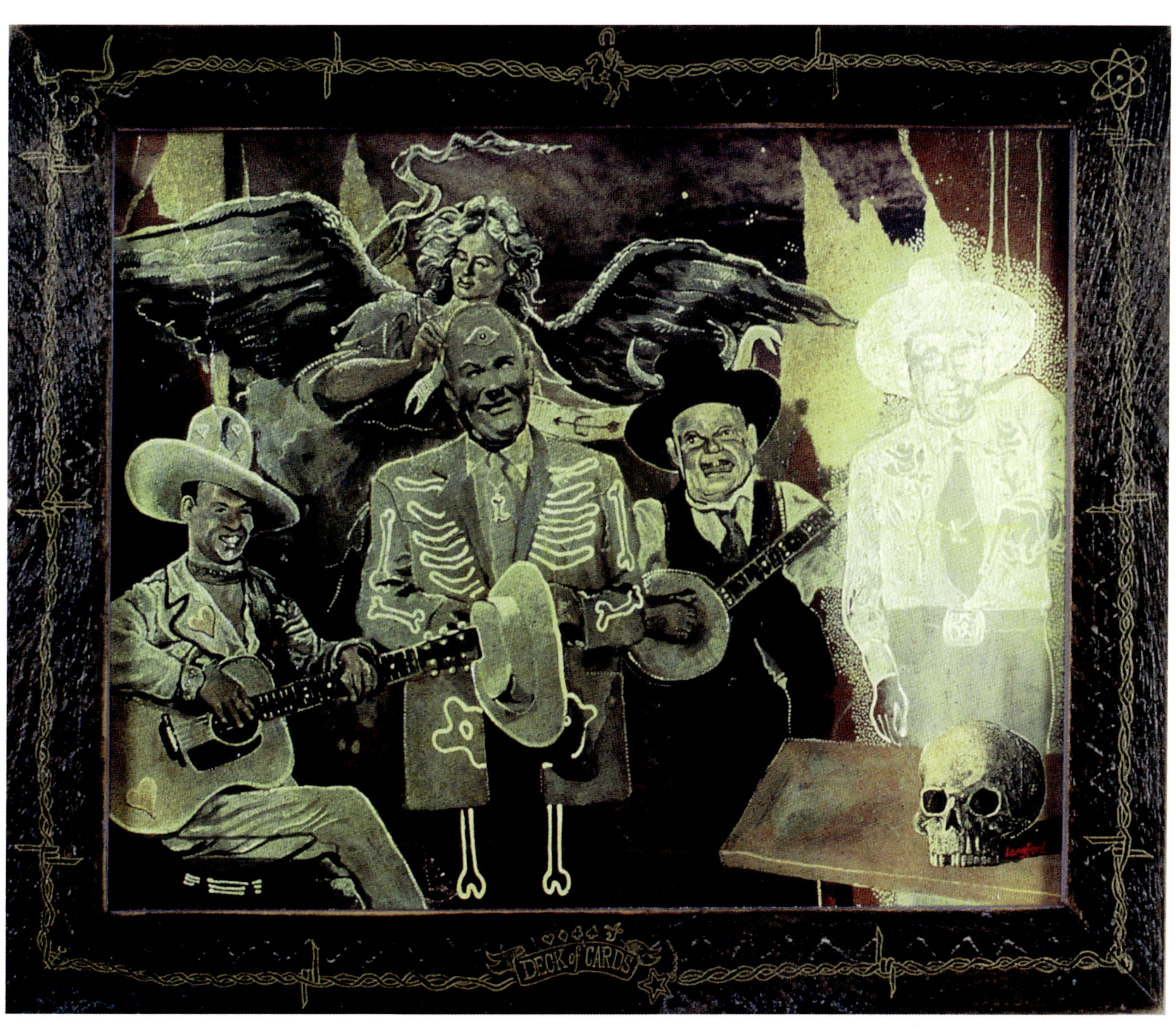
DECK of CARDS

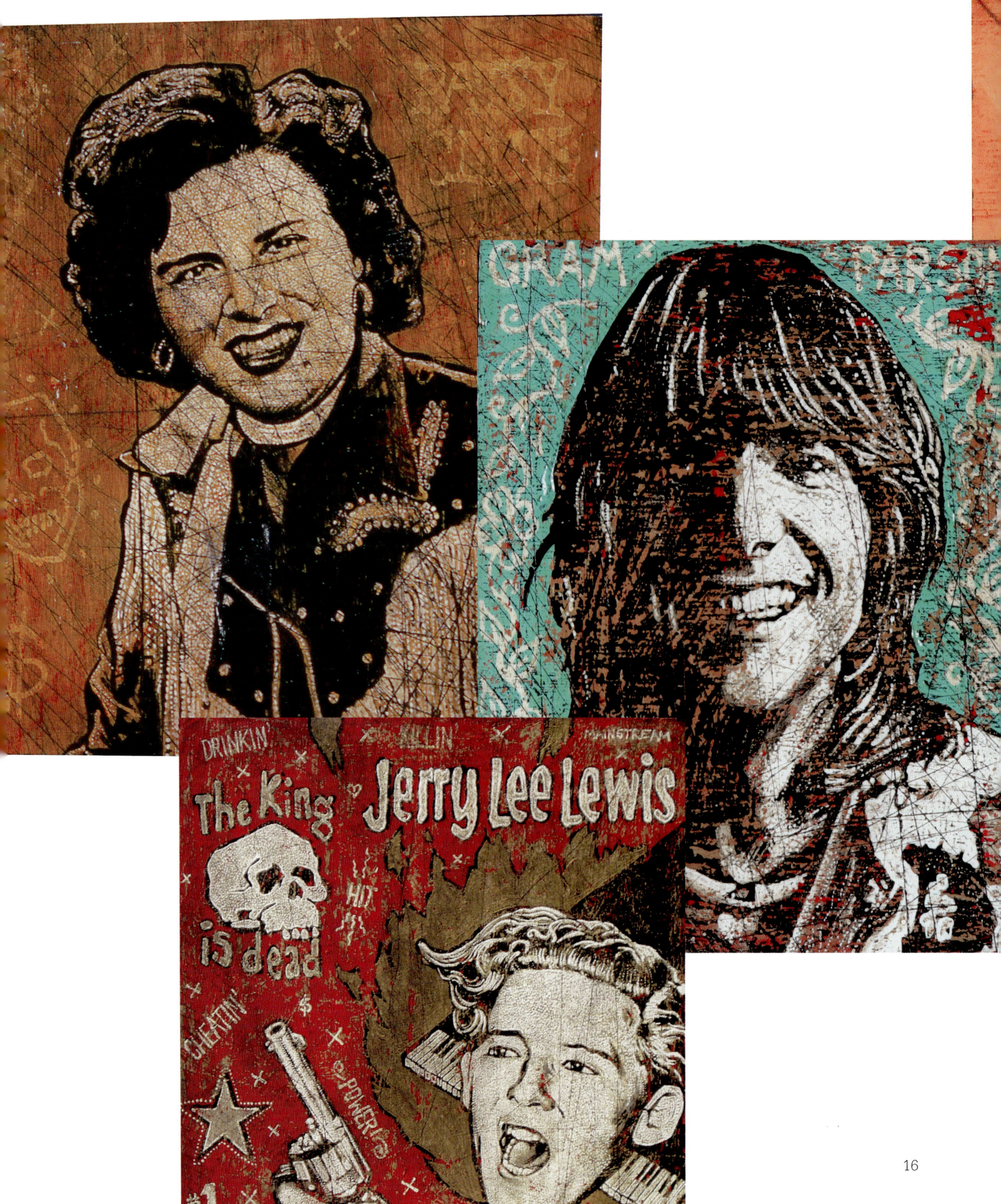
GRAM
PERSON
DRINKIN'
KILLIN'
MAINSTREAM
the King
Jerry Lee Lewis
is dead
HIT
CHEATIN'
POWER
#1
POP

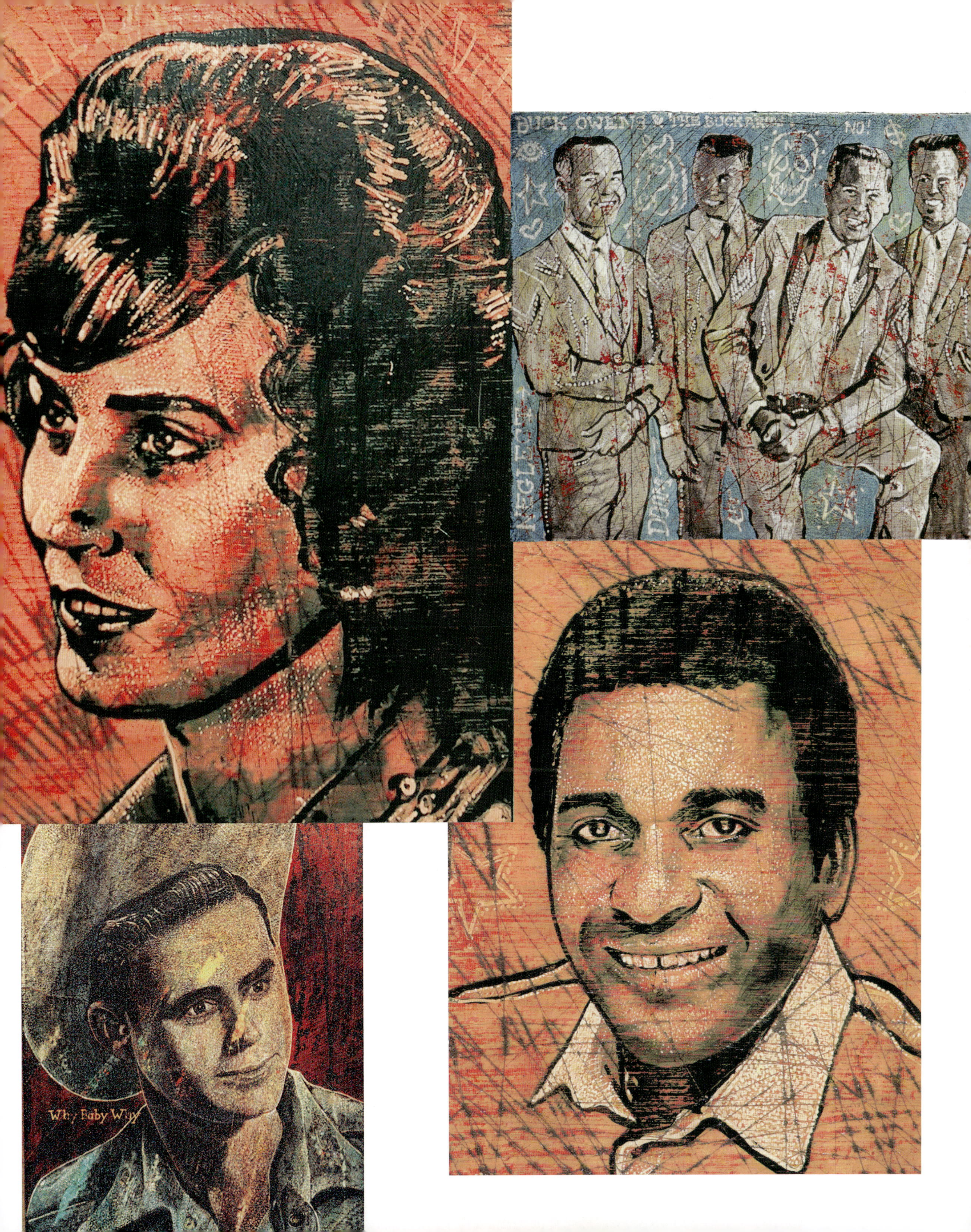
BUCK OWENS & THE BUCKAROOS
NO!
Why Baby Why

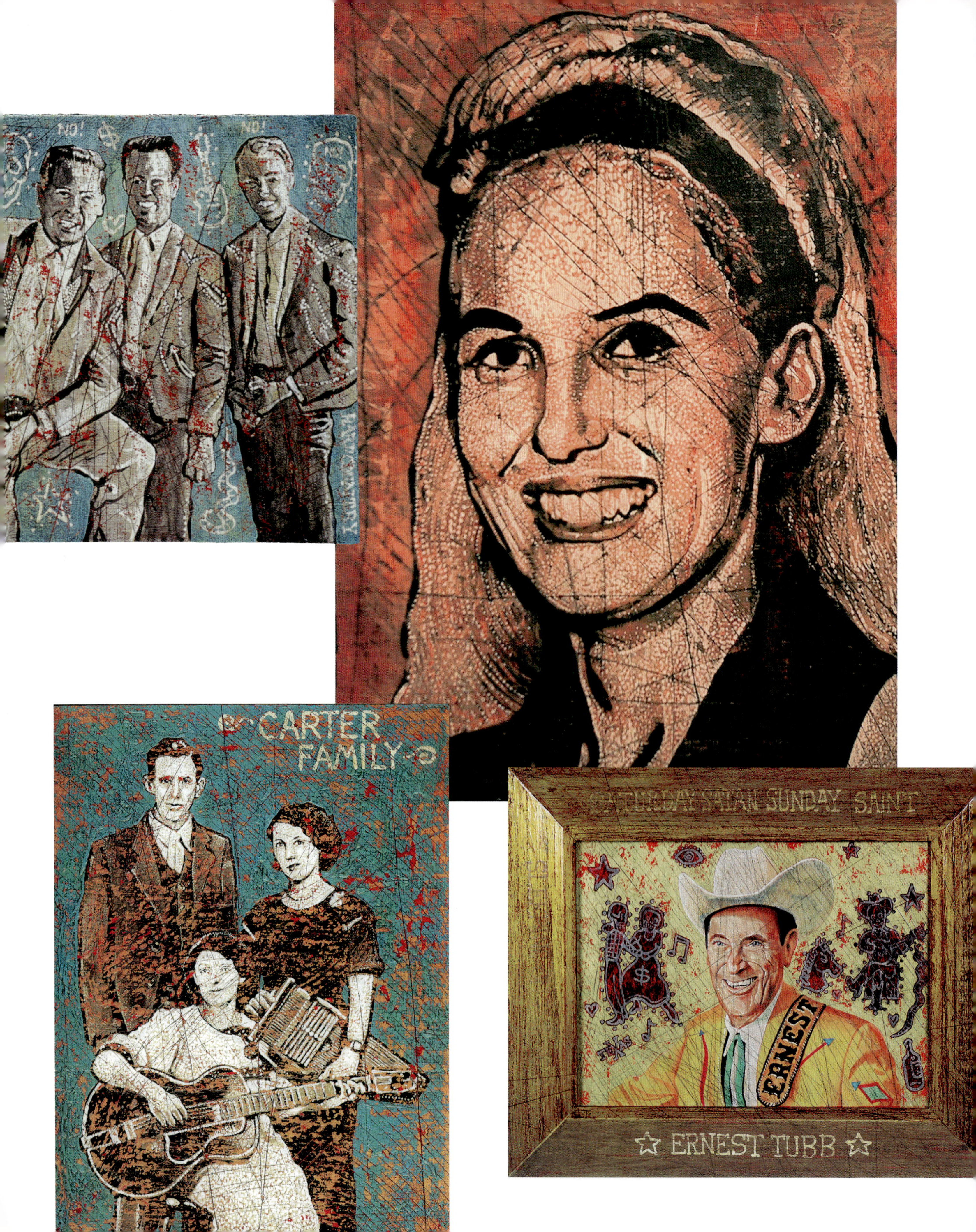
NO!
NO!
CARTER FAMILY
SATURDAY SATAN SUNDAY SAINT
ERNEST
TEXAS
ERNEST TUBB

For years I didn't paint at all. A painter needs a subject and for a long time I didn't have one. Maybe that's not quite true, but it'll do for my current purpose. When I went to university to study Fine Art, in the autumn of 1976, I was 18 and charmingly provincial (but to misquote Ernest Tubb, you'd better just remember to smile when you call me that). Straight out of high school via the cluttered back bedroom of my parent's house, I arrived in Leeds just in time for Punk.

Even as I sat in the back of my Dad's Volvo, heading north up the M6, the Sunday tabloid headlines screamed OUTRAGE & HORROR! A band called the Sex Pistols had just broken the tea-time fuck barrier on some local London TV show. Horror & Outrage! Suddenly Punk came soaring like some scabby-legged buzzard over the drab British horizon to fix us all with its crazy polarizing stare. In a country with only 3 TV channels (one of which just showed a potter's wheel going round and round and round) Punk became instantly inescapable for both the kids on the street and their parents back indoors. The former, with pants aflame, commenced spitting and hopping up and down on the spot to sever all ties with the past and fumble ungratefully for control of their own culture & entertainment, while the latter, sniffing Armageddon in every Oxfam shirt and safety pin, kicked their 9-inch black & white steam-powered TV sets around the living-room floor.

All Sex Pistols' guitarist Steve Jones had said was "What a fuckin' rotter," but oh yes, I knew right then how I'd be spending the next 27 years of my life! Me and my mate Tom immediately ceased nailing apples to the art-room wall to watch them rot, or setting our boots on fire with dangerous flammable materials—in fact, we stopped showing up at our painting studios at all.

As a kid in Wales I'd painted happy sloppy landscapes of yellow sunlight dancing through the leaves of bluish green trees out on a lush private golf course near the Severn Bridge, while waiting for my Dad and Uncle to finish up their Sunday afternoon round of golf and sneak me an underage pint. When I arrived in Leeds I was a sub-impressionist hick, and well deserved the kicking I received from my smug modernist studio tutors. They quickly squeezed all the Monet & Pissaro out of my tubes with their giant rainbow light-bulb ladders, terrible beards, monkey boots, and indifference.

SOME HISTORY

And that was it, really. In 1977 we downed brushes and formed the Mekons. Or at least Tom, Kevin, Chalkie and Corrigan did—then they got me and Ros to join 'cos I had a drumkit and she had the painting studio next to mine.
—We're gonna start a band where no one can play. Do you wanna be in it?
—Yeah, OK.

It was a joke, a one-liner—the anti-band, a bunch of drunken art students scribbling daft songs about Outer Space, girls, and unemployment on beer-mats in the pub. We were going be the first Punk band to play only slow songs, but we compromised even before our first gig when the promoter told us to play fast or stay home. The accelerated tempos reduced our set to a cozy 12 minutes. Someone else's gear and someone else's van, but within a year we had a record out and people were calling us for gigs and interviews.

In my drafty bedroom with the sloping, pink-carpeted floor, I'd record John Peel's show on Radio One every night at 10, sticking a portable cassette player up to my transistor radio before running down to the pub for last call. It was the only show that mattered and my crude, hissing tapes of it were the bible: Buzzcocks, Beefheart, Prince Far I, Pere Ubu, the Fall, Ivor Cutler, Misty in Roots—all for the first time. 3 tracks from Bob Marley's KAYA, a Kevin Coyne session, the Only Ones, and Althea & Donna's "Uptown Top Ranking" on its way to number 1.

The day the Mekons' first single "Never Been In A Riot" hit the shops I came home to find a bunch of my housemates hunched over the record player laughing their arses off. I'd imagined something magical must take place during the transfer to vinyl, so we would suddenly sound like a real band on a real record . . . but no, no way. We sounded so raw and extreme that out of sheer embarrassment I began to laugh as well.

But somehow, and not for the last time, the Mekons managed to snatch triumph from the jaws of humiliation. Two nights later, Peel announces he's going to play our single. Bloody hell! No one else is home, and nobody will believe me in the pub—so I drag my neighbor Dinah up to my attic as a witness. We sit there doubtful & anxious for the best part of two hours, but by midnight I am fully vindicated and in possession of the elusive rock-star cool I still enjoy today. Thank you, John Peel, for ruining any chance I had of a normal life. I am truly grateful.

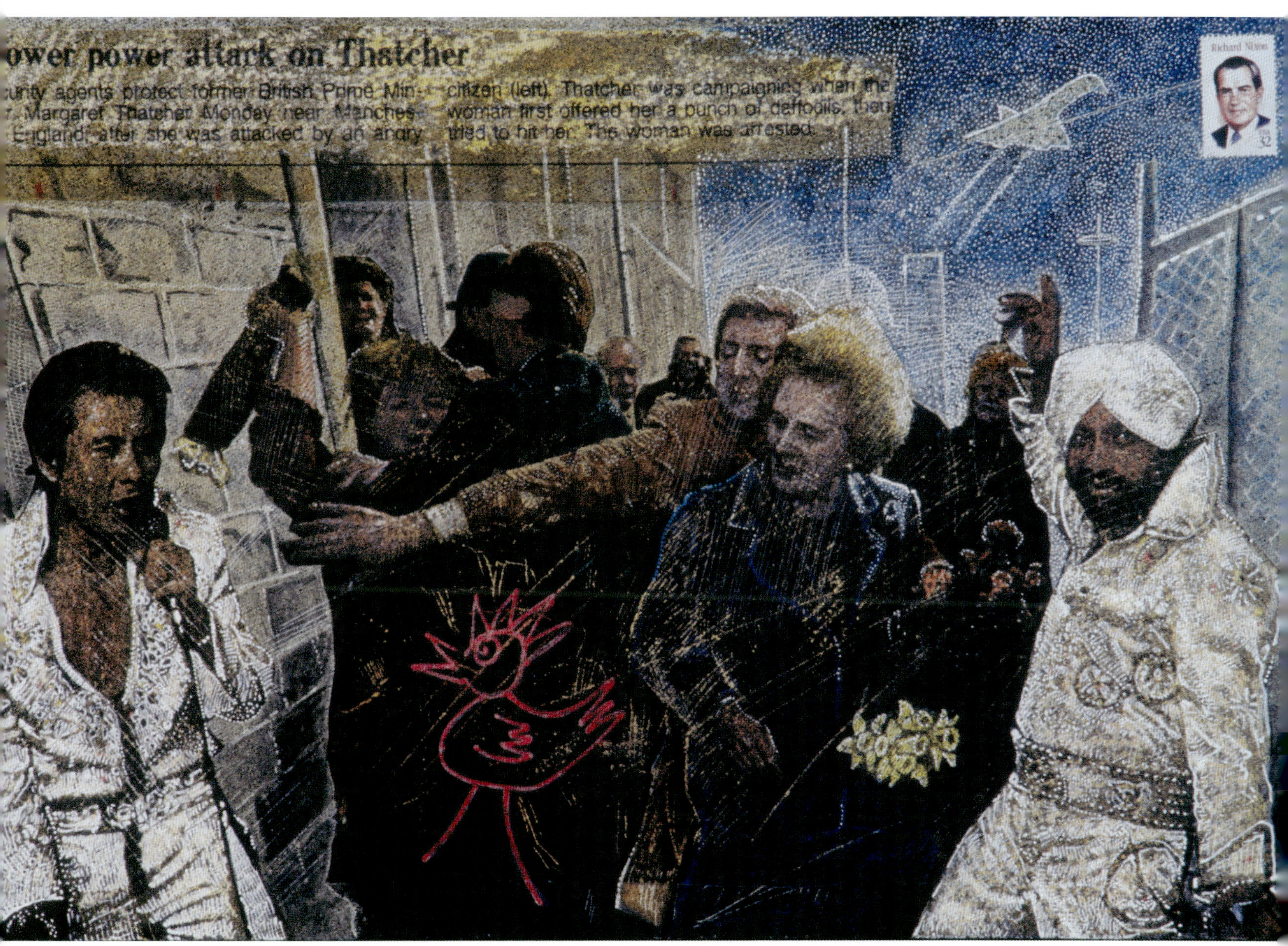
ower power attack on Thatcher
urity agents protect former British Prime Min-
r Margaret Thatcher Monday near Manches-
England, after she was attacked by an angry
citizen (left). Thatcher was campaigning when the
woman first offered her a bunch of daffodils, then
tried to hit her. The woman was arrested.
Richard Nixon
USA 32

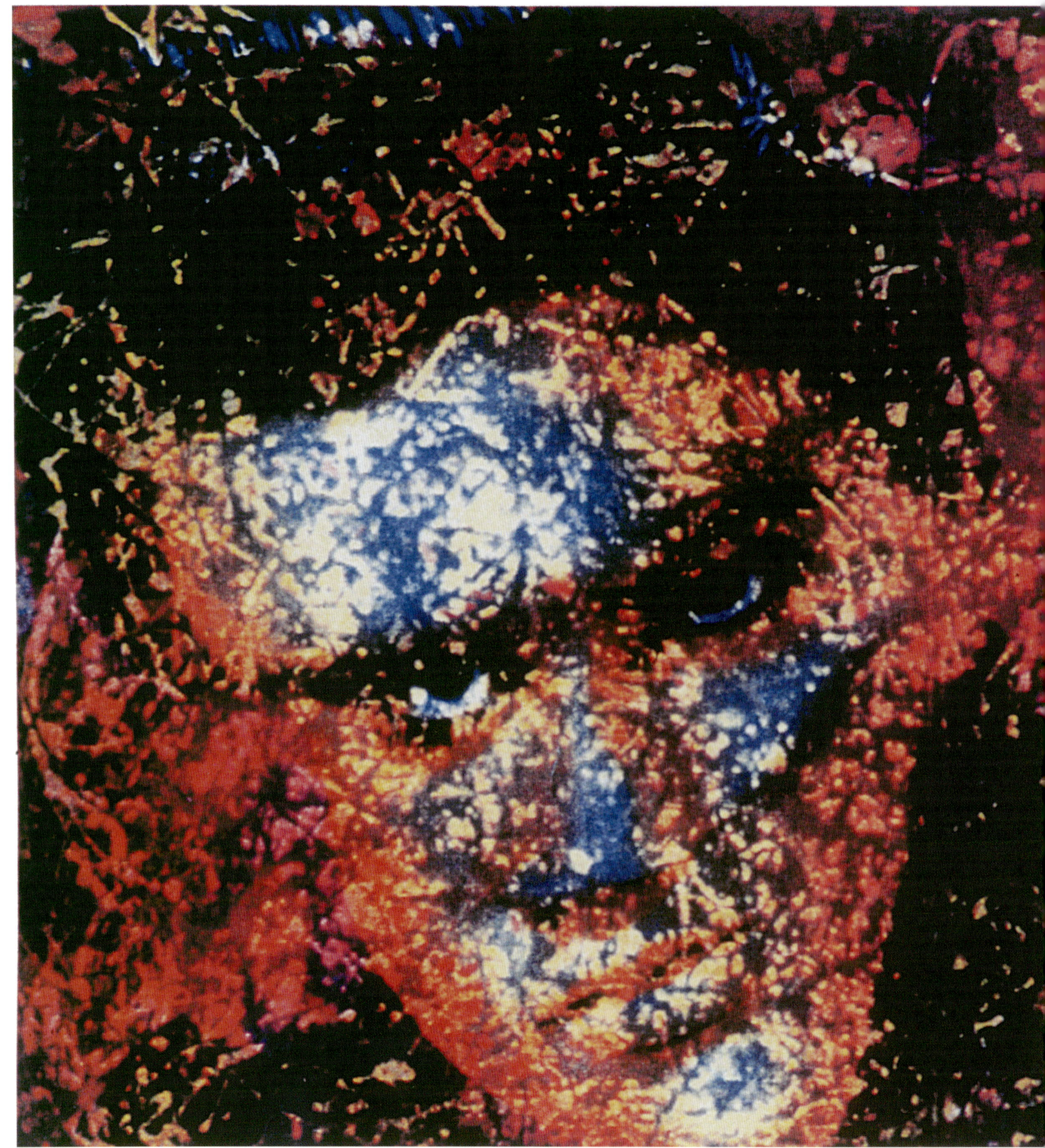

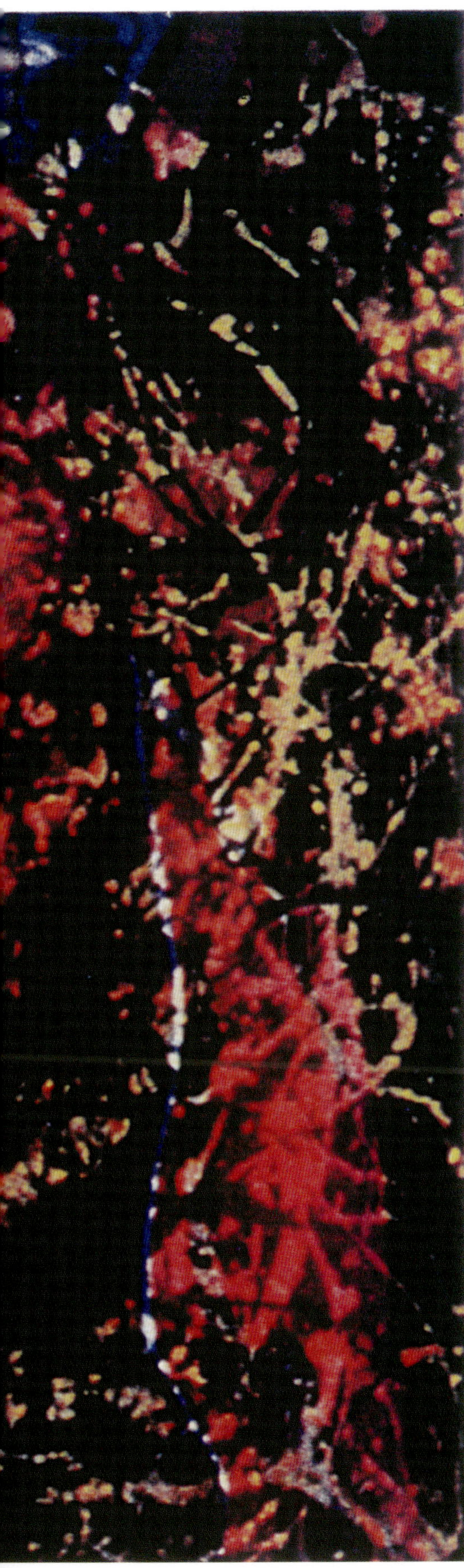

I wasn't entirely absent from art school all those years, I just didn't do any painting. T.J. Clark, the only British member of the Situationist International and a veteran of Paris '68, arrived as head of department the same week as me & Tom and proceeded to put some theoretical spine (Marxist, feminist, etc.) into a sloppy liberal arts program. It became a talking shop and we talked a lot. Us, the Gang of Four, & nearly everyone else we knew were art students who were in bands. We spent short days and long nights drinking and quarrelling about music and politics, all the while honing & sculpting our huge critical muscles and rigorously sleeping with each other. Whether we were in the Union bar, the Fenton, the all-nite cafe, the rehearsal room, the back of the van, or collapsed in bed for half the day listening to Graham Parker or the Clash, we talked a fierce game and sneered a good sneer.

Though punk now seems like a moment of limitless possibilities, we mainly obsessed about what we shouldn't do and only stumbled on what we should through a process of elimination. At Art School I read little, listened through a hung-over haze, missed vital reviews and tutorials but somehow managed to absorb the important things that actually stuck with me via some weird osmosis. It was intimidating and paralyzing for me as a visual artist, but I'm glad to have been through that ideological mincer; if not leading me to what I should do, at least it alerted me to what I shouldn't.

I remember Tim Clark interrupting a lecture I'd stumbled into bloodshot, bleary, & late—and lambasting me in his calm West-country brogue: "What's the matter Jon? Leeds getting to you?" But while the other teachers just seemed to hate us, he quietly cut us a lot of slack. We repaid this by disappearing for weeks on end in the van and finally dropping out to do the band full time.

When Mekons Mark 1 disintegrated after being dumped by Virgin Records, me and Tom went back to the Fine Art Department in Leeds with our tails between our legs—but found support and encouragement from Clark appointees like Terry Atkinson (Art & Language) and John Tagg who twigged that our punk rock adventures might actually be of some worth. I made some paintings, got my degree, and immediately formed another band called The Three Johns with painter John Hyatt and Belfast-born Phillip Brennan, an exile from the Troubles.

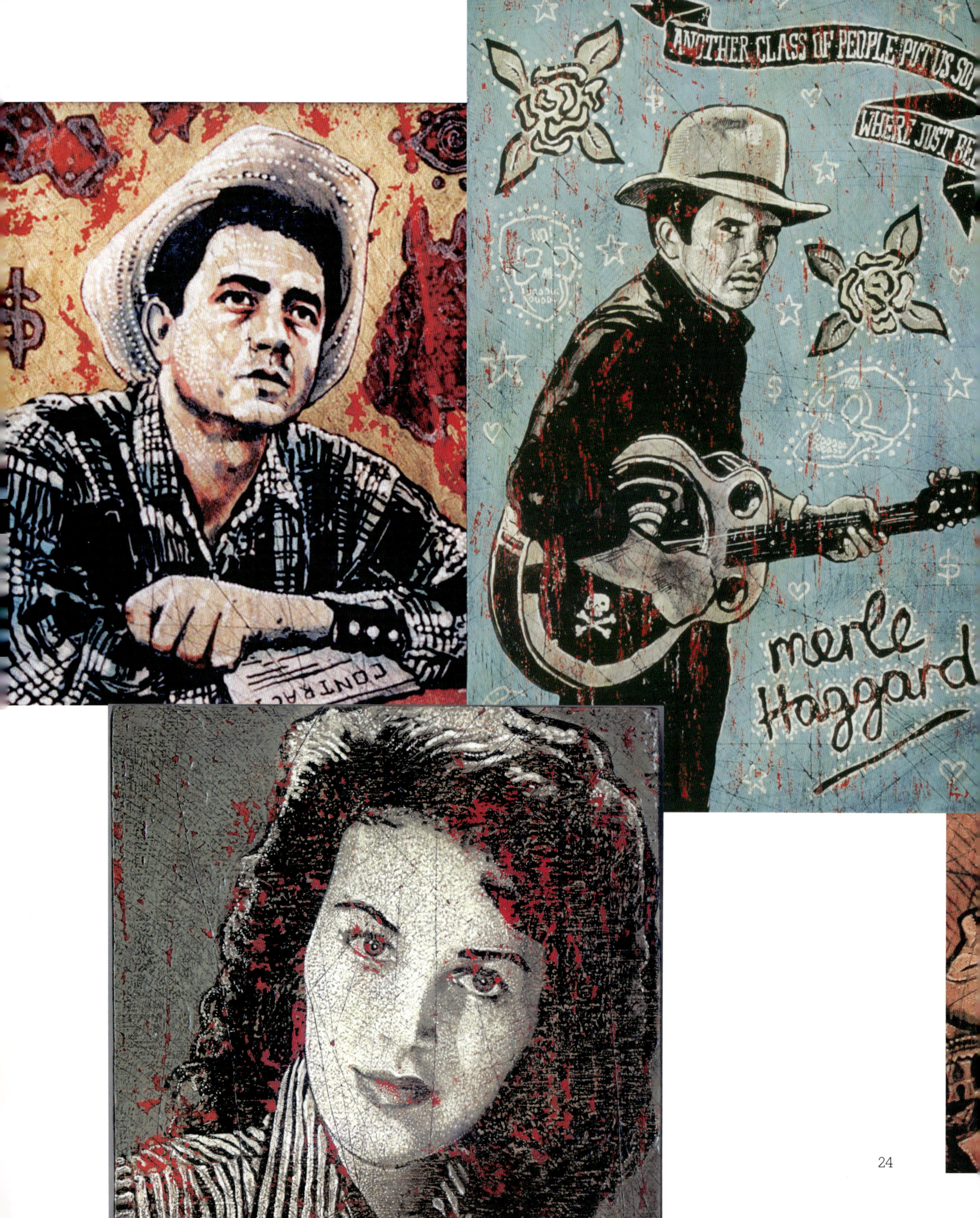
ANOTHER CLASS OF PEOPLE PUT US SO
WHERE JUST BE
merle
Haggard
CONTRACT

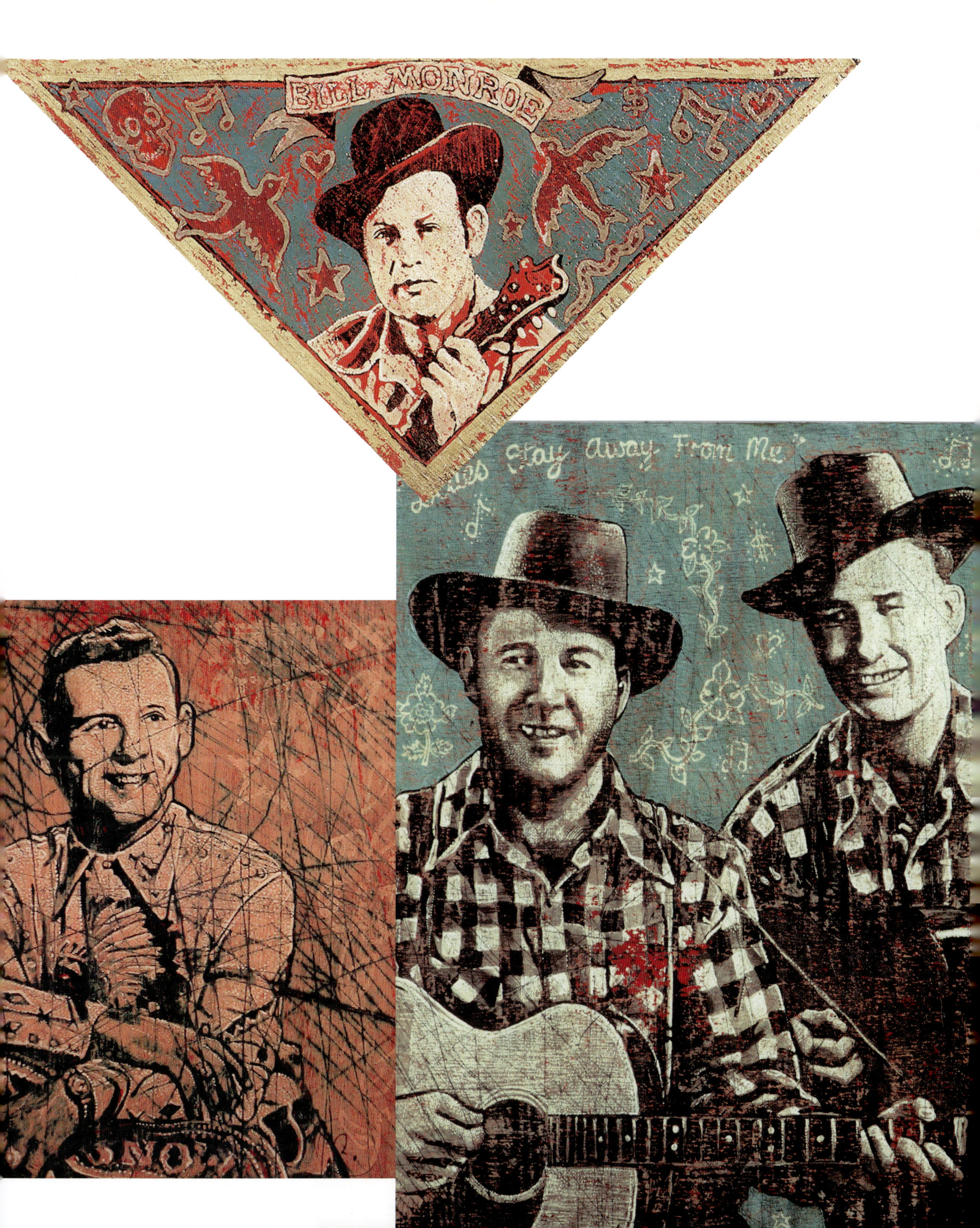
BILL MONROE
"Ladies Stay Away From Me"

Insignificance

A hologram of a naked man's eyes bat around the room
And fix you in their sights, proof of existence
A giant stirs to swat a fly that's lost its best defence
Insignificance

Damned if you do, damned if you don't
Don't drink that coke, it's really bad for you

A word slips out of Dallas in 1963
Spawns an industry – conspiracy
Initials ten feet tall just reinforce and underline
Insignificance

If they can kill Kennedy, what would they do to we
Stumbling into their attention
Walk into the shadows – a dim concealment

Down in the valley, the rich and the powerful
Blood runs down the plug-hole
Here's the burden, here's the proof
It's disappearing
A giant stirs the whirlpool
As it closes on the truth
Insignificant, insignificance

You have the right to lie awake at night
And hope that I am paranoid enough

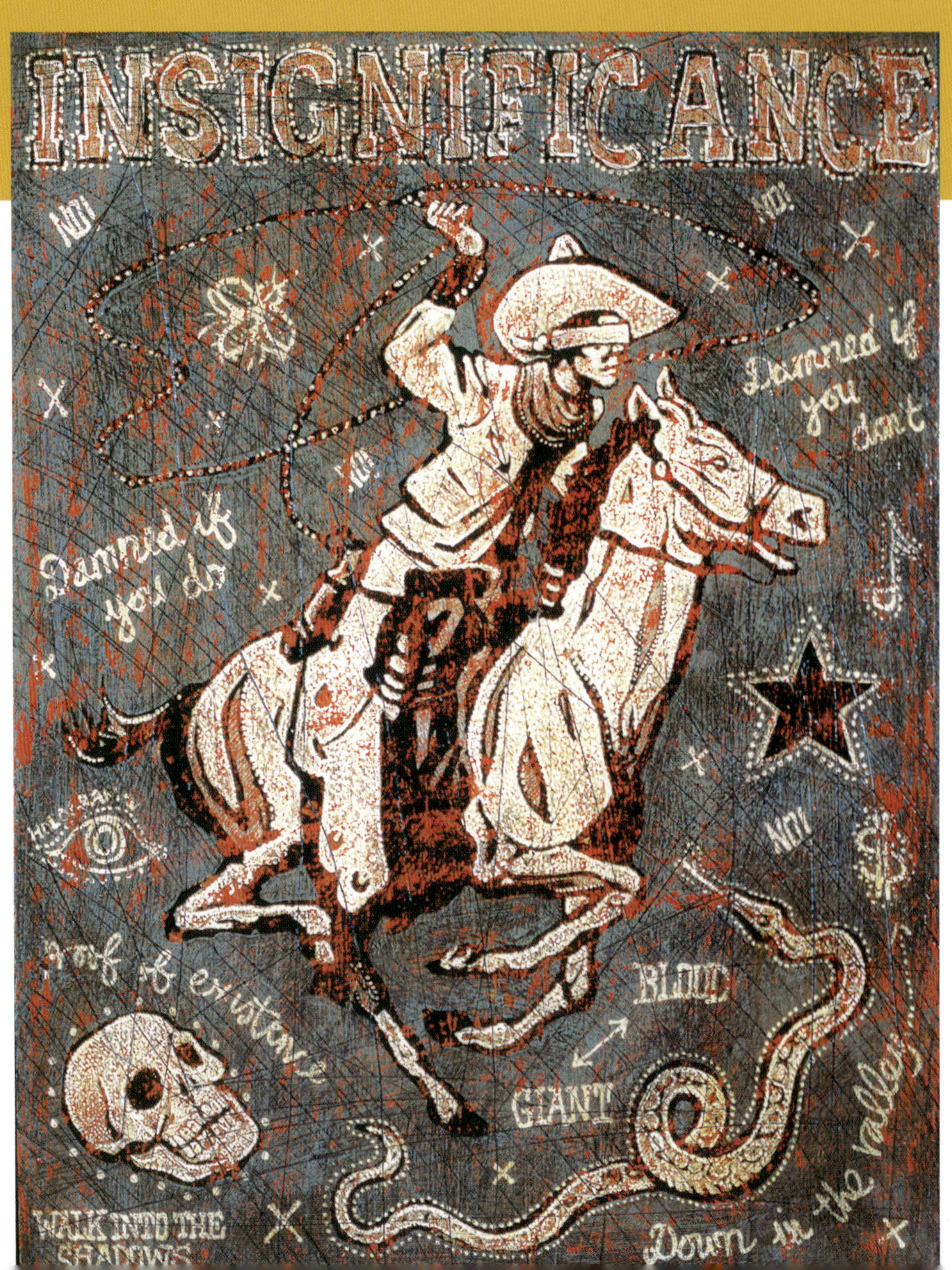

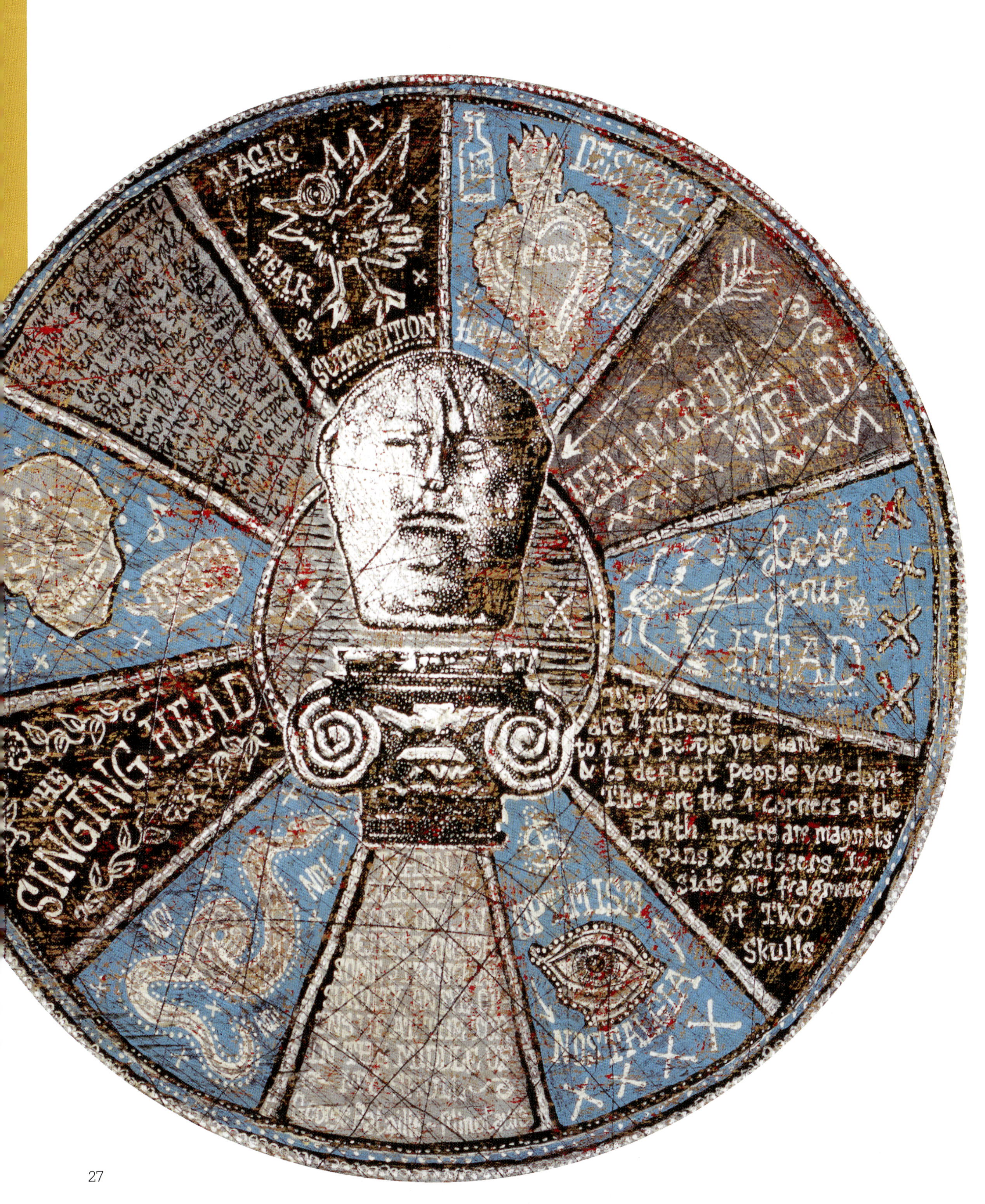

MAGIC
FEAR & SUPERSTITION
THE SINGING HEAD
Lose your HEAD
There are 4 mirrors
to draw people you want
& to deflect people you don't.
They are the 4 corners of the
Earth. There are magnets
pins & scissors. In
side are fragments
of TWO
skulls
OPTIMISM

THE PUNK/COUNTRY CONNECTION

We never heard Bob Wills, Merle Haggard, George Jones, Patsy Cline, Ernest Tubb, Kitty Wells, & Buck Owens in Leeds—we got Boxcar Willie instead. The mystery and misery of real hard country music only filtered into our strangely parallel punk-rock universe through some cassette tapes we were sent by an American college DJ in 1983.

At the time the Mekons were languishing in post-punk hibernation; not making records or playing live but far too lazy to actually split up. Some key members had quit the band after we were dropped by Virgin Records, but there was still a hard core that sat in the pub every night plotting revenge on a world that was resolutely not interested.

WZRD DJ Terry Nelson's favorite bands were the Mekons and the Pretty Things, and after a chance encounter with the Gang of Four's road crew he set off from Chicago for London to exhume them both. He had this idea that the Mekons were a Country band—'cos while proper Punk bands ranted about bondage and smashing the system, our simple clattering dirges mostly dealt with failed sexual relationships and drinking in bars. When he met us, Terry handed us a compilation tape of drinkin' & cheatin' songs he'd titled HONKY-TONK CLASSICS VOLUME 1 to illustrate his theory. The Punk/Country connection seemed a bit of a stretch, but we were hooked nonetheless. It was a total eye-opener, a confirmation that something dark, sinewy, and uncomfortable lurked beneath all that Nashville easy listening.

The tunes on Terry's Hard Country cassette lived up to our egalitarian Punk Rock ideals effortlessly. These Honky-tonk guys knew their crowd 'cos they lived in the same world as them, confronting the same realities head on every day with the same defiant humor & fatalism, the barrier between performer and audience melting away in a pool of common experience.

Corny as it seems, these stripped down honky-tonk tales of lust & loneliness, sex, drinking & death struck a chord with us (usually E-major) and connected our alienated, drunk, commie souls to a strident tradition we hardly knew existed.

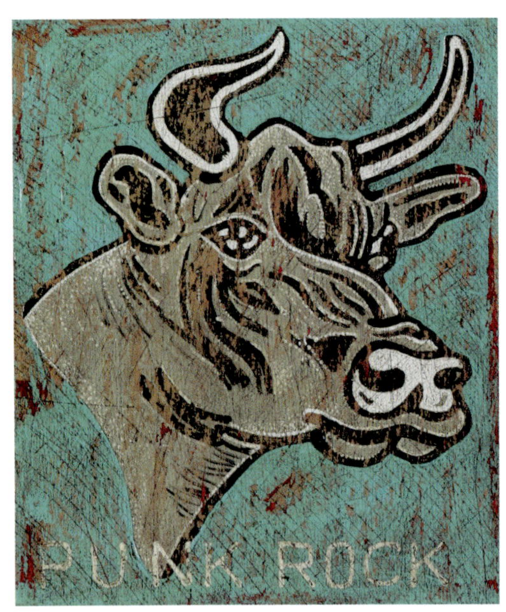

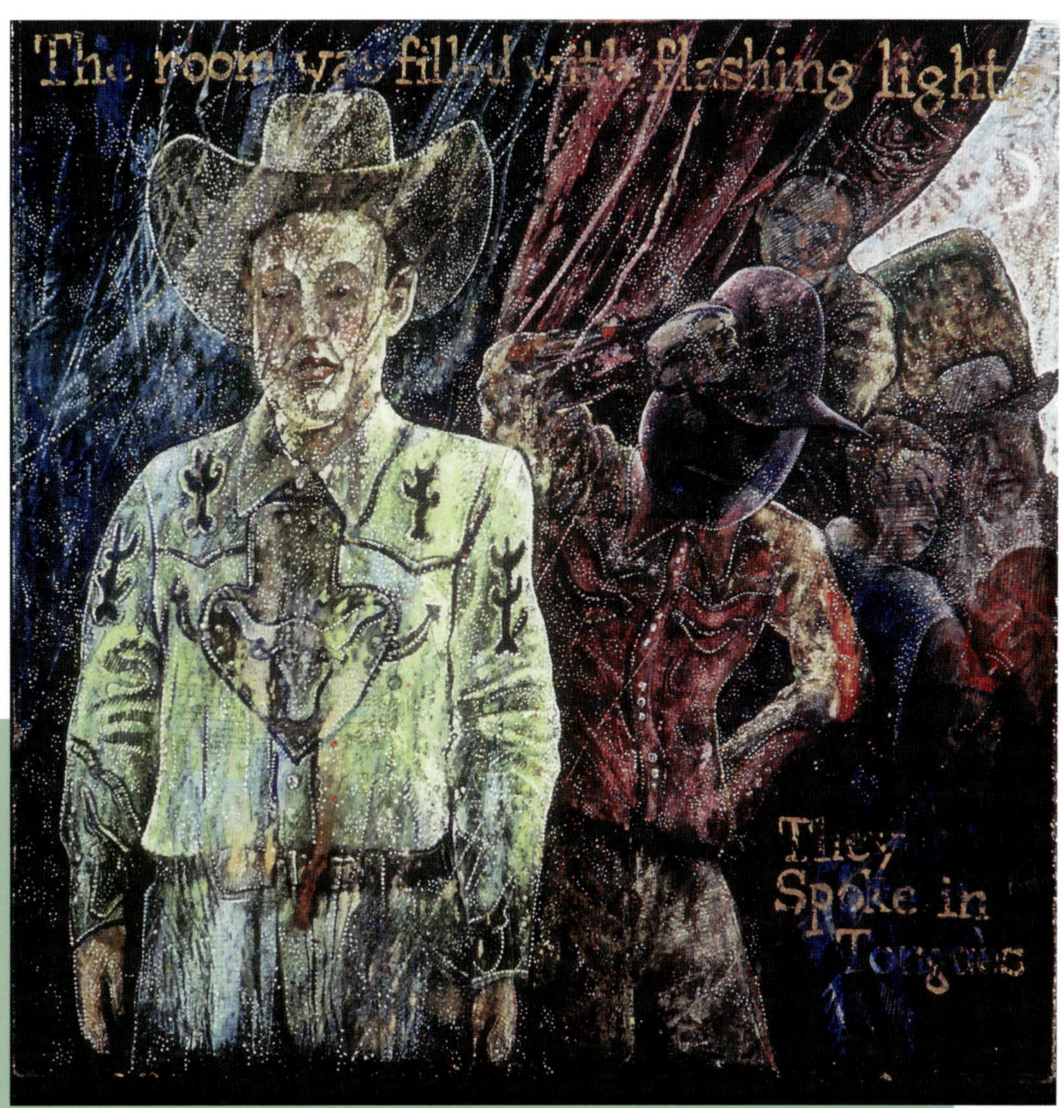

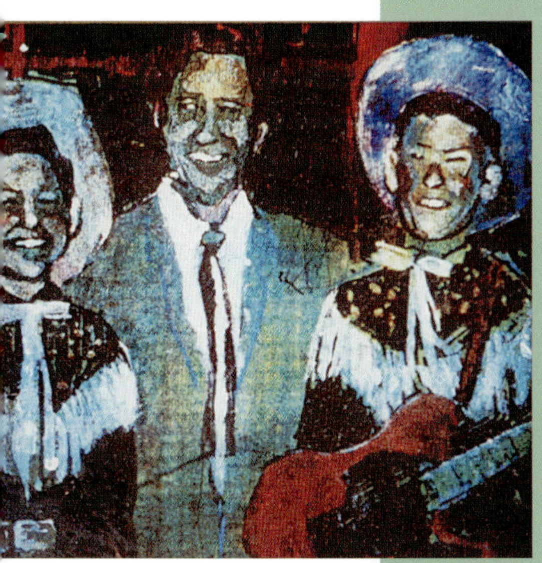

Ugly Band

Heat and dust
A shout above the din
Pushed into the corner
The creeping little thing
Down in the basement the ugly band plays

In the middle of the night
A light behind the door
Stubbing out some cigarettes
And stumbling to the floor
Outside in the desert
Out across the waves
We're listening to the country boys
And dancing on their graves
Down in the basement the ugly band plays . . .

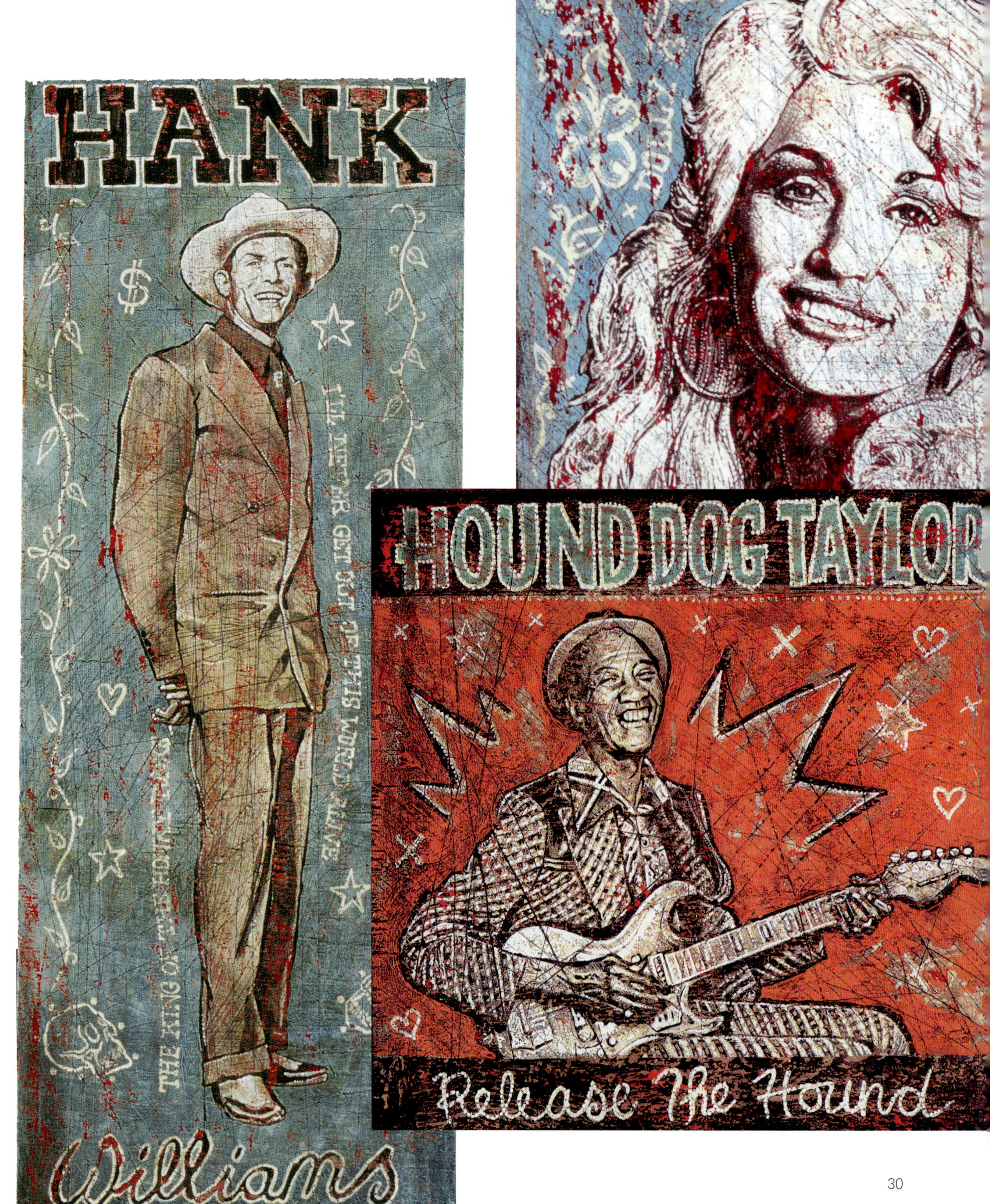

HANK
$
I'LL NEVER GET OUT OF THIS WORLD ALIVE
THE KING OF COUNTRY MUSIC
Williams
DOLLY
HOUND DOG TAYLOR
Release The Hound

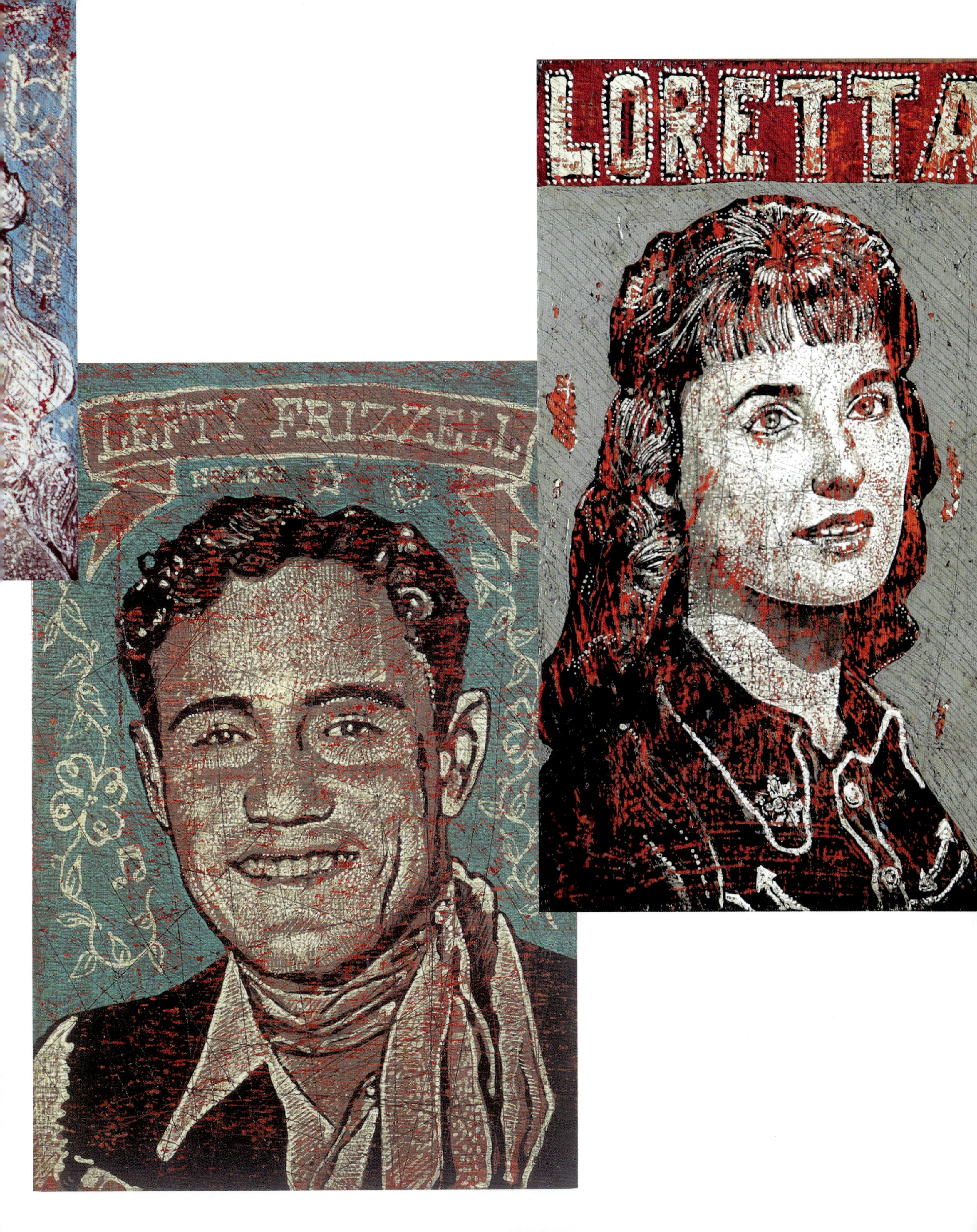
LORETTA
LEFTY FRIZZELL

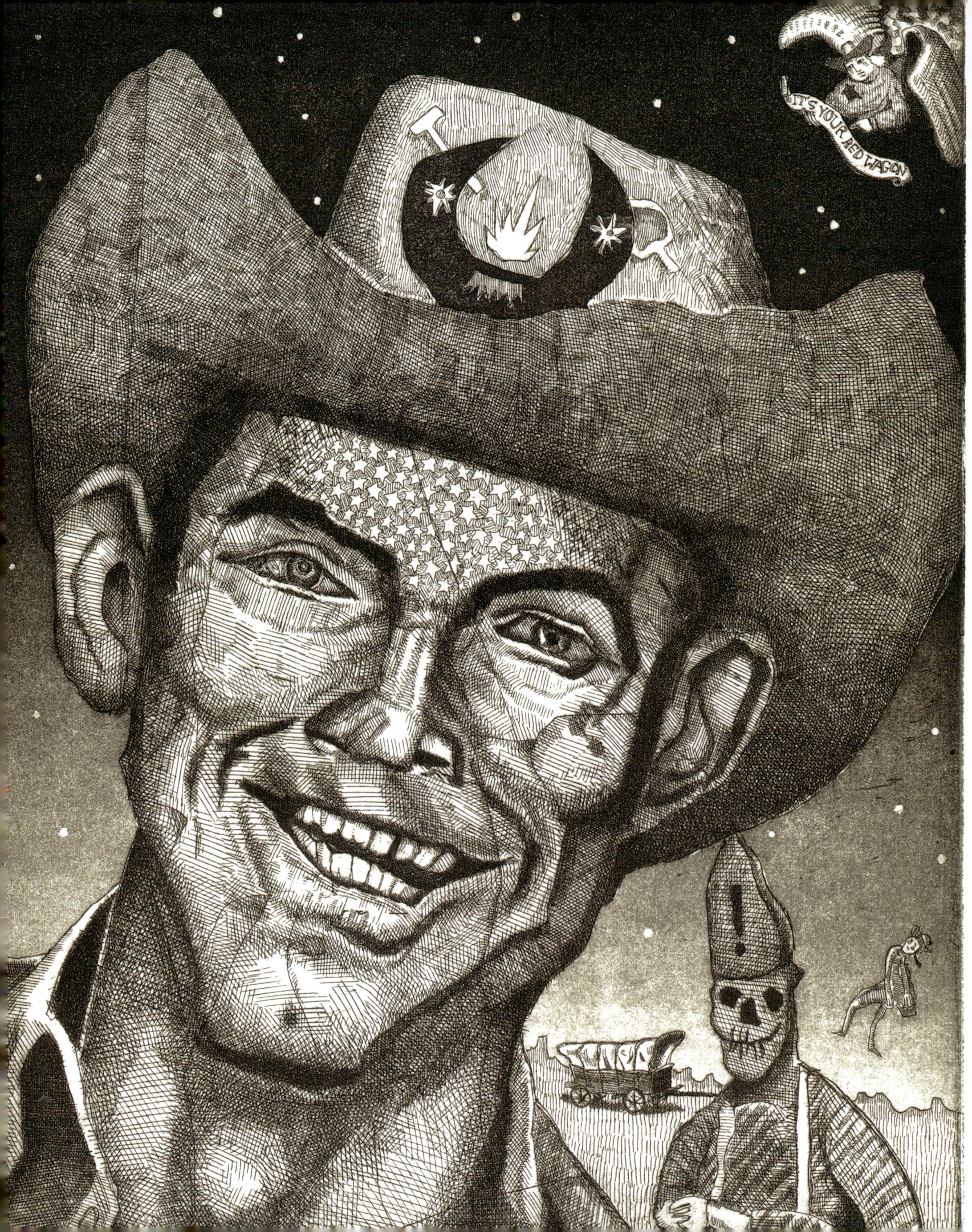
IT'S YOUR RED WAGON

Slightly South of the Border

So it's time we moved on
This geography has been so hard
Over mountains and out through the plains
Of this blighted land
We live in an old town
And our friends and acquaintances
Tell us those stories
That make us feel fine
It gets dark when the sun goes down
And it's cold underfoot
The electric comes up through the ground
It's paid for with words and tended with love

Shopping is easy and much can be bought
With some money you get from somewhere
But who makes the Sundays like stone
And decides where the new roads will go
Slow, the road bends at will
Plough through from crazy to sane
No education prepares you for this
You are born and you die
We go marching, coughing and croaking
So the smog cannot heal up our eyes
Great blank walls and dense prickly hedges
Paid for with words and tended with love

Small stupid children bring paper to life
And up on the damp walls there are patterns like fish
There's a time for arriving in old towns like these
And a time to be moving on . . .
So you see we should be glad
Just waiting with huge empty heads
Draw a map and tear it in half
It's paid for in words and tended with love

The land stretches out
You can feel with your hands and under your feet
Run your fingers through valleys and streams
Snapping fences and warm pools of blood
That's the history of all our dreams
Paid for with words and tended with love

Memphis, Egypt

Destroy your safe and happy lives
Before it is too late
The battles we fought were long and hard
Just not to be consumed by Rock 'n' Roll
Rock 'n' Roll!

Capitalismos, Favorite Boy child
We must apologize
Up in the rafters a rope is dangling
Spots before the eyes of Rock 'n' Roll
Rock 'n' Roll!

We know the devil, we have met him
& shaken him by the hand & thought
his foul breath was fine perfume – just
like Rock 'n' Roll.

East Berlin, you can't buy a thing
There's nothing they can sell me
I walk thru the wall, there's no pain at all
I'm born inside the belly of Rock 'n' Roll
Rock 'n' Roll!

Something to sell your labor for
When hair sprouts out below
I'm a microscope on that secret place
Where we all wanna go. It's Rock 'n' Roll
Rock 'n' Roll!

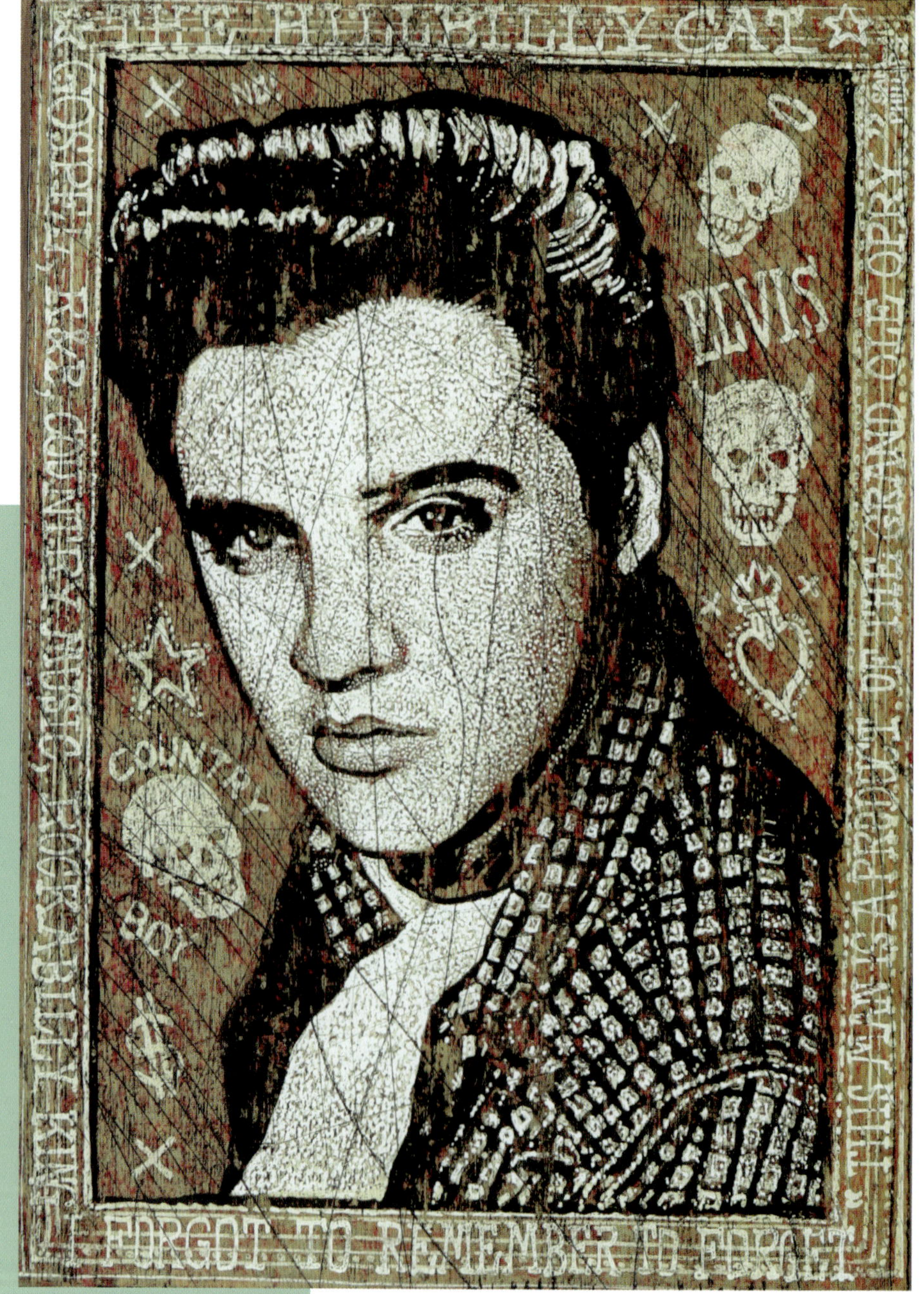

Going through Checkpoint Charlie into East Berlin in the late '80s, I'm pulled over by a border guard for having a Soviet-style hammer and sickle patch on the arm of my leather jacket.
—Where did you get this?
I told him I'd bought it in a Goth store on the Reeperbahn in Hamburg a few days earlier. I'd sown it onto the sleeve of my jacket out of boredom in the van.
—That is not possible . . .
—Oh yes it is. They sell this stuff all over Western Europe, even in Leeds.

There's much shaking of heads and pointing but finally we're let through. We soon find out that about the only place you can't buy cool Commie paraphernalia is in the East. Fur coats, perfume, watches, no problem—as long as you've got Western currency to pay for them. But all we've got is a pile of East German marks smuggled in inside somebody's knickers . . . and there's nothing here we can spend it on! Hey, we're from the West, products of capitalism, raised on Rock 'n' Roll, born inside the belly . . . We demand the right to purchase choice Stalinist nuggets, the souvenir bric-a-brac of your crumbling sector in exchange for this toy money.

If you come back in a few years, you can buy a chunk of the wall, slurp Miller Lite, and watch MTV at TGI Fridays in Karl Marx Platz with your previously owned Red Army tank parked outside, stuffed to the brim with contraband plutonium. And the same border guard will say, "Do you want fries with that?"

Herbert Marcuse said that whatever you throw at capitalism, it'll just sell it right back to you. And the music business is capitalism's muscular right arm with a big fat catcher's mitt on the end.

For a while—a brief, formative moment of opportunity and danger—Punk Rock was too hot to handle. But then the major labels donned their oven gloves, held their noses, and swallowed it whole. When the Clash signed to CBS, some PR guy came up with a marketing slogan, THE ONLY BAND THAT MATTERS, just to rub corporate salt into communal wounds. It was in papers and on posters everywhere.

The Mekons signed to Virgin Records in 1979. We thought we could climb into the dragon's mouth and piss out the flames.

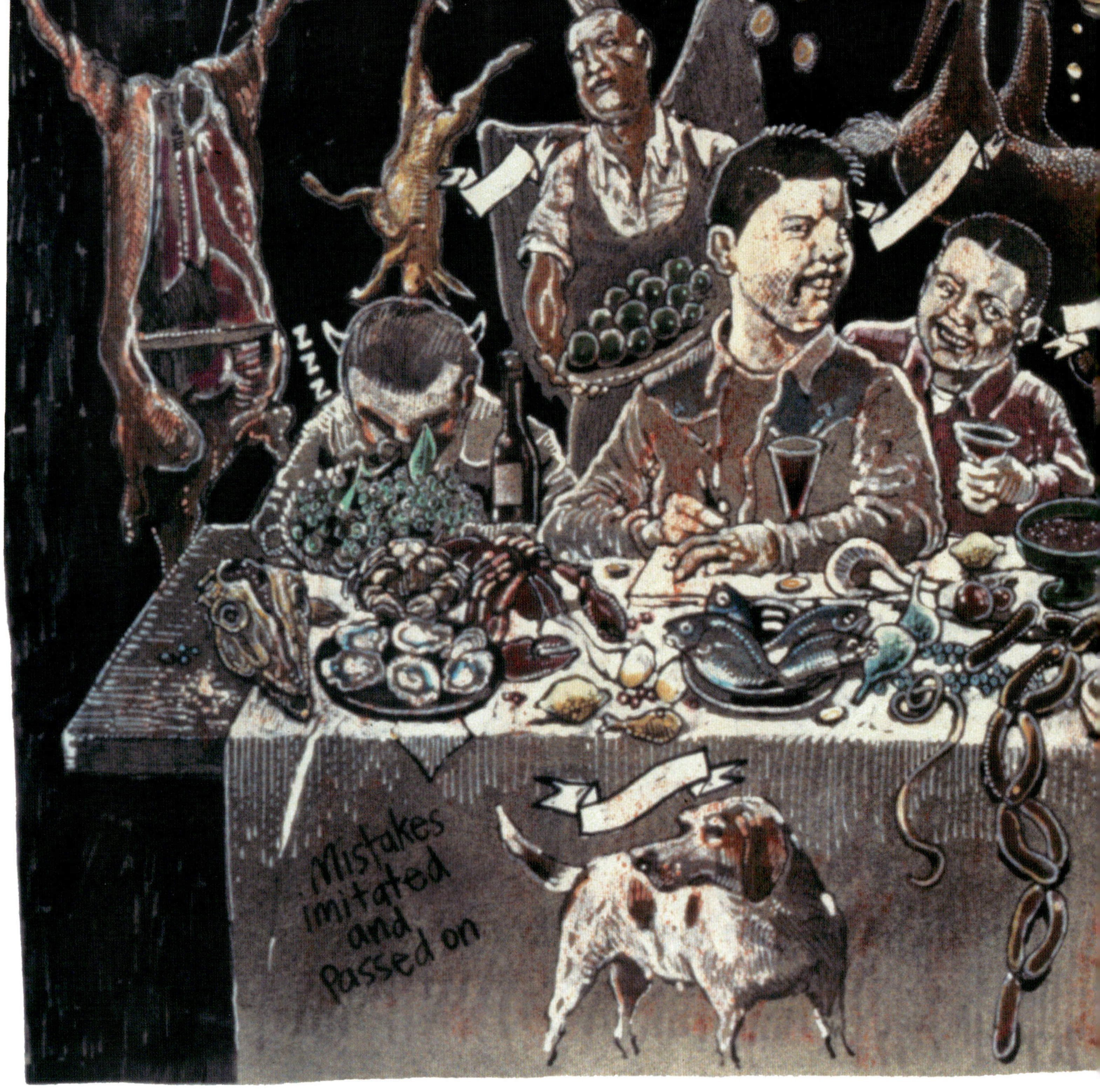

But we soon learned that the only band that matters is the one that makes the dosh. Punk Rock was reduced to Malcolm Mc-Claren's pointless swindle, which was reassuring for the industry: WE ALL WANT THE SAME THING.

Learning nothing from our own history, we signed with A&M in 1989 and made a concept album called THE MEKONS ROCK 'N' ROLL. It was an attempt to destroy the music industry from within while simultaneously charting our own demoralized capitulation. No one there had a clue what we were on about. I never met my new employer, but one day at the A&M offices,

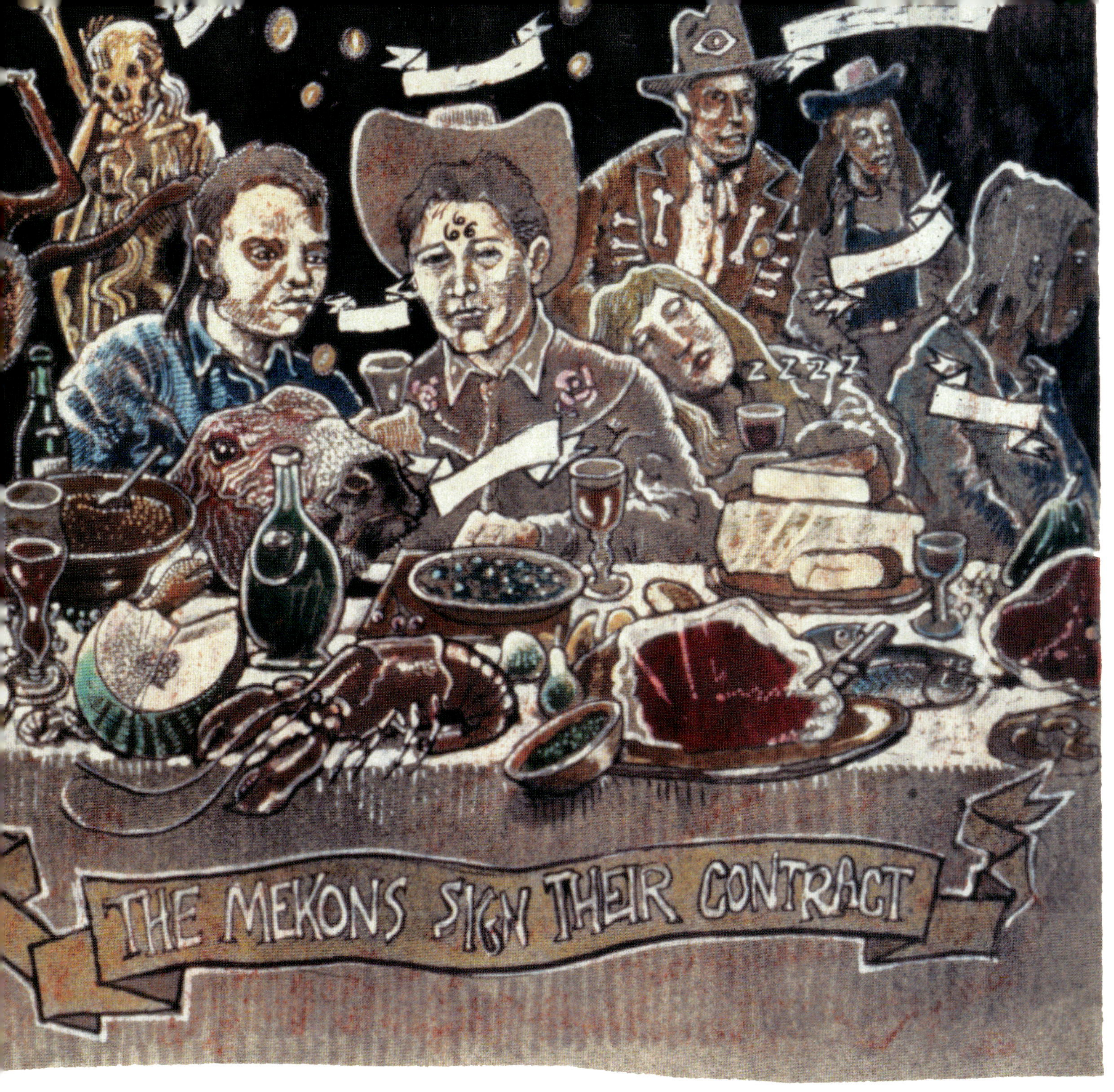

on the old Hollywood lot where Charlie Chaplin made the Great Dictator, the boss's personal secretary forged his signature on a CD for my Mother: Dear Mrs. Langford, You have a fine and talented son—Herb Alpert.

The secret of the Mekons' success was our lack of success . . . confounding expectations while having none of our own, and as our first 15-year van ride puttered out, I woke up bruised and penniless in a one-bedroom apartment in Chicago's Bucktown, finally disillusioned and isolated enough to consider painting again.

JOHNNY CASH

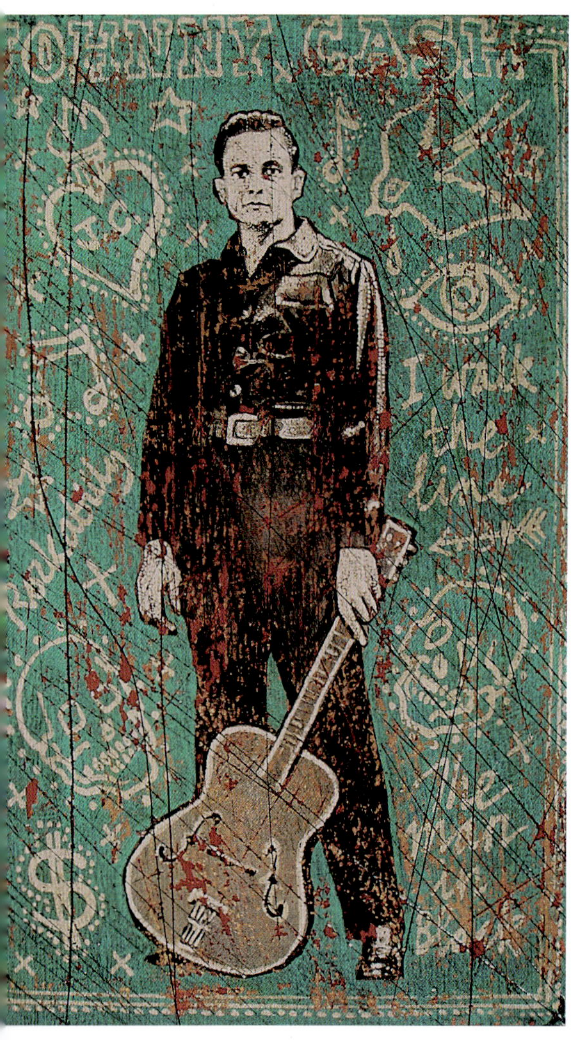

"I shot a man in Reno just to watch him die," sang Johnny Cash on "Folsom Prison Blues," trying to come up with the baddest line he could think of. But contrary to the prevailing myth, Johnny never spent more than one night in jail in his life—and that was for the heinous crime of picking flowers.

When Sundowner Curt Delaney's widow Joan comes to our shows she gets mad if we don't do "Cocaine Blues," another song recorded by Cash but with roots that go back darker and deeper. It's a nasty little song about snorting coke and shooting your girlfriend. It's also very funny, full of vicarious thrills for candy-assed, law-abiding wimps like Johnny Cash and me. I personalize my version to incorporate a flight from justice that ends in arrest at the Rainbow Club in Chicago and the incarceration of my fat Welsh carcass in Leeds' notorious Armley Jail. But I don't change the line "I can't forget the day I shot that bad bitch down"—'cos I couldn't come up with anything badder. I don't know if that makes me a sexist pig any more than it makes Johnny Cash a murderer, but there is gruesome pleasure to be had performing (and listening to) this sort of stuff, which is as uncomfortable as it is addictive (sniff!).

When Ice-T released "Cop Killer," he was savaged by media and politicians from both right & left. He pointed out this wouldn't have happened if he'd said what he said in a novel or a movie. But he didn't—he wrote a song, and even though I can't explain it I relish that difference. Songs are powerful and it's really hard to separate the singer from the song, the song from reality.

Rennie Sparks of the Handsome Family says: "I think of murder in songs as being like murders that take place in dreams. Just 'cause you dream you're an axe murderer doesn't necessarily mean you want to be an axe murderer. It's a language of symbols; it can't be deconstructed that easily. The words in songs are a language of dreams so the women tend to be the symbols of beauty, frailty, rebirth etc. That's why they need to die so much. All beauty must fade."

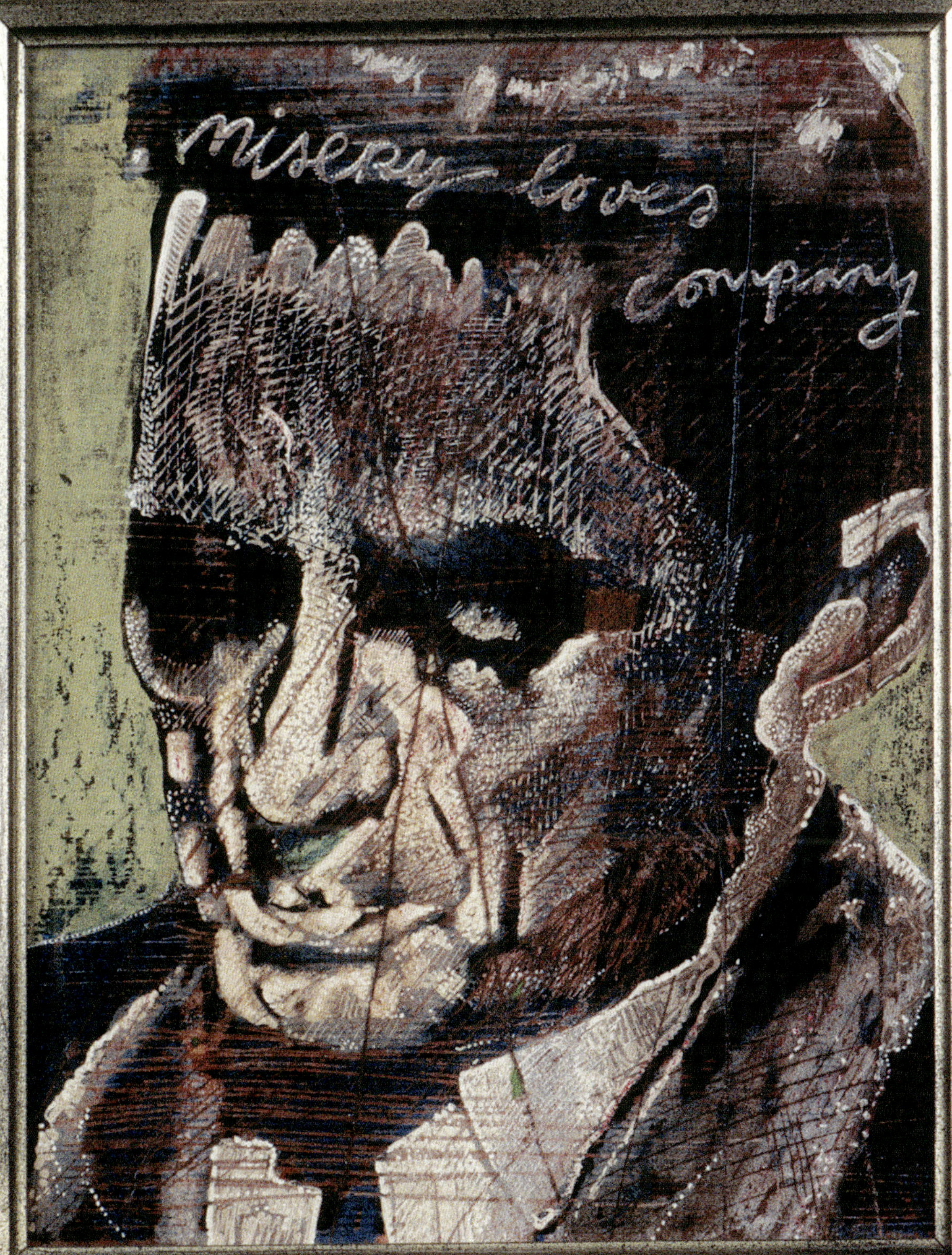

it's dark here at the home of the blues...
misery loves company
just around the corner there's heartache

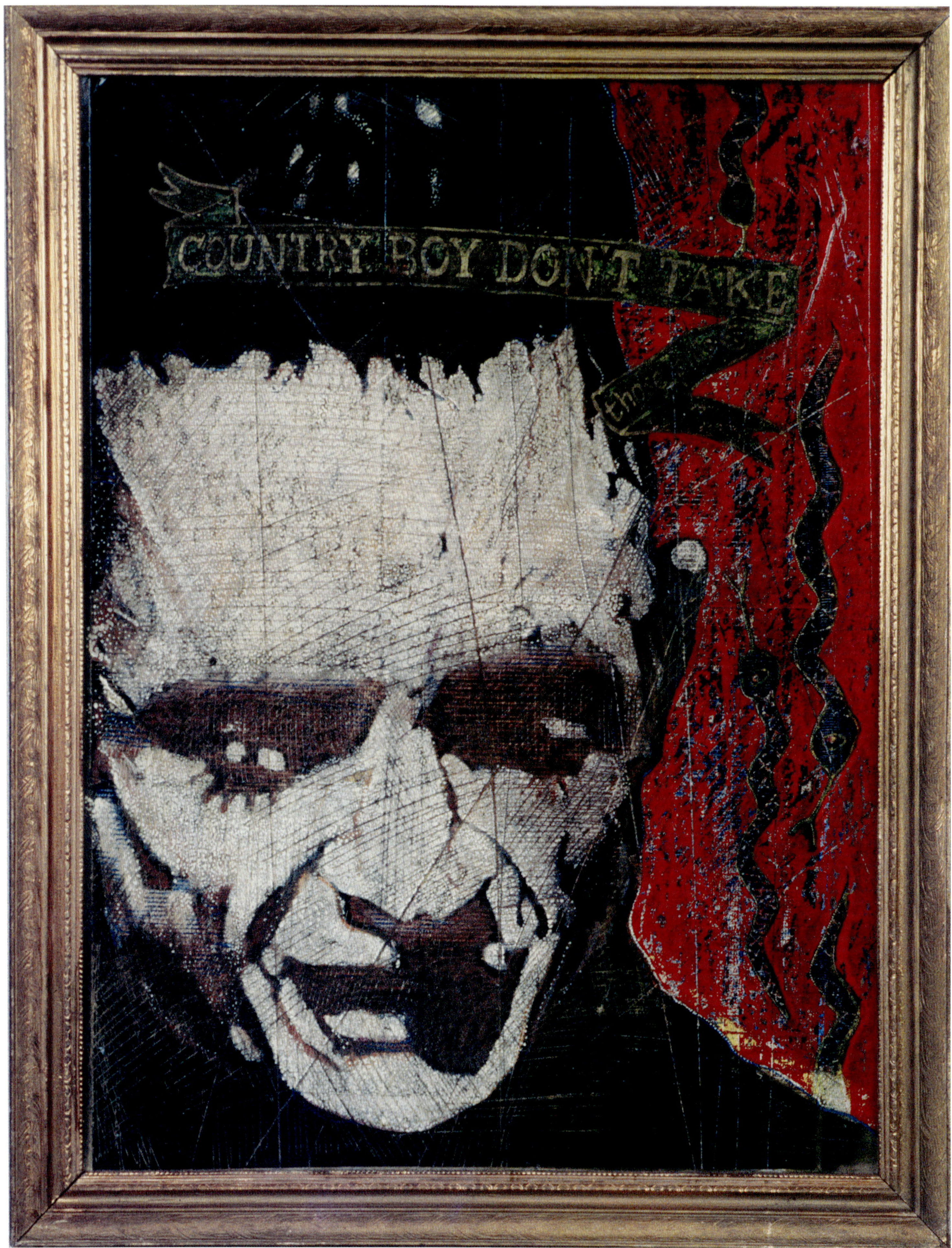
COUNTRY BOY DON'T TAKE
three

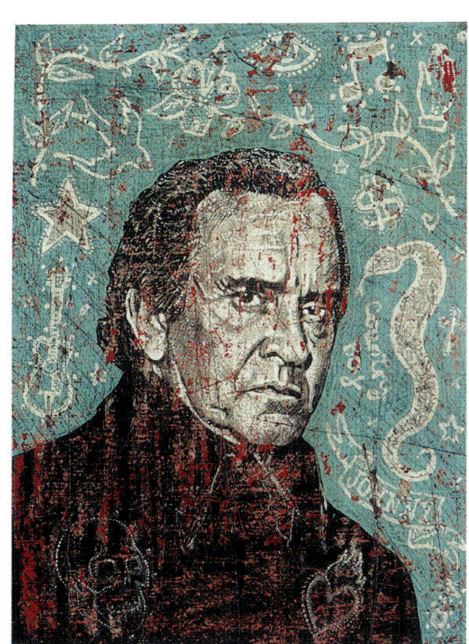

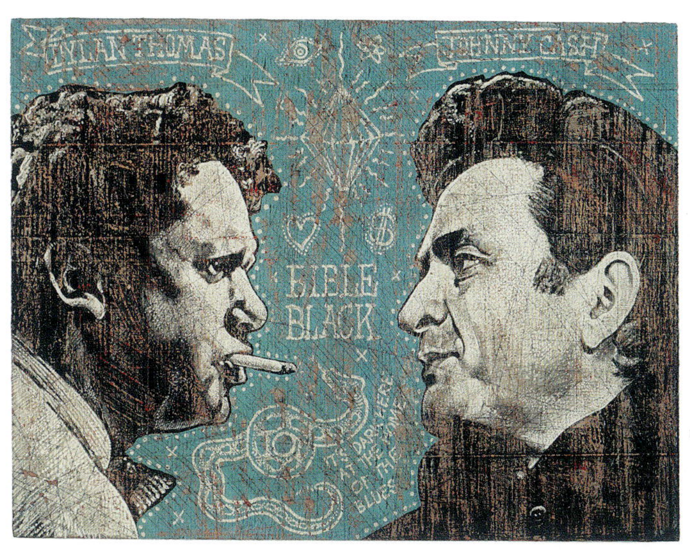
DYLAN THOMAS
JOHNNY CASH
BIBLE BLACK
IT'S DARK HERE AT THE BOTTOM OF THE BLUES

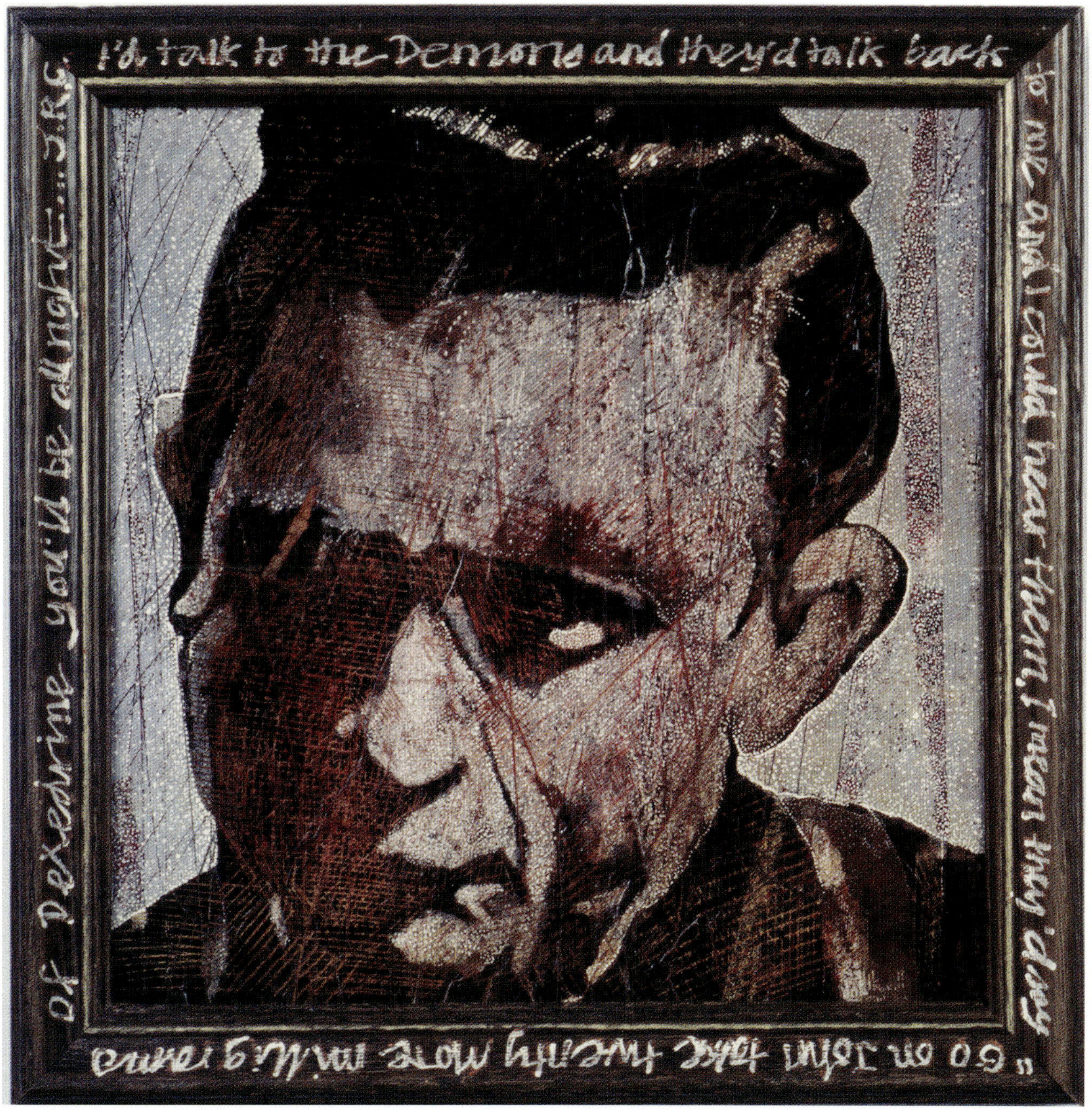

I'd talk to the Demons and they'd talk back to me and I could hear them, I mean they'd keep "Go on John take twenty more milligrams of Dexedrine you'd be alright...J.R.C.

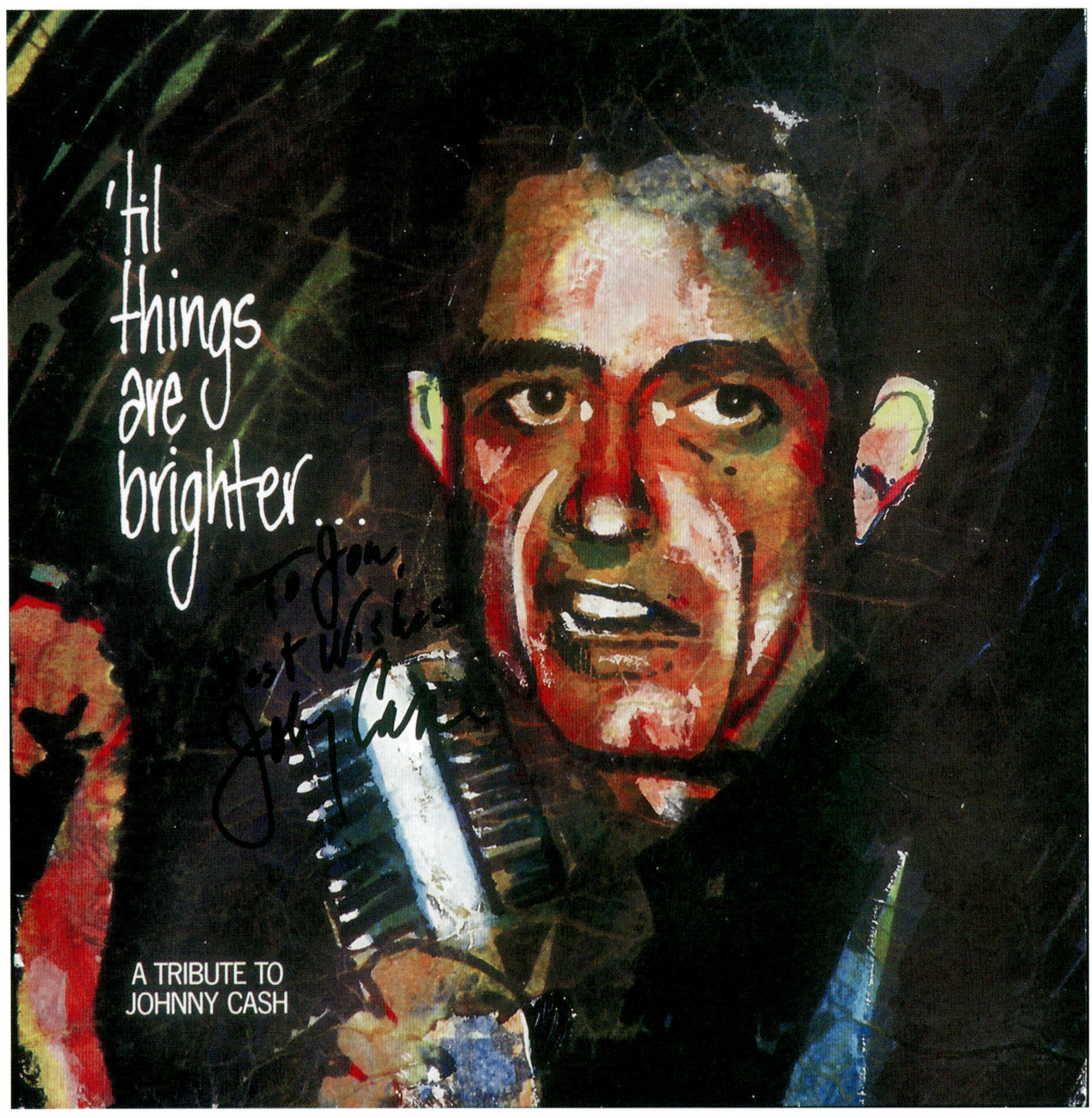

Johnny Cash was the only Country and Western singer to make a stand against the Vietnam War. Hillbillies, teddylads, acidheads, and mass murderers—Johnny has played for them all. He speaks out for the little man (and I don't mean Mickey Rooney). 'TIL THINGS ARE BRIGHTER is a compulsive collection of songs made famous by the Man in Black and performed by a varied collection of contemporary hillbillies, teddylads, acidheads, and mass murderers. It is both a tribute and fundraiser; with ignorance and bigotry so rife in certain elements of our society, AIDS is largely ignored or thought of as some kind of punishment "from above." The Terrence Higgins Trust is one of the few organisations getting to grips with the AIDS issue and all profits from this LP will go to that trust.

— sleeve notes for 'TIL THINGS ARE BRIGHTER

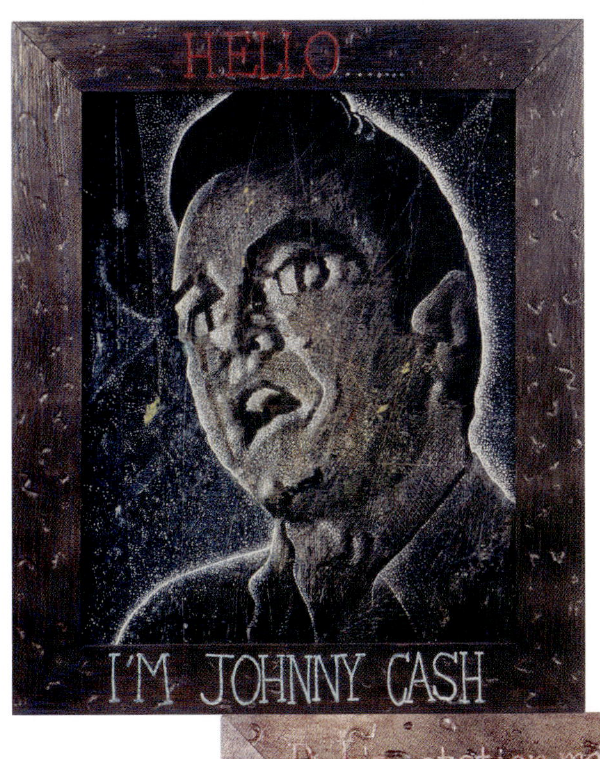

HELLO
I'M JOHNNY CASH

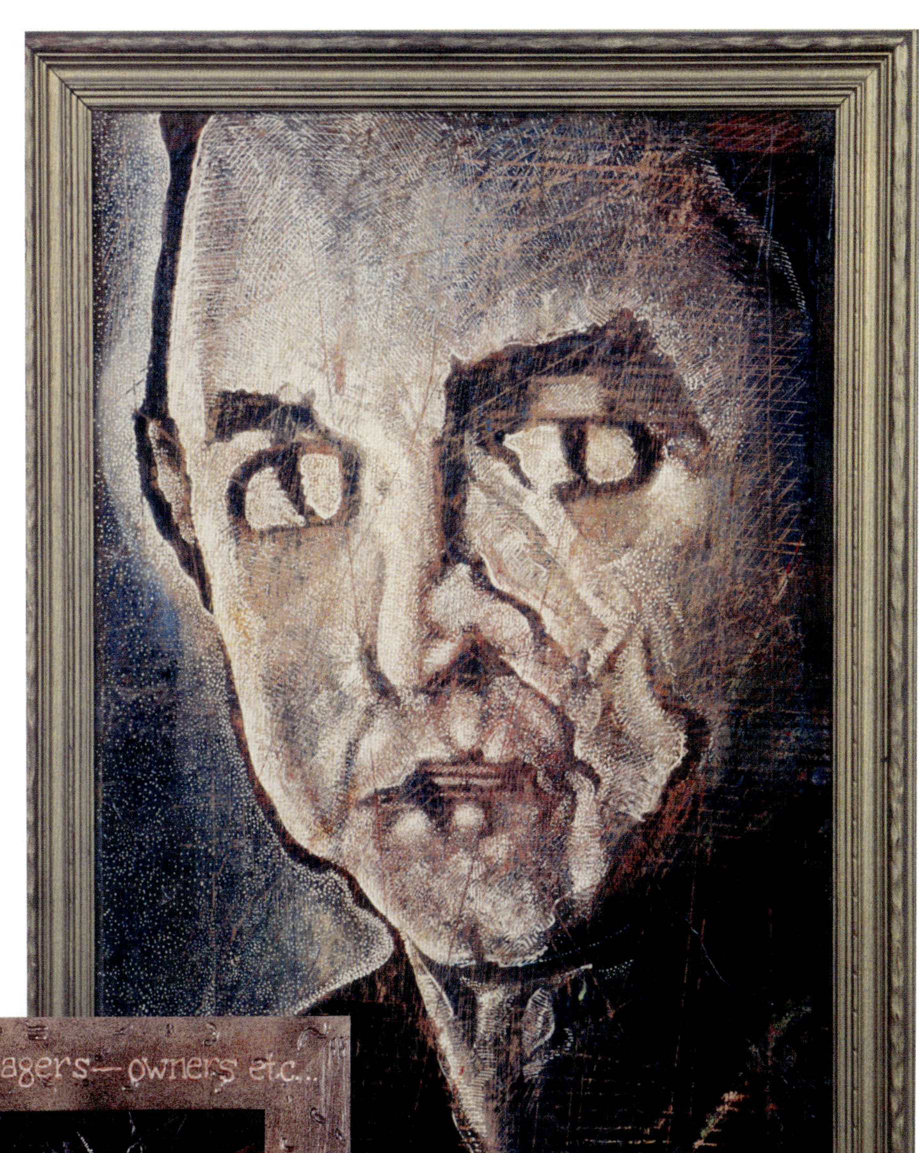

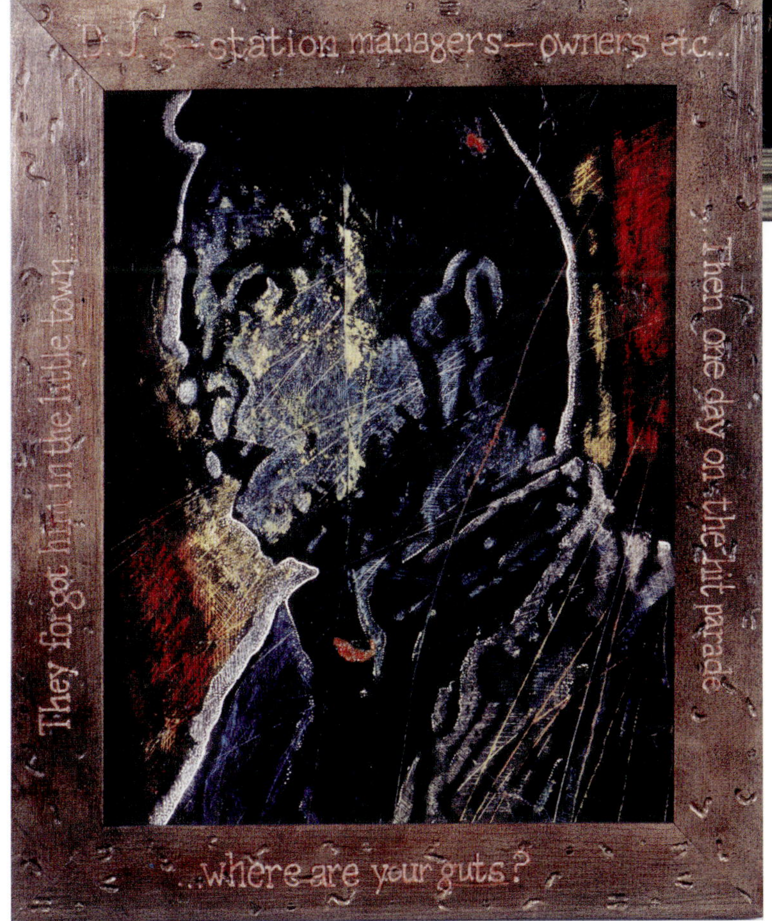

D.J.'s — station managers — owners etc...
They forgot him in the little town...
...Then one day on the hit parade
...where are your guts?

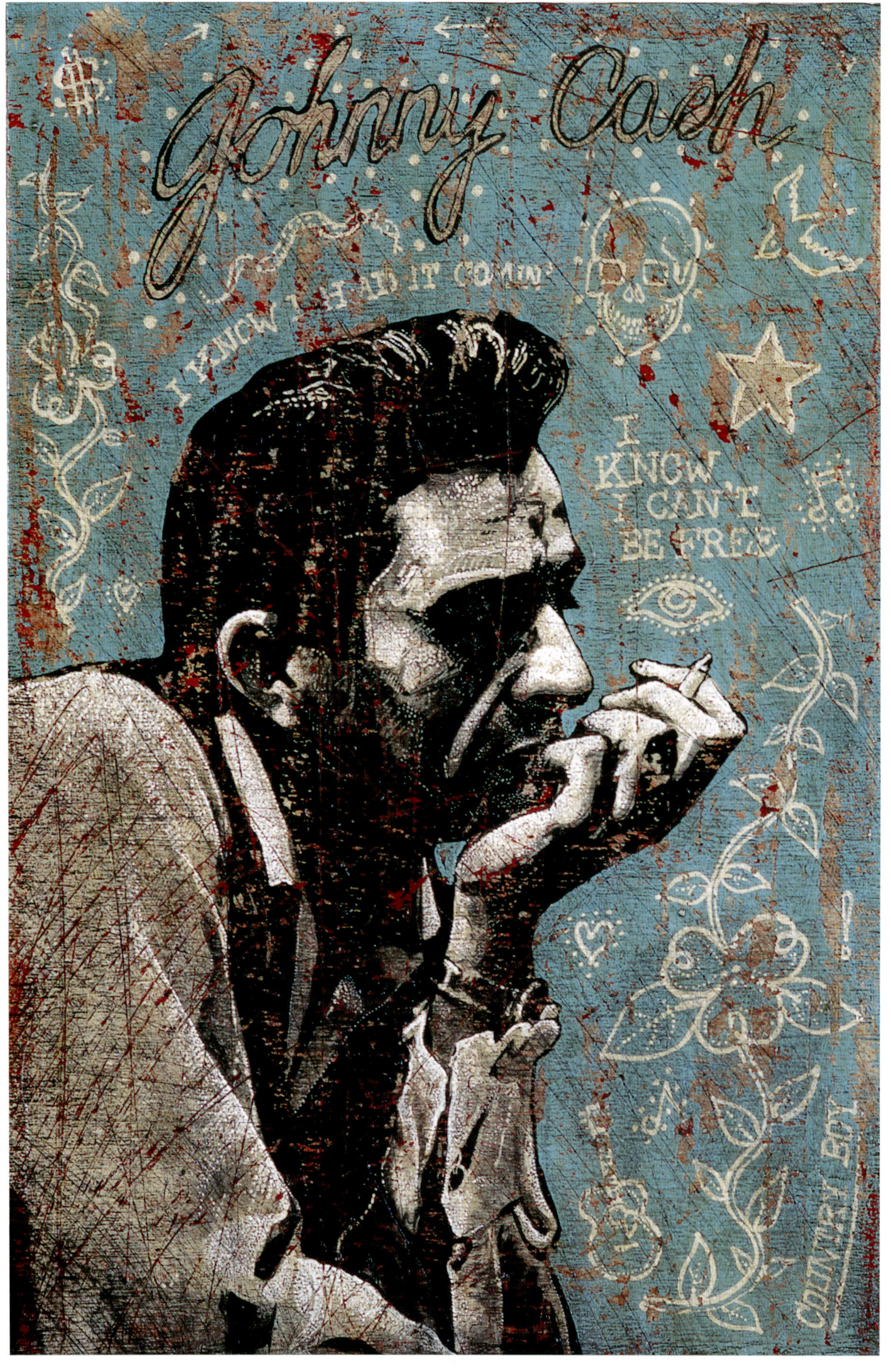

Johnny Cash
I KNOW I LET IT COMIN'
I KNOW I CAN'T BE FREE
COUNTRY BOY

"Back in 1986 in Chicago watching late-nite videos of Tex Ritter's "Ranch Party" in weird, grainy, harsh-contrast black and white . . . It is 1957, I am being born and out steps Cash, up there with the Sputnik, visibly ill at ease amidst the hilarious hick extras and hyperactive cornball novelty acts that populate the bleached out cardboard barnyard set . . . He sings a song, taut and twitching, and then just stands there, uncomfortable, humble and wired. He is the polar opposite of the cozy, safe, sexless and bland that White America usually clutches to its all-purchasing, suffocating breast . . . Decency, truth, honesty—around him these gutted terms retain some of their original meaning and in a country that fears self-criticism above all else he holds a mirror up to its rotten hide . . . Ironically it is patriotism and terrible guilty grief that fuels this righteous rage at totalitarianism, racism, genocide . . . You name it! . . . Going into the prisons & reservations, putting his own wildness and weakness under the same microscope . . .

"Once he kissed my mum on the lips backstage at the Newport Centre and she never gave me a hard time again about the punk rocking."

—from a postcard sent to Scout Records in Germany, August 2nd 1994, from the Dude Rancher Lodge in Billings, Montana. Used as sleeve notes for Misery Loves Company: Jonboy Langford & the Pine Valley Cosmonauts Explore the Dark & Lonely World of Johnny Cash

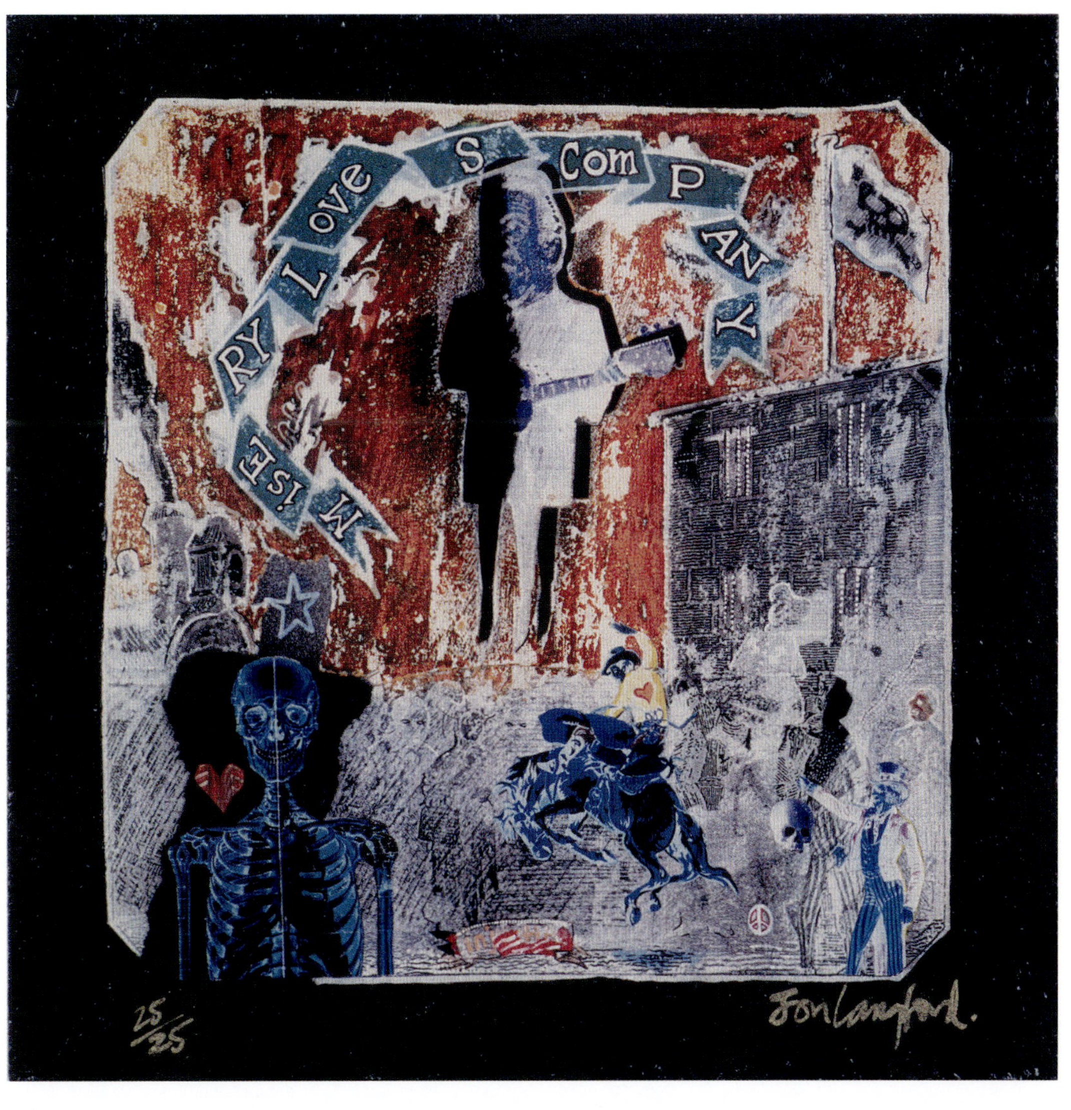

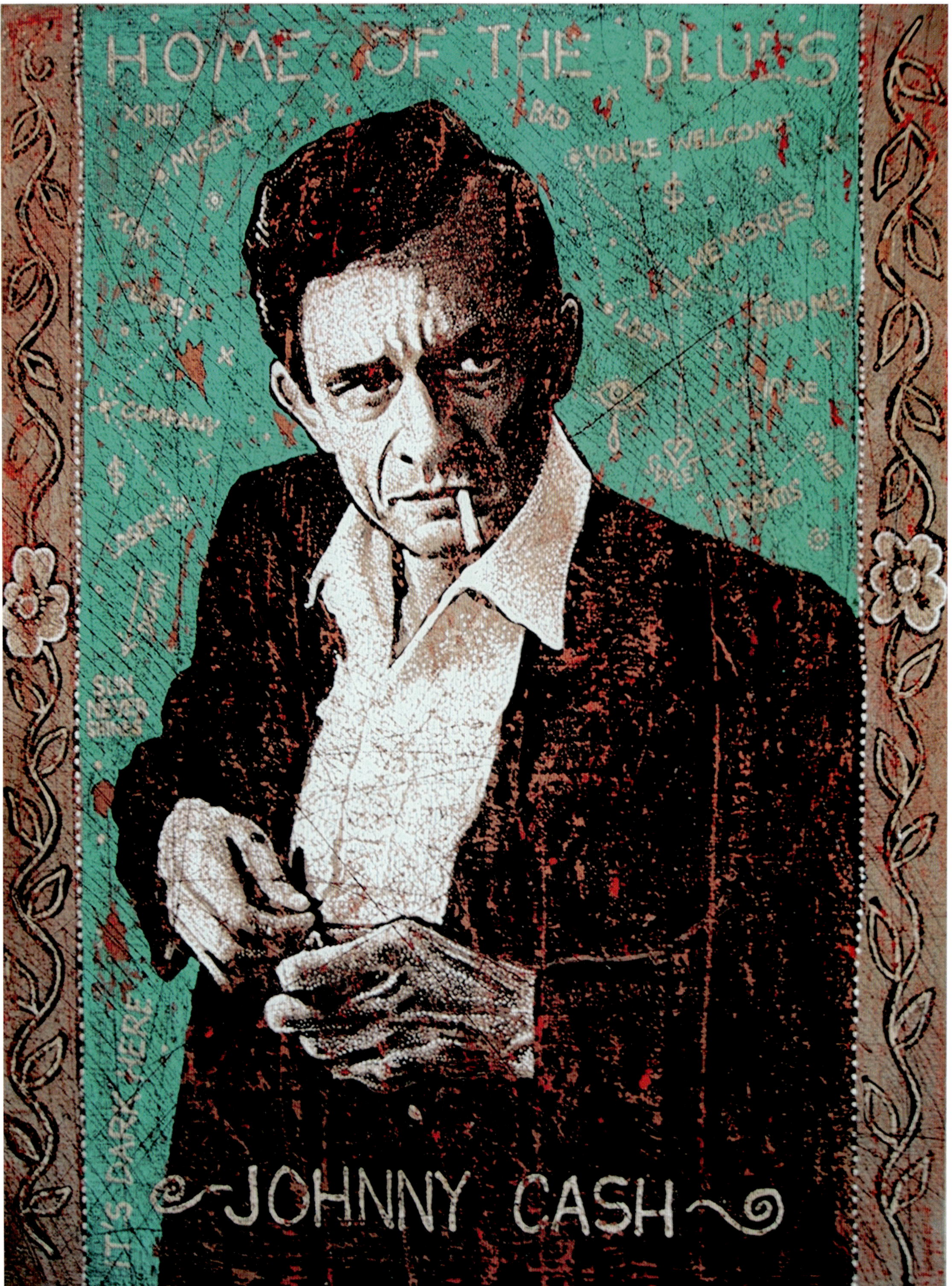

HOME OF THE BLUES
JOHNNY CASH

BORN TO ETCH

Memphis 1988: I meet Tony Fitzpatrick for the first time as he is being ejected from Graceland for running upstairs and jumping on the bed, an act he deems crucial to the pilgrimage he's making across the Old South on a credit card and a prayer. This huge ex-boxer/junkie/jailbird/car thief looks like trouble to us. He demands to know what the fuck the Mekons are doing hanging around outside Elvis's house.

Painting and drawing saved Tony's life—got him out of prison and provided a focus for his limitless hoodlum energy. He was the one who would bully me into making art seriously, so it's fitting that I ran into him on a trip that took me to Nashville for the first time.

Me, Sally, and Marc Riley from the Fall are busy failing to promote an album of Johnny Cash covers that we put out to raise money for an Aids Foundation in the UK. A few days earlier, we had wandered into Tootsie's Orchid Lounge, the beer joint across the alley from the old Ryman Auditorium, where inspired lushes like Patsy Cline, Hank Williams, Roger Miller, & Faron Young came to get wasted between sets at the original Grand (but dry) Ole Opry.

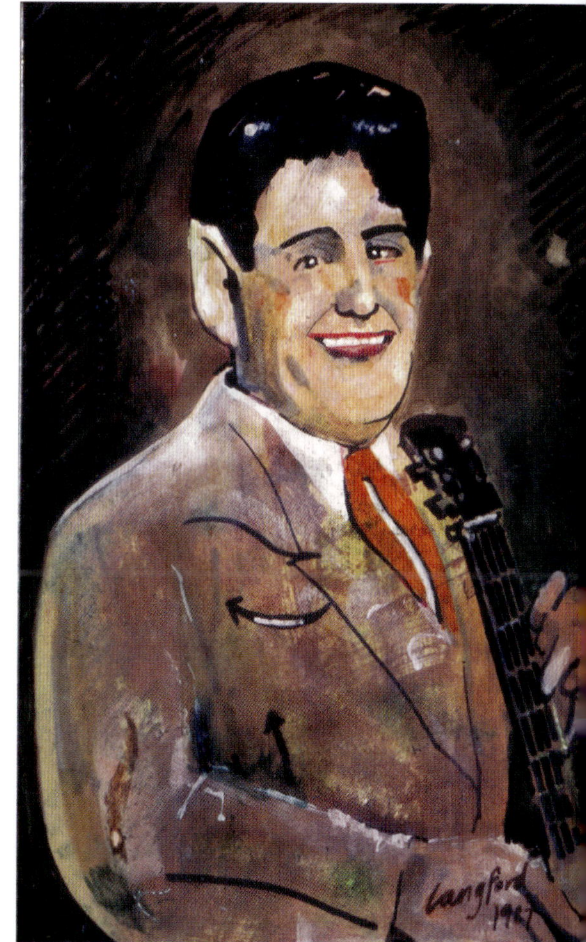

Every inch of Tootsie's walls is covered with old publicity photos, the icons and relics of a culture that buried its dead high on bar-room walls—framed, tattered, and embalmed in amber layers of nicotine snot. Rabbits frozen in history's headlights, signing their contracts and signing away their souls, used up, spat out, and finally forgotten like the waste products of any other industry or theatre of war. Teeth and pearl buttons gleam, eyes gaze out hopefully from glazed promo-shot grins. Old stars, dead stars, non-stars—cannon fodder glimpsed thru the murky paranoid depths of America's neglect, lost in a fog of dim lights, thick smoke, and cold, cold war.

As you stand and stare, trying to take it all in, blind optimism and hopeless nostalgia race in opposite directions like freight trains, oblivious to the logs that have fallen on the tracks up ahead and the tidal wave of mediocrity that will sweep away everything but the memory of a time when visionaries & pioneers thrived at the heart of the mainstream and the lid wasn't on so tight.

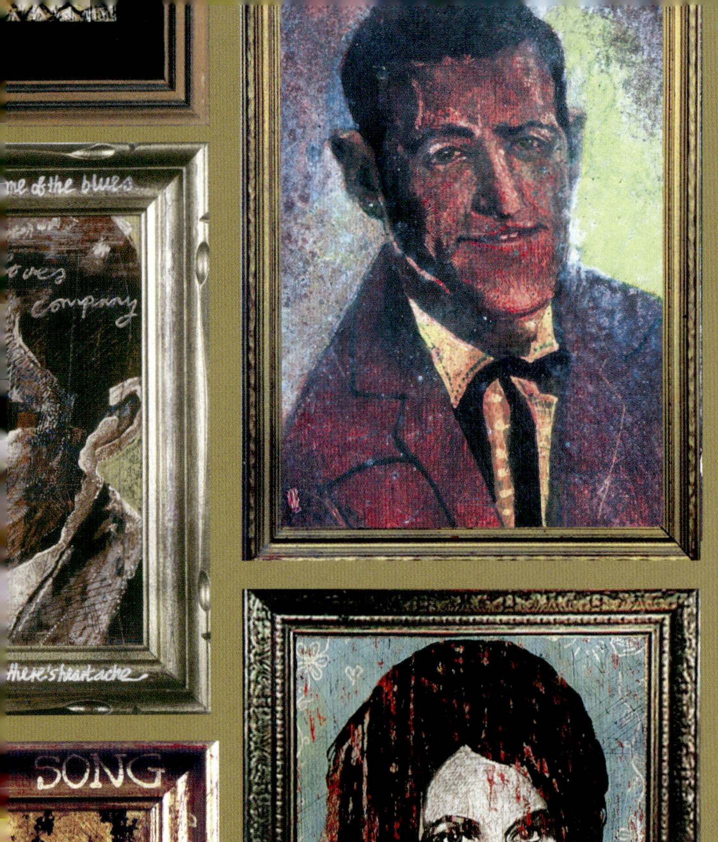
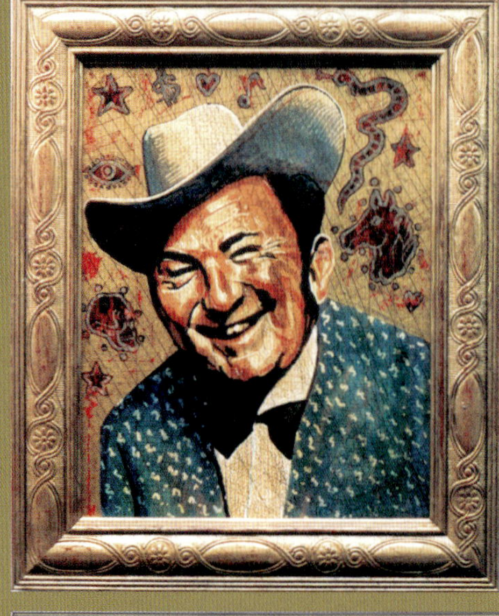
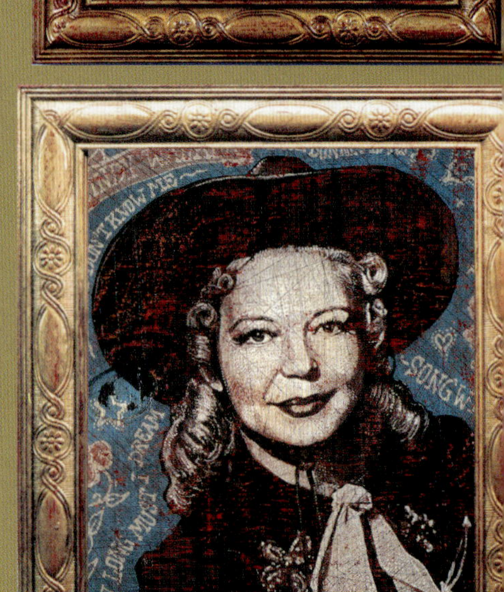
SONGW
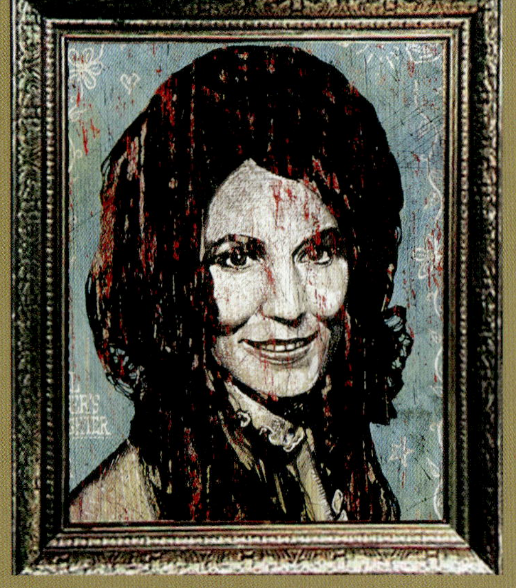
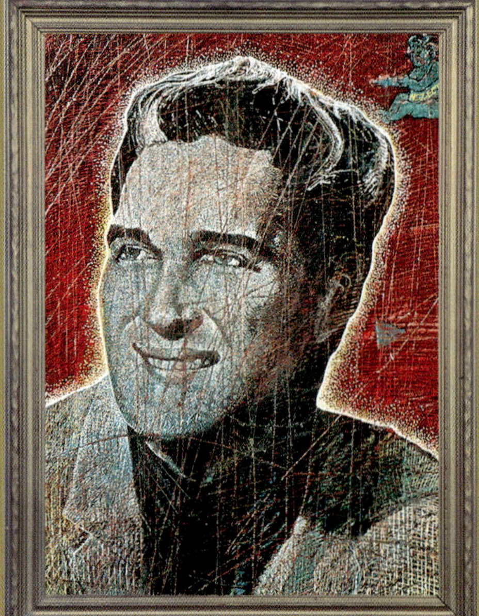
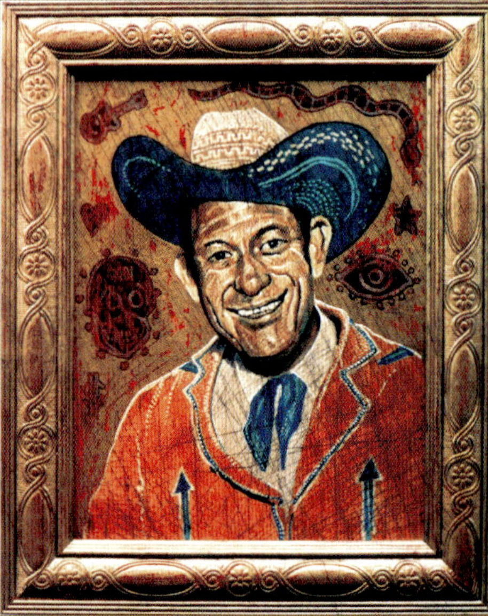
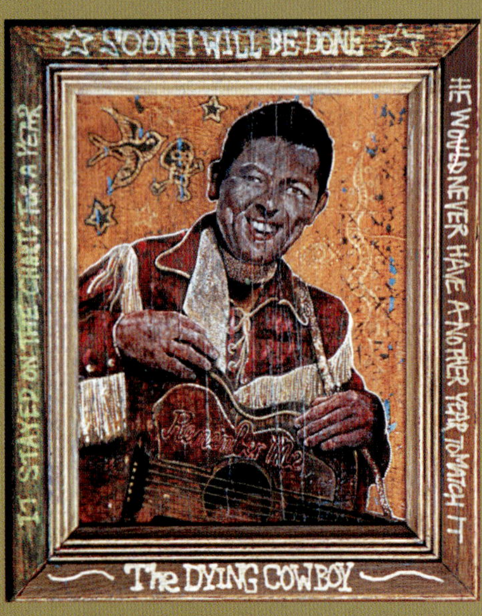
SOON I WILL BE DONE
IT STAYED ON THE CHARTS FOR A YEAR
HE WOULD NEVER HAVE ANOTHER YEAR TO MATCH IT
The DYING COWBOY
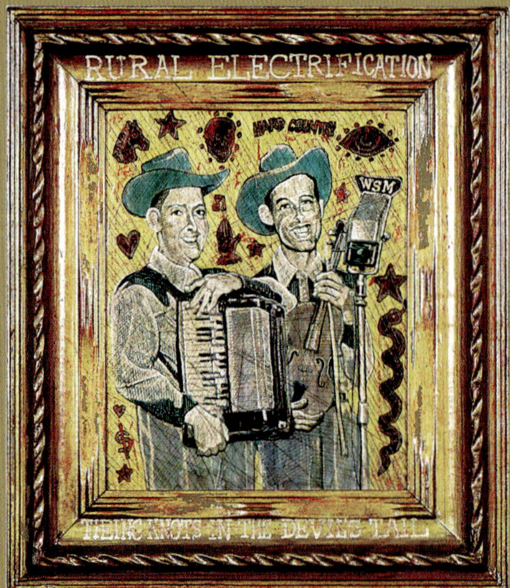
RURAL ELECTRIFICATION
HARD COUNTRY
WSM
TIEING KNOTS IN THE DEVIL'S TAIL
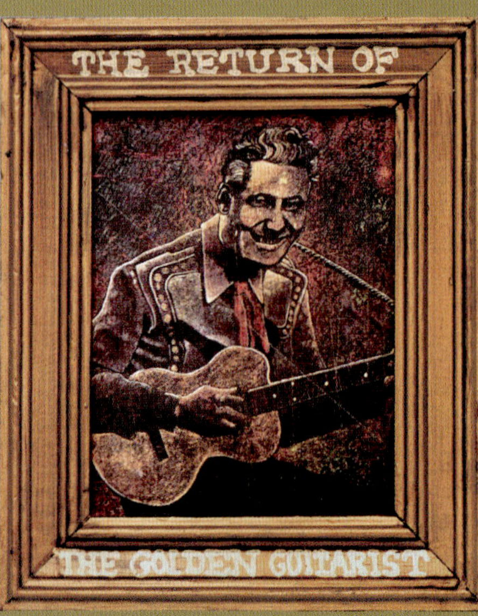
THE RETURN OF
THE GOLDEN GUITARIST
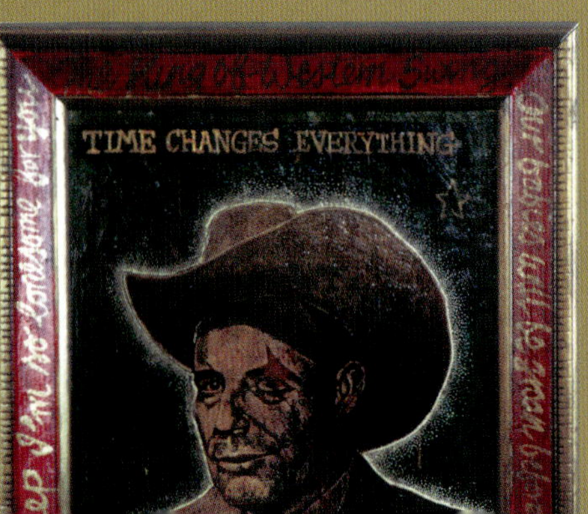
TIME CHANGES EVERYTHING
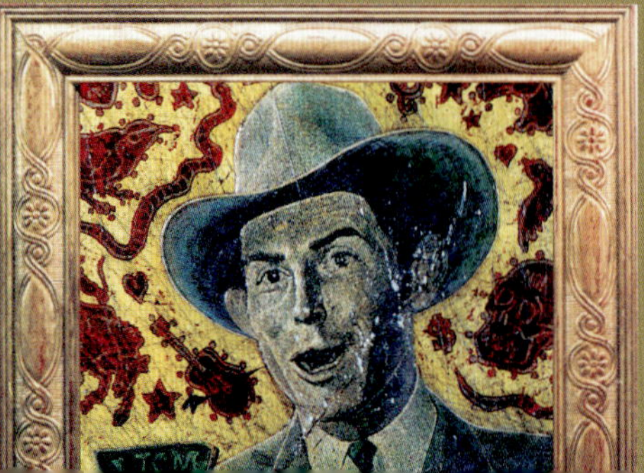
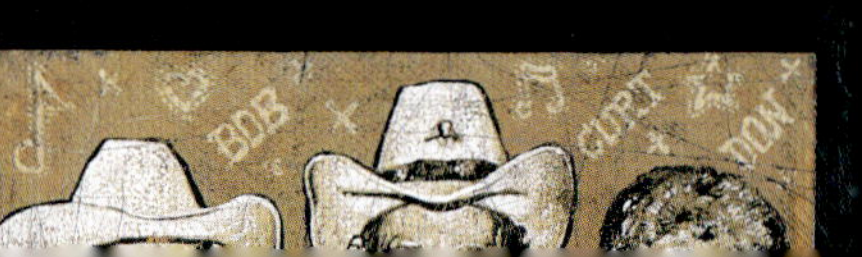

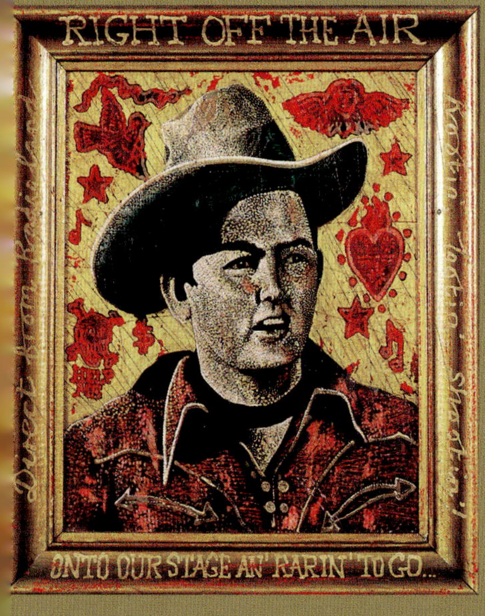
RIGHT OFF THE AIR
ONTO OUR STAGE AN' RARIN' TO GO...

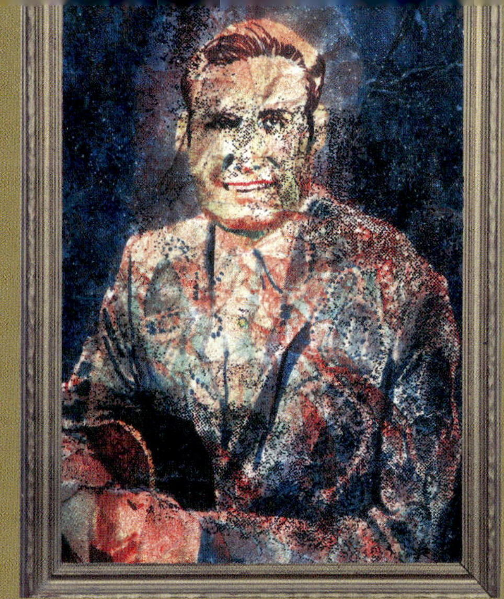

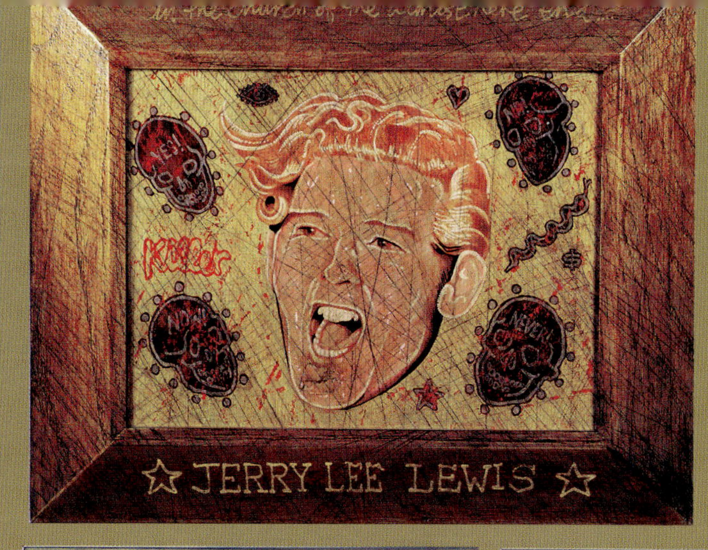
☆ JERRY LEE LEWIS ☆

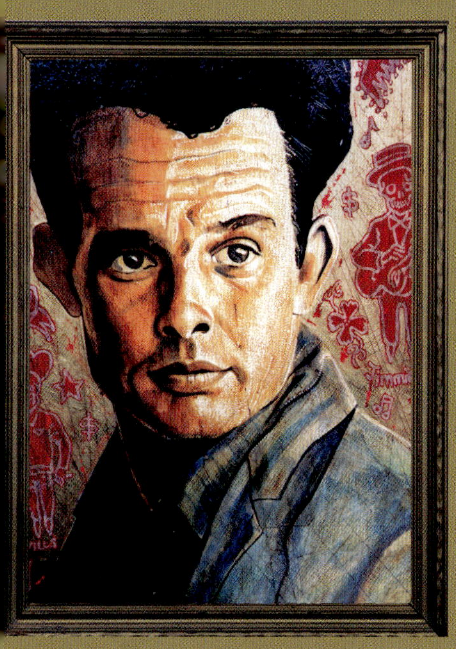

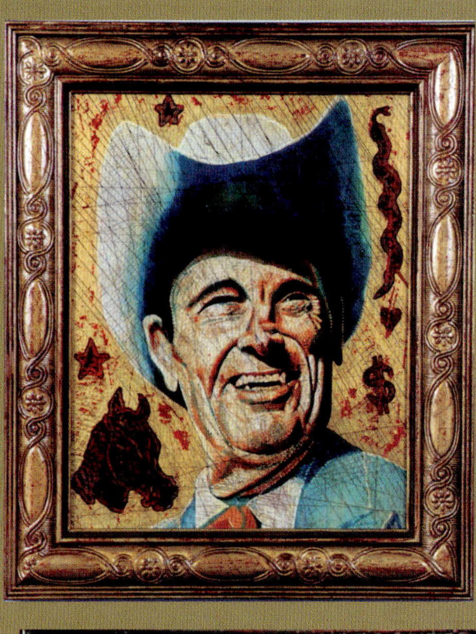

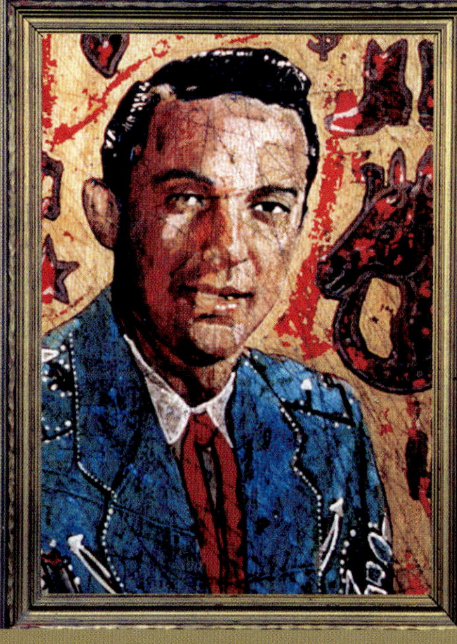

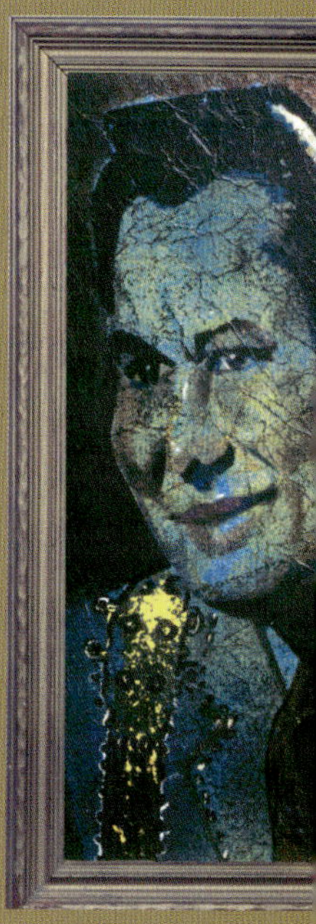

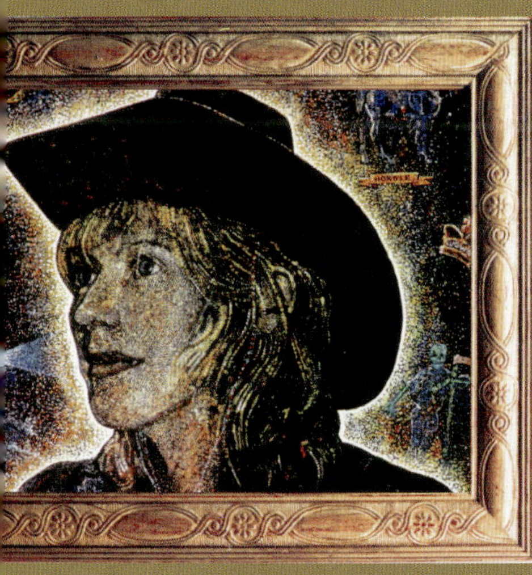

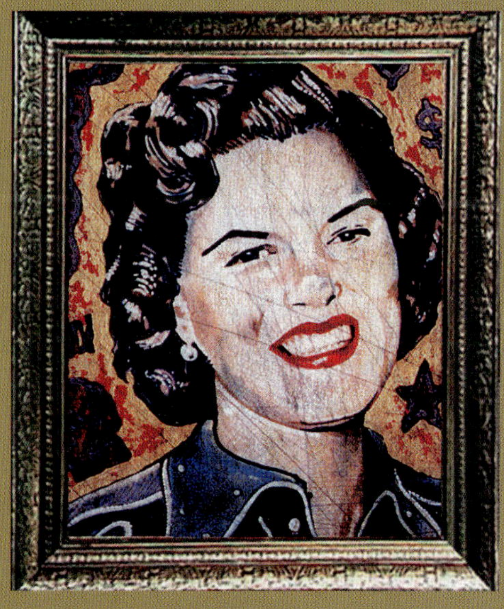

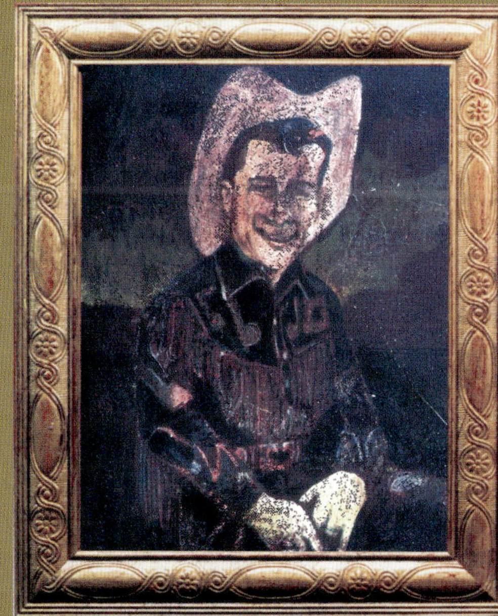

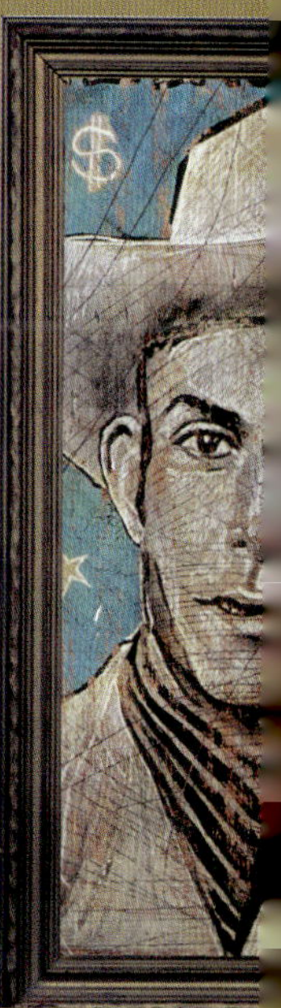

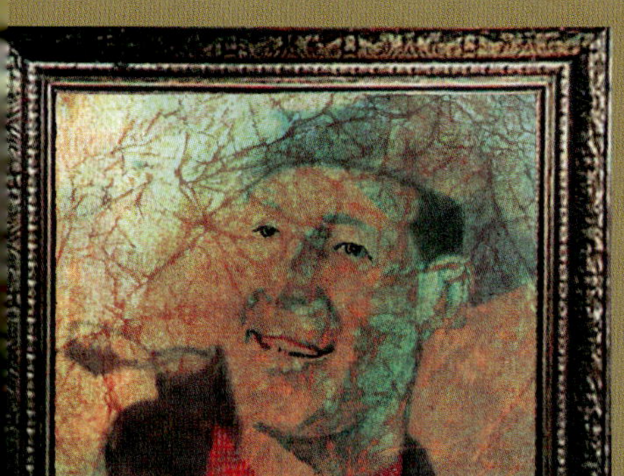

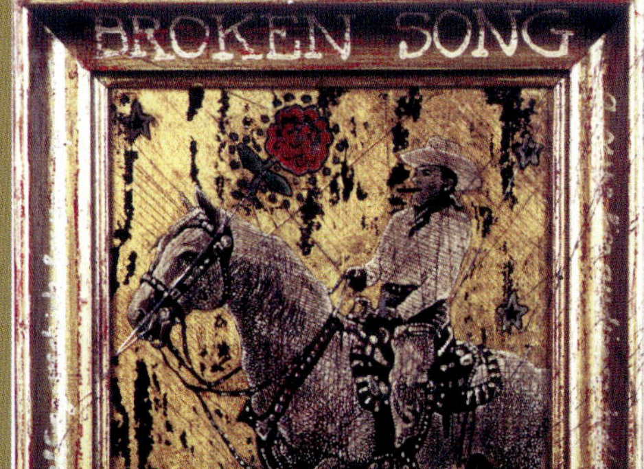
BROKEN SONG

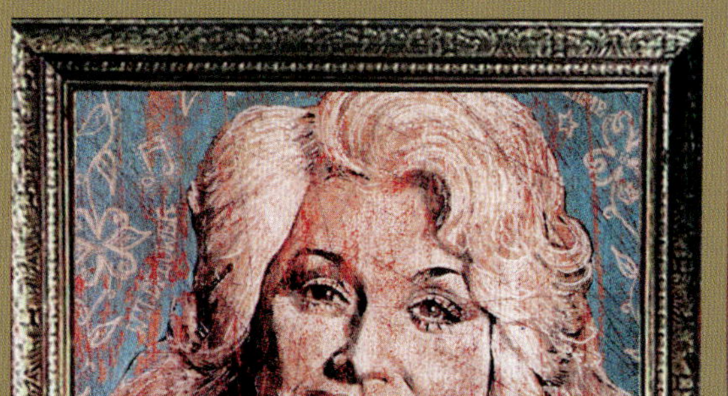

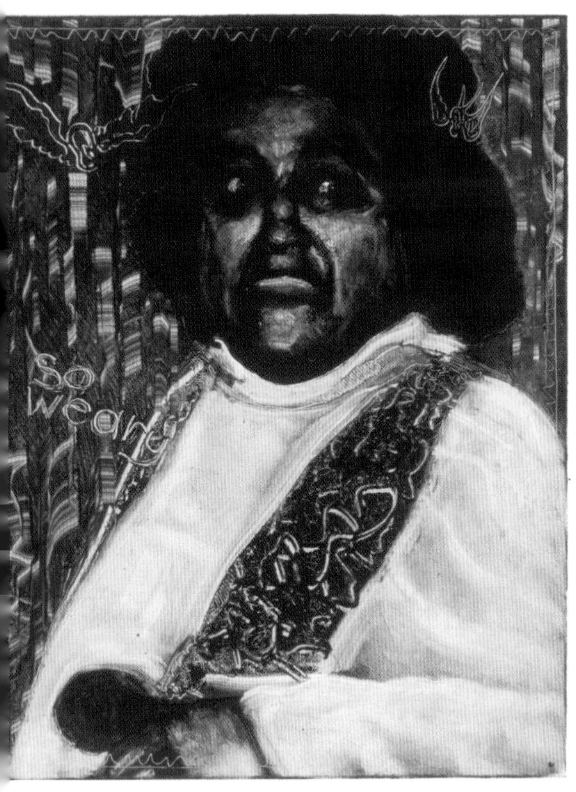

Back in wild West Yorkshire, the Texas of Britain, I try to recreate the images I'd seen at Tootsie's. I make paintings of Country & Western publicity photos. Not paintings of people, but paintings of photographs that had been left on a wall to decay. I start to think of them as semi-religious icons, so I add gold to the frames and backgrounds. Then I spit on them, rub coffee grounds and gunk into them, slash their surfaces with knives, and toss them round the room to imitate the corrosive power of time and deliberate neglect. I never thought of selling or exhibiting these works. Mostly, I gave them away to friends.

But later, in Chicago, working artist Tony Fitzpatrick hunts me down and tells me I was "born to etch!" I start going to his studio every Saturday (where I'm tutored by fantastic printmakers Theresa Mucha and Steve Campbell) and turn out a sheaf of black and white copperplate etchings of scratched-up entertainers surrounded by details from Dutch still lifes, classic western wear, and the cold war.

There's Tom Jones levitating over South Wales, Bob Wills fast asleep, Louis Armstrong, Yuri Gagarin, Dorothy Love Coates. And Hank Williams—as St. Sebastian, shot through with arrows; signing his contract; and going head to head with Josef Stalin while an ugly angel whispers "All the fame of lofty deeds must perish like a dream."

Country music has a great tradition of answer records, songs that comment or cash in on someone else's hit, so I imagined the Soviet dictator responding to Cold War Hank's big political number "Oh No, Joe!" with his own "Hank Williams Must Die"—like Kitty Wells slinging "It Wasn't God Who Made Honky-Tonk Angels" back at Hank Thompson, except with a big moustache and hands drenched in blood. The fact that Uncle Joe never had a hit with that song & probably never ordered the hit on Hank Williams says something to me about the gnat-like impotence of political pop. In case it isn't obvious already, all these images are deeply autobiographical.

1993: Tony shows my etchings at his World Tattoo gallery— and people actually buy them! Which causes some rusty old cogs to turn in my brain: CLICK! Make art. WHIRR! Sell it!

This came at a very good time: a time when the Mekons were quite possibly signed to Warner Brothers' Latin division, but nobody really knew or cared except some distant and invisible gaggle of lawyers squabbling over tiny slices of nothing.

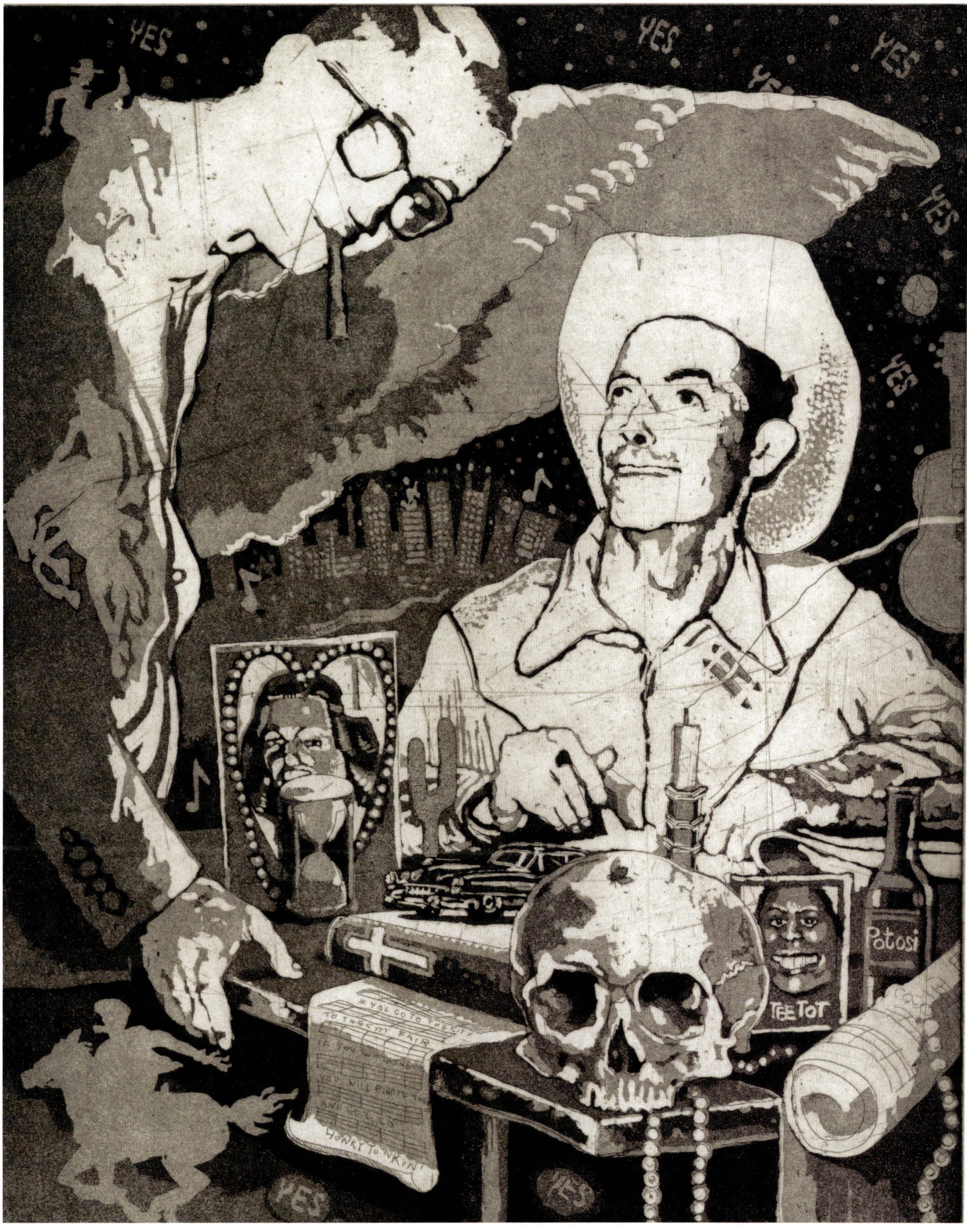

YES
YES
YES
YES
YES
Potosi
TEE TOT
IF YOU GO TO THE CITY
TO THE CITY FAIR
YES
YES

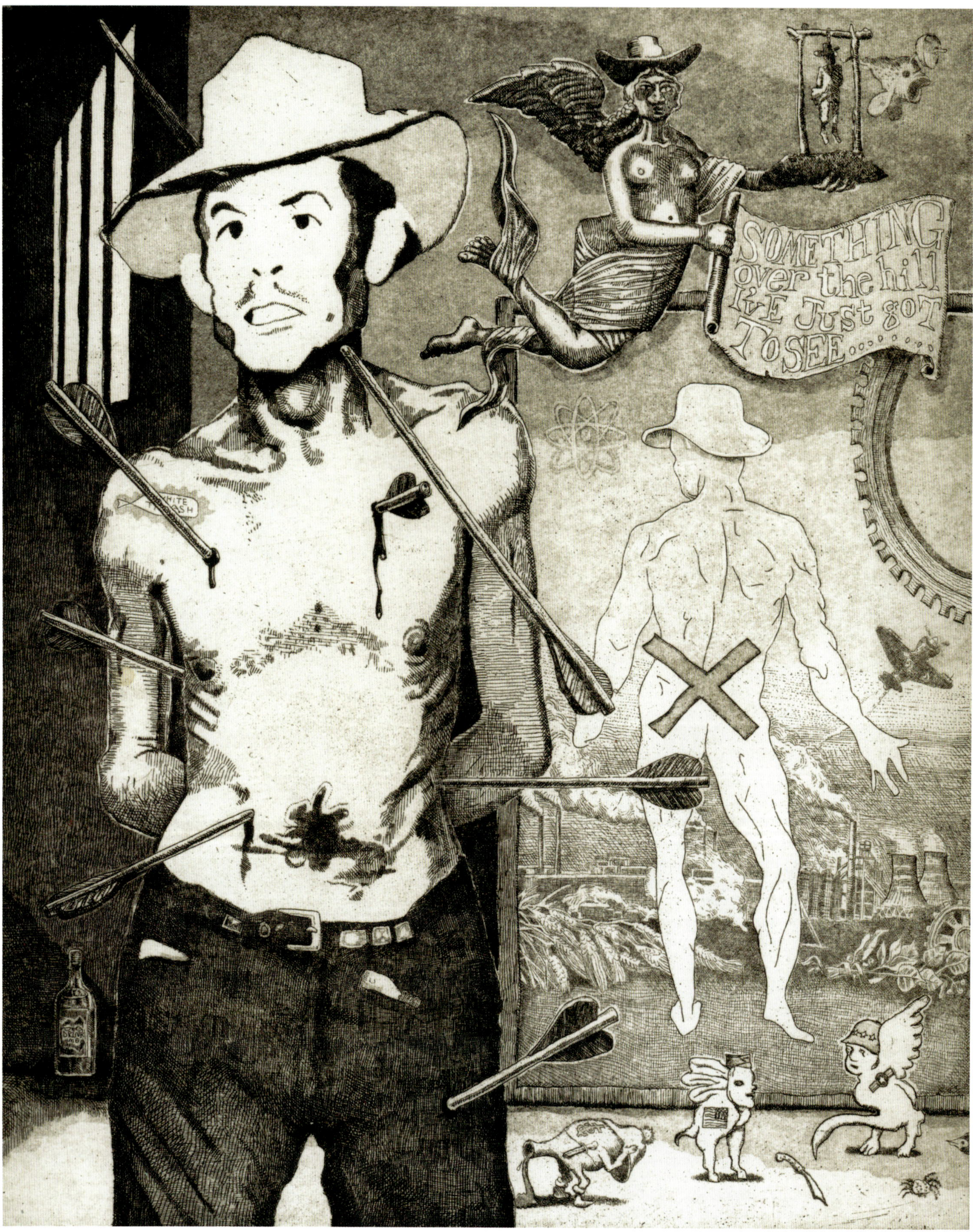
WHITE TRASH
SOMETHING
over the hill
I've Just goT
TO SEE...

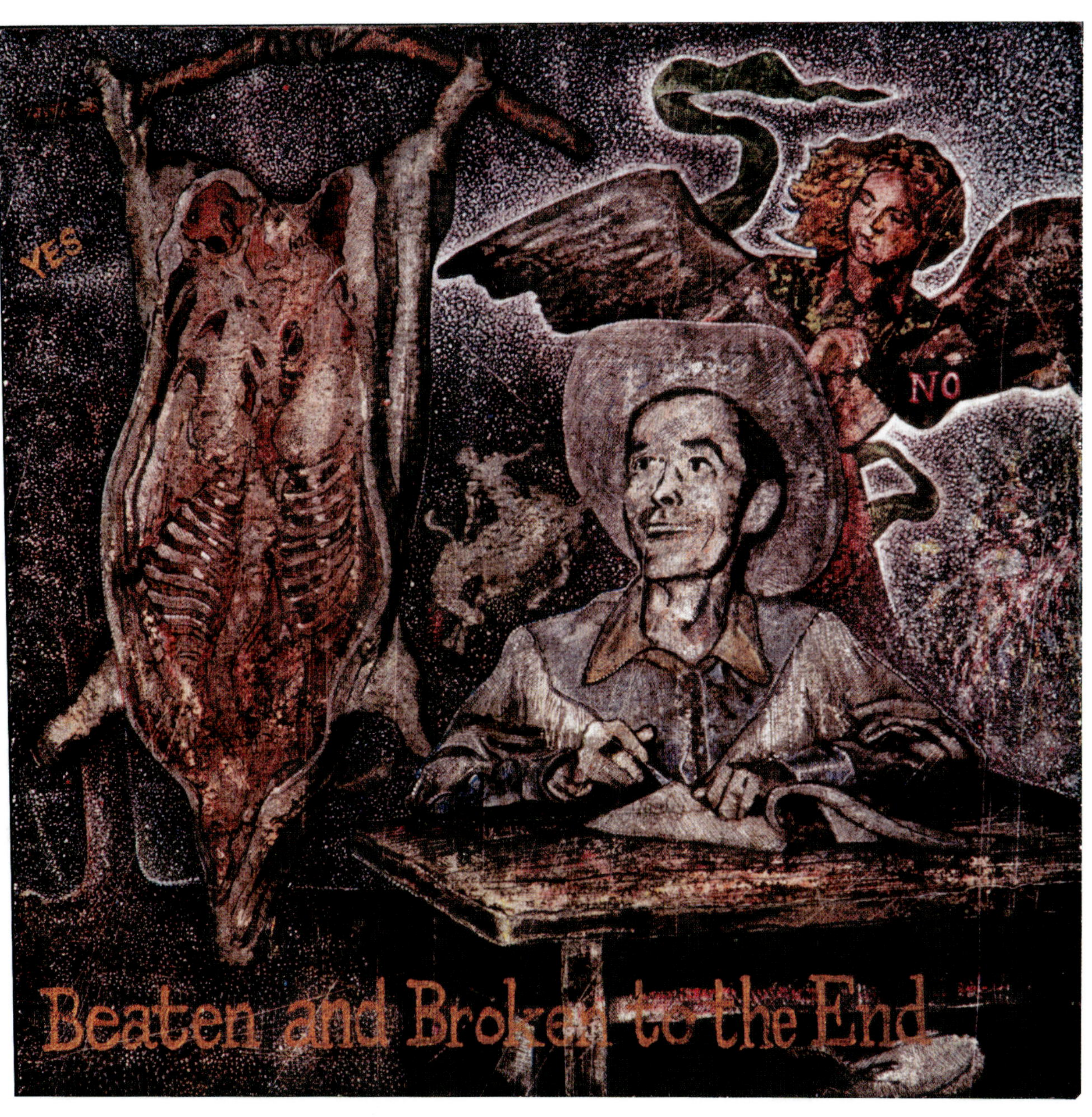

Hank Signs His Contract

Sat down at the table with papers and pen
A flashlight explodes in his eyes
To bleach the flesh white on a hand poised to write
His signature in blood on the line

At the fulcrum, on the seesaw, what goes up comes down
& If he'd even read it he'd find
That each cut of meat has been bought by the pound,
By the someone who smiles at his side ➡

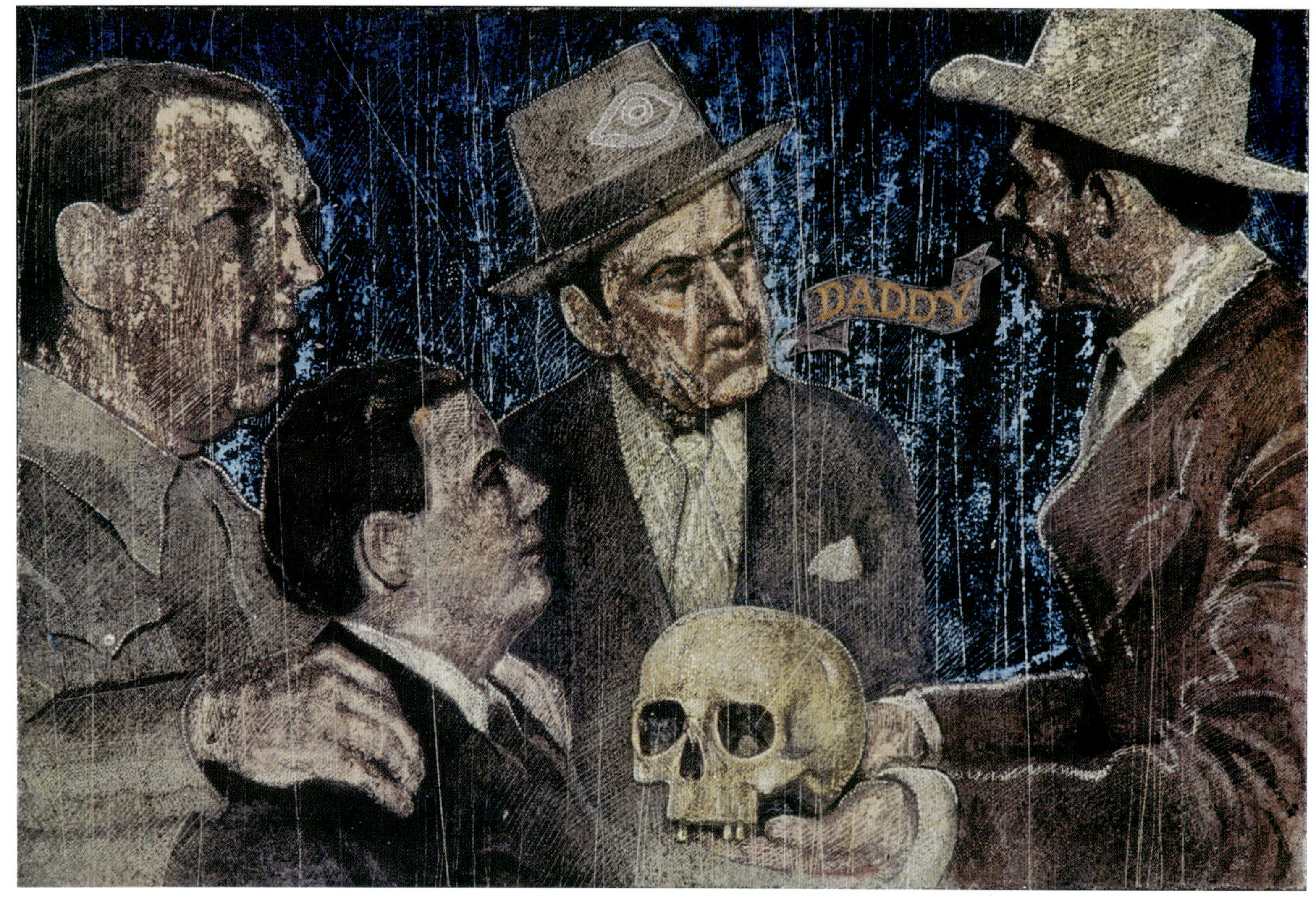

A great eagle's wing will close over him
Curving from the shoulder of that man
Whose other arm extends in a show of force
As it shakes & takes the reins from his hand

Just like a blind man robbed of his cane
Shoved through the wrong door today
Through a minefield of type, the enemy's terrain
Down in the vault locked away

With a stroke of that pen how the engine will roar
& He'll rise above the stiffs and nobodies
& Wake up one day in the back shot away
A stone dead & prized employee

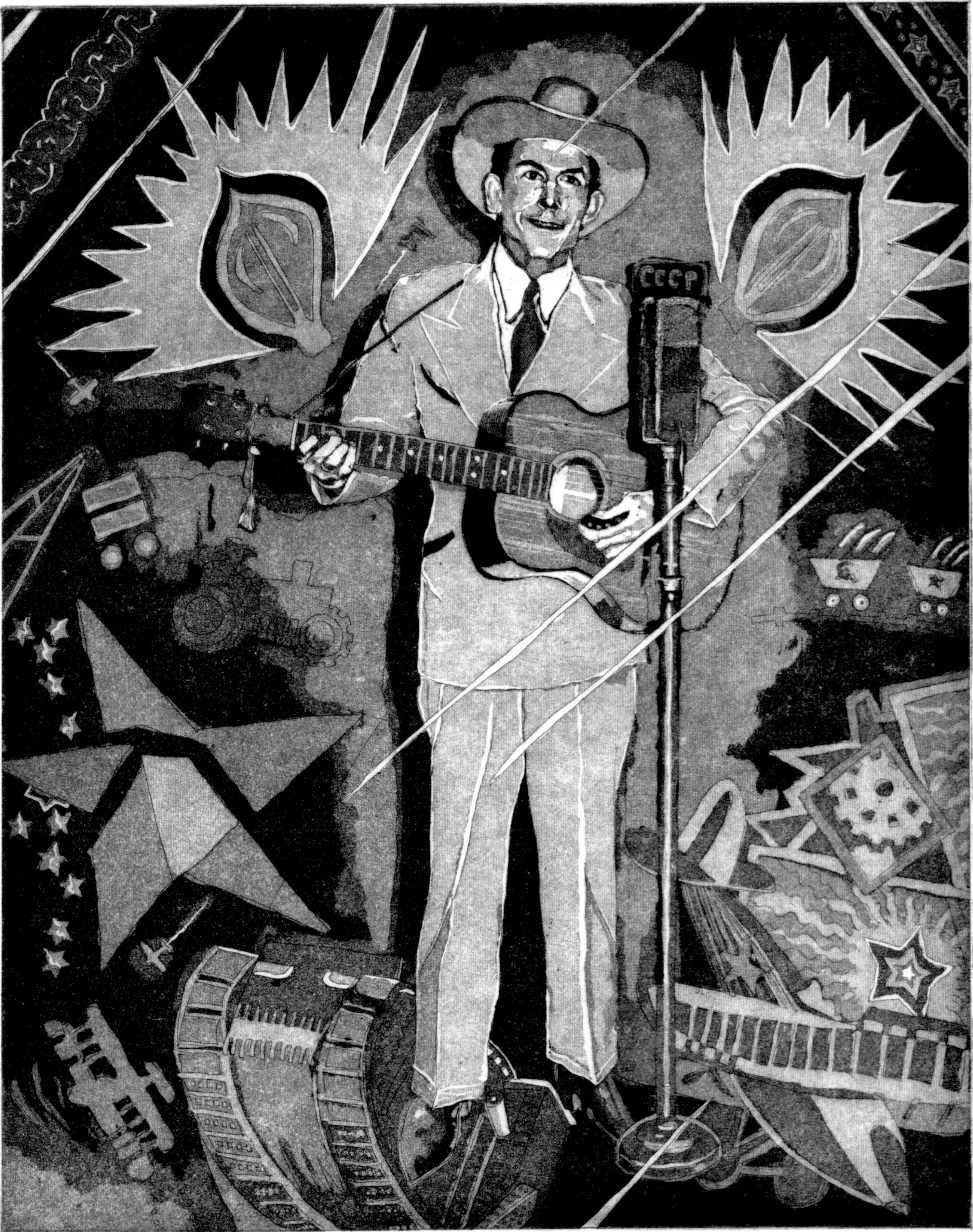

CCCP

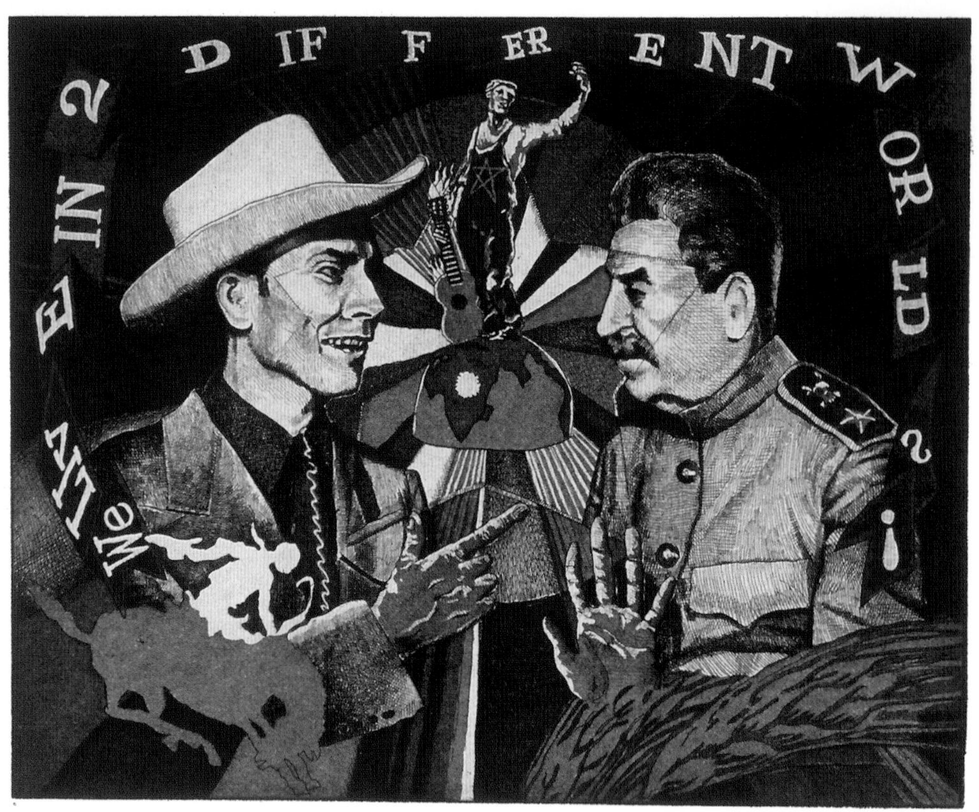

Oh No, Hank!

Silence you fools
Silence! Silence!
The creek it is dry
Don't no one ask why
The cat's in the bag and the bag's in the river
Don't no one ask why
Hank Williams must die

Shot thru with arrows
Howling in ecstasy
Thru the looking glass I saw his spine
Moving on over to the Soviet side

The corn is as high as an elephant's eye
Shooting down mosquitoes with an elephant gun
No, no one ask why
Hank Williams must die

He's somewhere out there
Happy and alive

BOB WILLS

Bob Wills once rode 50 miles on horseback to hear Bessie Smith sing the blues.

He was the first man to use drums on the Grand Ole Opry, and he was ready to pack up and go home if they wouldn't let him.

When he was asked what he thought about rock 'n' roll, Bob said he'd been rockin' since 1928.

And he never hollered on demand.

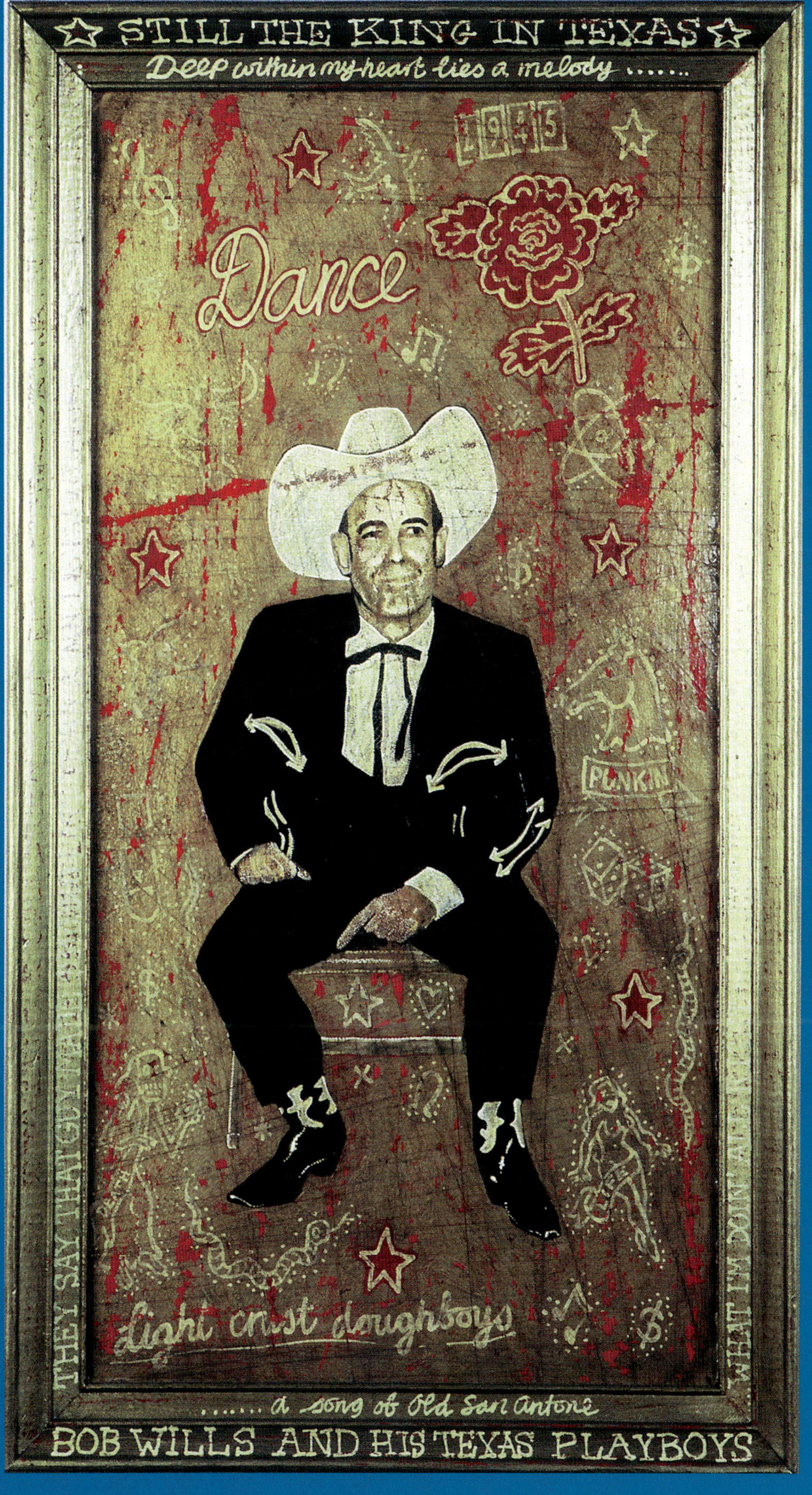

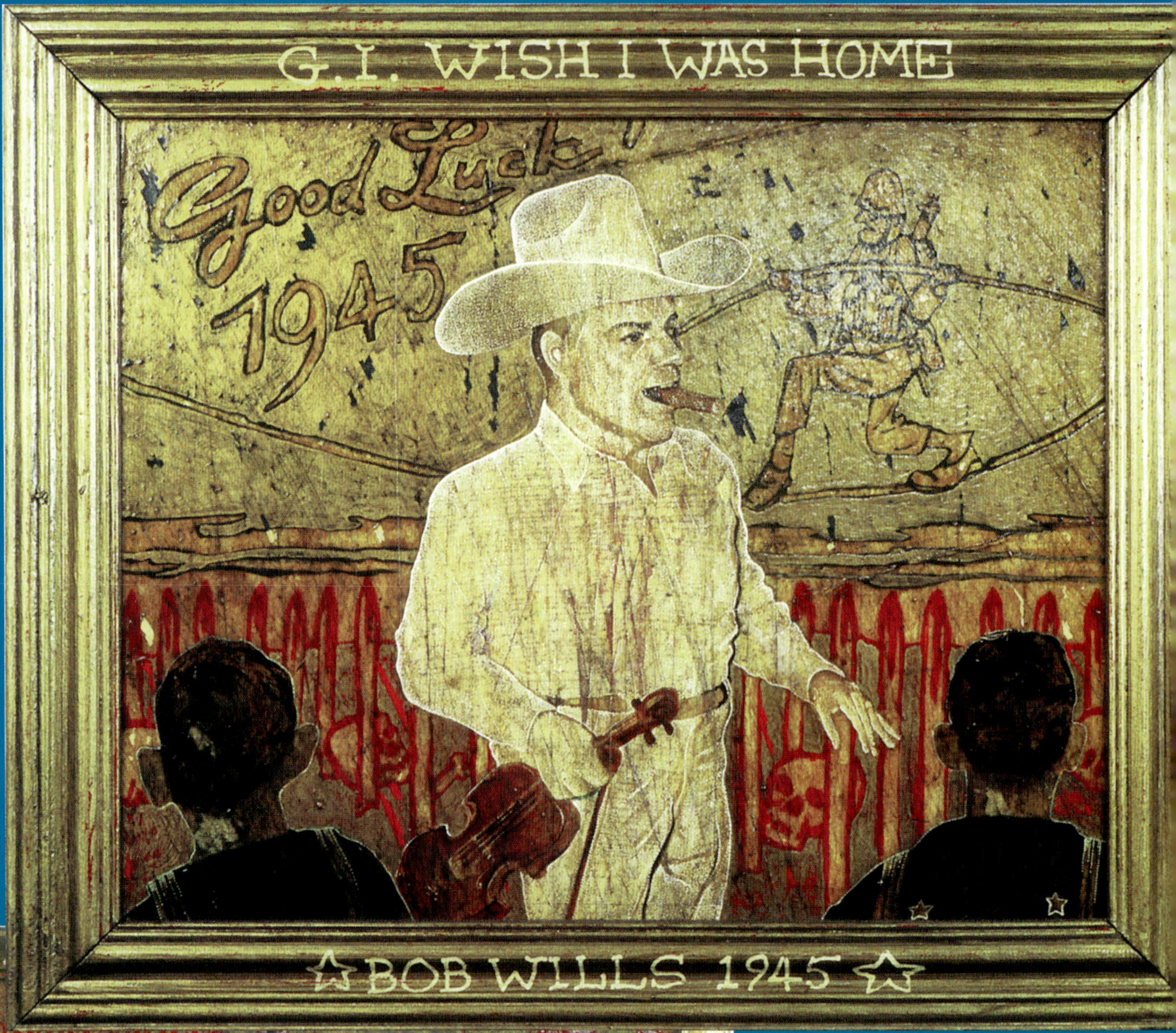

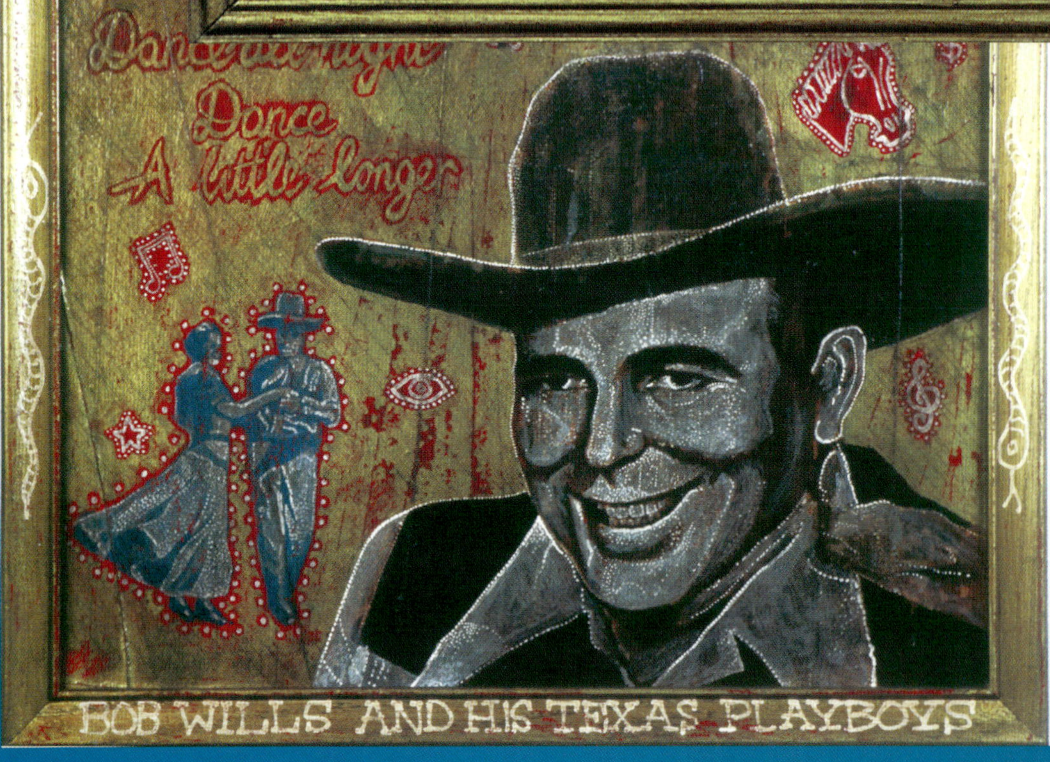
G. I. WISH I WAS HOME
Good Luck!
1945
☆ BOB WILLS 1945 ☆
Dance all night
Dance
A little longer
BOB WILLS AND HIS TEXAS PLAYBOYS

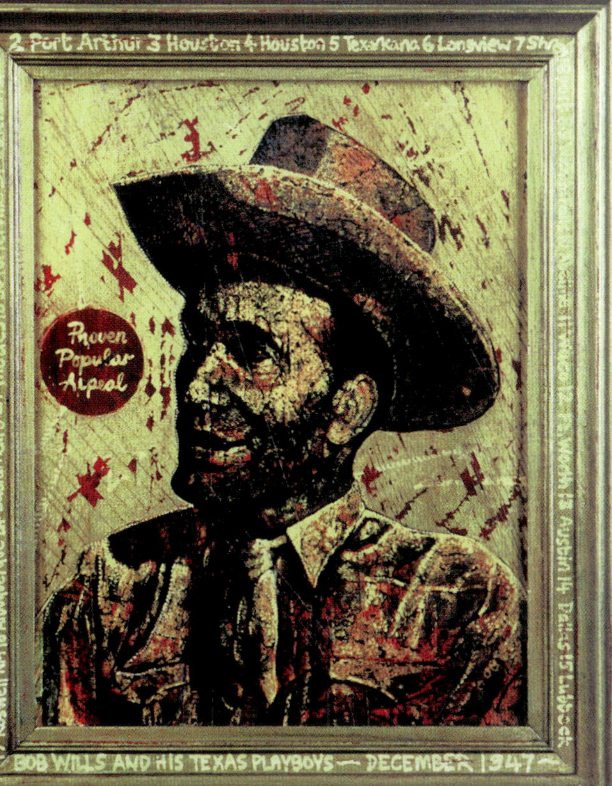
Proven Popular Appeal
2 Port Arthur 3 Houston 4 Houston 5 Texarkana 6 Longview 7 Sh
BOB WILLS AND HIS TEXAS PLAYBOYS — DECEMBER 1947
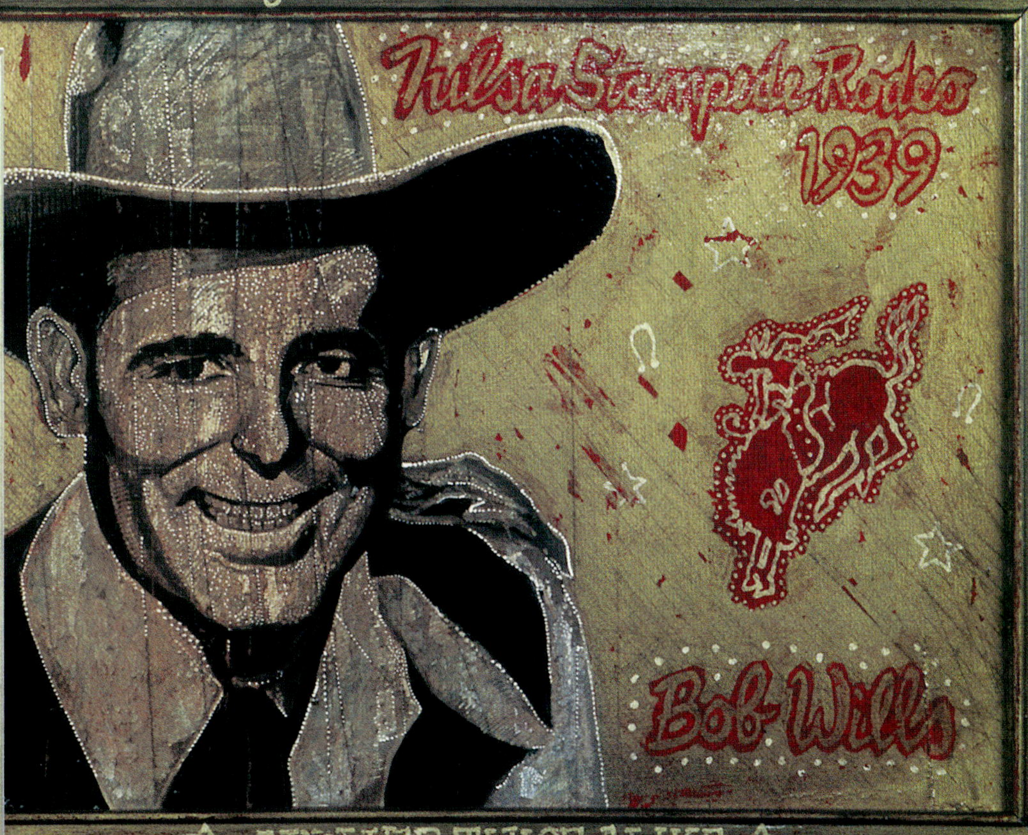
PRIDE of the SOUTH WEST......
Tulsa Stampede Rodeo
1939
Bob Wills
☆ NEVER TWICE ALIKE ☆

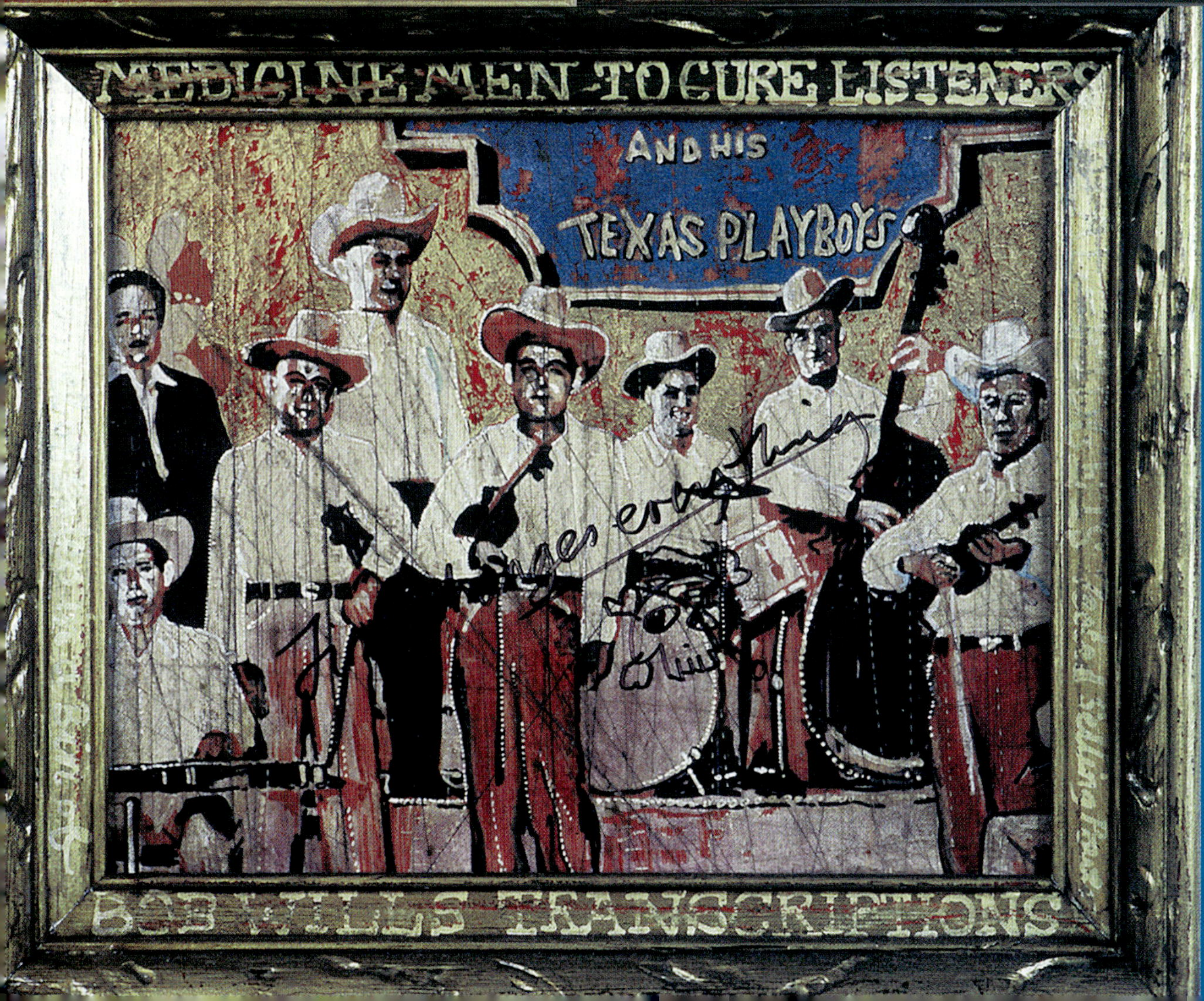

MEDICINE MEN TO CURE LISTENERS
AND HIS
TEXAS PLAYBOYS
BOB WILLS TRANSCRIPTIONS

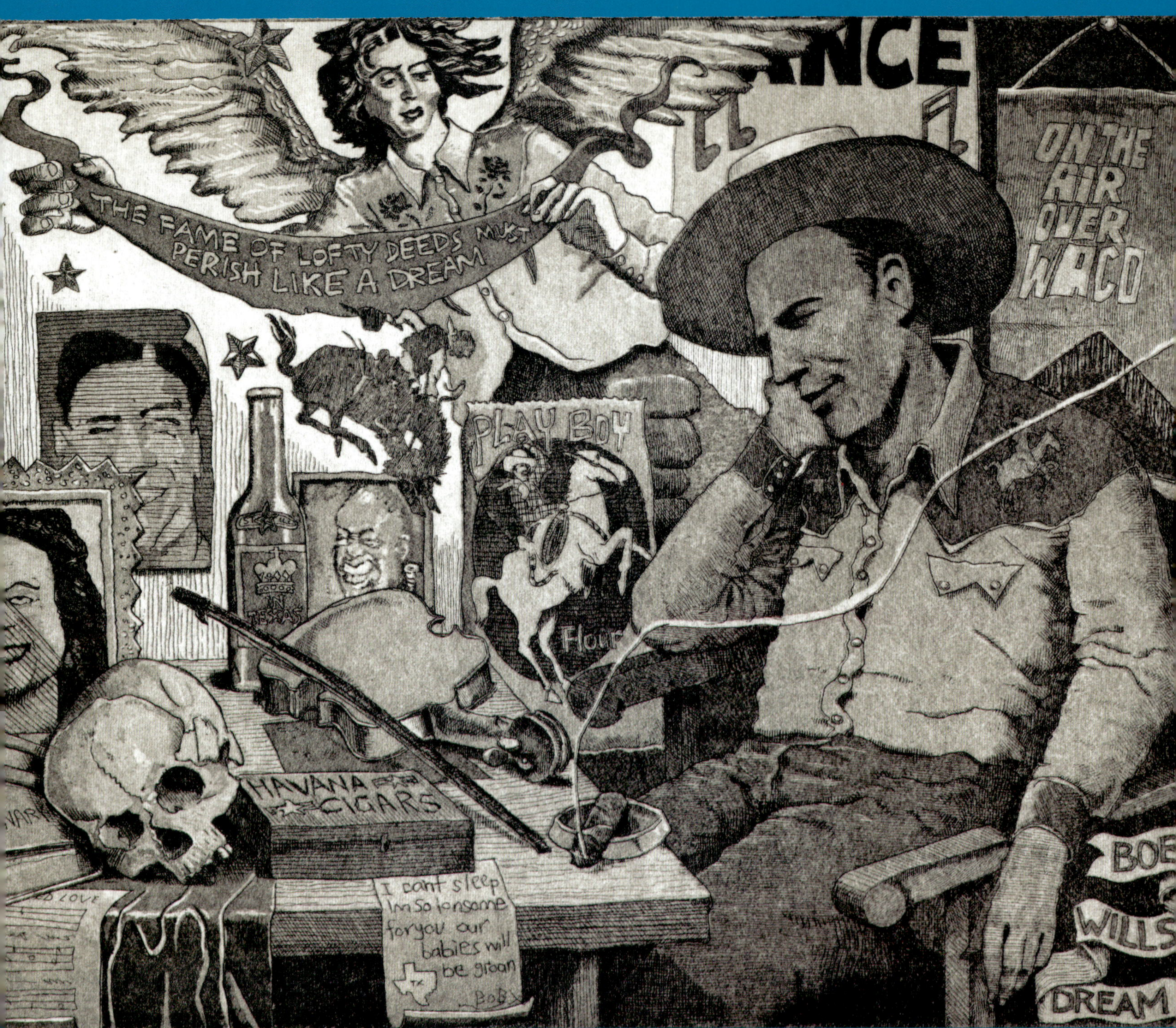

THE FAME OF LOFTY DEEDS MUST PERISH LIKE A DREAM
LANCE
ON THE AIR OVER WACO
PLAY BOY
HAVANA CIGARS
I can't sleep
I'm so lonesome
for you our
babies will
be groan
BOB
BOB
WILLS
DREAM

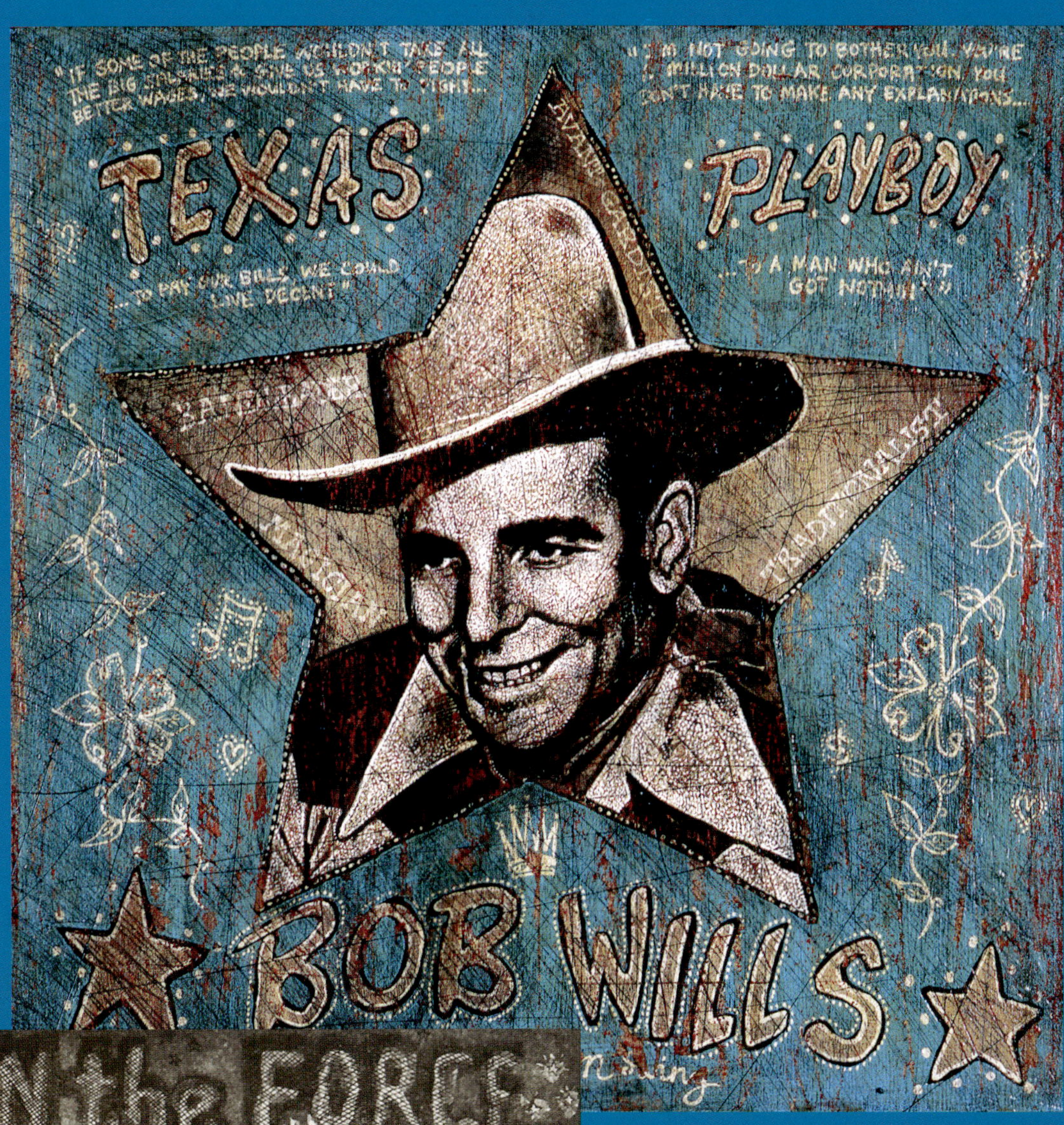
"IF SOME OF THE PEOPLE WOULDN'T TAKE ALL THE BIG SALARIES & GIVE US WORKIN PEOPLE BETTER WAGES, WE WOULDN'T HAVE TO FIGHT..."
"I'M NOT GOING TO BOTHER YOU, YOU'RE A MILLION DOLLAR CORPORATION, YOU DON'T HAVE TO MAKE ANY EXPLANATIONS..."
TEXAS
PLAYBOY
"TO PAY OUR BILLS WE COULD LIVE DECENT"
"IS A MAN WHO AIN'T GOT NOTHIN'"
BOB WILLS

DISTURBANCE IN THE FORCE...
ONGING & MADNESS & LUST

See Willy Fly By

In this suburb of Babylon, they don't like to wait
They kill the messenger 'cos the message was late
Kill the child starving at the gate
Predicting the ruin of the state

See Willy fly by, in the by and by
In the never you mind, in the dollar store light
In the there you go, in the wait and see
In the us and them, in the them and us, in the them and me
He's the exception that proves the rule
All your dreams are a lie
How much will you swallow when Willy flies by?

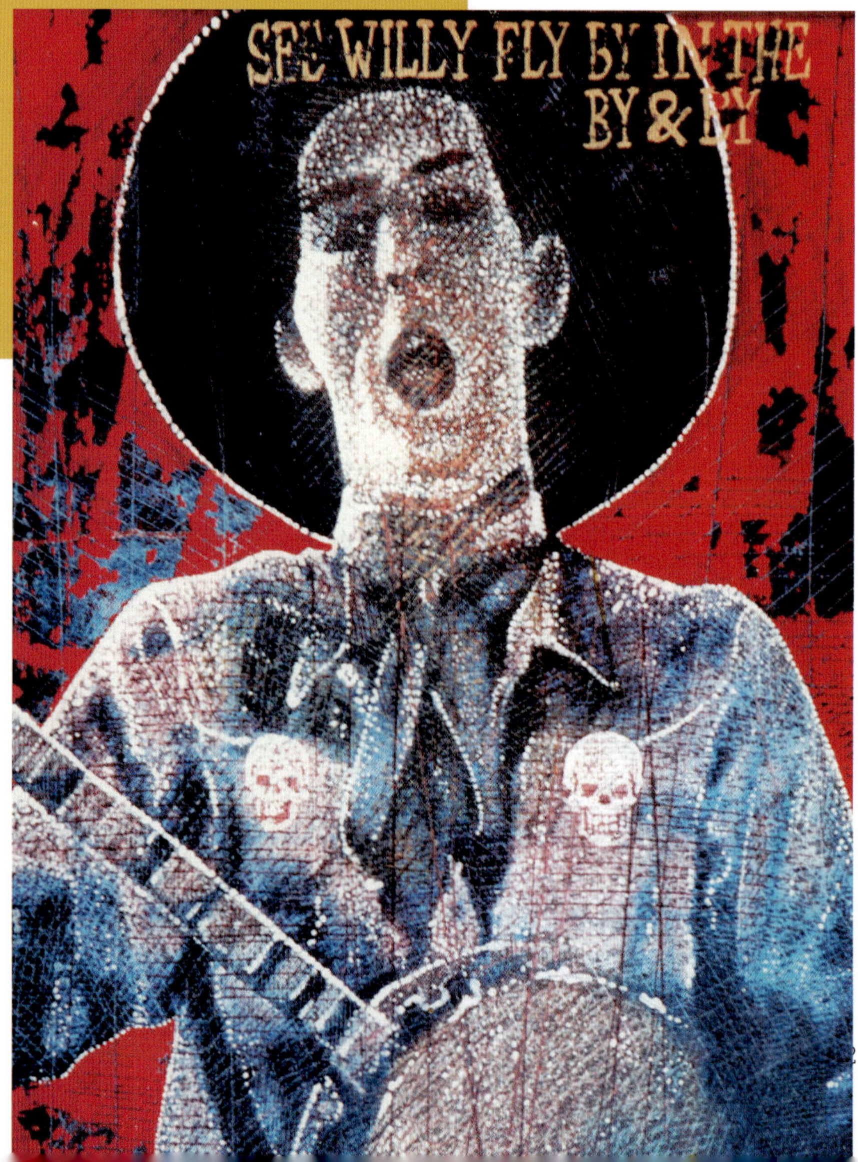

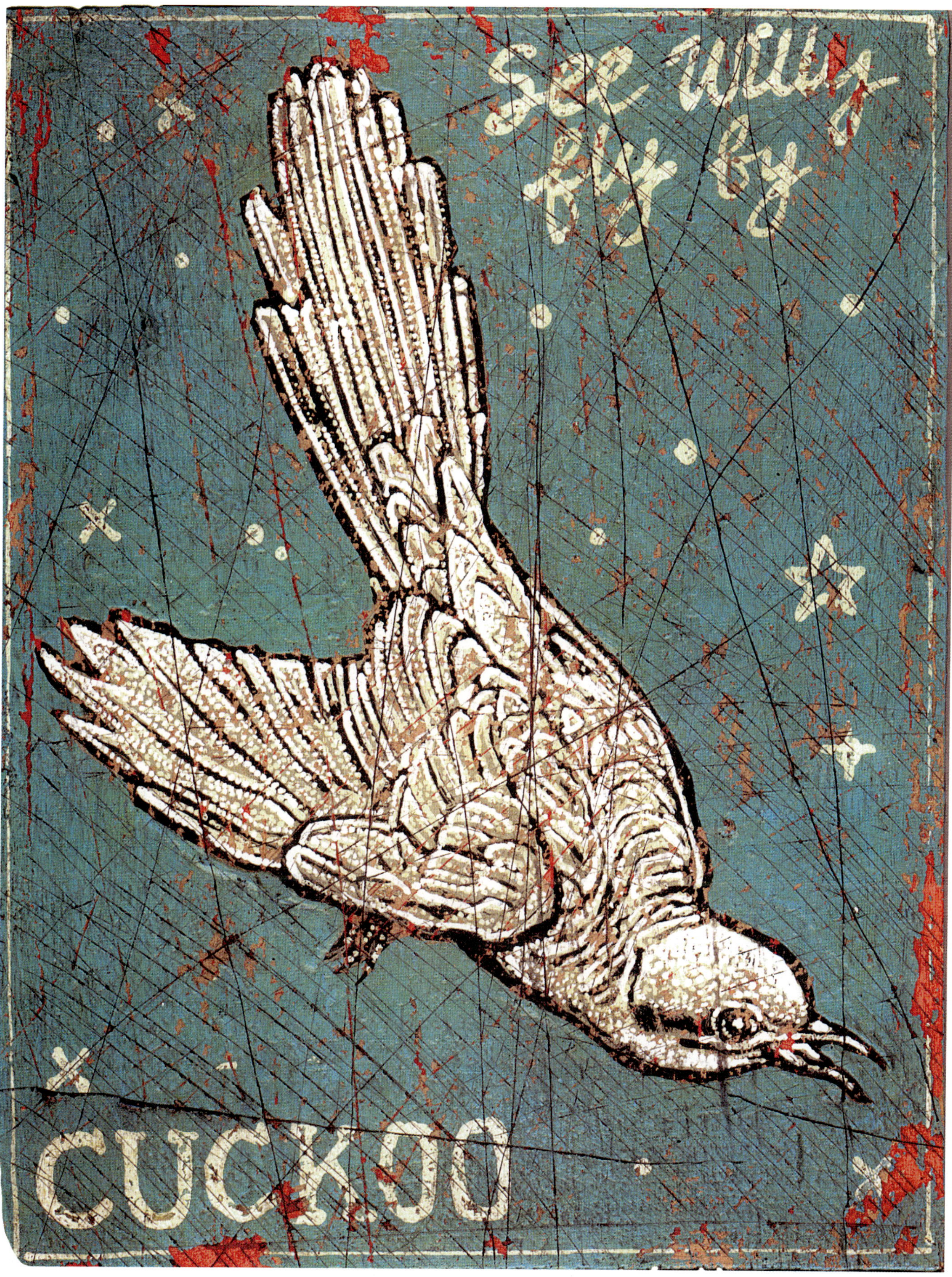

see will
fly by
CUCKOO

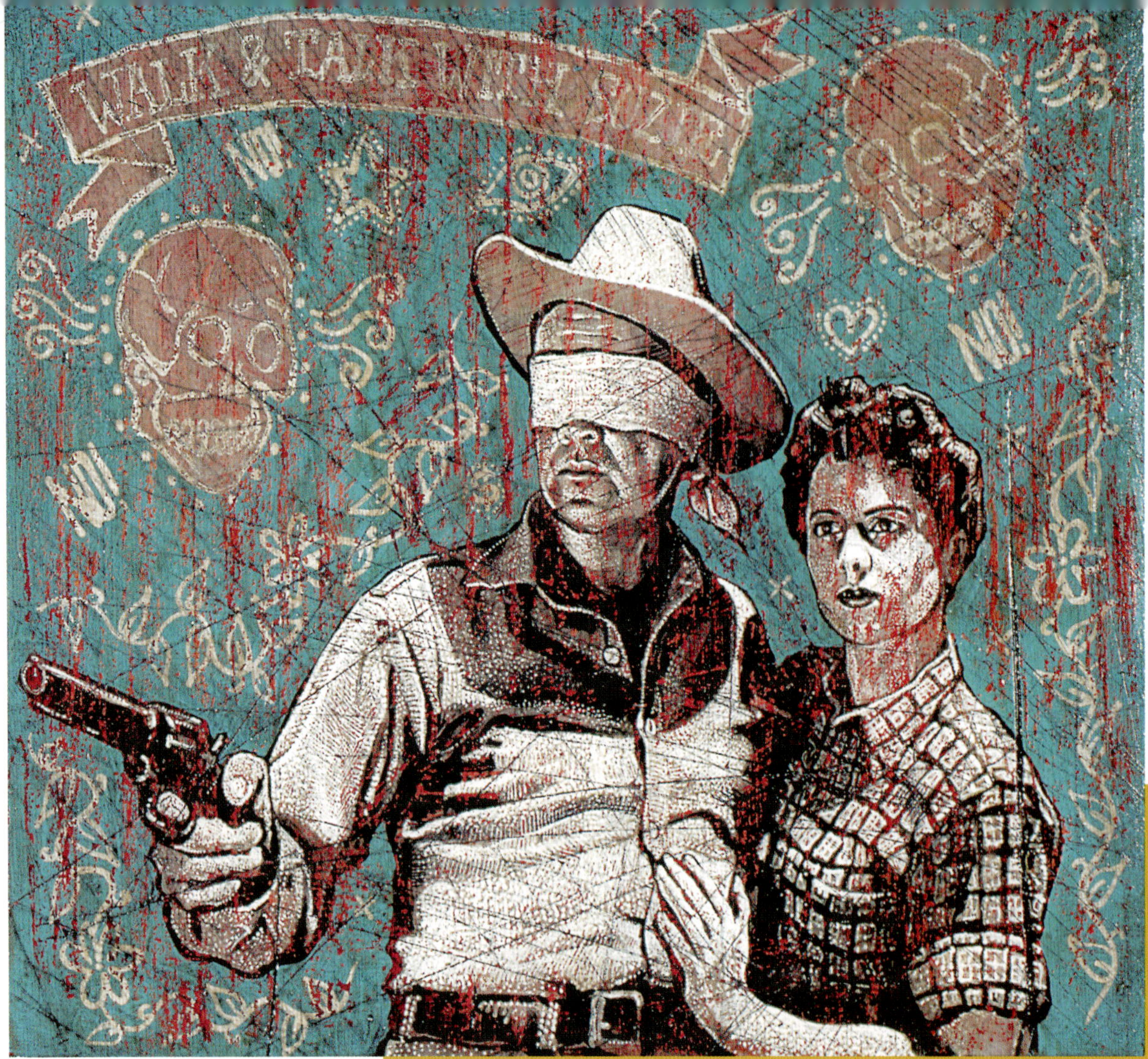

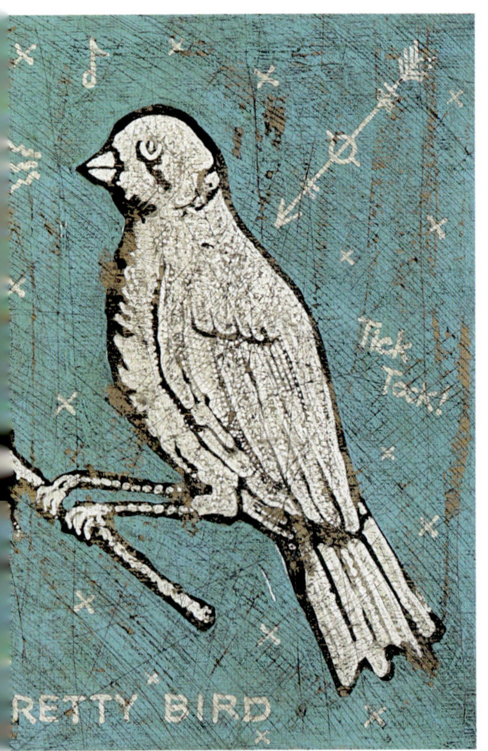

There's something rotten round here, nobody forgot
All the rest on the bottom, white men still on the top
Walk and talk with Suzie, shoot to cripple and maim
Shoot to kill again and again and again and again

Gonna build me a house, on a mountain so high
Sit in my car and stare up at the sky
The dream is a lie, put it to the test
One man rising up on the backs of the rest
On the backs of his family, all the duds and the Does,
'Til the sun melts his wings and down we all go

See Willy fly by, in the by and by
In the never you mind, in the dollar store light
In the there you go, in the wait and see
In the us and them, in the them and us, in the should have been me
He's the exception that proves the rule
All your dreams are a lie
See the trains all leaving without you, when Willy flies by

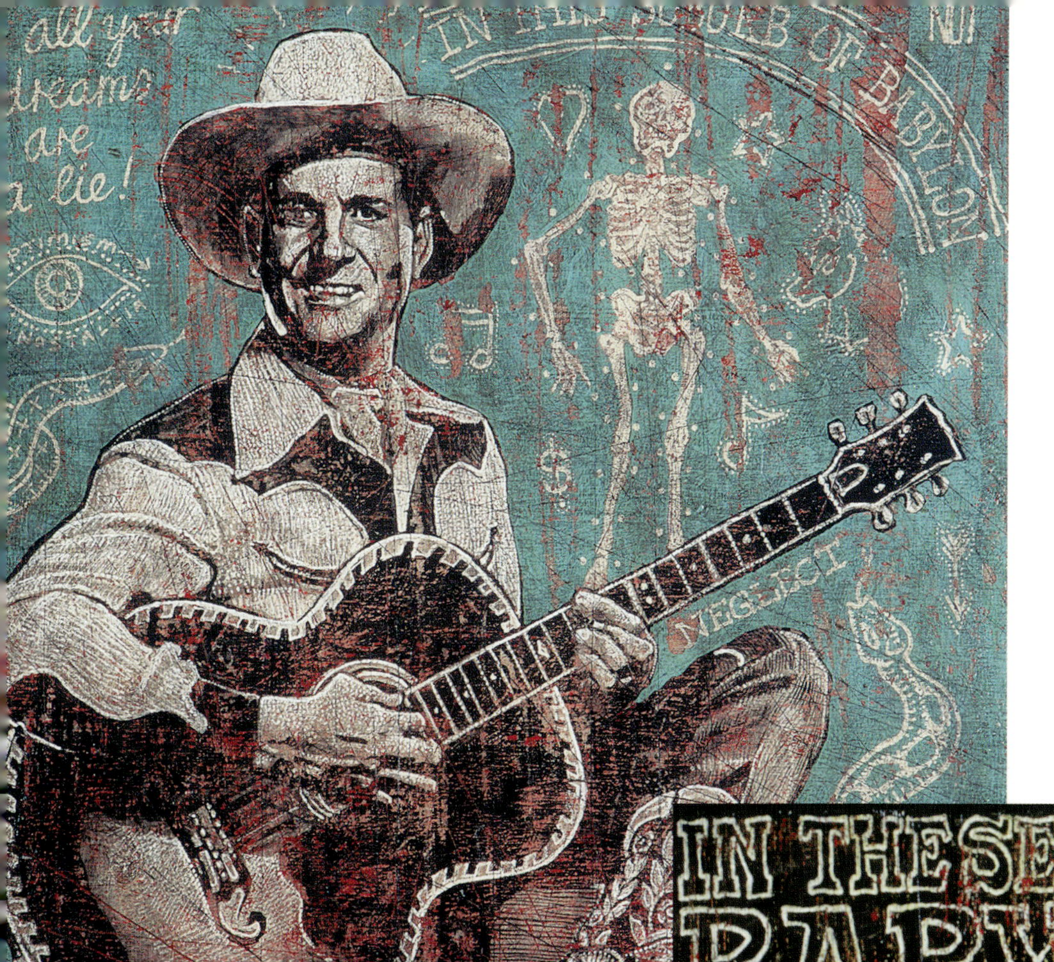

all your
dreams
are
a lie!
IN THESE SUBURBS OF BABYLON
NEGLECT

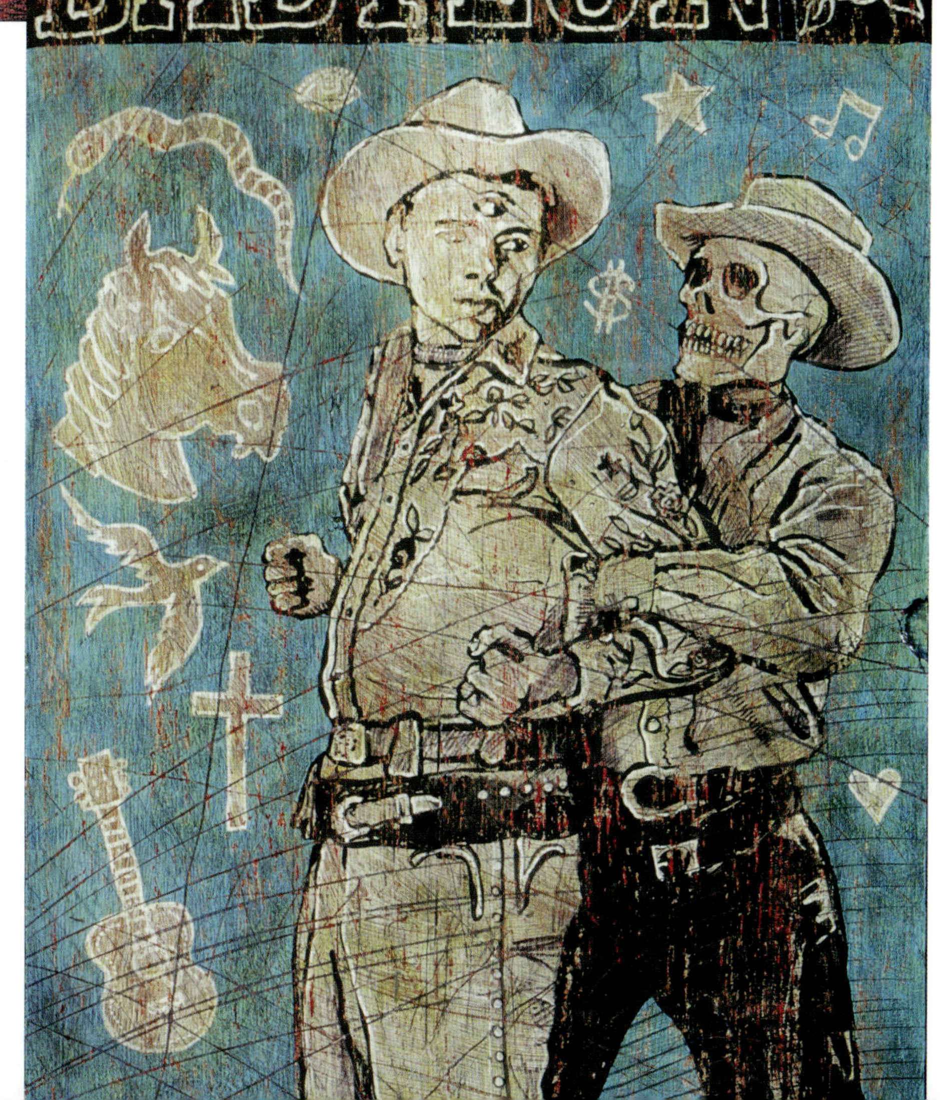

IN THESE SUBURBS OF
BABYLON

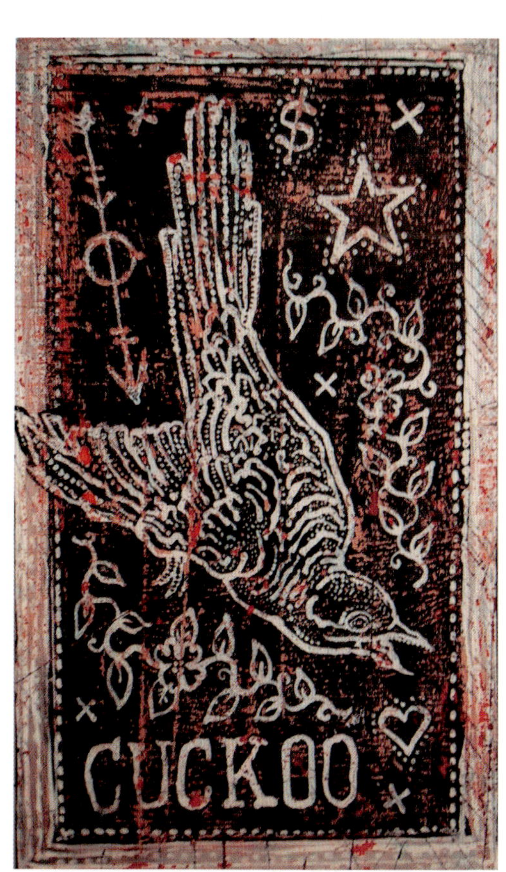

$
CUCKOO

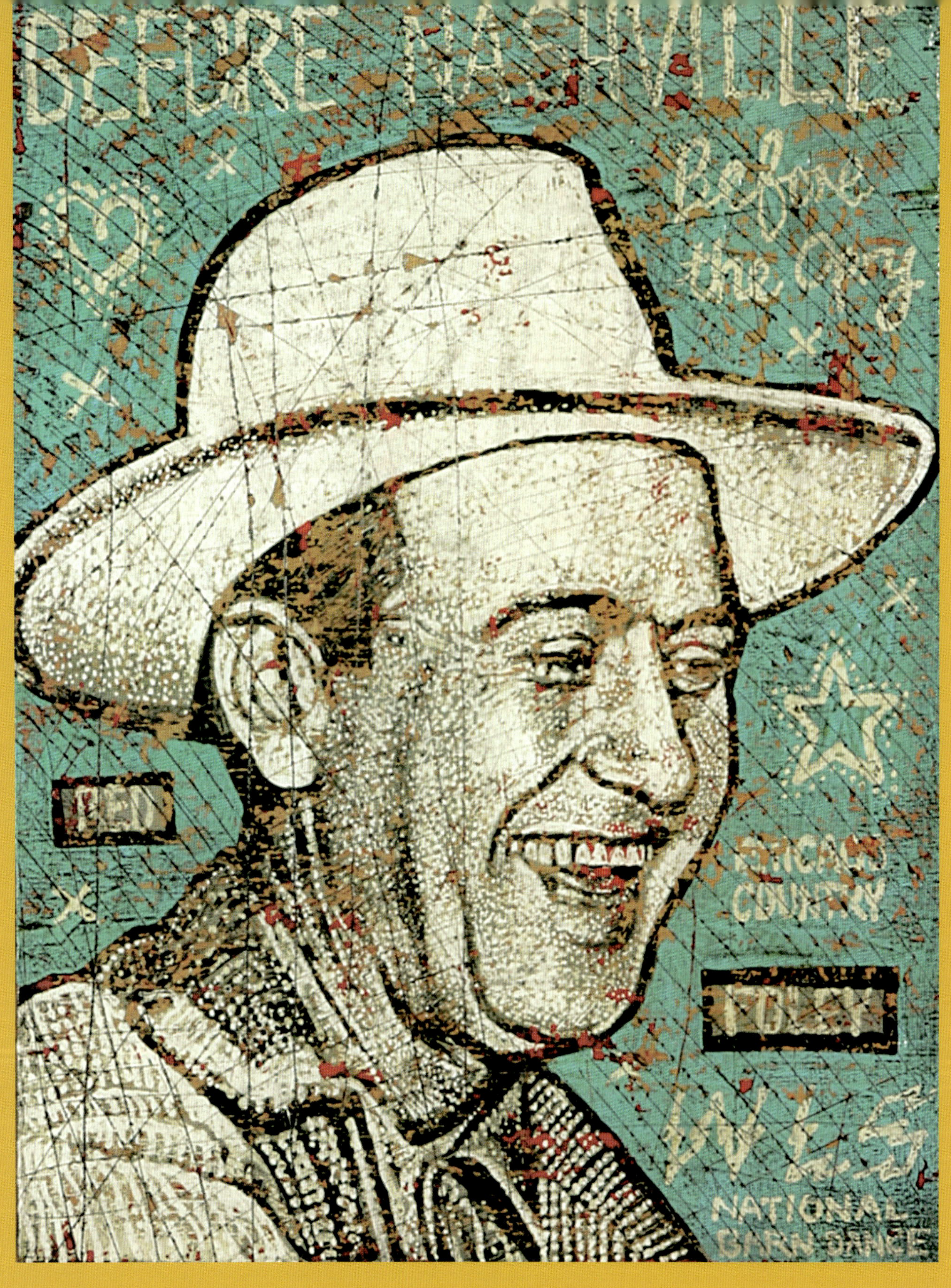

BEFORE NASHVILLE
Before the City
Chicago Country
NATIONAL BARN DANCE

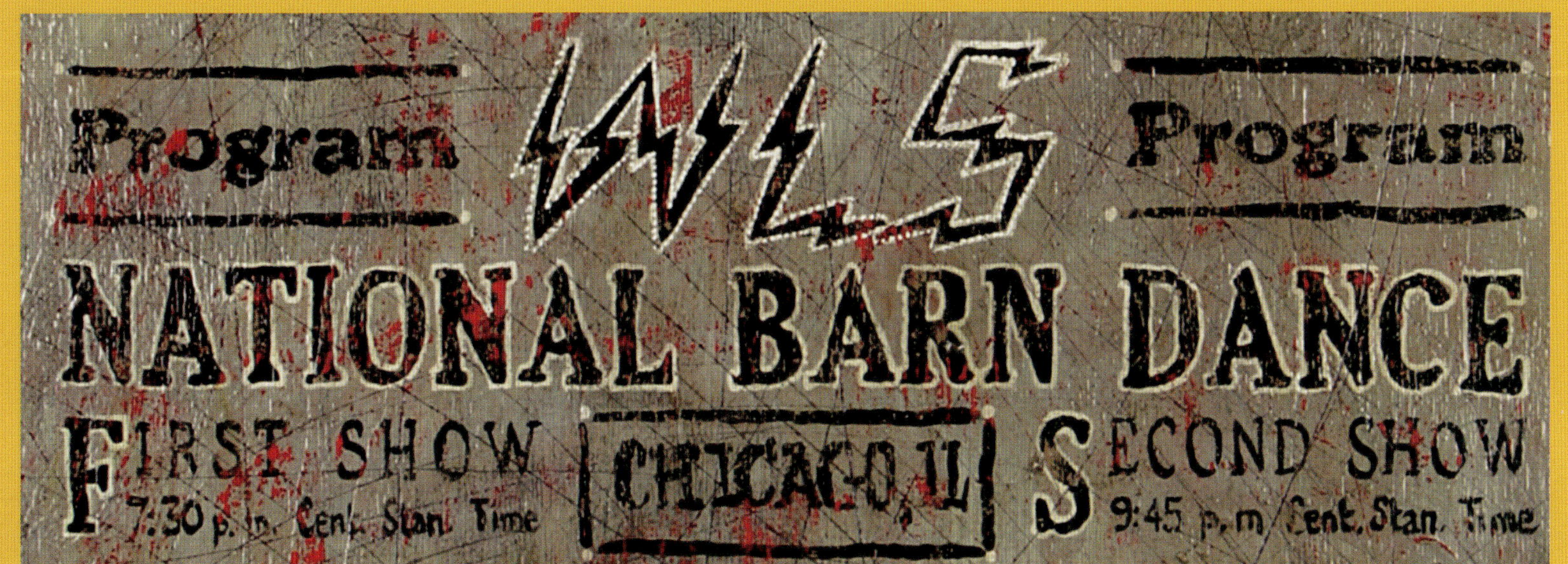

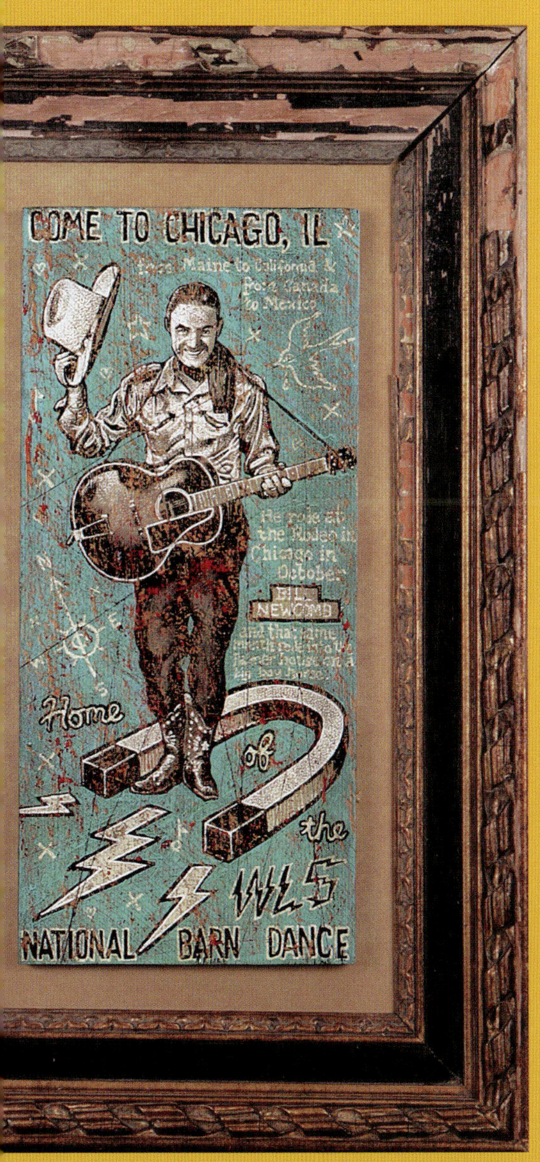

A thriving punk-country scene coalesced around Chicago's Bloodshot Records label in the early 1990s. While Nashville bolted its doors to anything but the most banal, a bunch of Chicago musicians and recent transplants (Freakwater, Neko Case, Kelly Hogan, the Handsome Family, the Waco Brothers) were busy repossessing rural American music for their own nefarious purposes.

To many it seemed like this scene had just dropped out of the sky, but there's some secret (or forgotten) history here, because in the middle of the 20th century Chicago acted as a lightning rod for country music just as it had more famously for blues and R&B.

Before Nashville's Grand Ole Opry ever went on the air, WLS in Chicago began broadcasting a show called the National Barn Dance. It ran uninterrupted for 36 years & became the most popular Country music variety show in the US, blasted into the newly electrified parlors of rural America on 50,000-watt lightning bolts of sound and drawing huge crowds to its Saturday night live broadcasts where cast members like Gene Autry and Patsy Montana became national stars.

Enormously popular but never Pop, the National Barn Dance was eventually outflanked by the Opry in the 1950s, scrapped in favor of Rock 'n' Roll and news radio in 1960, briefly revived as a regional TV show, and then soundly forgotten, its die-hards banished to the clubs and bars where rumors of Chicago's great legacy as a Country music town have been whispered persistently ever since . . .

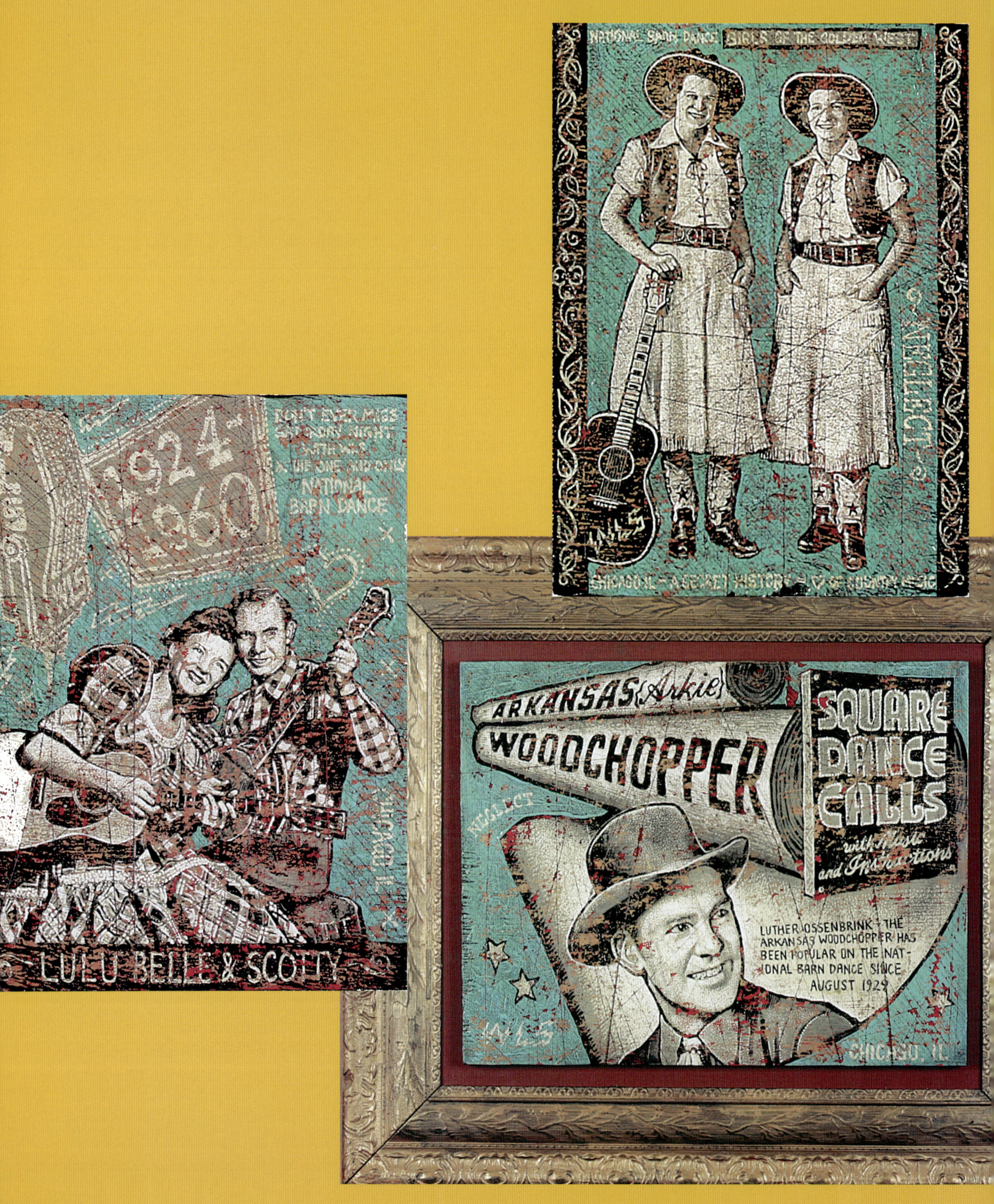

NATIONAL BARN DANCE
GIRLS OF THE GOLDEN WEST
DOLLY
MILLIE
DETECT
REFLECT
CHICAGO IL - A SECRET HISTORY OF COUNTRY MUSIC

1924
1960
DON'T EVER MISS
SATURDAY NIGHT
NATIONAL
BARN DANCE
LULU BELLE & SCOTTY

ARKANSAS (Arkie)
WOODCHOPPER
SQUARE
DANCE
CALLS
with Music
and Instructions
LUTHER OSSENBRINK - THE
ARKANSAS WOODCHOPPER HAS
BEEN POPULAR ON THE NAT-
IONAL BARN DANCE SINCE
AUGUST 1929
REFLECT
CHICAGO, IL

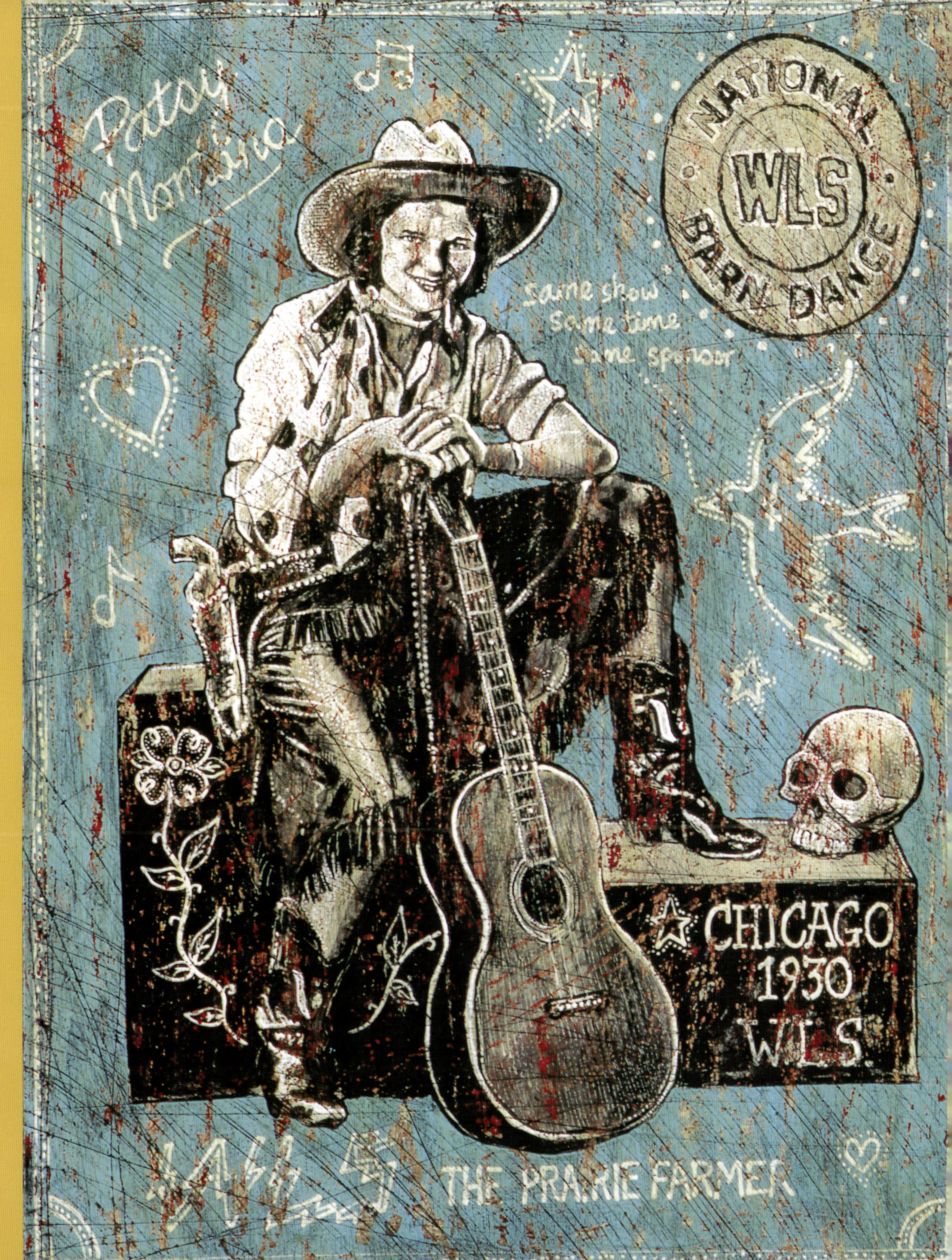

Patsy Montana
NATIONAL
WLS
BARN DANCE
same show
same time
same sponsor
CHICAGO
1930
WLS
THE PRAIRIE FARMER

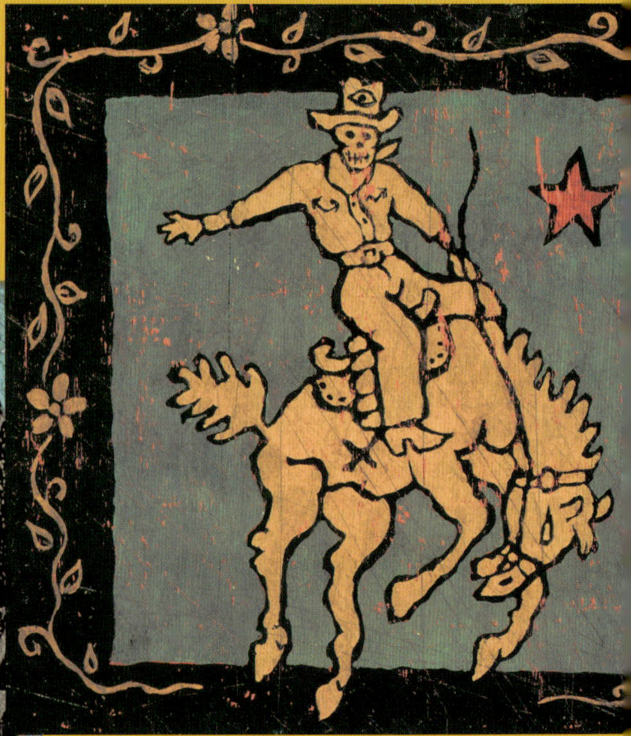

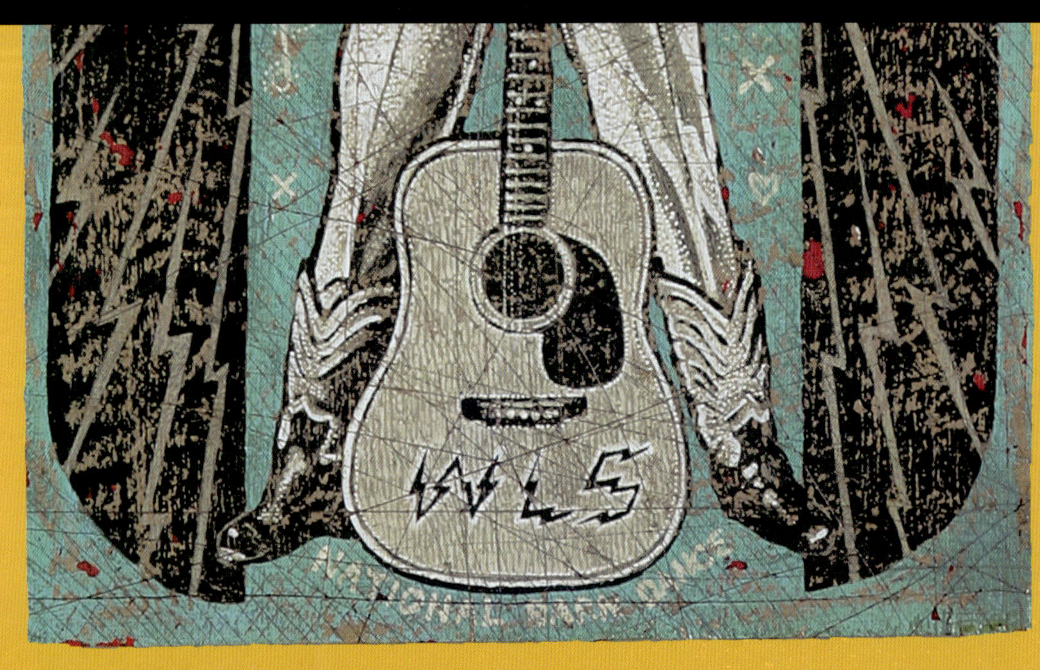

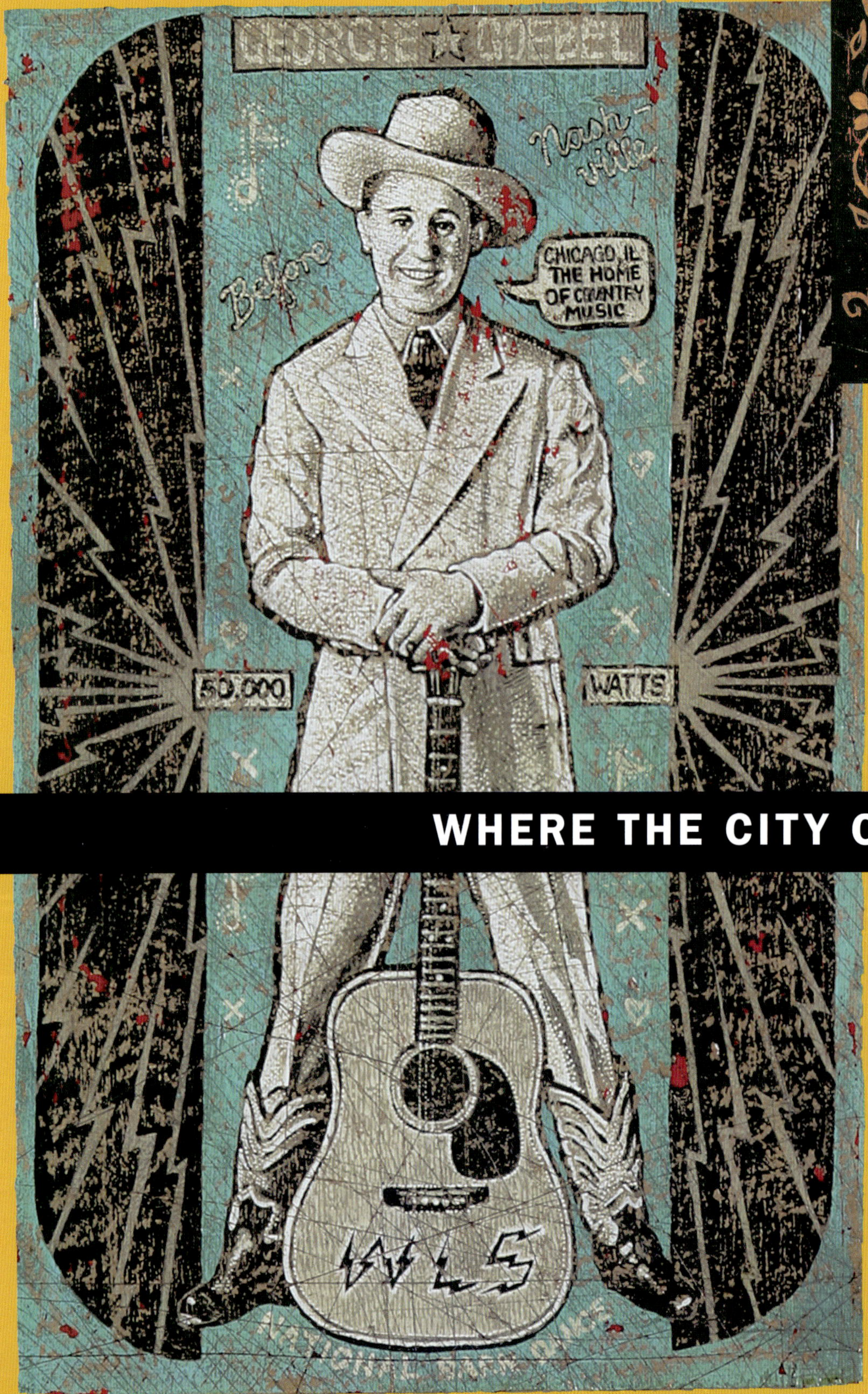

WHERE THE CITY CASTS ITS SHADOW

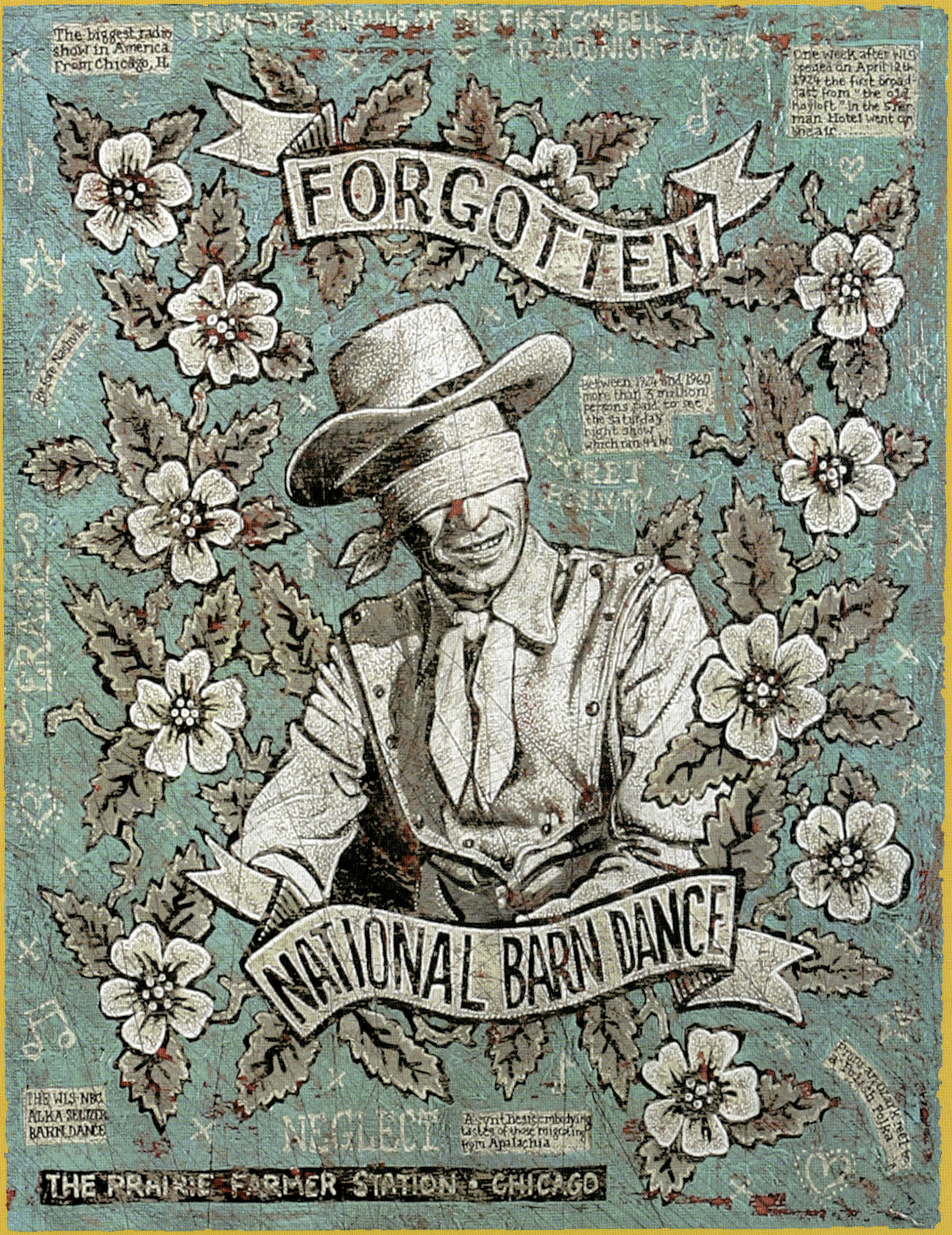

FROM THE RINGING OF THE FIRST COWBELL
TO MIDNIGHT LADIES

The biggest radio
show in America
From Chicago, IL

Before Nashville

One week after WLS
started on April 12th
1924 the first broad-
cast from "the old
Hayloft" in the Sher-
man Hotel went on
the air.......

FORGOTTEN

Between 1924 and 1960
more than 3 million
persons paid to see
the Saturday
night show
which ran 4 hrs

NATIONAL BARN DANCE

THE WLS-NBC
ALKA-SELTZER
BARN DANCE

NEGLECT

A synthesis embodying
tastes of those migrating
from Apalachia

THE PRAIRIE FARMER STATION · CHICAGO

Tom Jones Levitation

Wherever you wander
Wherever you'll be
Up there in the Rhondha
Down here by the sea
We're calling you home
We're calling you home
And this time it's to stay

And I, I can fly
Over the clouds and over the rain
And I can see the greedy hand
Of the vandals who ravaged the land

It's just waiting to happen
The equation's the same

And the rules are as dirty
Though everything's changed
I see it all, You're still so small
And disasters will take new names

And I, I can fly
Over the valleys and over the hills
And I see the secrets
The kisses and the quiet
I see the moonlight in the valley
It's taking me back
Where the earth is still black
And the murderer lies under your feet

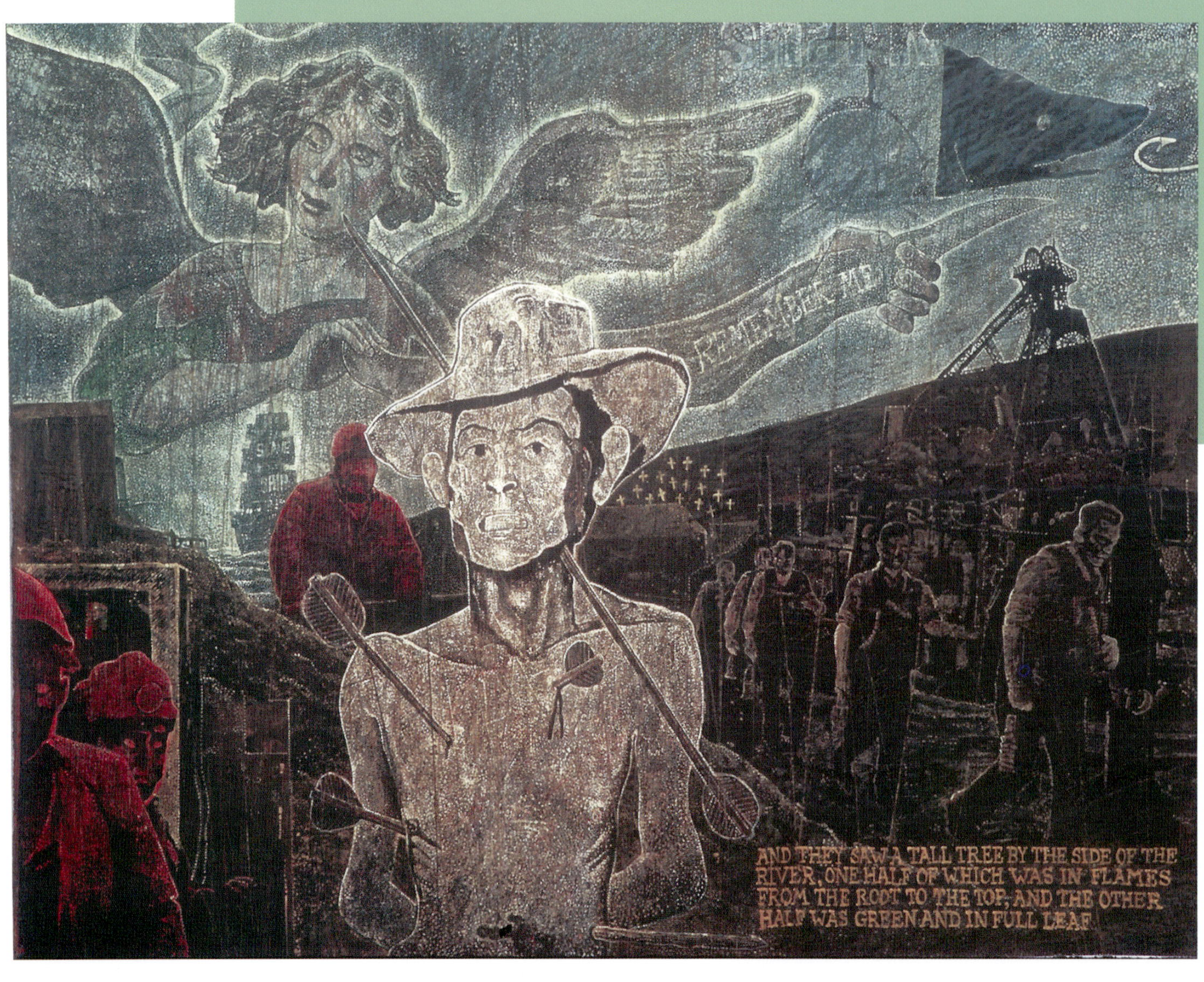

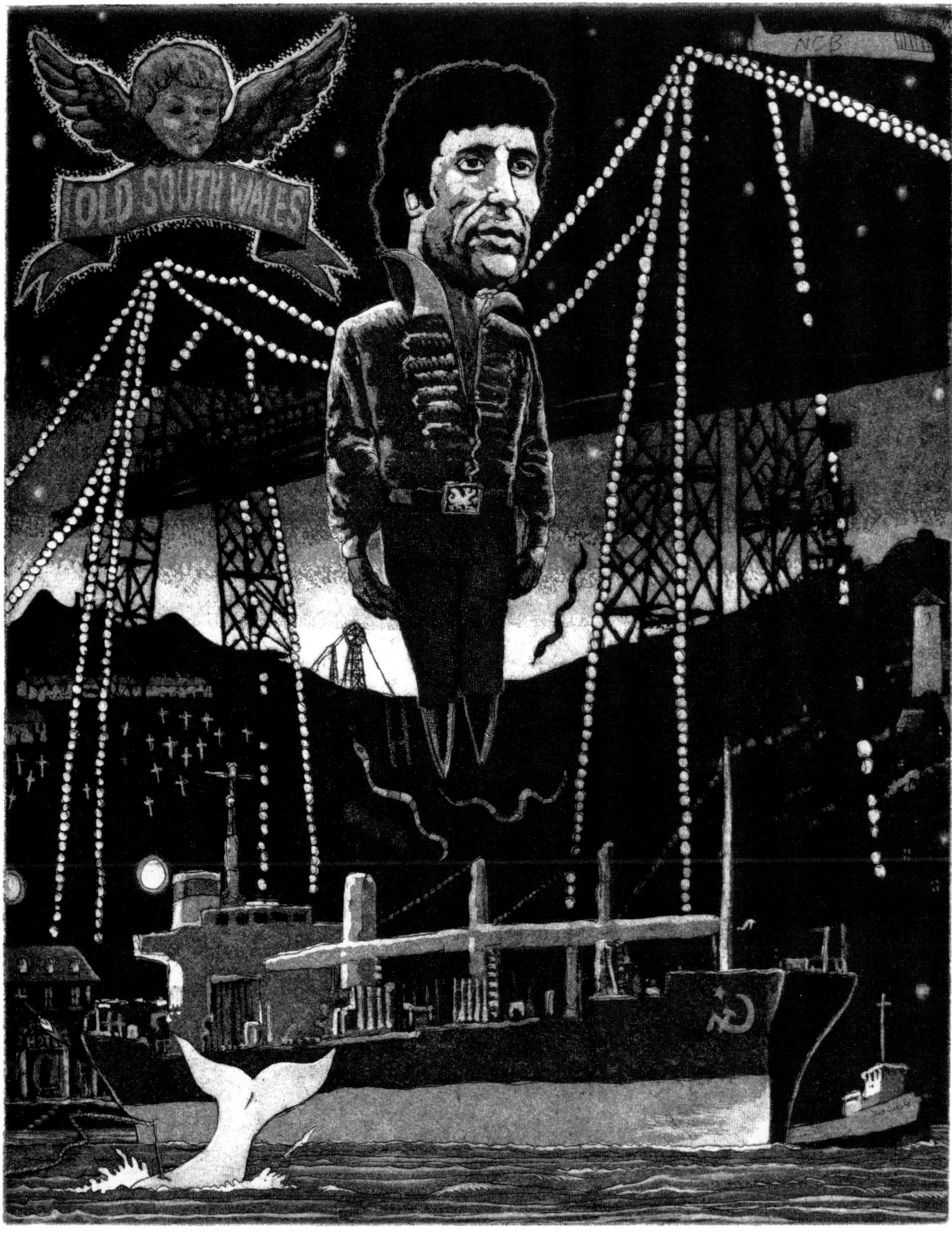

OLD SOUTH WALES
NCB

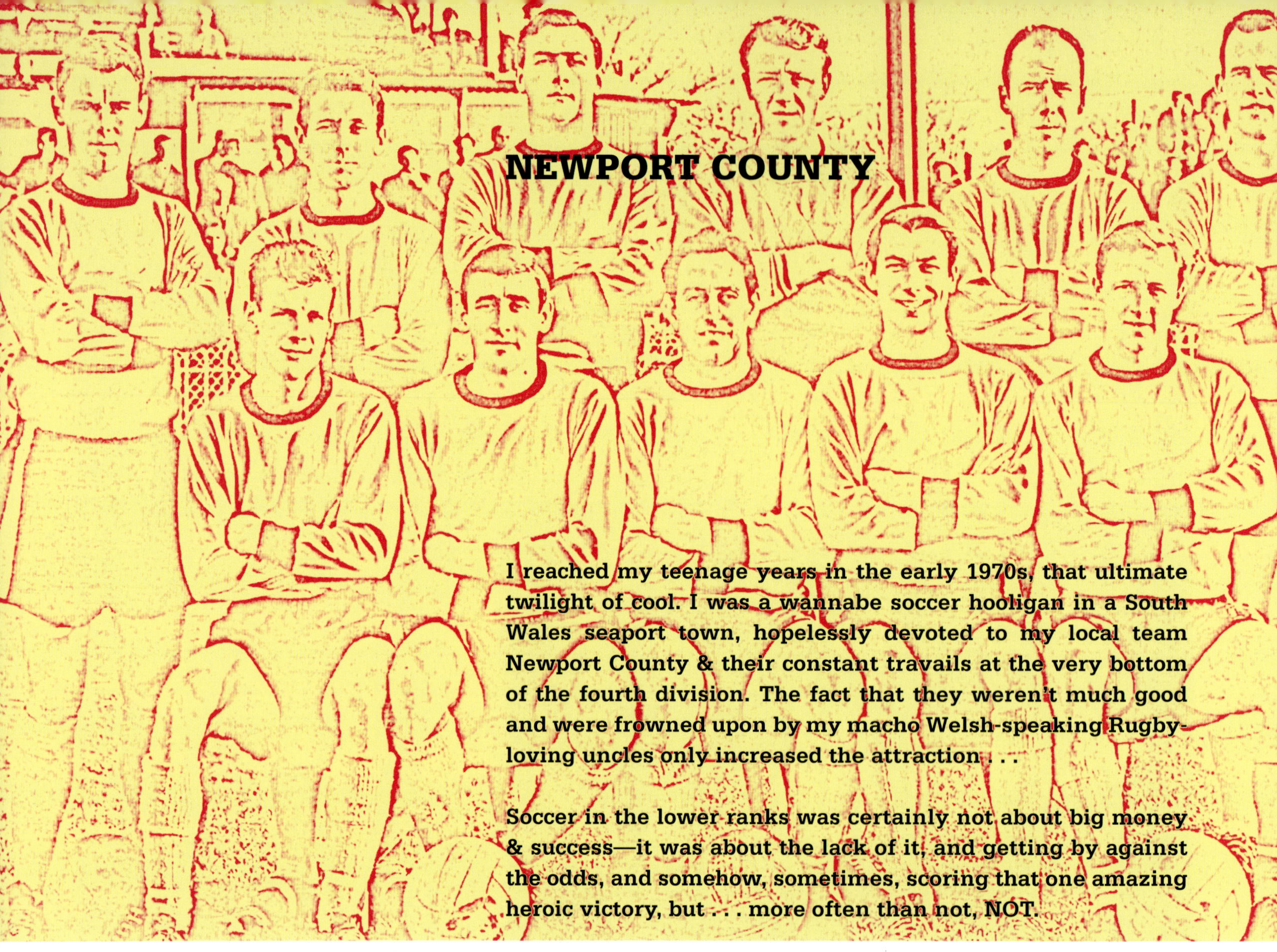

NEWPORT COUNTY

I reached my teenage years in the early 1970s, that ultimate twilight of cool. I was a wannabe soccer hooligan in a South Wales seaport town, hopelessly devoted to my local team Newport County & their constant travails at the very bottom of the fourth division. The fact that they weren't much good and were frowned upon by my macho Welsh-speaking Rugby-loving uncles only increased the attraction . . .

Soccer in the lower ranks was certainly not about big money & success—it was about the lack of it, and getting by against the odds, and somehow, sometimes, scoring that one amazing heroic victory, but . . . more often than not, NOT.

Blind with optimism we'd be back again the next Saturday, waiting around for something to change. It was as accurate and poignant a representation of the working-class experience as any poet, folkie, or painter could ever muster, playing itself out week after week in the pissing rain and driving wind, a clumsy backbeat to the choking routine of daily life.

Mostly me and my friends ate chips, drank pop, & shouted sarcastic abuse at our own players, competing in this with other gaggles of sorry local youth scattered sparsely across the rotting wooden railway-sleeper terraces of Somerton Park.

It was all about feather cuts, Doc Martens, A Clockwork Orange, Bowie, Roxy, T. Rex, and Slade. Most of the kids I knew who went to the footy back then became punk rockers at the same time as me. We left town, got into bands, & followed our noses down new roads to nowhere, unconsciously carrying something of Newport County with us.

Sentimental Marching Song

In the barber's shop
In the game
In the lair of the wrinkled old worm
All men the same
All men the same
Born to brutalize
On every scale
On every scale
Passing down the iron line
Cocooned in a fist

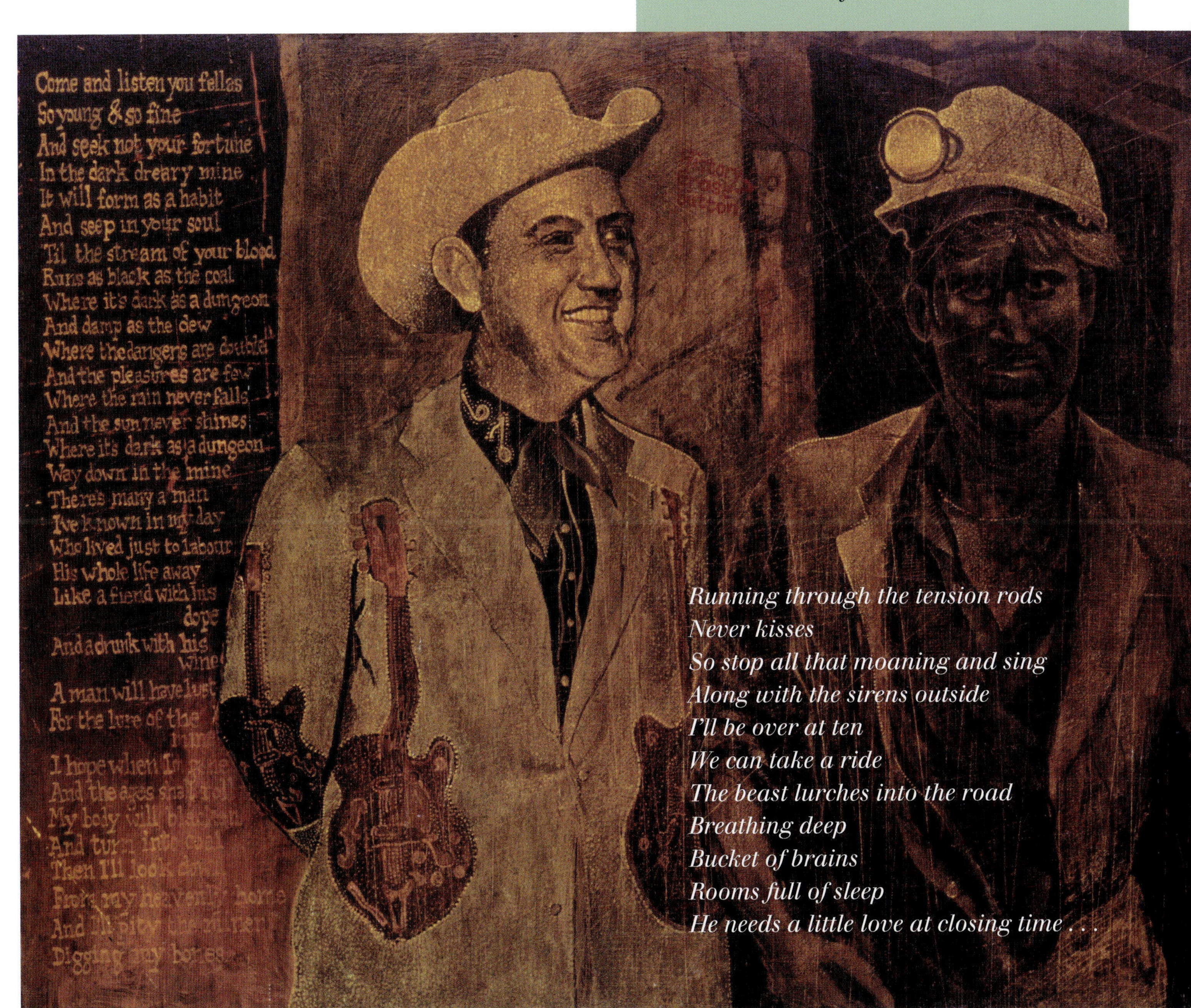

Running through the tension rods
Never kisses
So stop all that moaning and sing
Along with the sirens outside
I'll be over at ten
We can take a ride
The beast lurches into the road
Breathing deep
Bucket of brains
Rooms full of sleep
He needs a little love at closing time . . .

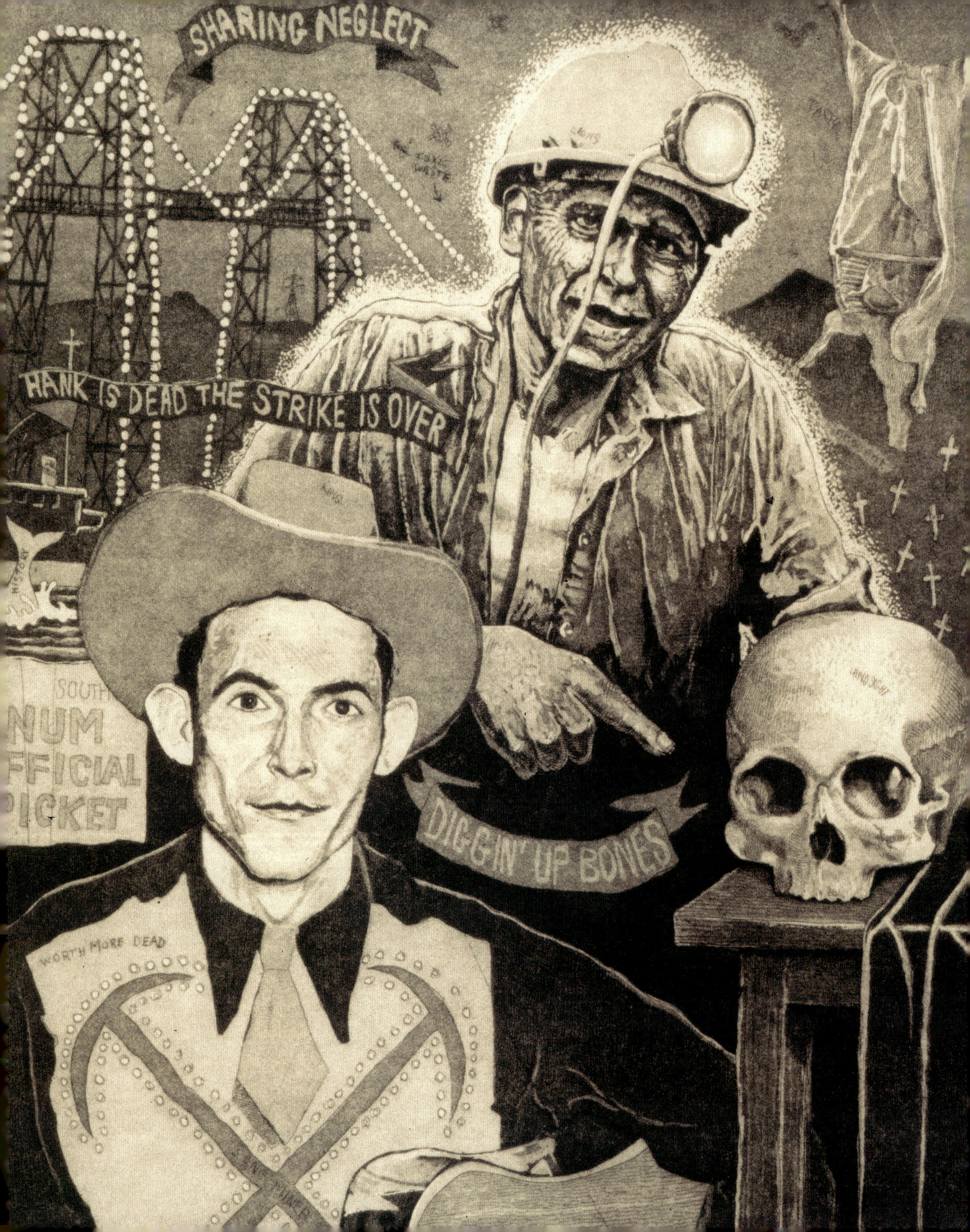

SHARING NEGLECT
HANK IS DEAD THE STRIKE IS OVER
DIGGIN' UP BONES
WORTH MORE DEAD
SOUTH
NUM
OFFICIAL
PICKET

Tubby Brothers

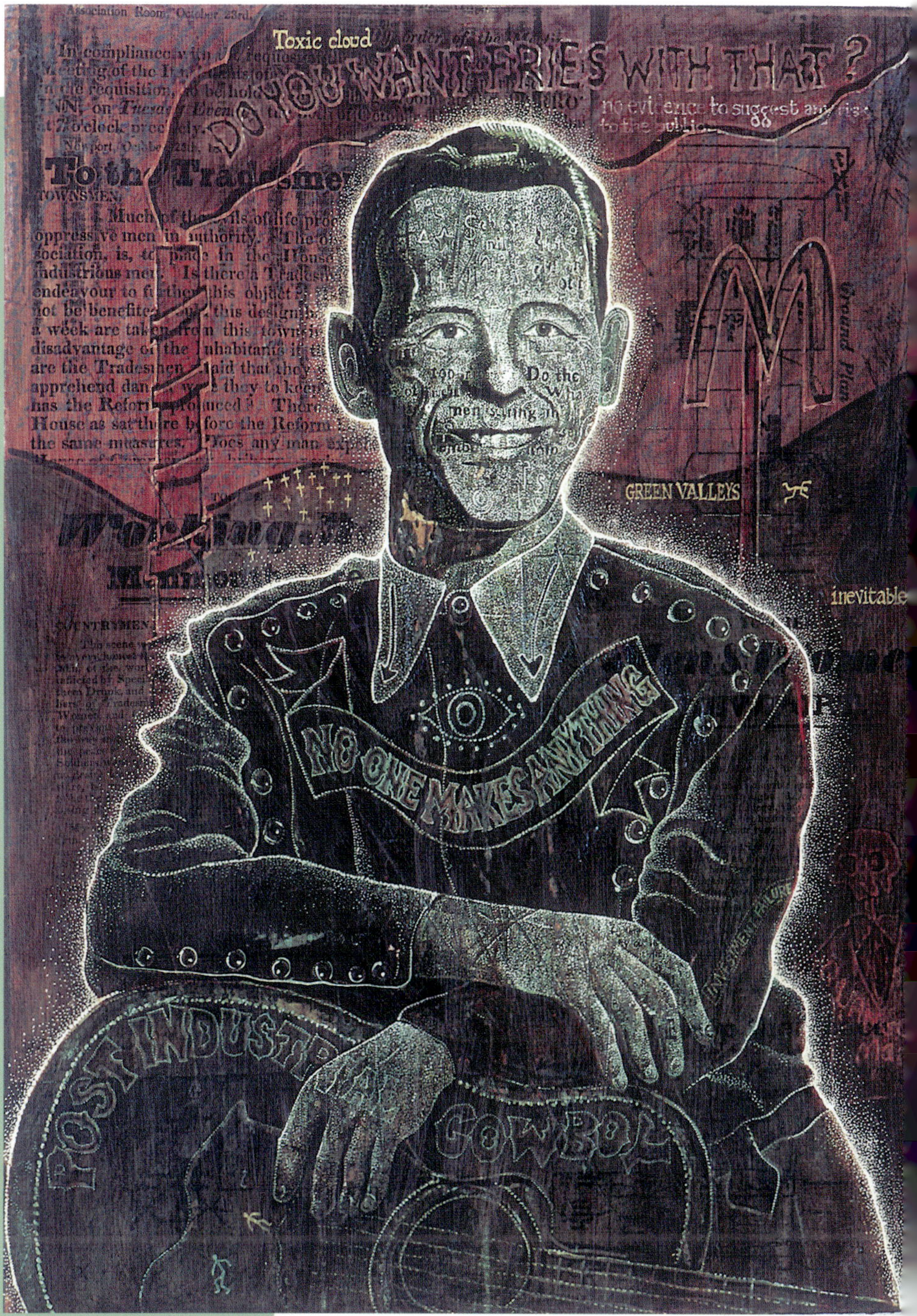

Someone's dead in Blewitt Street
Down the stairs we chipped some paint
Declined sweet sherry, had some tea
And hovered silently

Someone's dead in Caldicot
They dug their grave on a brand
*   new plot*
See the footbridge has been taken
*   down*
It only takes five minutes to drive
*   through the town*
But the flowers look like wounds
And the roads cut deep and direct
The railways change their names and
*   don't connect*

I remember Aberfan
Rows of little crosses up the hill
I wouldn't swim in the channel
*   though now*
People paralyzed at Oxwich Bay
Two containers full of chemicals
Can't take the boy down there—
*   what would his mother say?*

Someone's dead in Clarence Place
A dry palmed handshake and a face like a well-kept grave
There was some problem with the feet
But we were soft spoken, formal and discreet
When the lid is down and you're underground
We wait and watch hanging around
And dream of horses in black feathers
Breathing heavy at the front of the motorcade

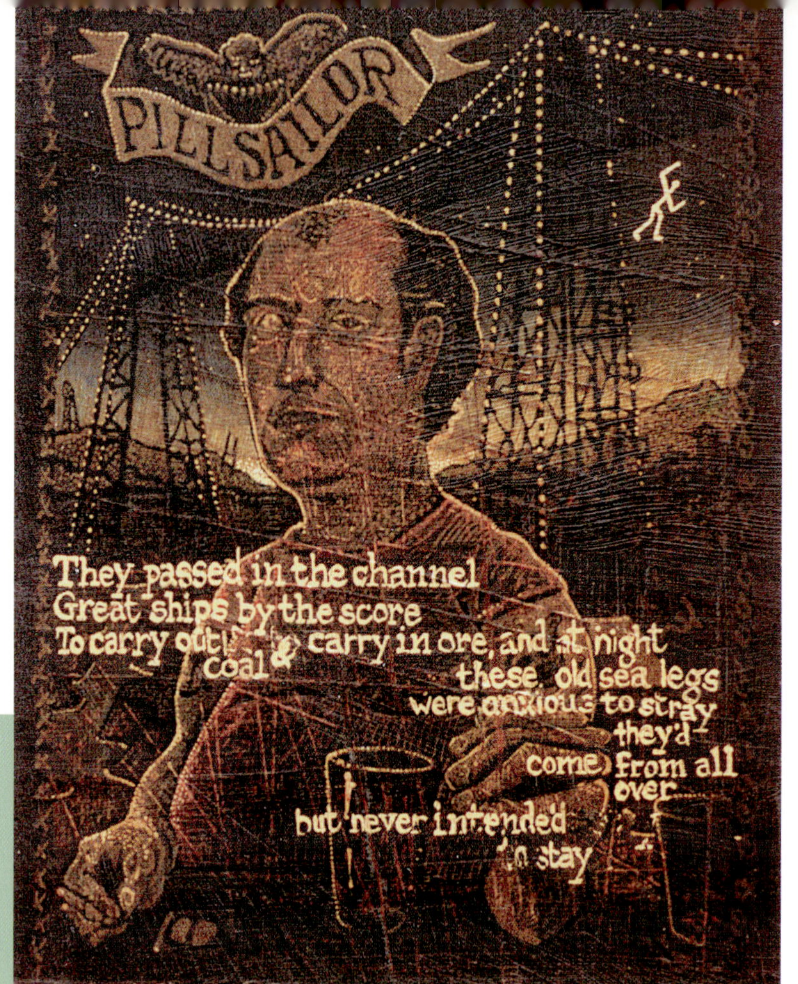

Pill Sailor

A pit bull tattoo
One good eye of blue
That's wandering still
But what can you do
These ropes are all knotted and tangled round me
I'm a sailor who wandered a little too far from the sea
Did they raise up this child just to die
To stare for too long into one sky
Shirley Bassey's from Tiger Bay
But I'll spend my nights down in Pill
They've shut down the docks
Thrown our lives on the rocks
But my good eye is wandering still
Past the pubs where I festered all day
Transporter bridge transport me away
'Cos these rope are all knotted and tangles around me
I'm a sailor who wandered a little too far from sea

They passed in the channel great ships by the score
To carry out coal and carry in ore
And at night these old sea legs were anxious to stray
They'd come from all over but never intended to stay
So tell me something I don't know
And find me a skipper with somewhere to go . . .

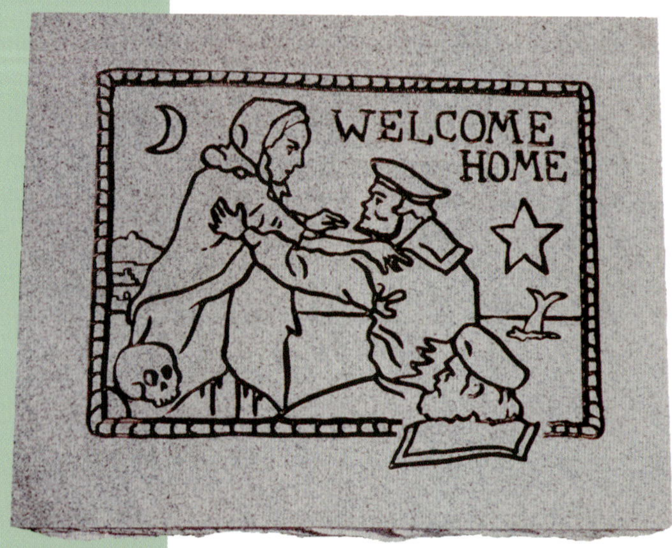

The Return of the Golden Guitarist

His grip is now frozen in one old G chord
Looking for pals and for parties
With luck he might make it without losing his way
The return of the golden guitarist

His eyes are as flat as an old forty-five
That somehow never quite charted
And out of his mouth spews vinyl and wax
The return of the golden guitarist

It's time to come clean, to come back this way
It's time to come back in the harness
Whether stolen or lost, now he is found
The return of the golden guitarist

What gives him the right to talk that way
Pray silence, now don't get me started
You got freedom of speech, but you got nothing to say
So welcome the golden guitarist

His eyes are as flat as an old forty-five
That somehow never quite charted
Out of his mouth spews vinyl and wax
The return of the golden guitarist

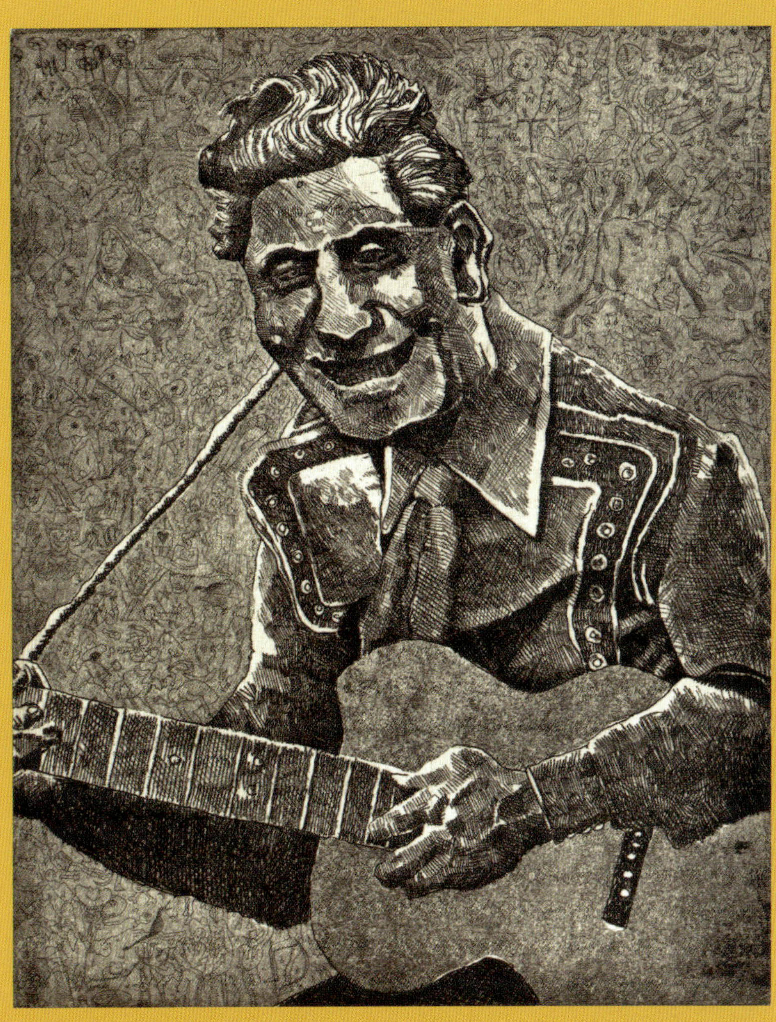

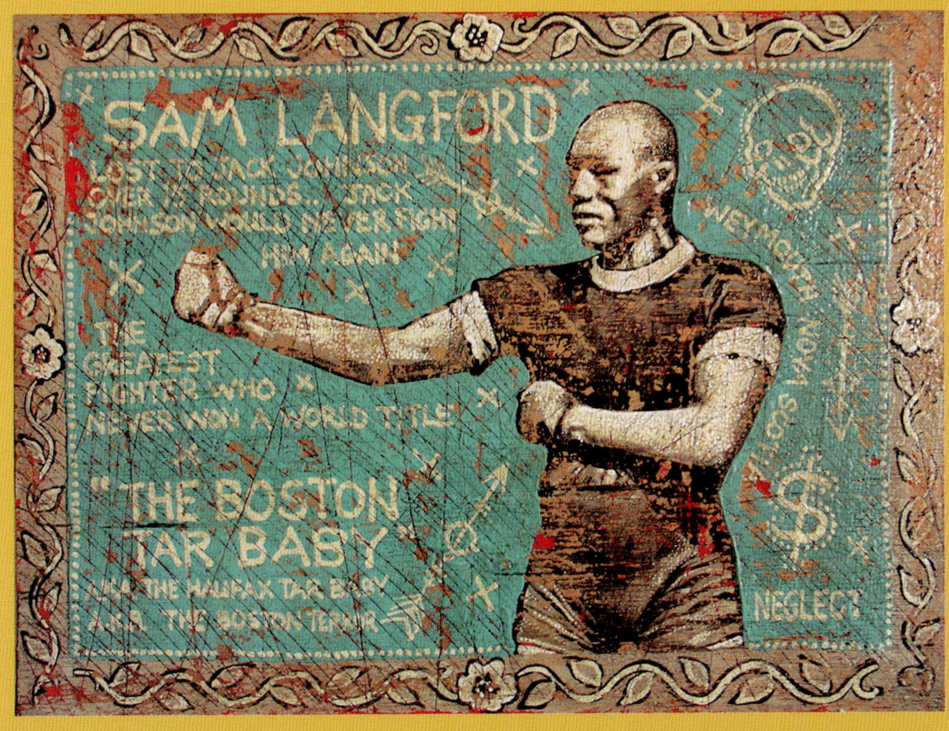

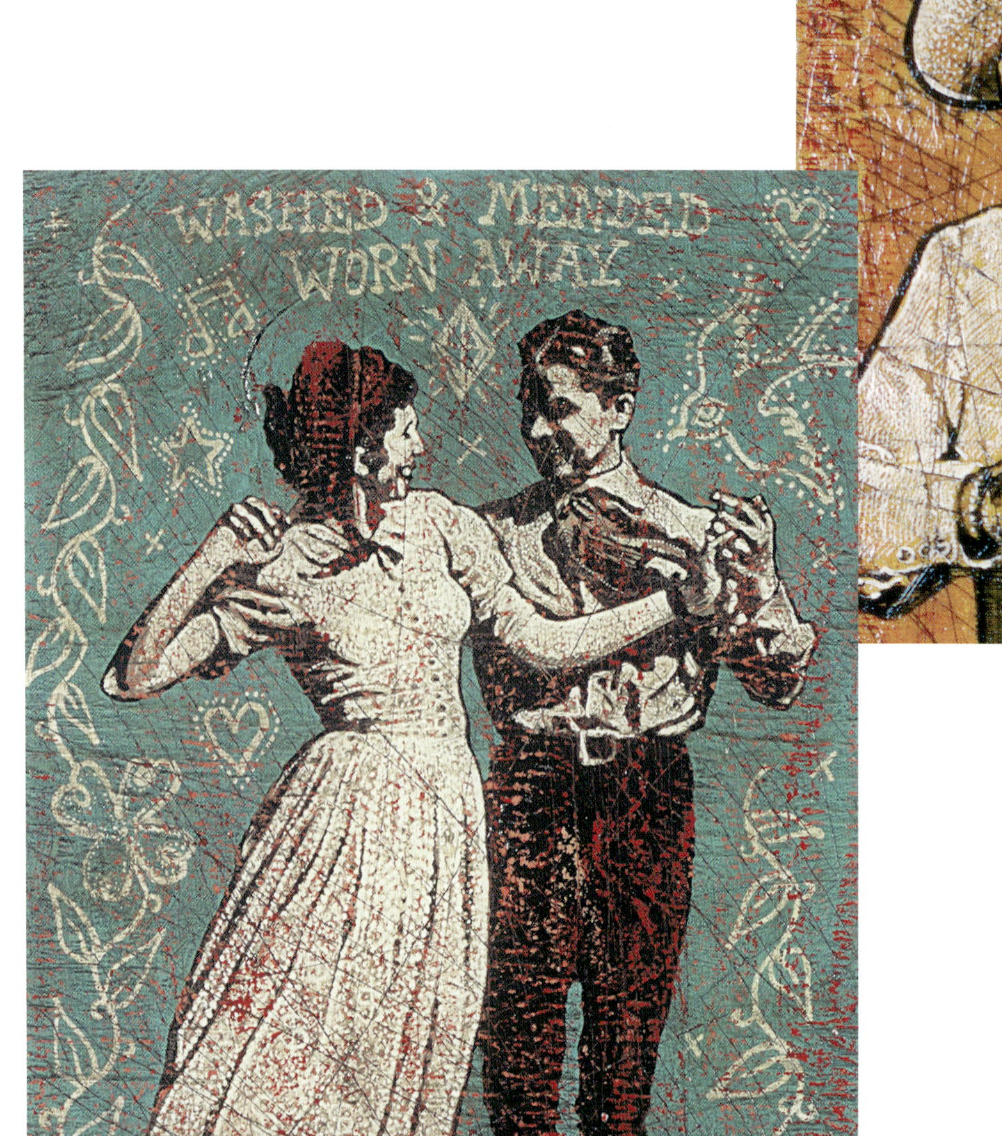

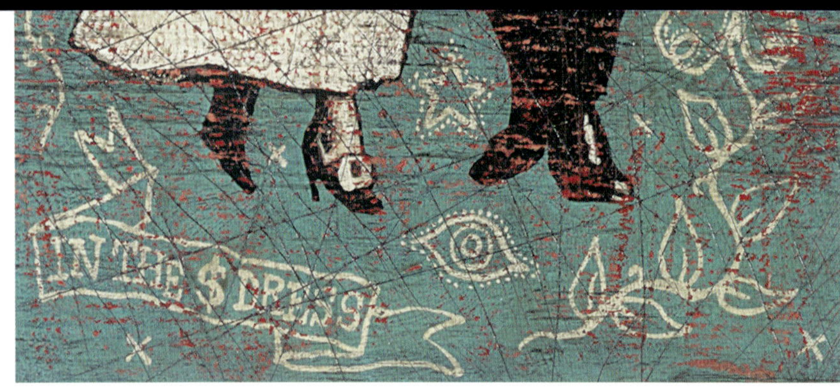

CAN YOU PROVE YOU'RE ALIVE?

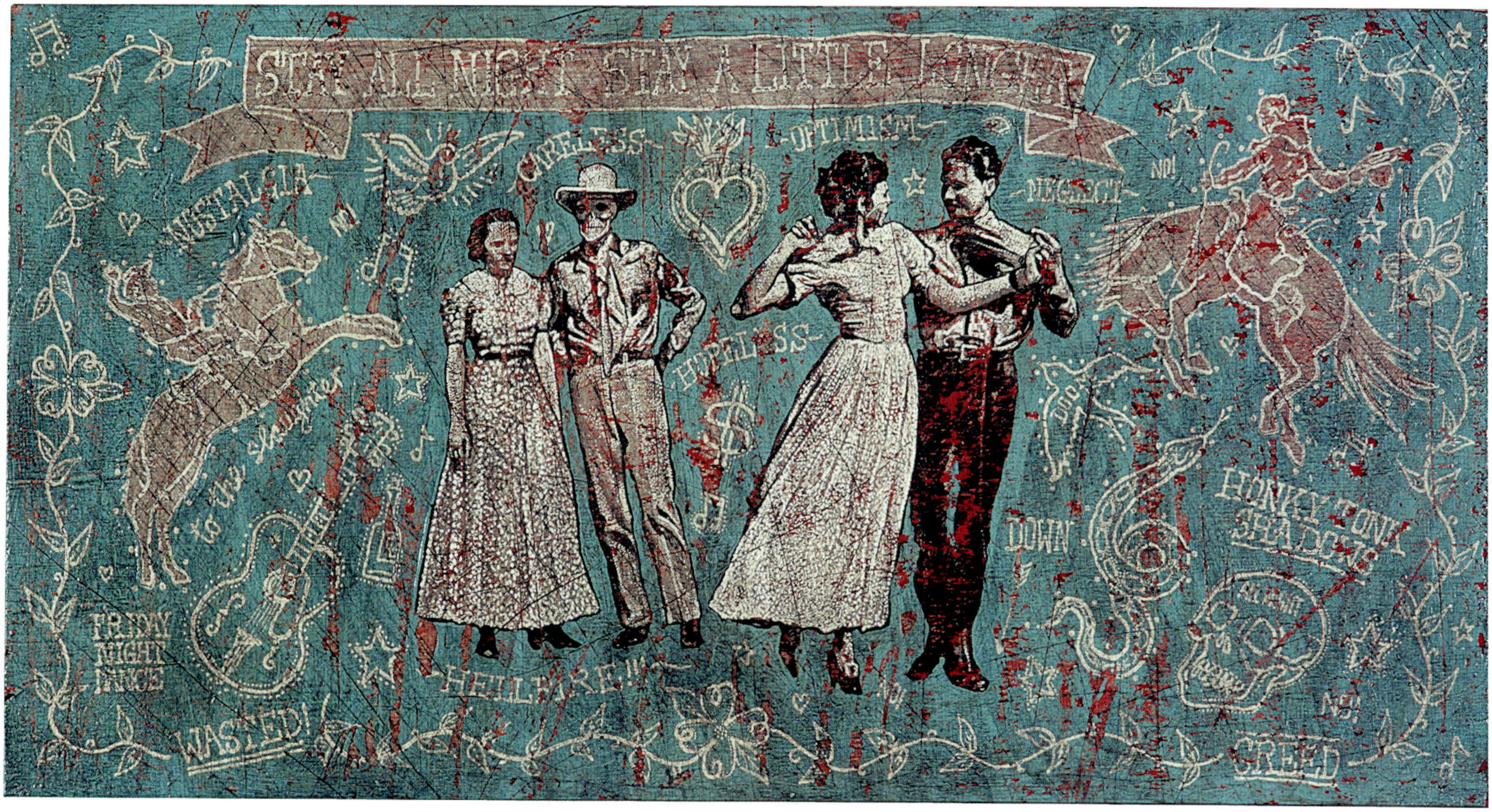

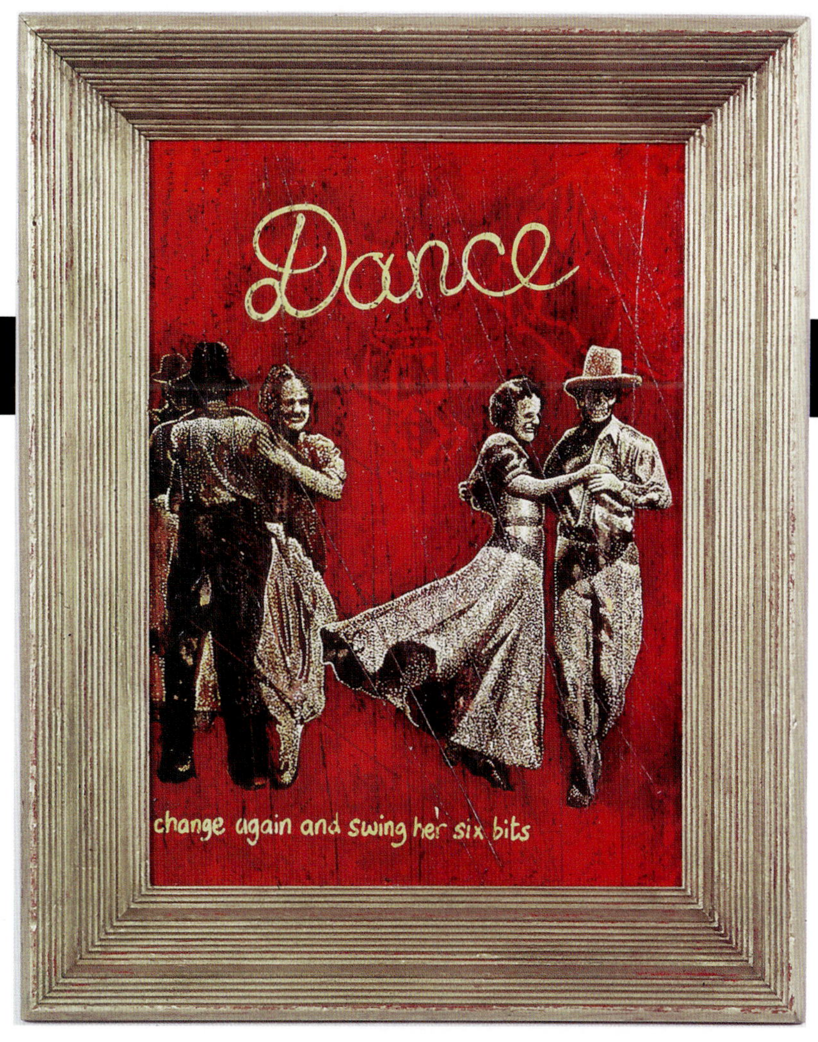
Dance
change again and swing her six bits

Dollar Dress

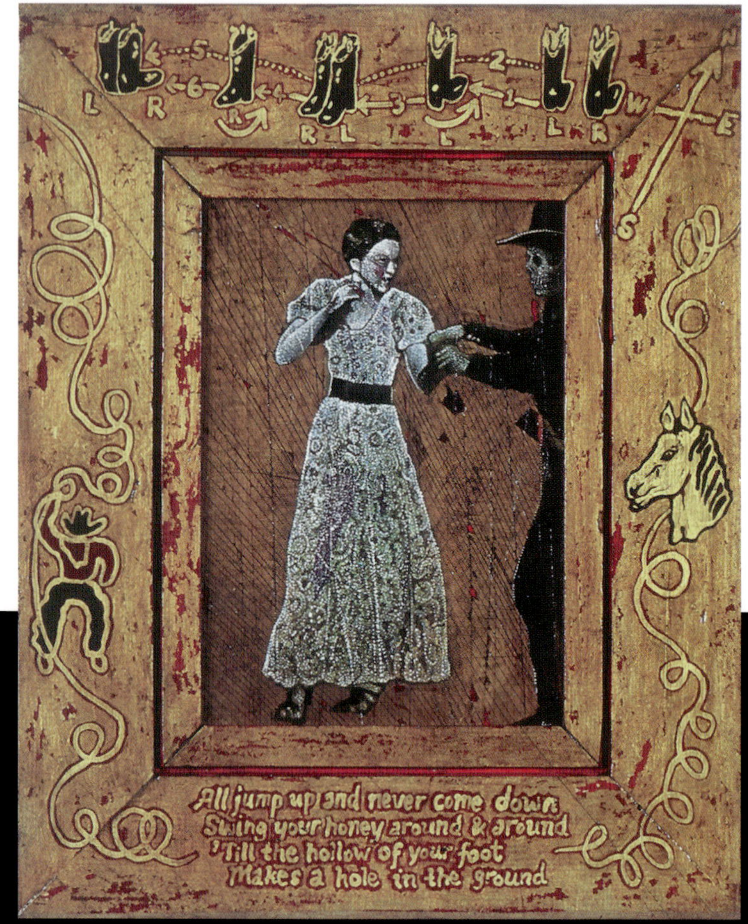

She is dancing with death in the dollar dress

There's a box in an attic in a run-down northern town
And there's a key on the shelf so you can look inside
There's a song that will pick you up and spin you around
A photograph and some letters left behind

Can you prove you're alive?
Do you know where you've been today?
It's sown into the fabric of your life,
Washed and mended, worn away

She's dancing with death in the dollar dress

The hooter sounds and the whole town shakes again
A line of ghosts clock out at the gates
Cousins, sisters, and brothers are spirited home
They fill the streets and make the traffic wait

Will the flag still fly if the wind don't blow today?
It's sown into the fabric of your life,
Washed and mended, worn away

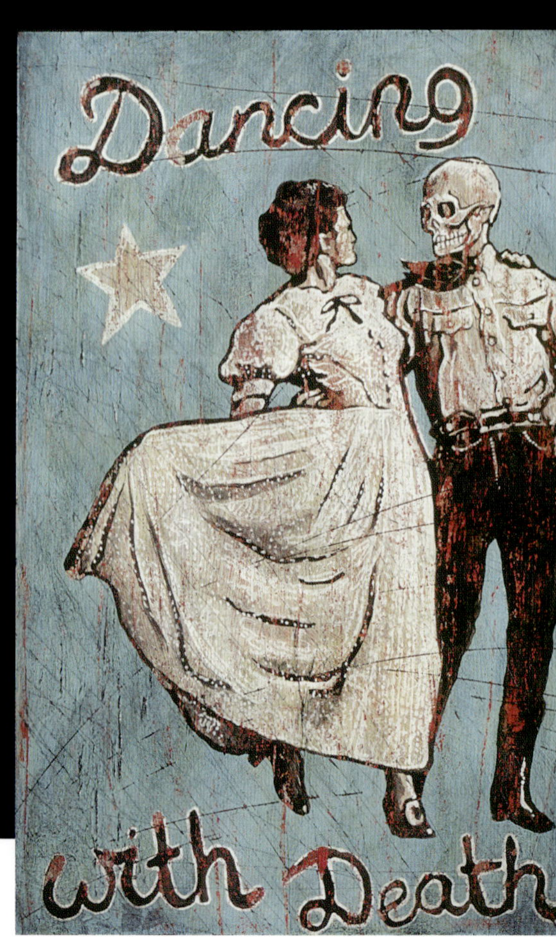

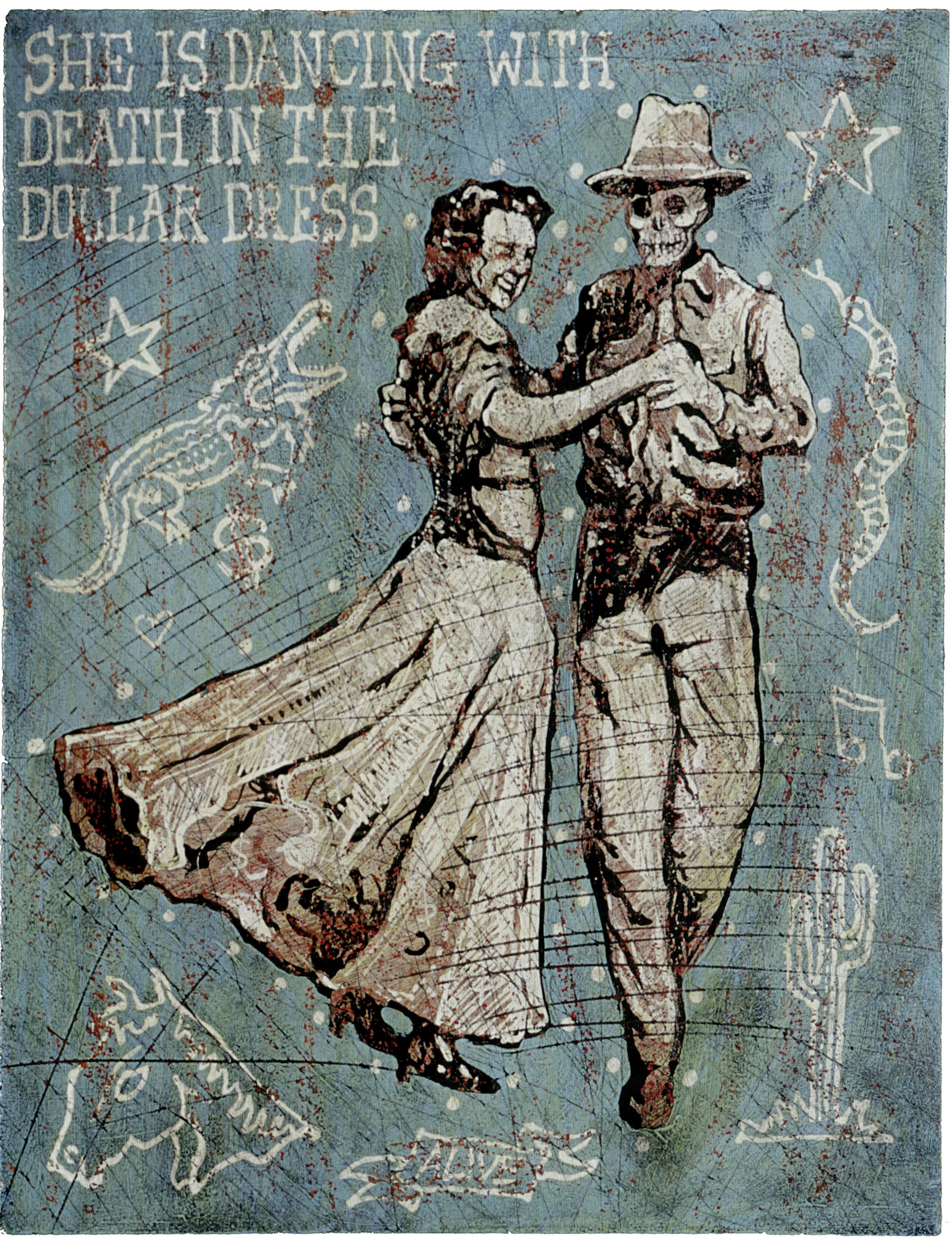

SHE IS DANCING WITH
DEATH IN THE
DOLLAR DRESS

Drugstore

Step out here and take my hand
Across the floor where there's space to move
I don't care who's playing in the band
I just want to get closer to you
Well I don't mean to sound pedantic
But what are we going to do now?
I came back & built this wall
So you could tear the whole thing down

Just for a day everything makes sense
Feel your ankles grinding on the floor
And every tune seems so familiar
We must have heard them all before
Looks like that big clown's got a gun
He walked right back into the room
He's the master of the world
& We've been living on the moon

Sonic booms out over the channel
People lock themselves inside
But the air tastes good and it's the same air
*   that you breathed*
When you were dancing by my side
Hey, hey, the band just keeps on playing
I hoped things wouldn't get this far
My energy is going nowhere
Sucked back up into the stars

Come on down to the drugstore
Come on down, sweet Jerry Lee
Come on down to the drugstore
Someone's waiting there for me
Hey, hey, the band just keeps on playing
& No one knows that I'm still here
I'm melting back into the crowd
Waiting for the dust to clear

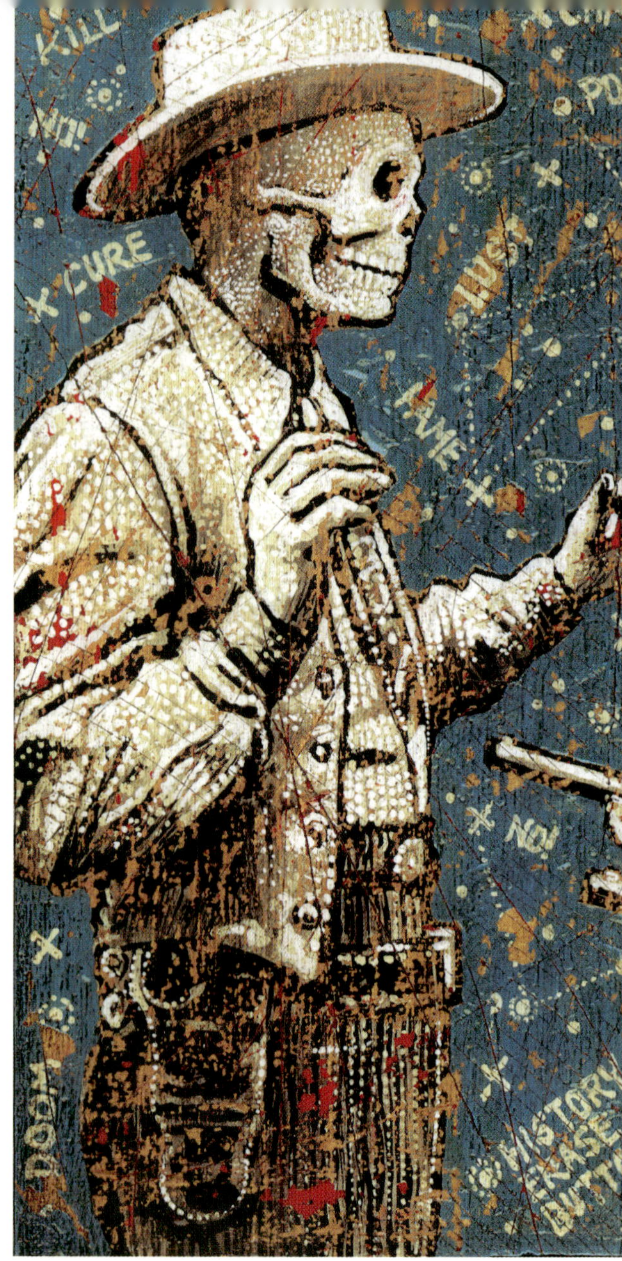

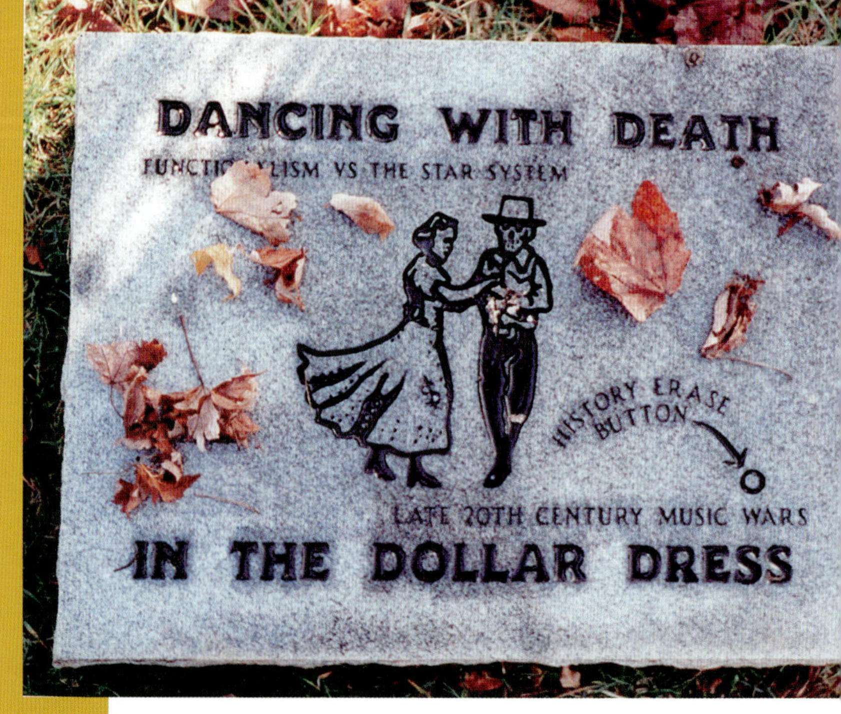

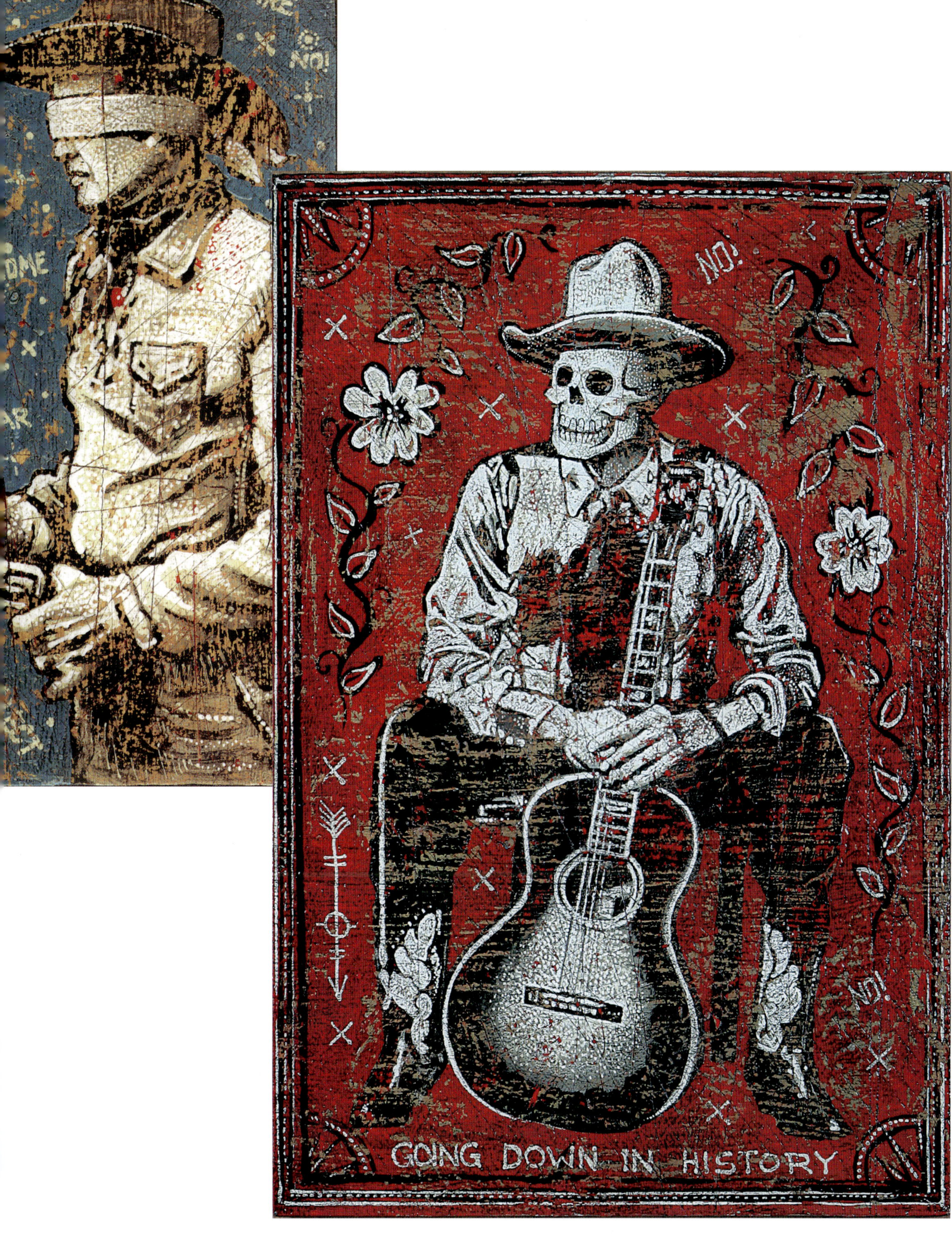

NO!
NO!
GOING DOWN IN HISTORY

Blink of an Eye

John Doe fat and snarling (anag.)
Every little mother's darling
Falling like a bullet from the sky
A joke he told up on the gallows
Plays out in the midnight shadows
Gone in the blink of an eye

A love song to the maladjusted
Doors kicked down, Johnny's busted
Hush little baby don't you cry
'Cos the president's just half a man
Riding in some giant's hand
He's gone in the blink of an eye

Gone, gone, gone, gone
Gone in the blink of a eye

In the time it takes for doors to shut on
Fingers poised above the button
Longing for a fatter fish to fry
Where everybody's sat around
With all the pretty things they found
You're gone in the blink of an eye

You're sawing through the cradle branches

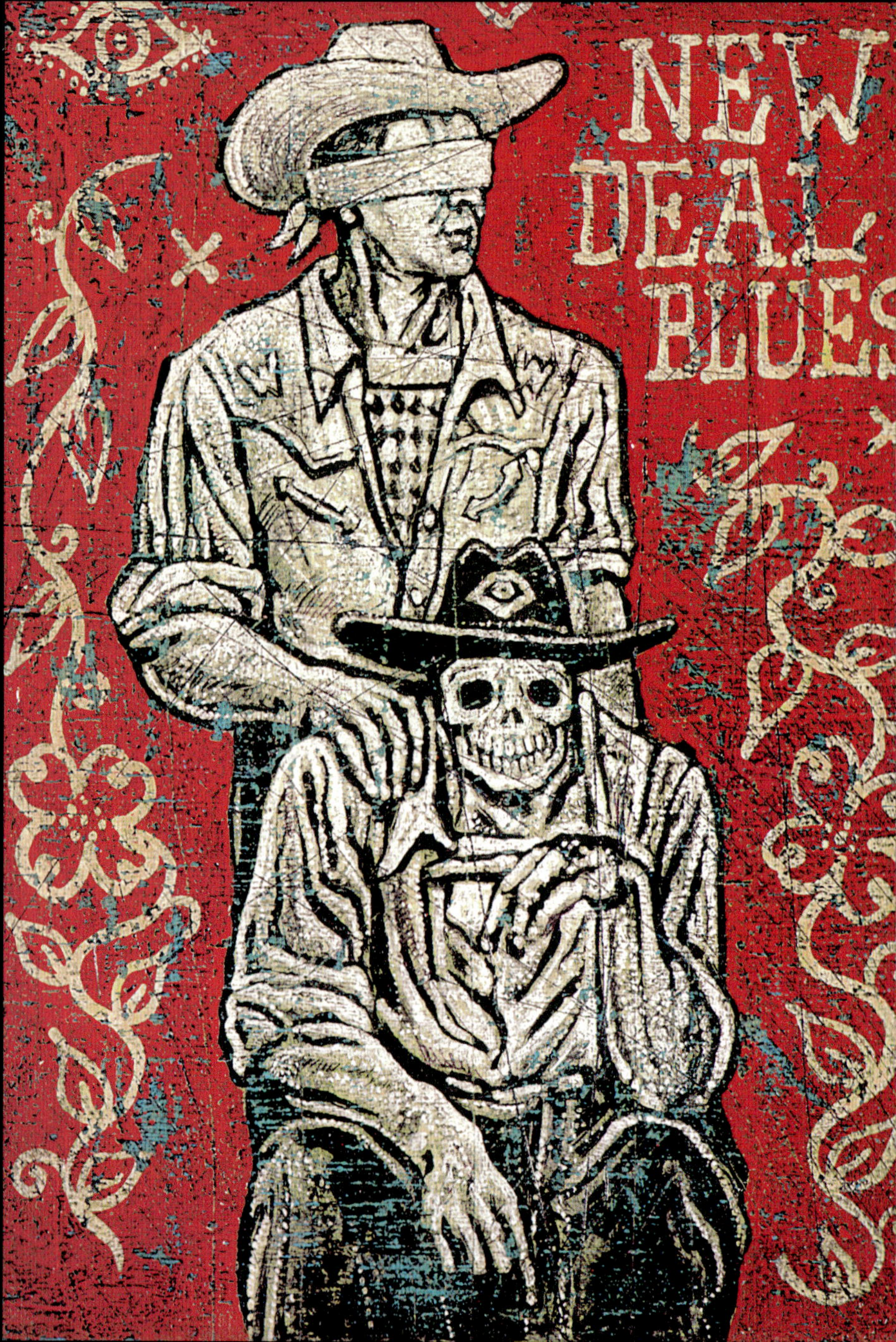

Cowboy in Flames

You feel disgusted and confused
Manipulated and abused
You're not the reason, you're just the means
It's a brutal little lesson in being free
40 days & 40 nights, out of mind is out of sight
Talking trash, conspiracies
Handing all your weapons to your enemies

I claw at another door and everything will slip away
There's so much money washing 'round out there
Can't a little bit come my way?
Uh, uh, uh, oh! Punishment, punishment!

Earthbound & heaven sent
Brainwashed, lobotomised
Cowboy in flames, bombs in the sky

General Custer's on the trail
His last letter's in the mail
It's propaganda, it's marketing
Oooh, General Custard died for your sins
And the good old rock where we once stood
Has got too old to be much good
And the good old ways are sick and lame
Third world on horseback
Cowboy in flames

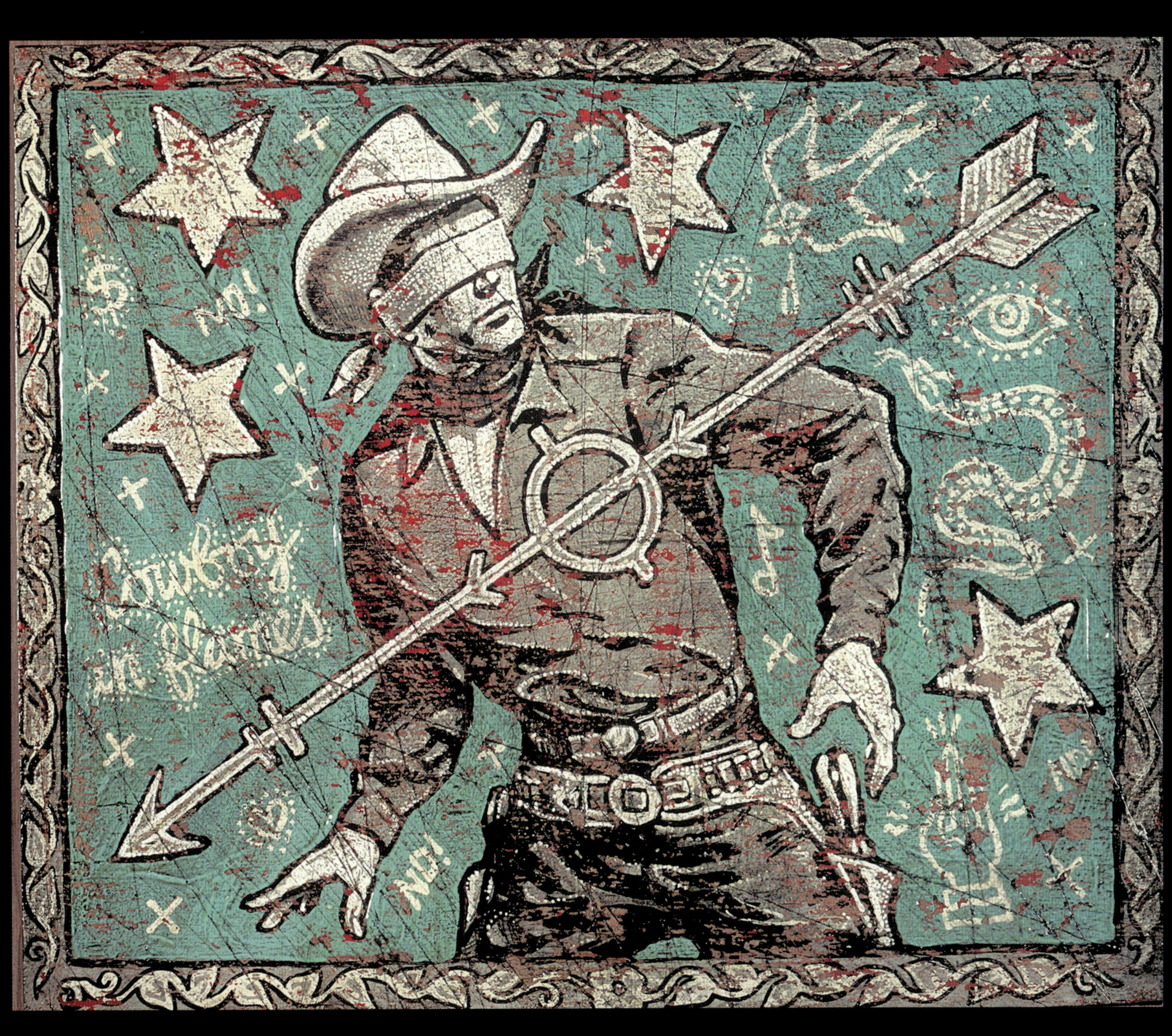

Last Fair Deal Gone Down

You are yourself at the center of the story
Your fate falls through your hands
& At the heart of all this faded glory
Scattered on the land
The Deal was done on a bright blue morning
The how and why and when
So out of step as those forces beyond you
Go whipping up the dustbowl again

This jealously defended domestication
Turns out to be a temporary situation
This little calm, this precious quiet
Gives way to a riot

Work 'til your back is breaking
Don't try to tell me that your faith's not shaken
You have your reasons to believe in people
But people aren't all the same
They're not the same today

We lost a piece of the puzzle
We lost one of the team
Who really knows who caused this trouble?
Turned us all around
Last fair deal gone down

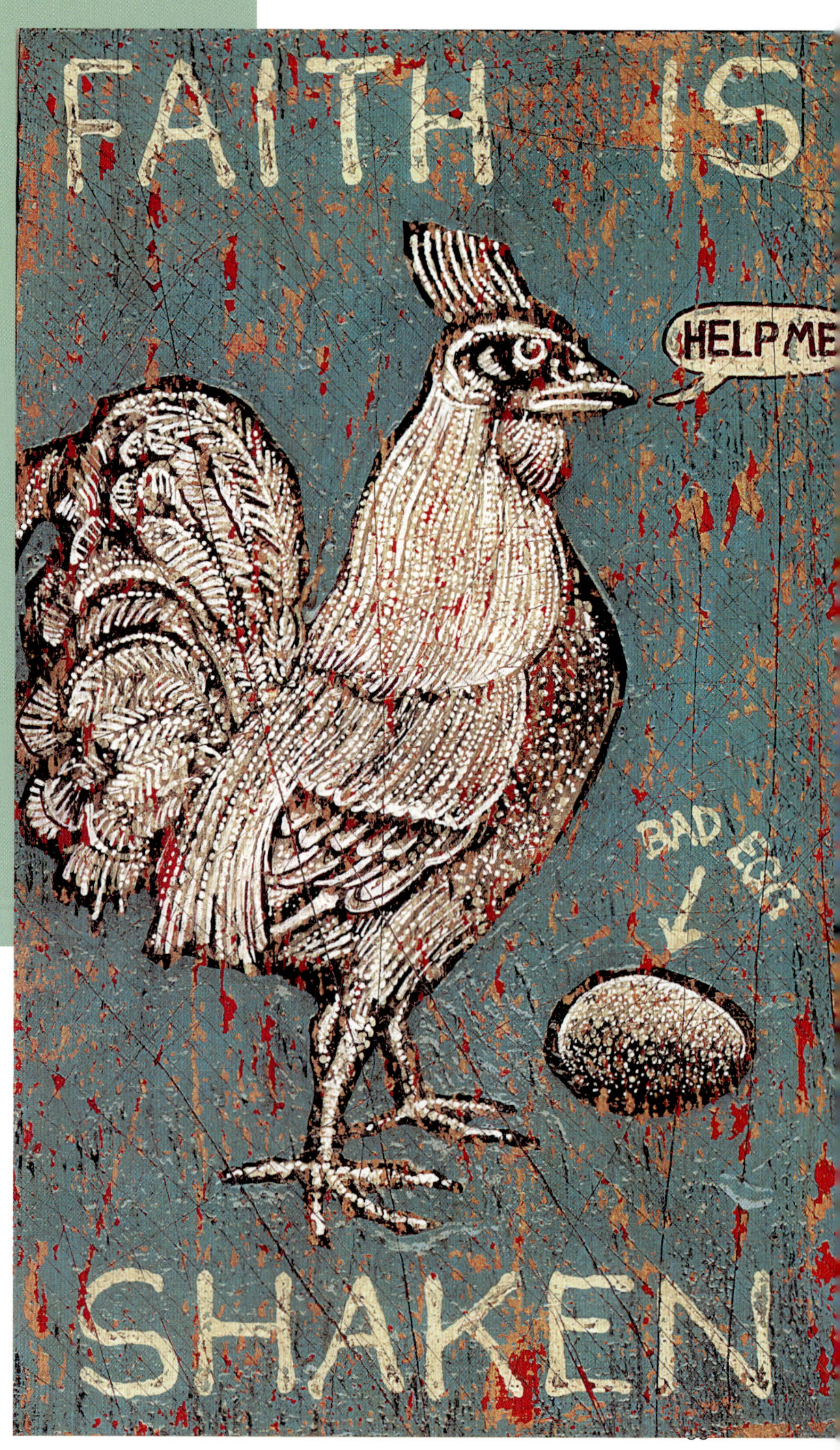

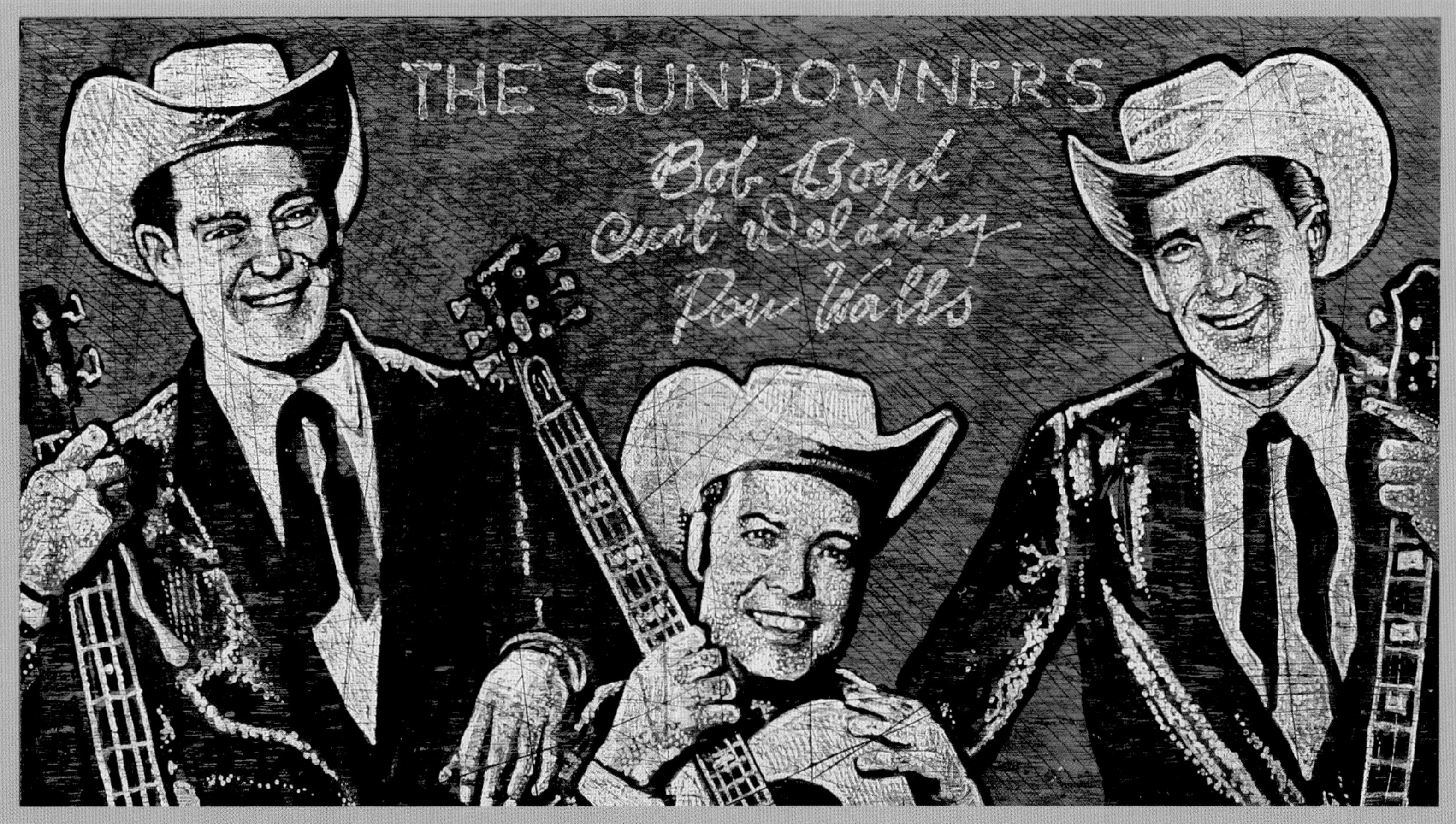

THE SUNDOWNERS

1987: The Mekons' second tour of the United States. Decked out in big hats, pearl buttons, black embroidered western shirts, pointy boots, and collar tips—the cool civilian uniform that offers outsiders a direct line to the core of the American cowboy myth—we stumble into the Double R Ranch, a sub-terranean honky-tonk deep beneath the shiny skyscrapers of Chicago's Loop.

Up on stage, below wall-mounted longhorns & cowhide maps of Texas, a band of old guys called the Sundowners are half-way through an all-nite set, their lovely rasping western harmonies guiding a crew of sozzled city-folk down the long trail to dawn.

"Looks like we've got a band here!" says singer Bob Boyd, and invites us up to play a few numbers!!! Two out of three Sundowners duck into the shadows and hit the bar, grateful for a break. But guitarist Don Walls stays & plays with us; his beautiful, fluid guitar lines hold us together like a powerful glue & pass our racket off as something the regulars can tolerate. He smiles encouragingly and does not seem alarmed by how crap we are. Maybe he recognizes kindred spirits? Maybe we're all just smashed? Who cares? In a hard city, a million miles from the country, we're all exiles trying to keep our feet out of the corporate dogshit & forget all the divisions, injustices, and casual brutalities that make this place so terrifying.

Like so many hillbilly hopefuls, the Sundowners had been drawn to Chicago by the magnet of WLS's National Barn Dance. They'd headed north with big dreams, but they hit town on the wrong side of the curve and were left to earn a workingman's living in a shrinking scene that had been all but paved over by the time the Mekons came stalking the honky-tonks looking for authentic cowboy thrills.

For 30 years Curt, Bob, & Don played grueling 8-hour, 5-night-a-week shifts in the clubs on Madison Street and the Double R Ranch in the Loop. Finally they tried their hands at running their own place on Mannheim Road out by the airport, where with never a cuss word spoken on stage they plucked a thousand drunken requests from bulging folders of handwritten lyric sheets that spanned the breadth & depth of American music. They projected their 3-part harmonies out over the pissed-up chatter & clinking of glass thru the hovering nicotine fog & watched as visiting baseball stars and obscure Midwestern TV cowboys carved their names in the

THE TRAIL IS HARD BUT IT LEADS EVERYWHERE

furrowed table-tops, always gracious & aloof even when lame local anchormen & British punk rockers stumbled onstage to murder the classics.

They'd each had opportunities to break for the big time, to play the Nashville game, but they stuck it out in Chicago—comfortable in each other's company—and stood their ground together. For us that was half the attraction.

I was not quite at home when I moved to Chicago a while later. My band was in legal limbo, and I was stuck out in the deep suburbs, broke & sleeping in my girlfriend's parent's attic. We liked to hang out at the Sundowner's Ranch, perched on bar-

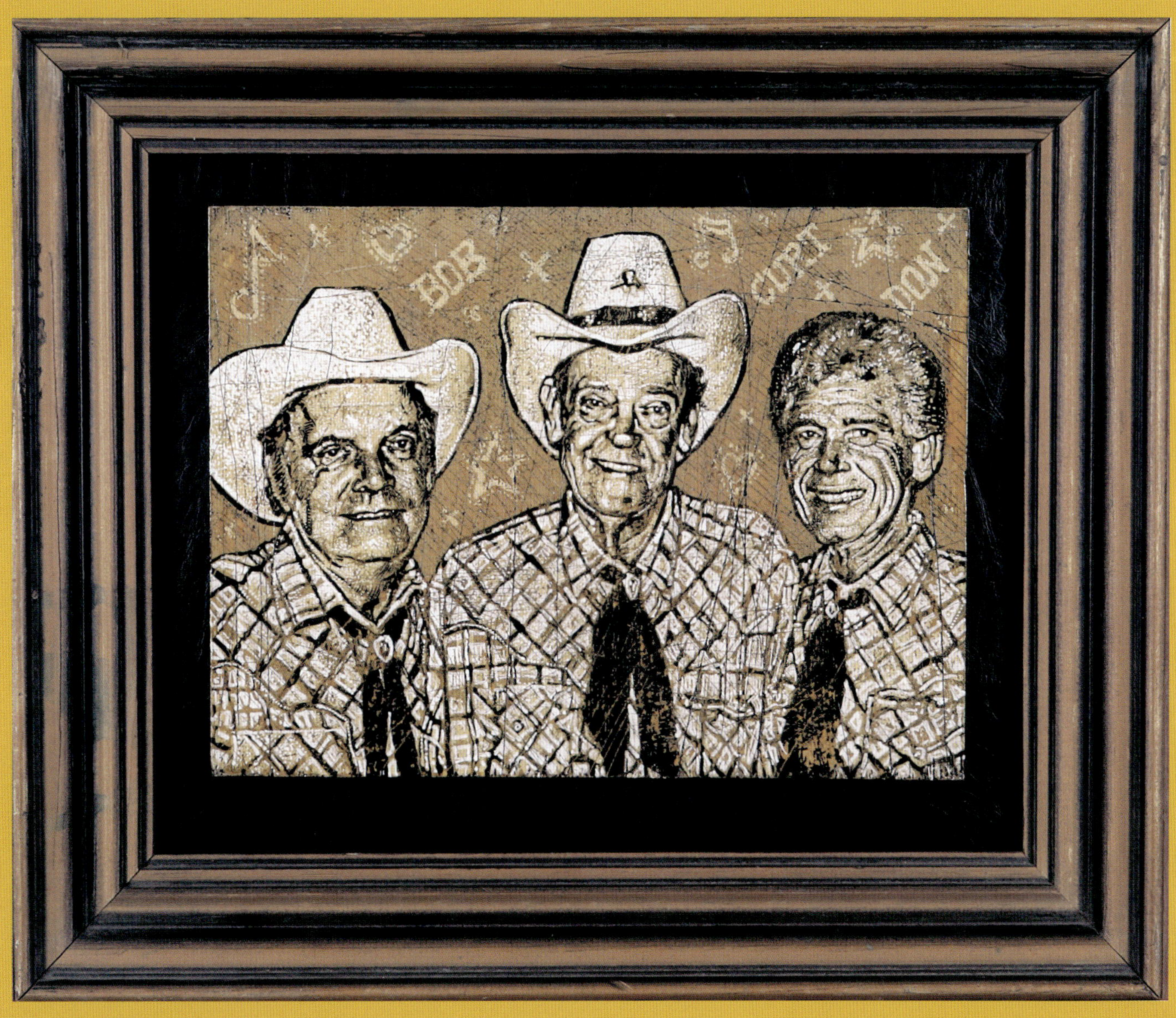

stools just around the corner from the swingin' doors marked
Bulls & Heifers. It was the only place where I knew anybody,
our little oasis in the sprawl with its relentless John Wayne
rec-room décor and a surreal food menu that climaxed with
something called a Chili Mac Salami Tamale Perch Bowl – the
house special!

After playing George Strait's "All My Exes Live In Texas,"
Curt would announce, "Two of my ex-wives live in Illinois,
one's in Indiana and the other one . . . well, she's in hell, I
guess!" He said that every time they played the song, which
was every time I saw them. Also: "My first 2 wives left me
but this one just won't!" & (a personal favorite) "This song's
called 'Never Hit Your Grandmother With A Shovel!'"

And they'd always ask me up to play, which was flattering, scary, and ultimately educational. Back in Leeds, Rico Bell & me would do Buck Owens covers in pubs—and even our friends wouldn't come. So to get onstage and sing Hank & Johnny with the Sundowners in front of a crowd of genuinely mean and inebriated Americans meant tangible vindication—a rite of passage. That acceptance of me coming here and doing what I wanted to do was what I loved most about this contradictory place, where ordinary people go dancing and drinking on a Saturday night under the flags and guns and skulls that give just the faintest glimpse of that dark, violent face America shows the rest of the world.

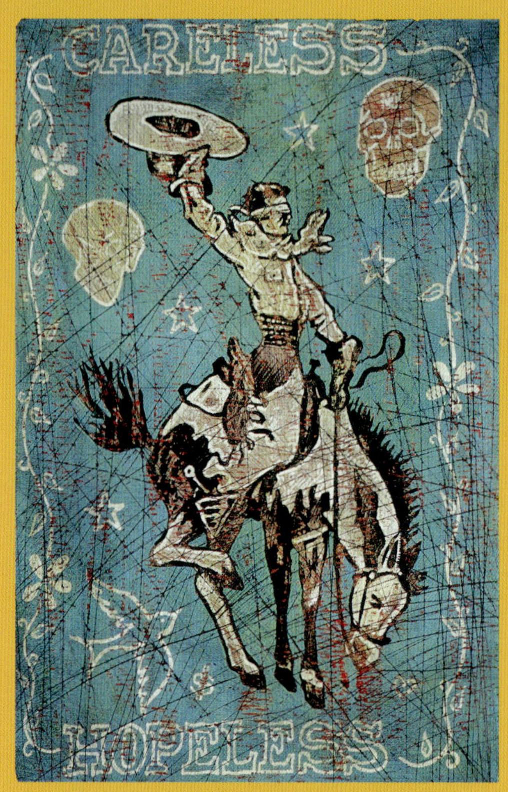

The Sundowners said they'd play our wedding—sort of—but we never knew if they were coming till they came. As dark clouds gathered in the June sky, they rolled up the driveway in a big gleaming station wagon, all decked out in matching silk bomber jackets with the Sundowners logo on the back. They played a set and my friends & family from Wales, London, & New York danced around & yelled until the temperature dropped and the band retreated into the house to stuff their weathered faces & shmooze with people their own age. They were very popular with the Welsh ladies . . .

Hours later I coaxed them back outside for a short second set. They didn't want to be paid, of course, so I gave them matching bolo ties I'd picked up at Alcala's Western Wear and they went away & one by one over the years they got older & sick and the ranch closed down. The mayor made December 4th "Sundowners Day" and we celebrated it with a couple of big parties. Then Don had a stroke & lost the use of his picking hand and Curt died . . .

Bob Boyd came & sang on the Pine Valley Cosmonauts' Bob Wills tribute album. We were recording at Kingsize, a punk-rock studio in hipster Wicker Park. Bob walked right in, took off his Stetson, spiked up what little hair he had left, stuck a metal ring in his nose, and said "just thought I'd try and fit in." But he was already sick & he died the following year. At his wake we sat with the families and the regulars, looking at pictures. We drank & smoked by the Coke machine in the back of a grim suburban funeral parlor, told old stories, and somehow felt at home. My 3-year-old stared unafraid into the open casket and asked: "Daddy, who's that cowboy?"

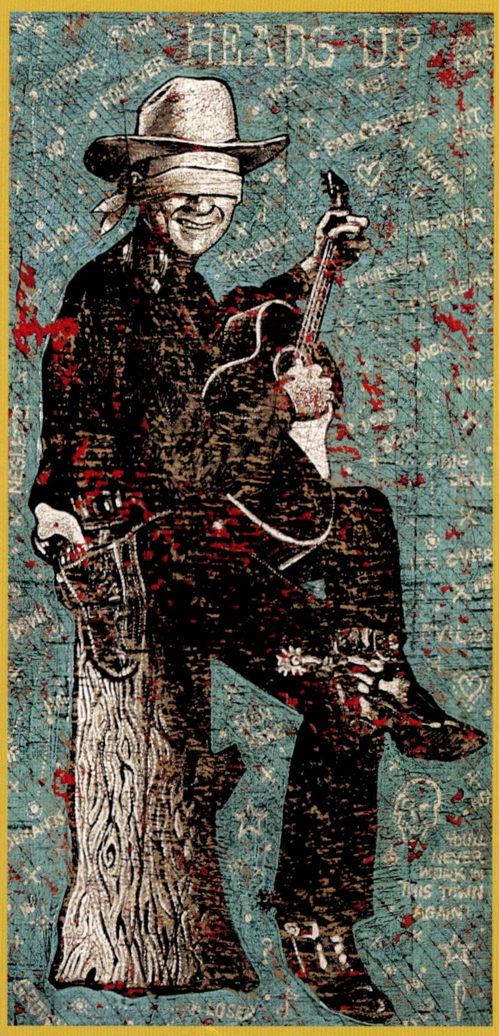

The Last Dead Cowboy

I'm a careless, hopeless, hard drinking man
Frightened of the thunder and the cold
Many times you've seen me out there on the land
I'm a man who died a long, long time ago

The trail is hard but it leads everywhere
Out in the desert glare
I pull my hat down over my eyes
Hypnotized by the image on the screen
That shirt so white and clean, silver pistols at his side

Take a trip, to the wide-open spaces
Looking for the traces of the wild frontier's call
Riding out, feel the rain on our faces
Through familiar places, the truck-stop and the mall

This country starts to look and sound the same
There's a singer on the radio and I don't like his name

I'm a careless, hopeless, hard drinking man
Frightened of the thunder and the cold
Many times you've seen me out there on the land
I'm a man who died a long, long time ago

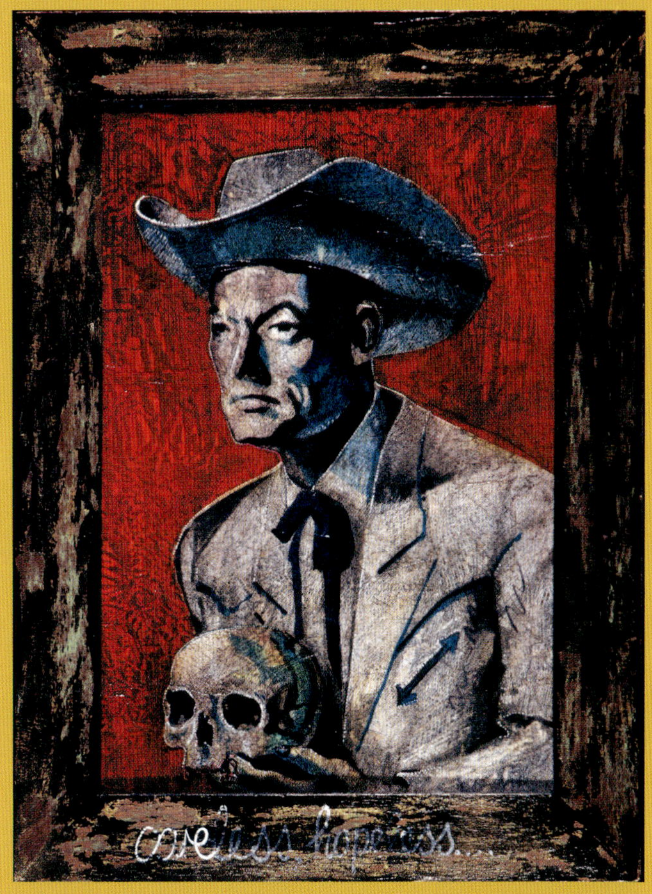

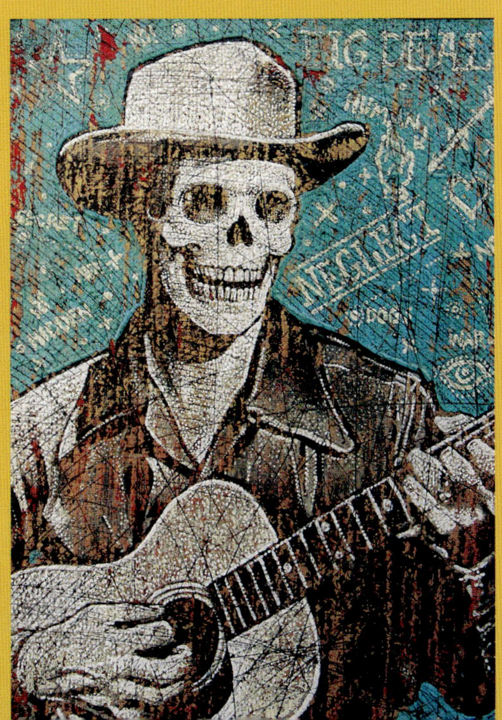

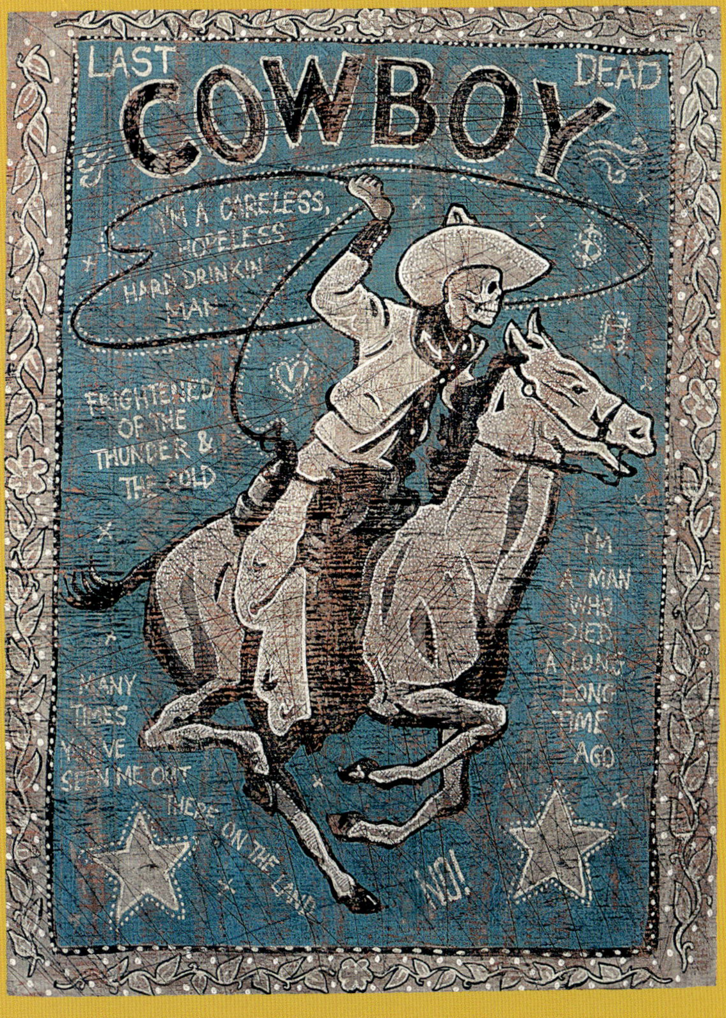

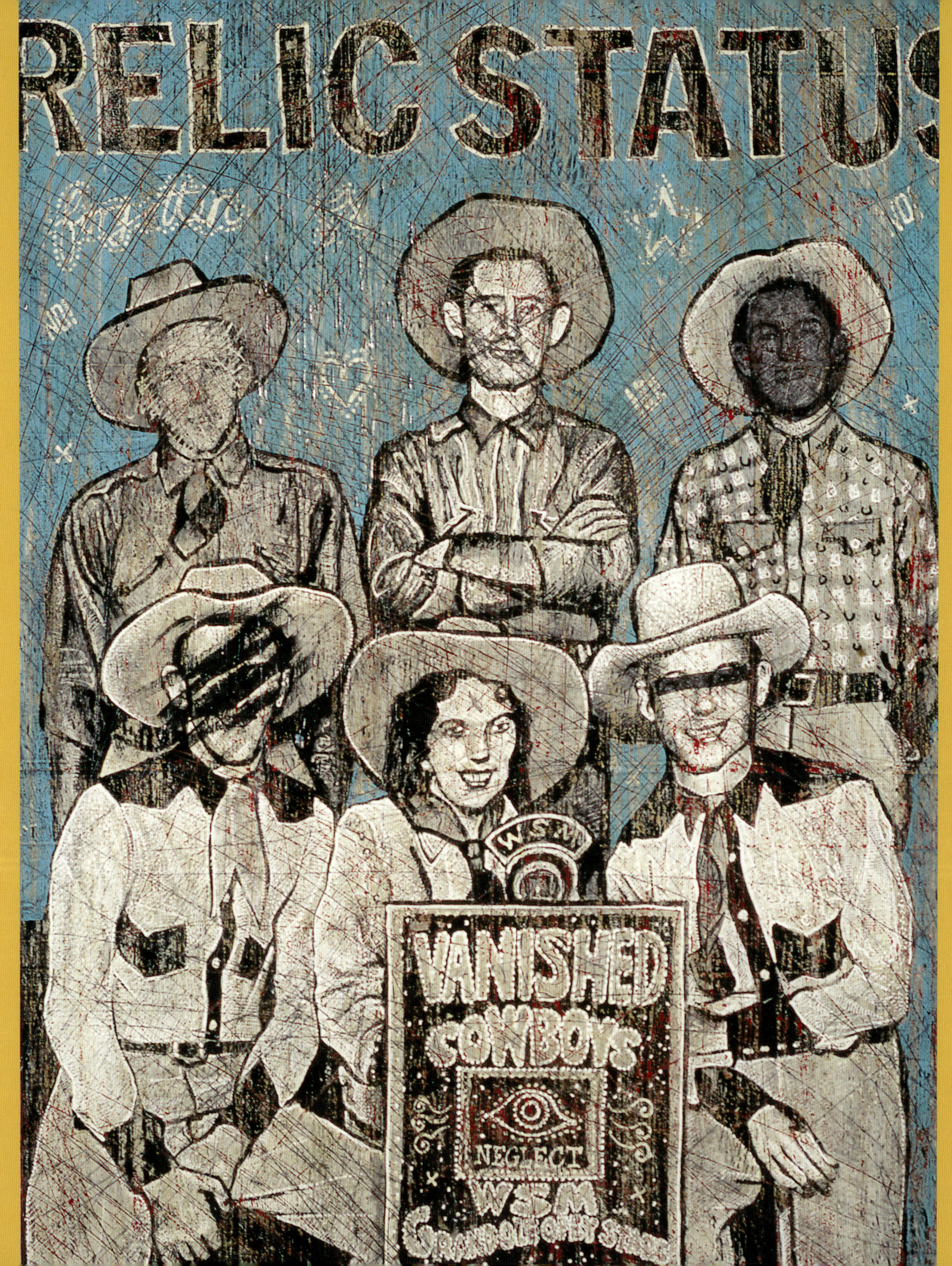
RELIC STATUS
WSM
VANISHED
COWBOYS
NEGLECT
WSM
GRAND OLE OPRY STAGE

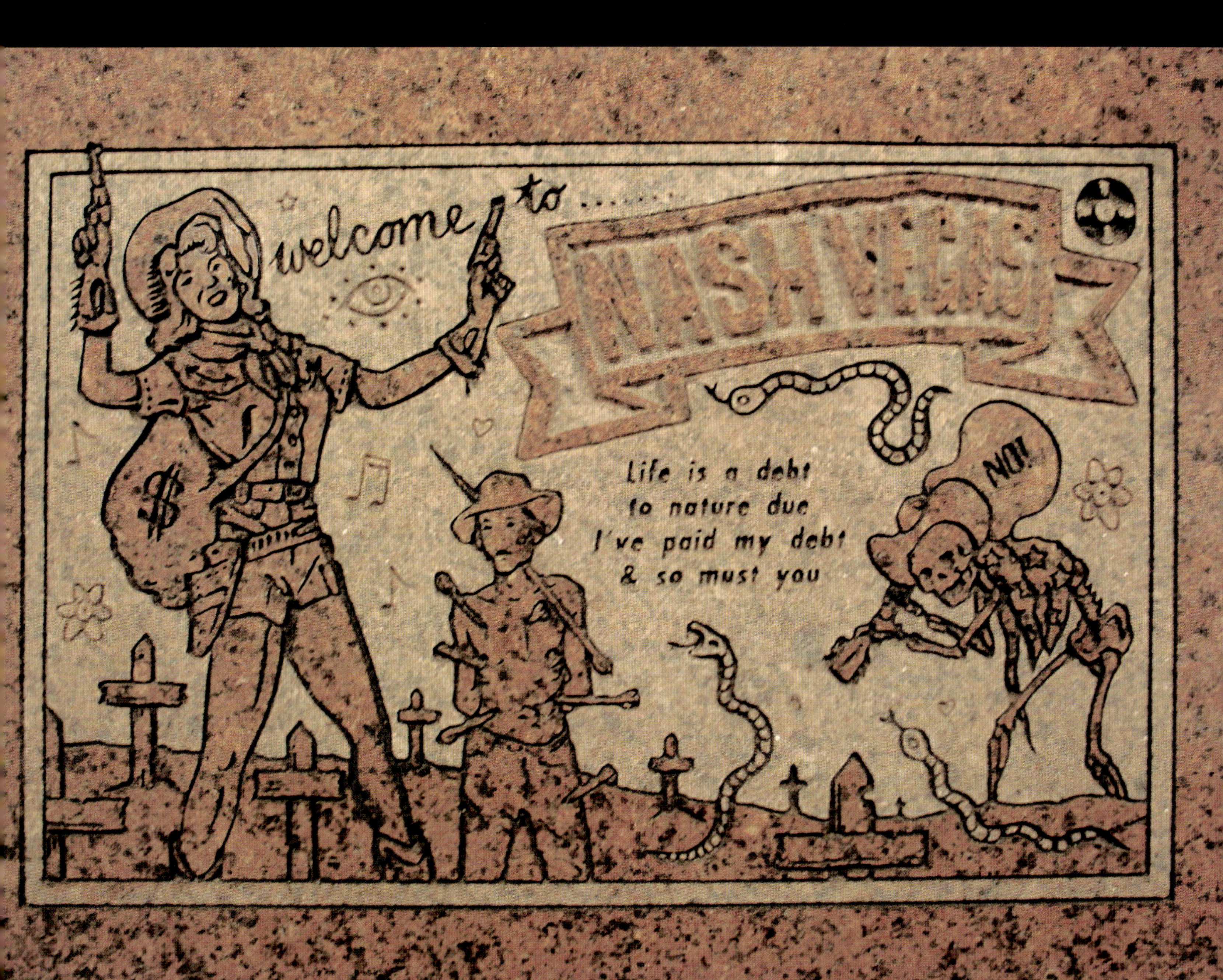
welcome to
NASH VEGAS
NO!
Life is a debt
to nature due
I've paid my debt
& so must you
$

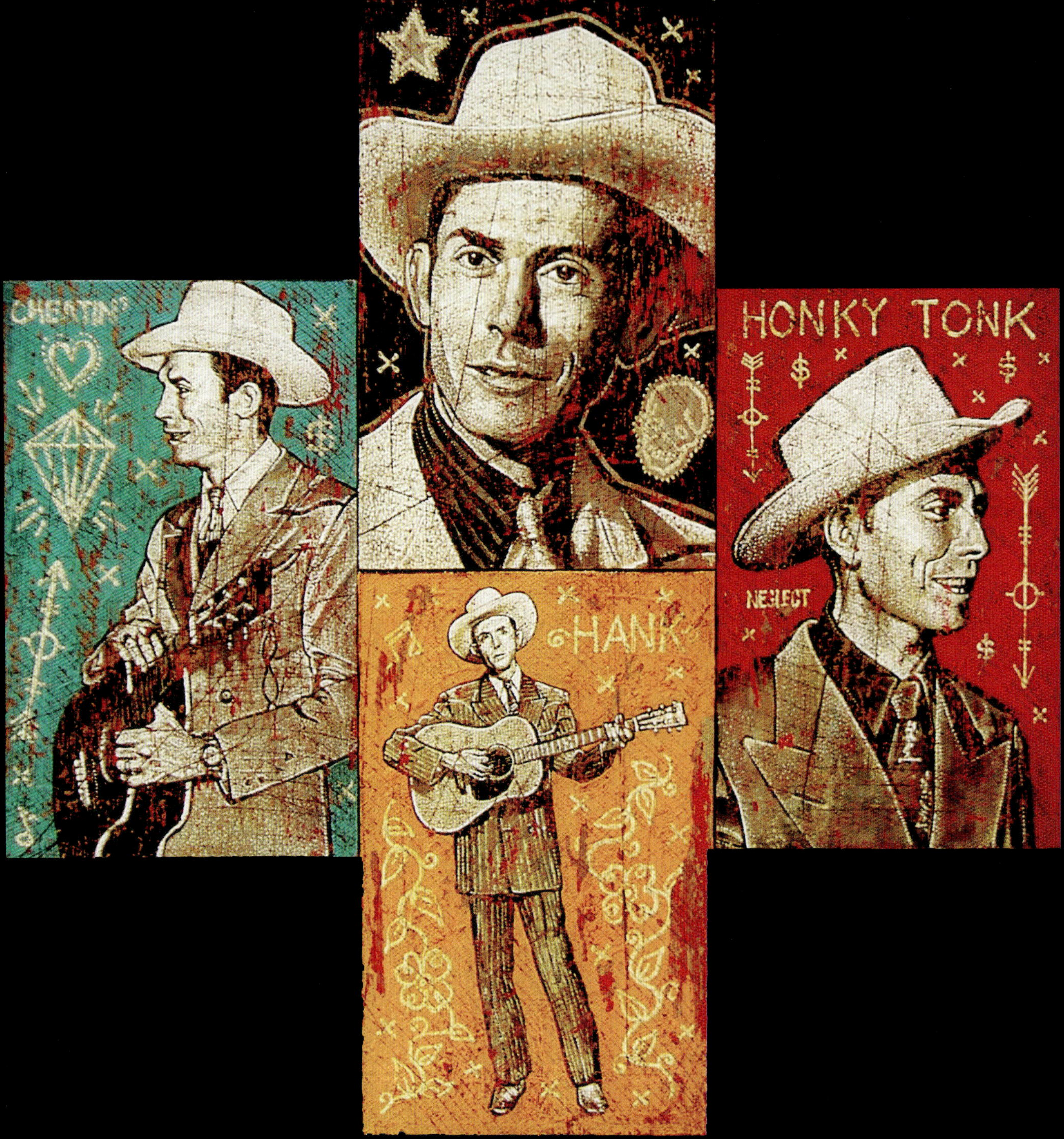

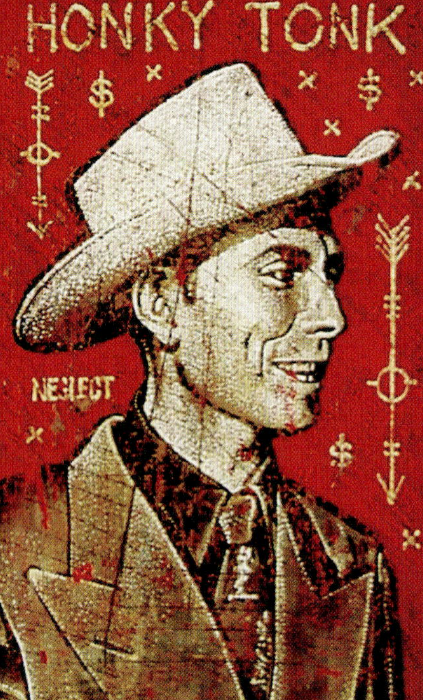

Nashville Radio

Drink and pills and Nashville radio, my life'll never be the same
Chills and spills from Maine to Mexico, riding on my funeral train
In every town there's the same tribulation, in every state I wake up in
The night before is a dim recollection of powders and bottles and sin
There's a bored little stranger heading out the door just about half my age
Blood on the walls and glass on the floor;
I don't think I even made it on stage
Doctor Doctor sign my prescription, I'm in trouble again
Ever since I was a tiny little baby, I couldn't get rid of the pain ▶▶

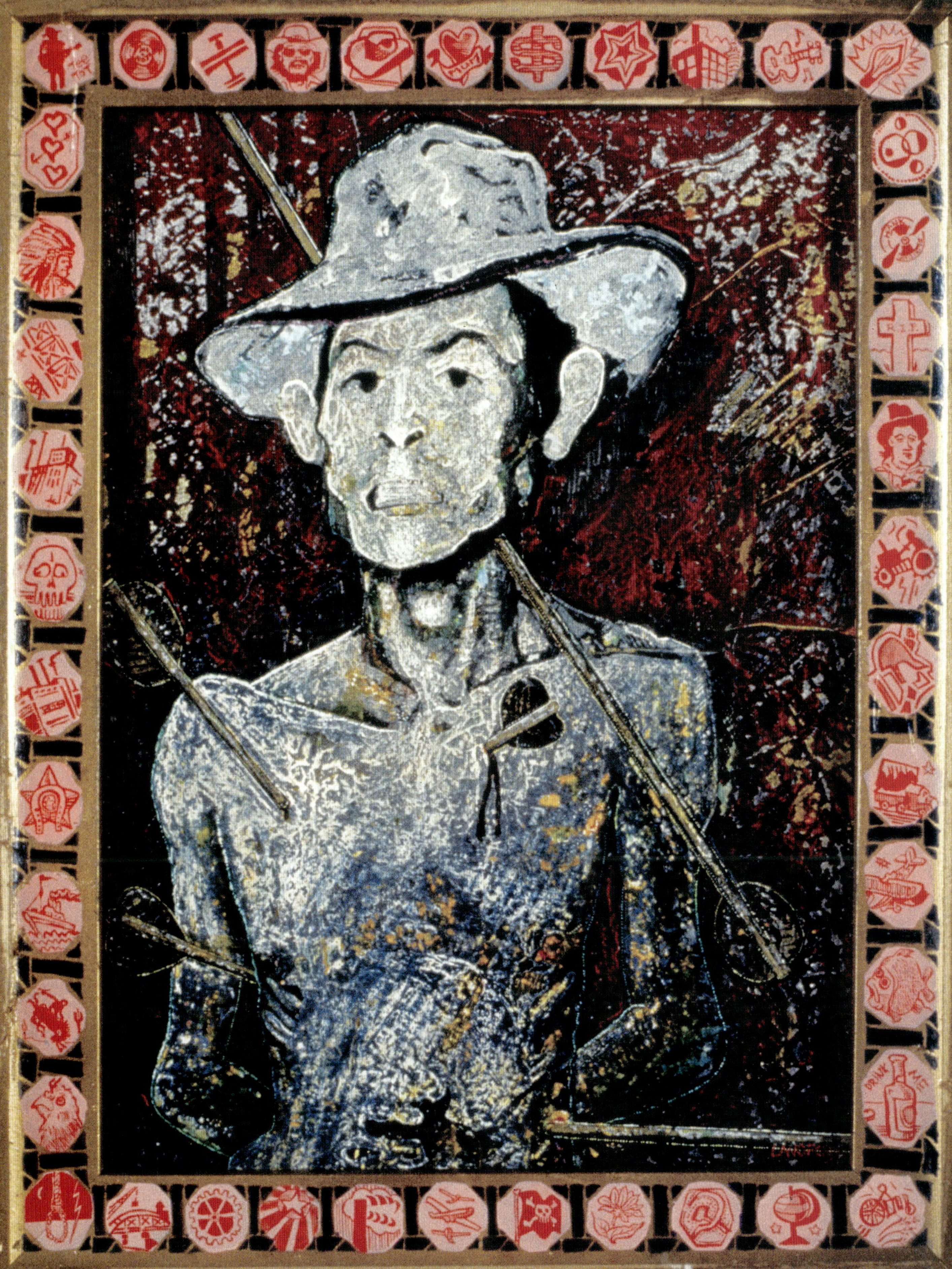

Drink and pills and Nashville radio, life'll never be the same
Chills and spills from Maine to Mexico, riding on my funeral train
I can shake my hips but I walk like a cripple and my body is getting too thin
I can count every one of my bones in the mirror
Poking through my cold white skin
There's a shiny star on the dressing room door
But I'll be hiding in the back of the car
'Cos I don't know a soul I can trust with the money or to tune up my guitar   ▸▸

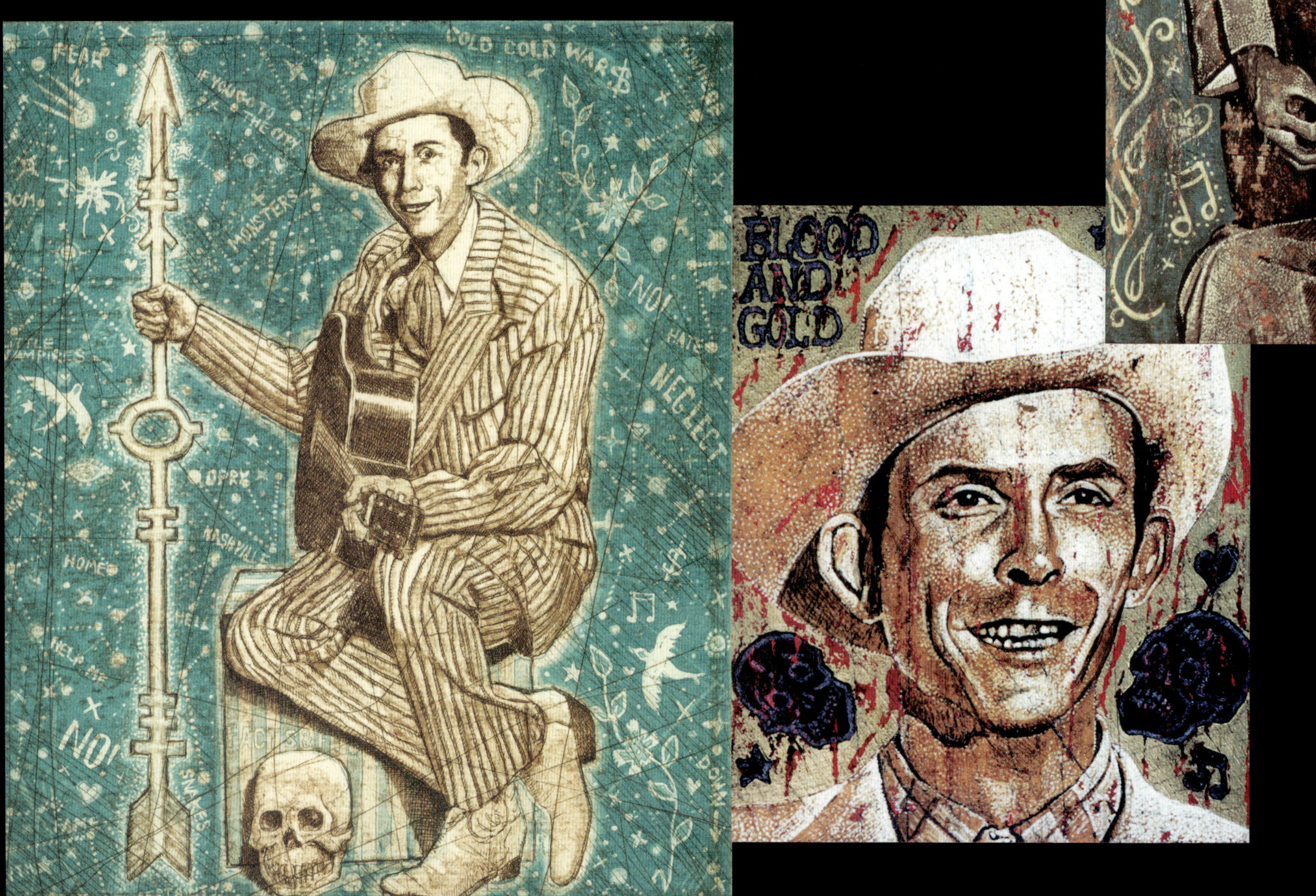

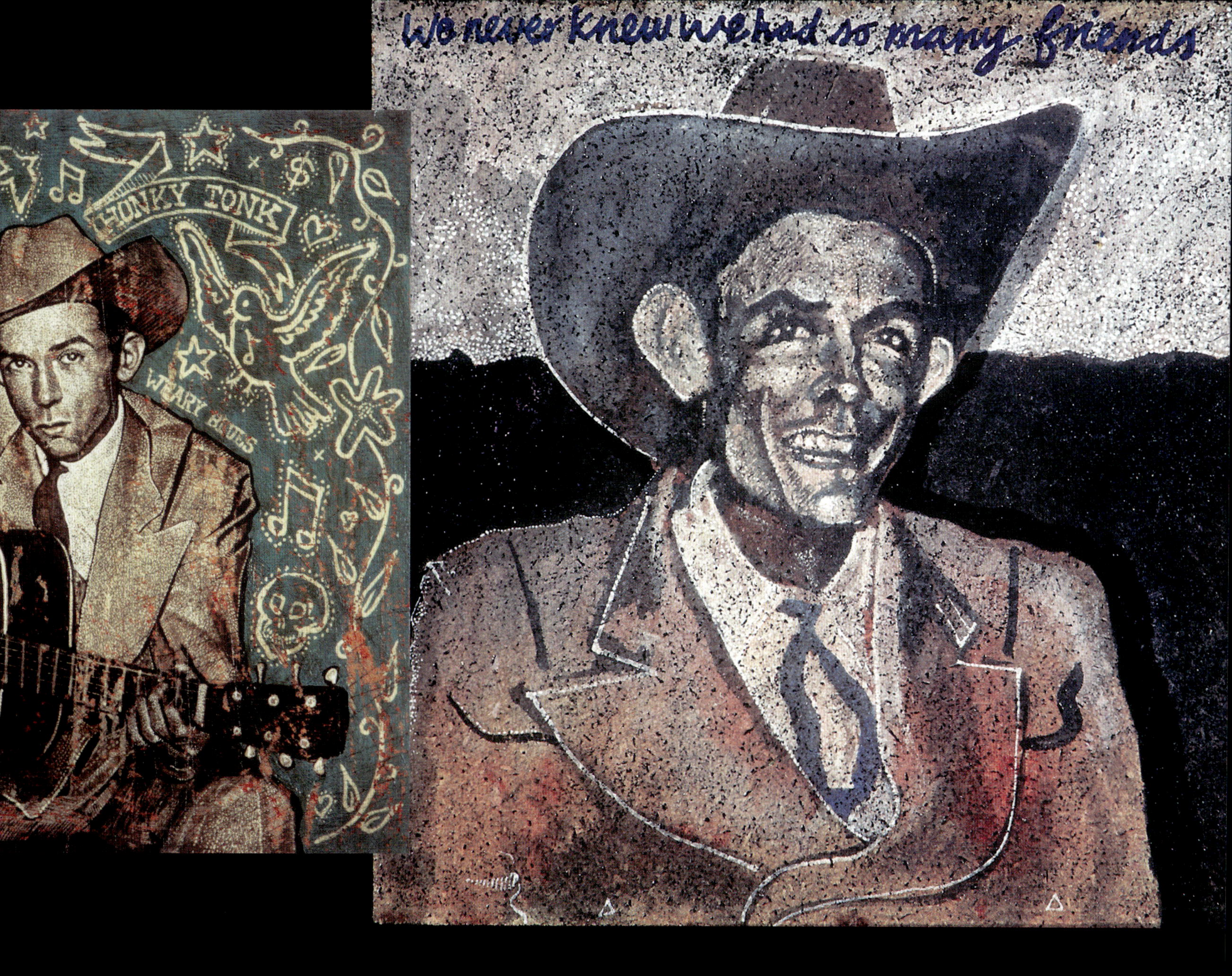

Drink and pills and Nashville radio my life'll never be the same
Chills and spills from Maine to Mexico, riding on my funeral train
I can't sleep without the engine humming

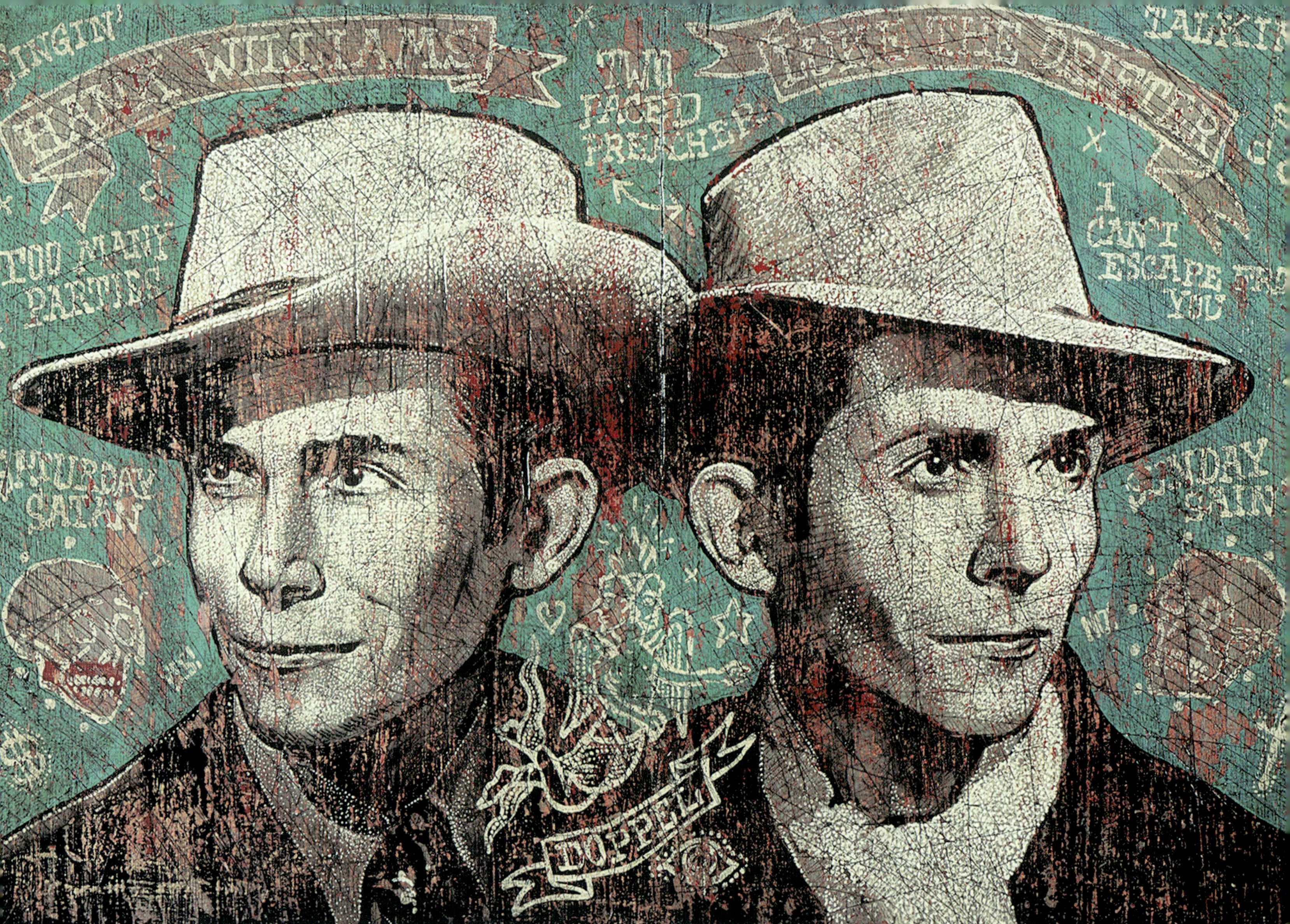

Ever since I was a tiny little baby, I couldn't get to sleep at night
Listening to the Nashville Radio hours before daylight
They threw me off the Grand Ole Opry 'cos I couldn't behave
Didn't know how many friends I had 'til I was lying in a cold dark grave
I gave my life to Country music, I took my pills and lost
Now they don't play my songs on the radio, it's like I never was
Fat sweaty cop in an Alabama lockup looked at me and laughed
Heard my records on the Nashville radio, asked me for my autograph
He said "Doctor, Doctor sign my prescription, I'm in a lot of trouble again
Ever since I was a tiny little baby I just couldn't get rid of the pain."
Drink and pills and Nashville radio, my life'll never be the same
Chills and spills from Maine to Mexico, riding on my funeral train

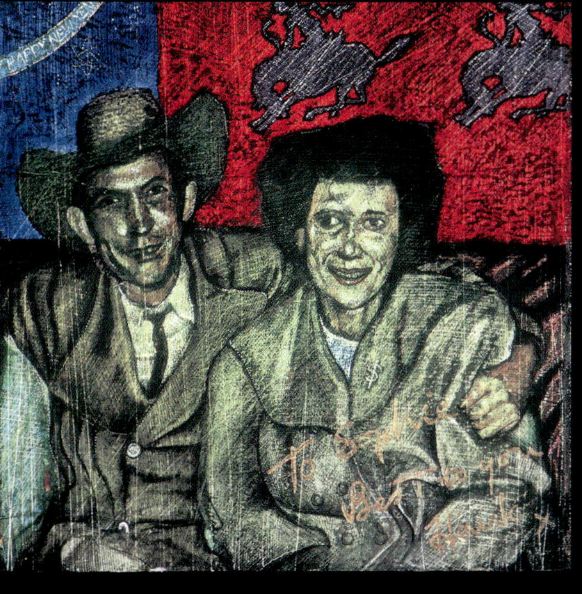

HAPPY NEW YEAR

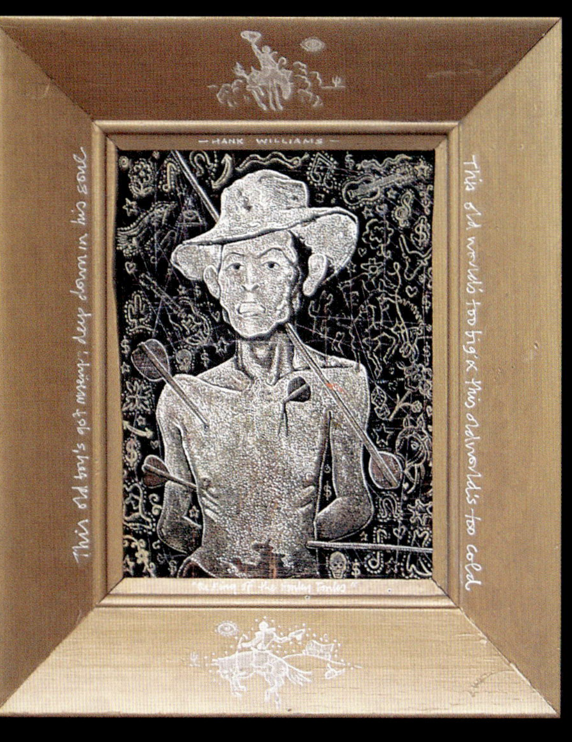

— HANK WILLIAMS —
This old world's too big & this old world's too cold
This old boy's got money; deep down in his soul
"The King of the Honky Tonks"

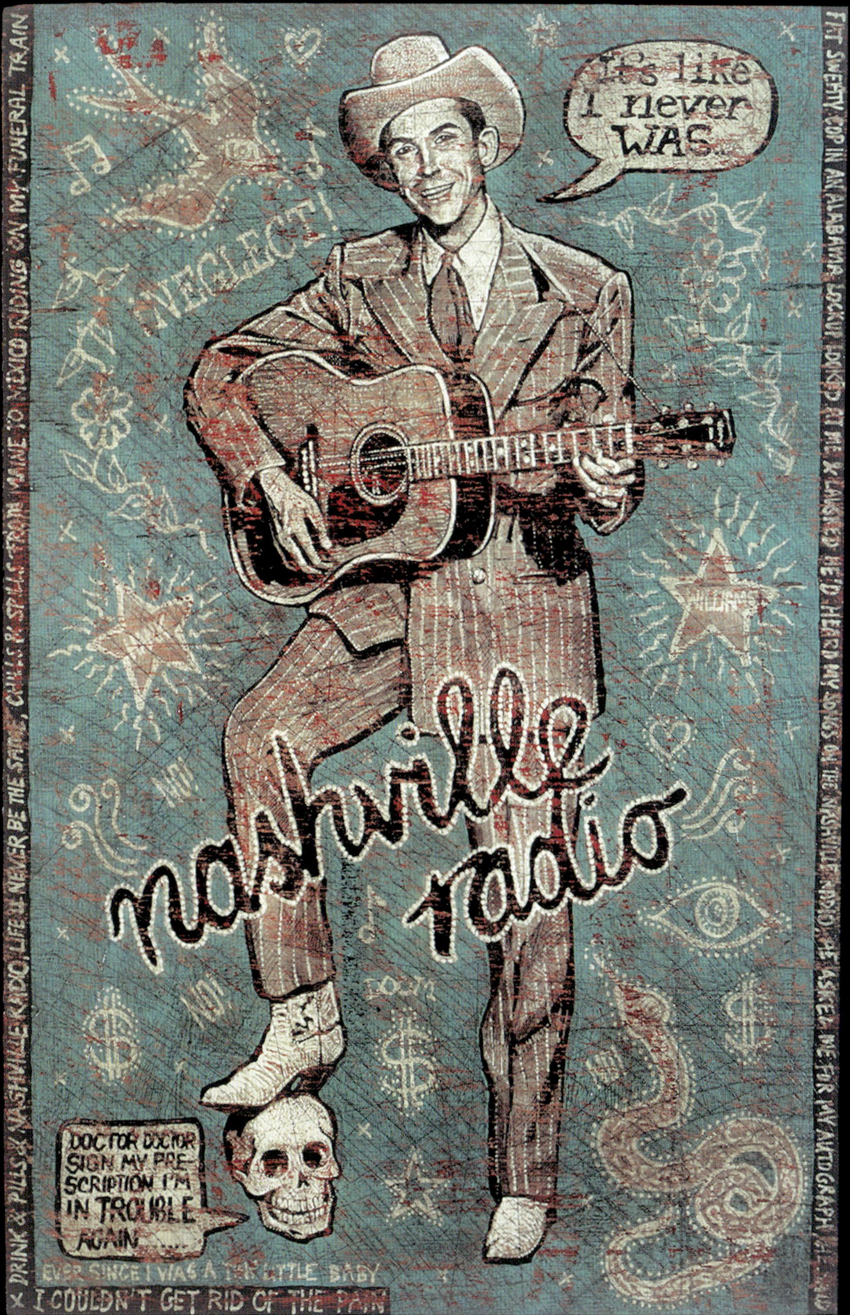

It's like I never WAS...
NEGLECT!
nashville radio
DOCTOR DOCTOR SIGN MY PRESCRIPTION I'M IN TROUBLE AGAIN
DRINK & PILLS & NASHVILLE RADIO LIFE'LL NEVER BE THE SAME, CHILLS & SPILLS FROM MAINE TO MEXICO RIDING ON MY FUNERAL TRAIN
EVER SINCE I WAS A LITTLE BABY
I COULDN'T GET RID OF THE PAIN
FAT SWEATY COP IN AN ALABAMA LOCKUP LOOKED AT ME & LAUGHED HE'D HEARD MY SONGS ON THE NASHVILLE RADIO, HE ASKED ME FOR MY AUTOGRAPH
WILLIAMS

Sputnik 57

I was born in 57 and somewhere in the heavens
The Sputnik started beeping night & day
A shiny little ball that could never ever fall
Floating slowly by the window where I lay
I went out there on the launch pads
Up there with the Sputnik
I stayed up all night when the men walked on the moon
I was born in the trail of the rocket's fiery tale
I saw a brighter future coming soon
The winners of the human race
Floating weightless up in space
Above the poor and the heavy and the doomed
One small step for man a giant leap from Vietnam
Up there when the men walked on the moon

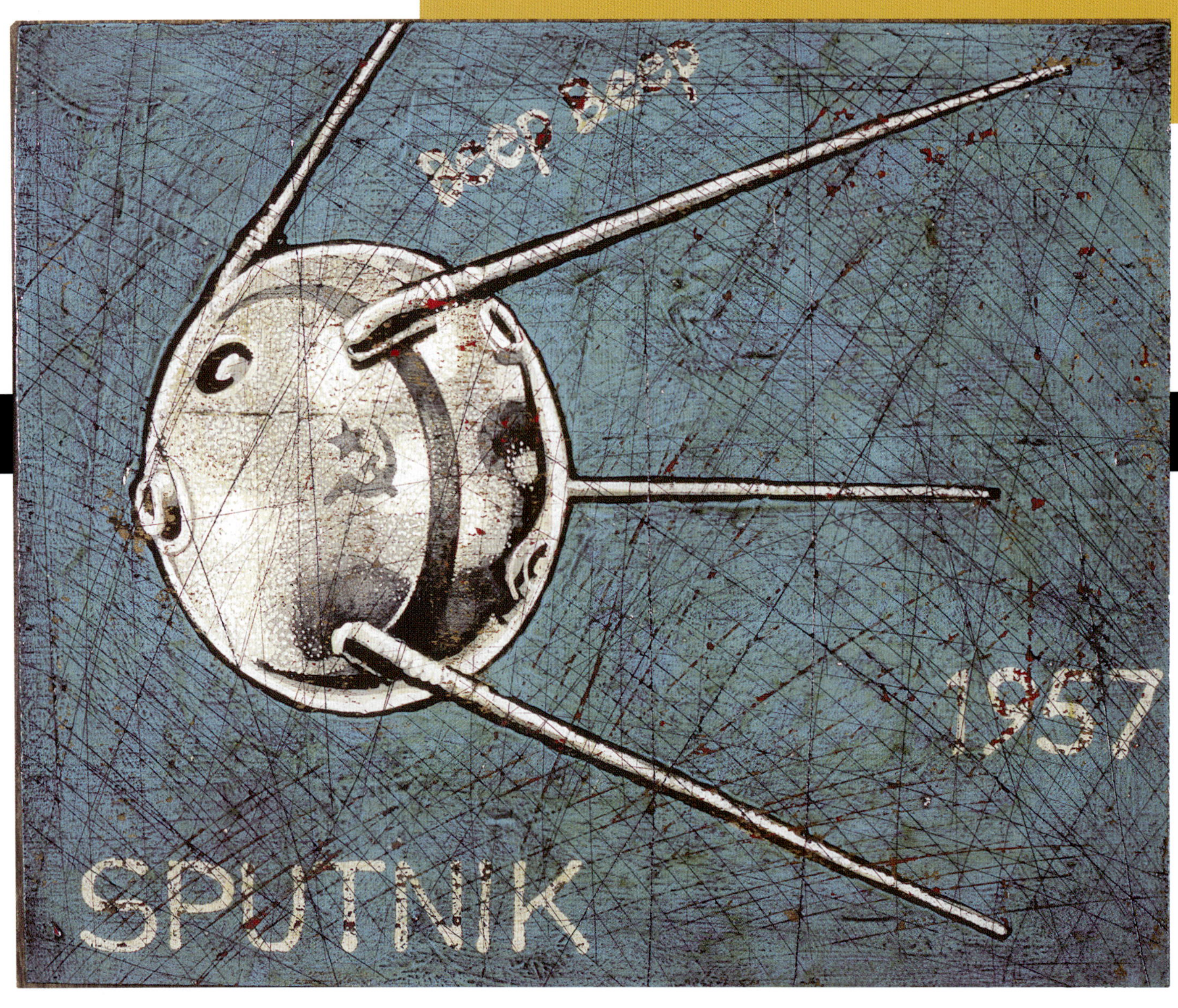

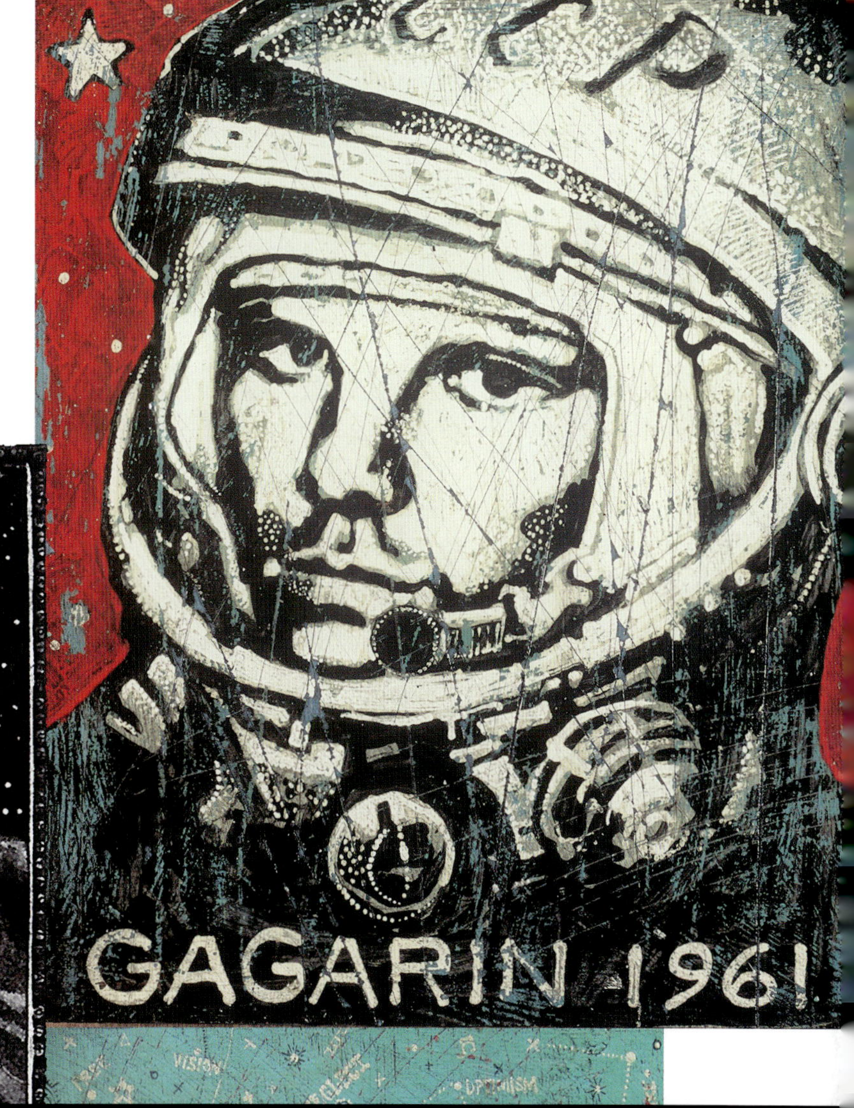

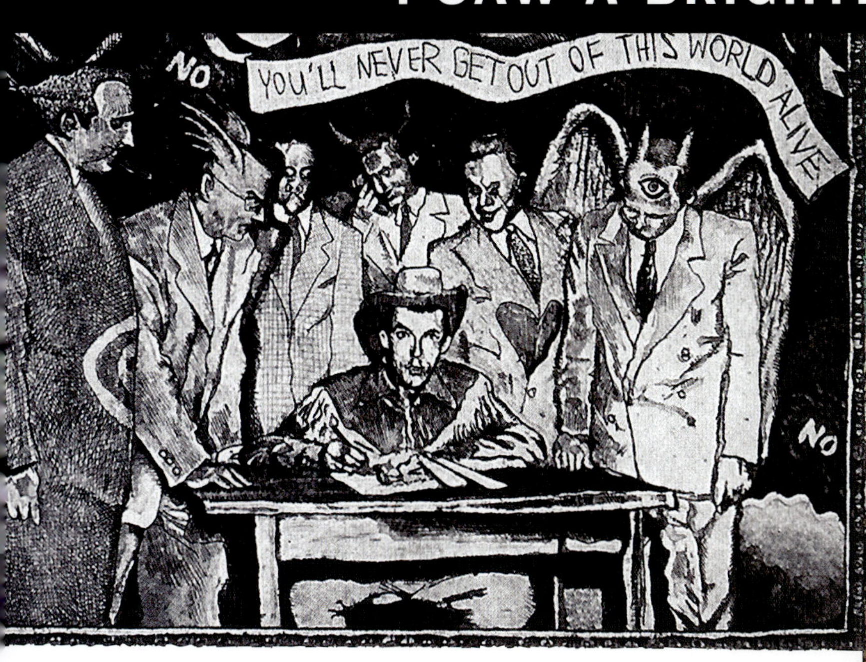

I SAW A BRIGHTER FUTURE COMING SOON

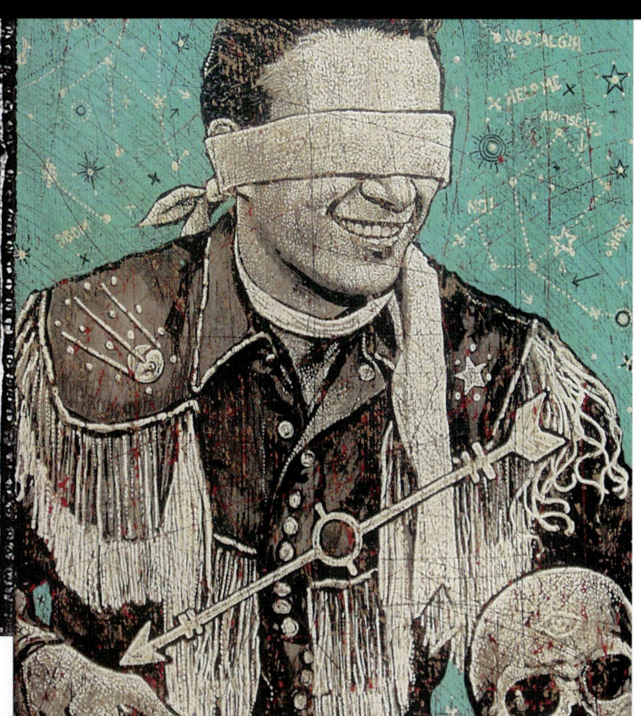

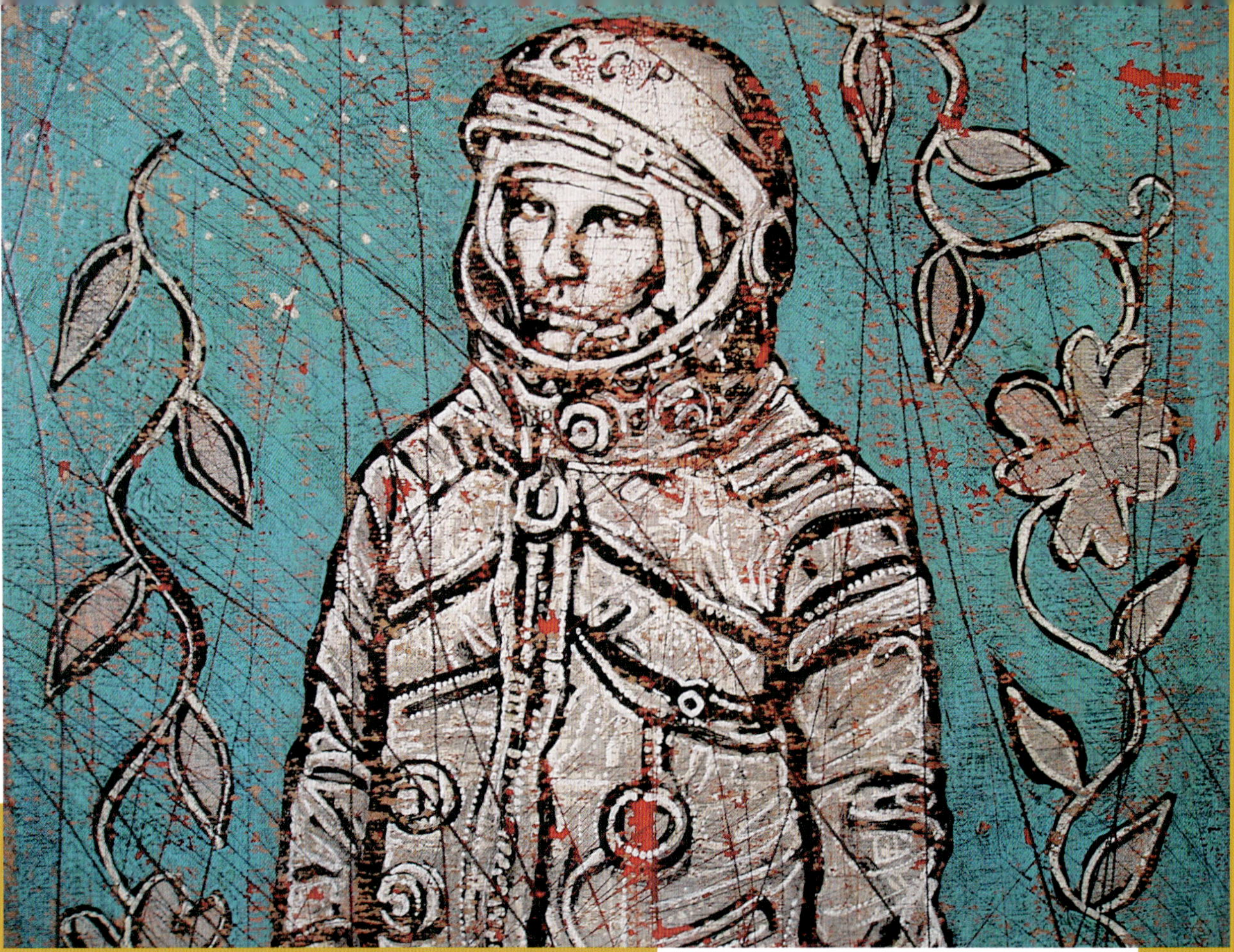

Inside the Whale

We saw a better world just around the corner
Time's arrow pointing down some happy trails
Big clear dreams arising over the event horizon
But no light escapes from inside the whale

Long blue summer nights, some basic human rights
The lunar landing craft, a donkey's ears and tail
All swallowed up as midnight struck
It's so dark down here inside the whale

An end to hunger – equality
Under the sea, inside the whale

Progress, progress, rose-tinted glasses
Cockeyed optimism, all cracked and paled
And all the astronauts and the Kennedys got caught
Down in the depths, inside the whale.

So naïve, this white boy's dream
Tucked up in bed, inside the whale

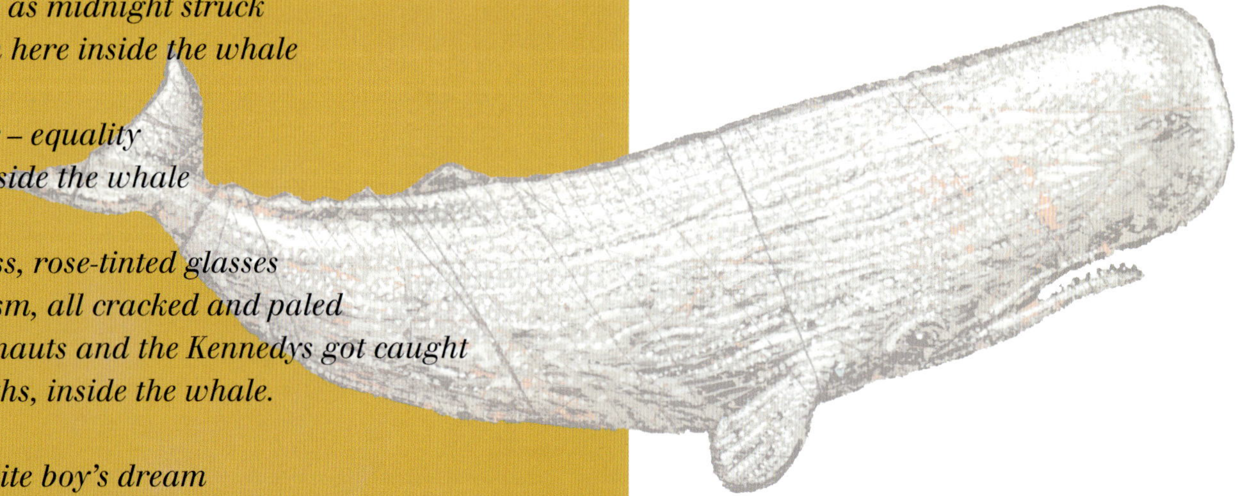

Now We Have the Bomb

Tie a red silk scarf around my mouth
This protest leaves the hearing and the sight
Fantastic place to be, a place to live in
Forgive them, they are young and rich and white

Cash rules everything around me
The slowest animals have upped and gone
An accident sits down with you for breakfast
Things are better now we have the bomb

A stranger pulls the white sheet from your body
Crutches tap the rhythm of a song
An accident sits down with you for breakfast
Things are better now we have the bomb

Lovely girls slip softly into ruin
The boys of summer scattered all around
We thought we were natural survivors
Forgive me if I go out with a bang

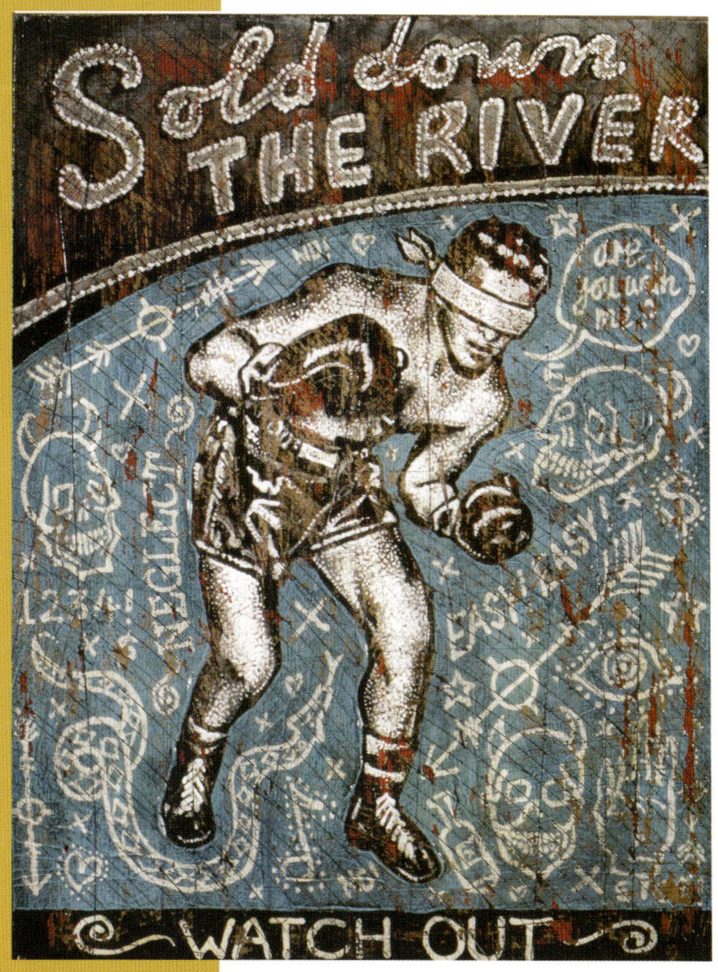

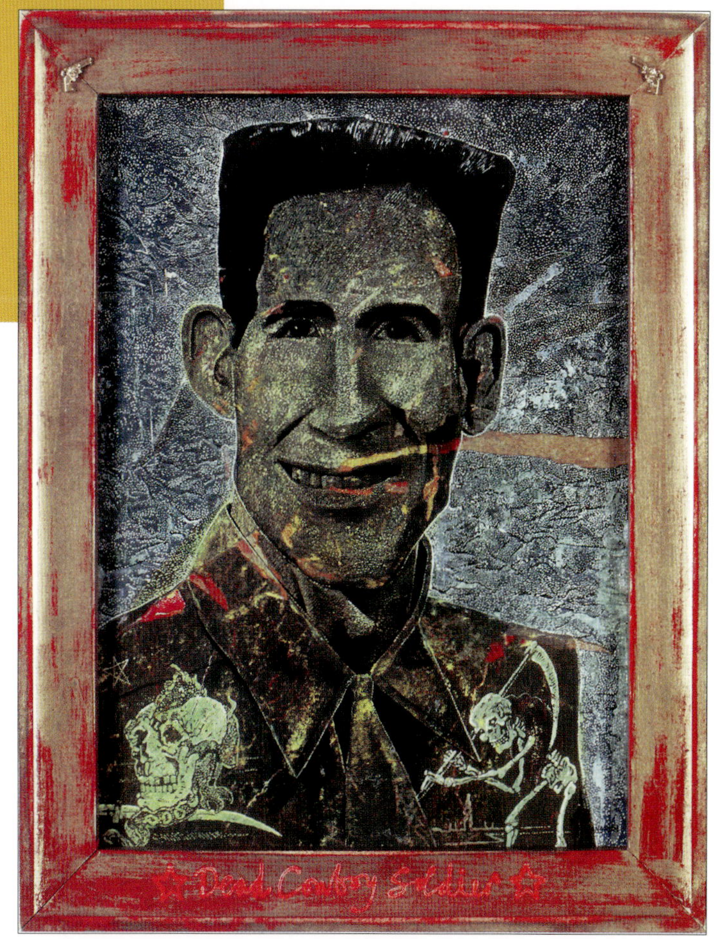

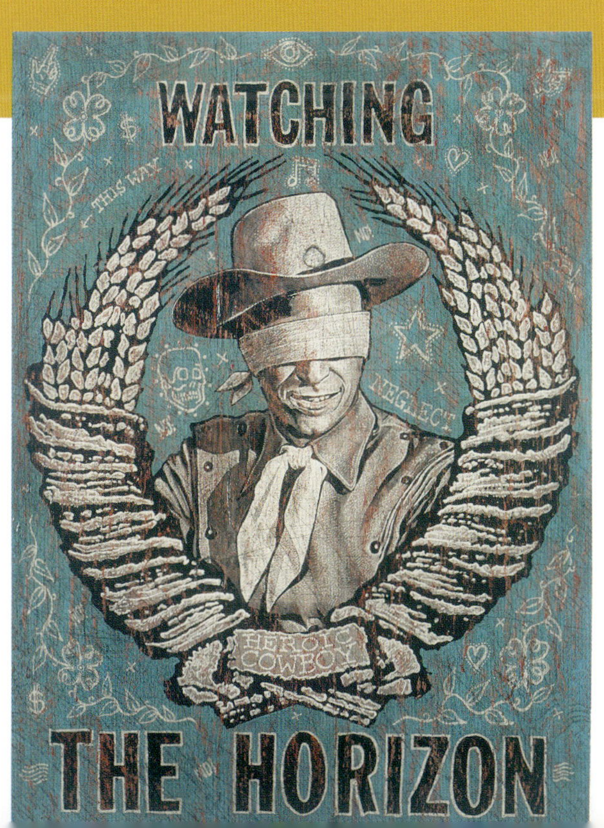

All the Fame of Lofty Deeds

Close up the house fit for a king
It's got everything anybody needs
His worldly gains up on display
All the fame of lofty deeds

He quit the band, went on his own
Got his own show, the rest is history
Made a few mistakes but took all the breaks
Charmed the snakes & burst the seams

And anyone who had a taste
Could cut his face from magazines
For the wind to suck and the sun to bleach
To fade and perish like a dream

& All his fans like grains of sand
Will fall through glass, God, truth & speed
To climb that hill and kiss or kill
For all the fame of lofty deeds

When the candle's snuffed & things get tough
Your enemies seek your company
When you're all alone, reach for the phone
I'm skull & bones – remember me!

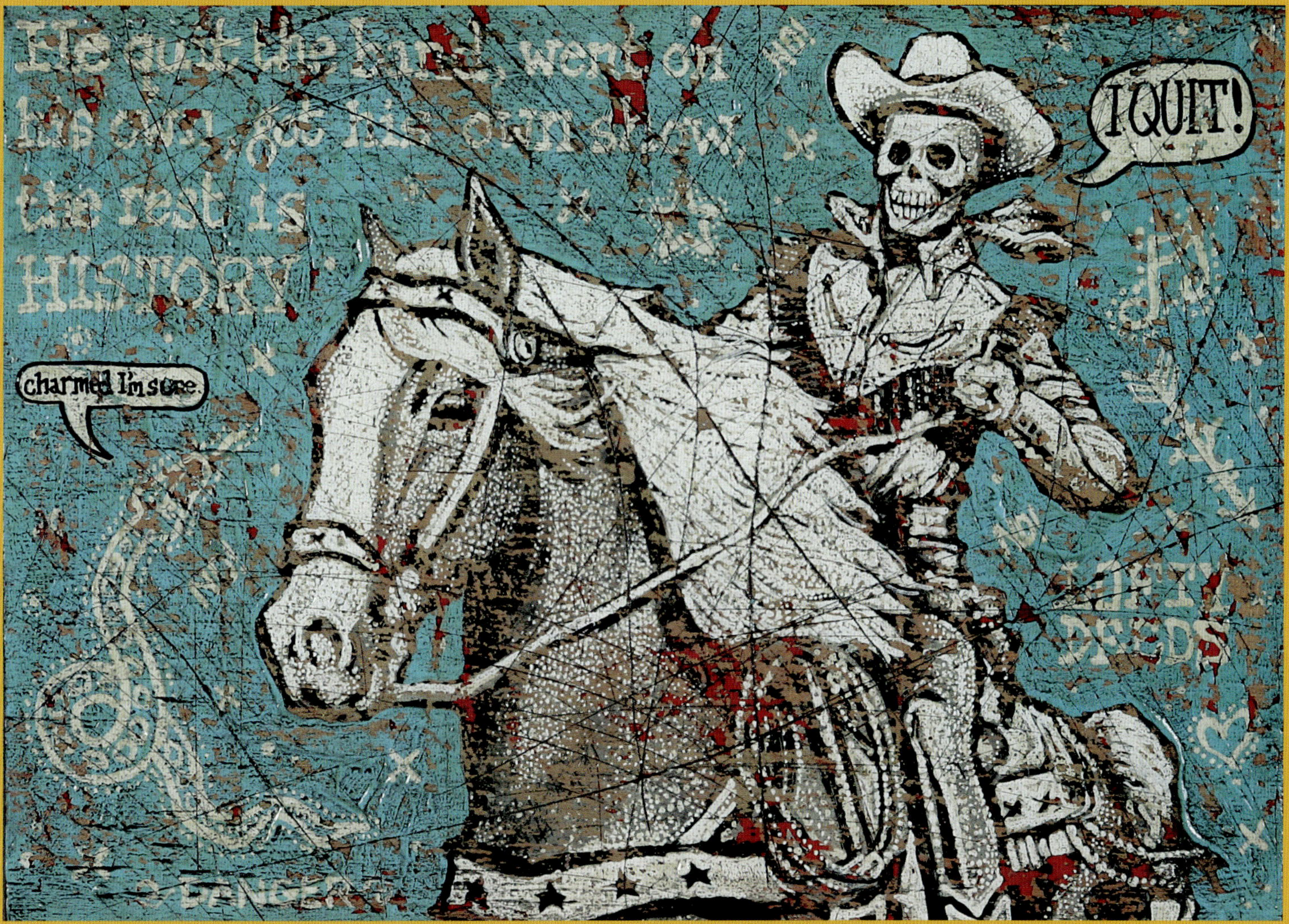

He quit the herd, went on
his own, got his own show,
the rest is
HISTORY
I QUIT!
charmed I'm sure
LOFTY DEEDS

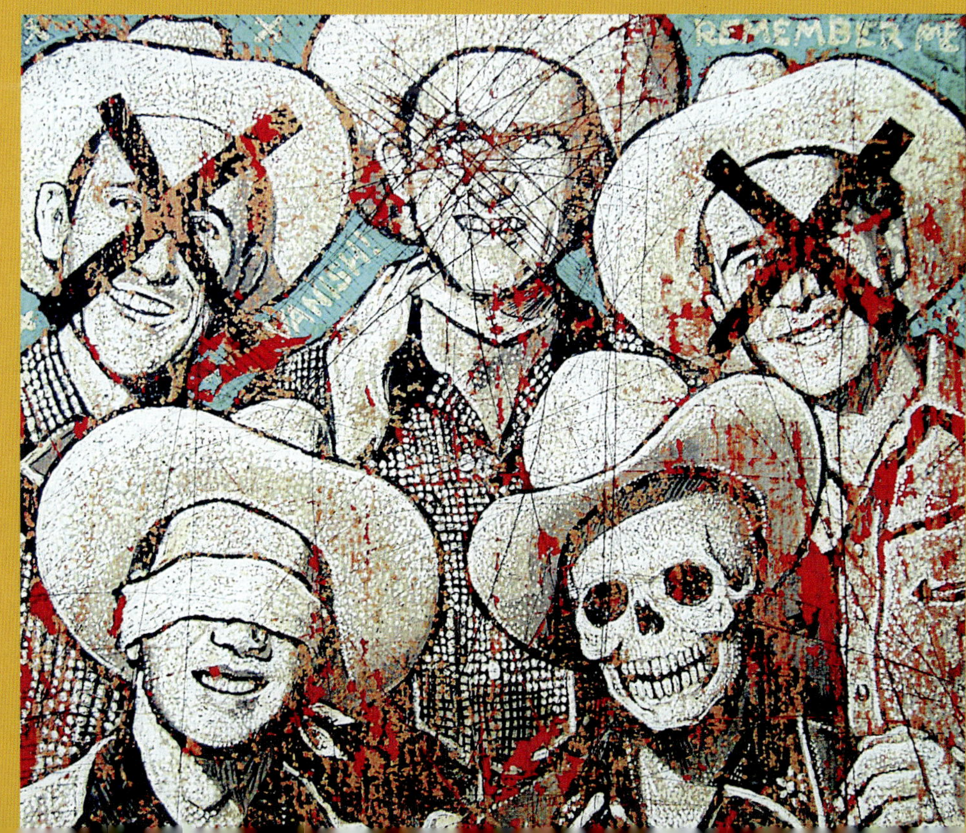

REMEMBER ME

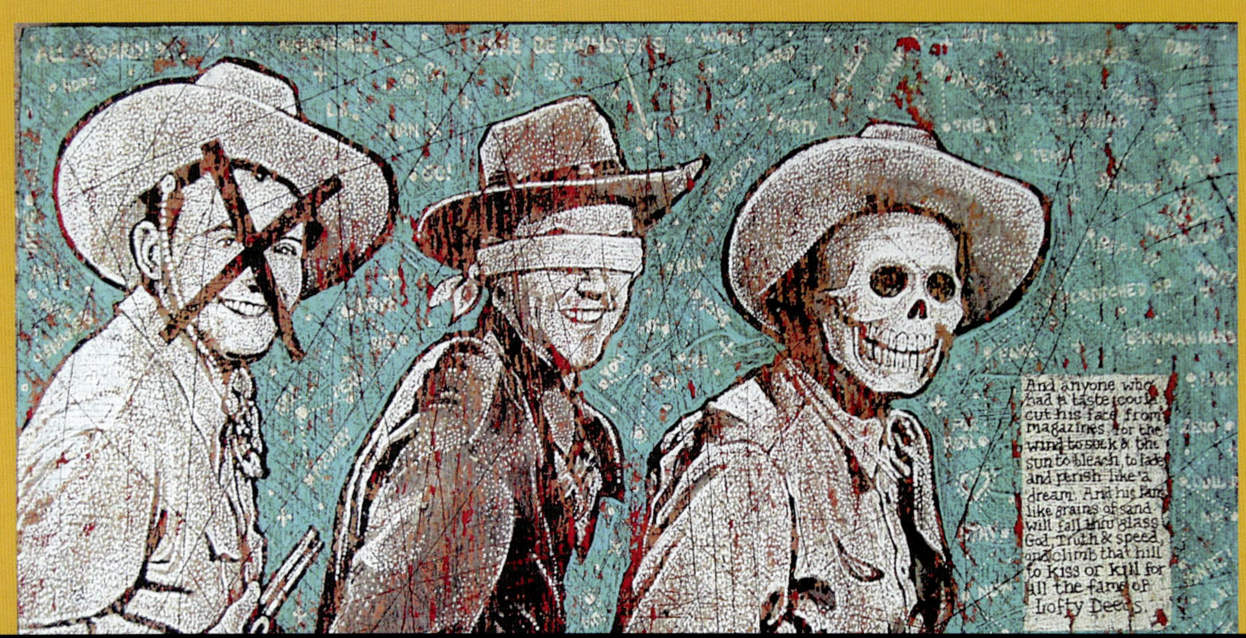
And anyone who
had a taste could
cut his face from
magazines for the
wind to soak & the
sun to bleach to last
and perish like a
dream. And his fans
like grains of sand
will fall thru glass
God, Truth & speed
and climb that hill
to kiss or kill for
all the fame of
Lofty Deeds

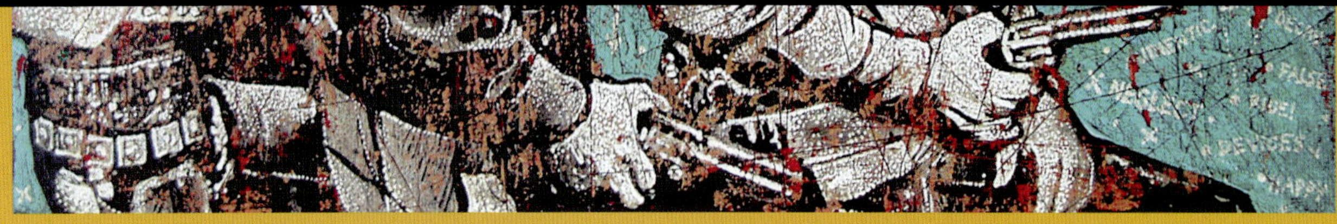
I'M SKULL & BONES—REMEMBER ME!

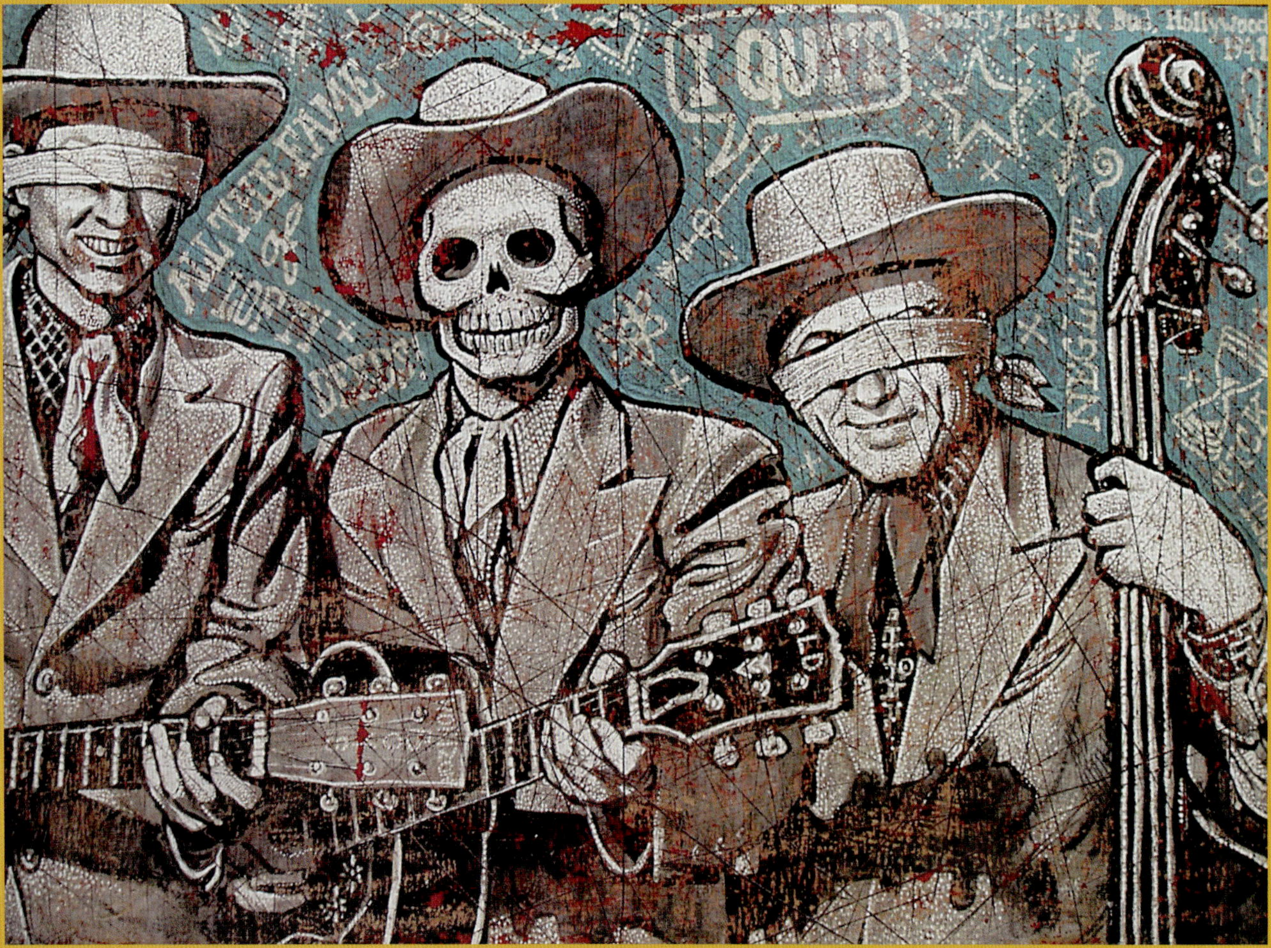

Over the Cliff

I work hard and I've got lots of money
I tried hard but I don't want to stay
I've seen too much trouble
Felt too much pressure bubble
I knew there had to be a better way

I wouldn't mind if you thought I was worth it
Or you slapped me down when I misbehaved
But everybody knows I've got flunkies here in tow
To clean up all the messes that I've made

I'm going over the cliff
Its hard to tell if life
Is a burden or a gift
I'm going over the cliff

So forgive me or forget me everybody
I guess I always had this honest streak
Sick of all the yawning
The bitching and the bawling
Sick of feeling powerless and weak

And please don't call me cool
Just call me ARSEHOLE!
'Cos I would be a beggar not a king
And the devil don't care if
You're a fish or you're a chip
I'm going over the cliff

I'm going over the cliff
Success on someone else's terms
Don't mean a fucking thing
I'm going over the cliff

In New York and LA they're sending faxes
So the company can wash their hands of this
But there was no one there
To look after me or care
I'm going over the cliff

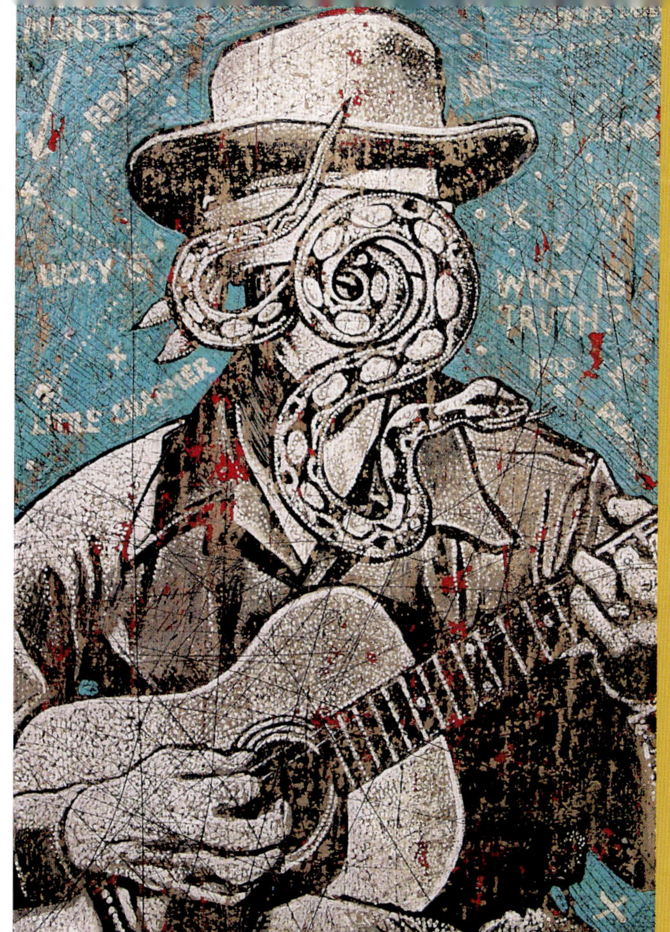

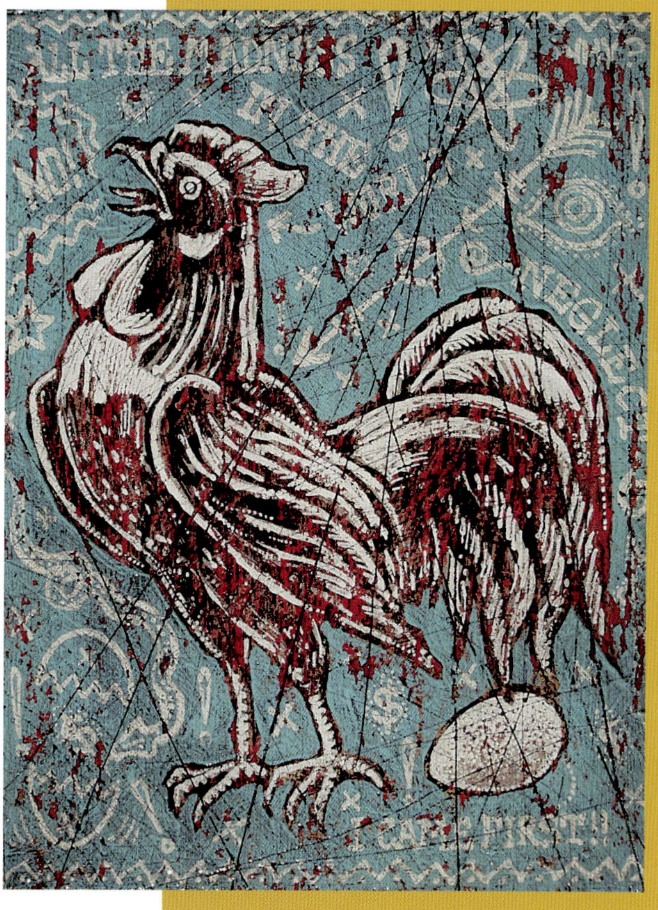

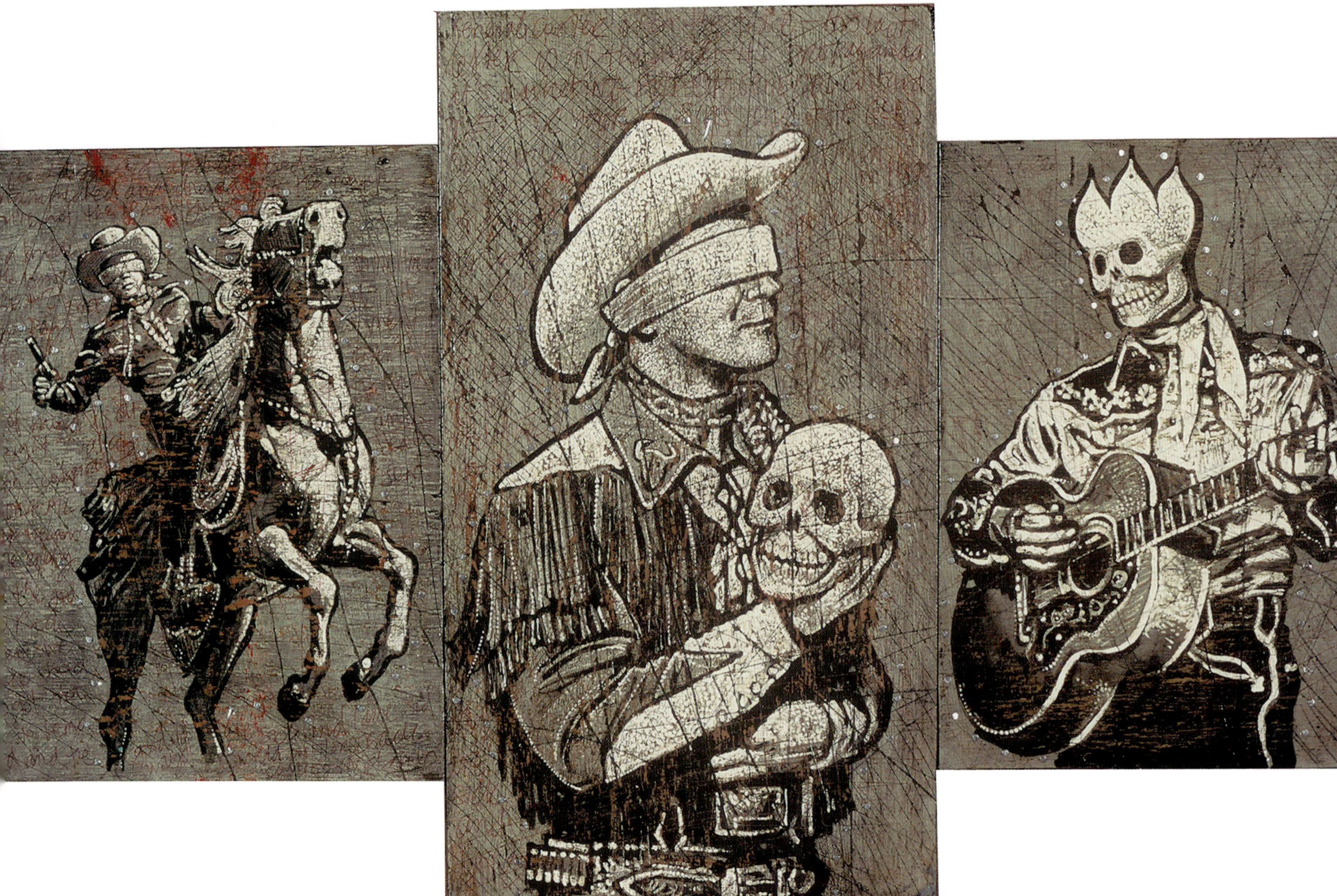

Horses

I'd be riding horses if they'd let me
Sleep outside at night and not take fright
I would ride the range and never worry
I would disappear into the night
Everybody needs an angel
But here's that devil by my side
Death's head rings upon his finger
Poor boy hanging on the line

They'll be drawing straws outside the courthouse
As the southern twilight turns to black
Torches burn into the sad eyes
On the wrong side of the tracks

Make those horses jump through hoops of flame
They won't kick and they won't scream
Let the good lord do the driving
Poor boy sinking in the stream

I can smell the campfires burning
But I'll go out walking on my own
By day and night the world keeps turning
Frightened people hiding in their homes
Everybody needs an angel
But here's that devil by my side
Death's head rings upon his finger
Poor boy hanging on the line

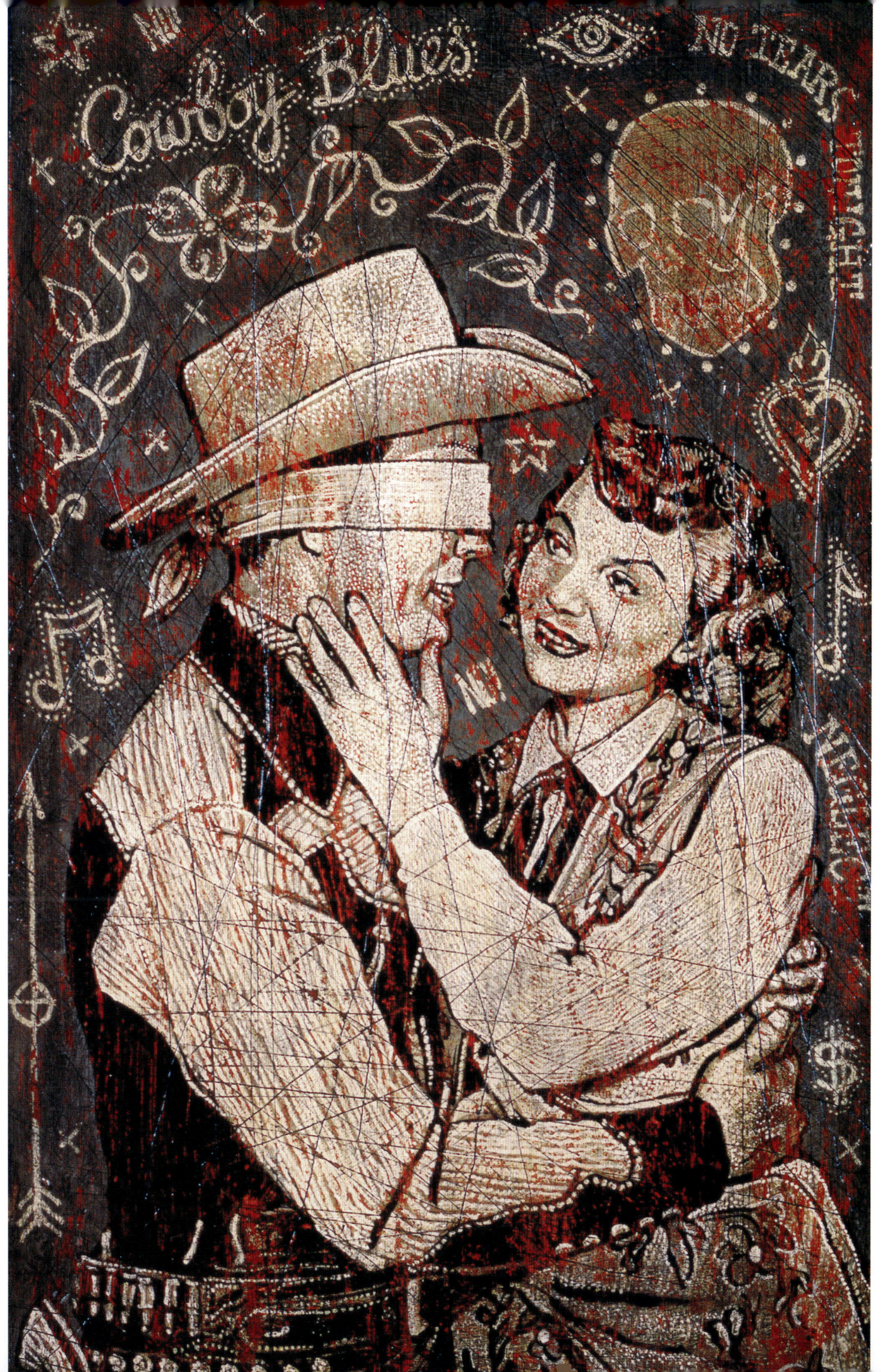

Cowboy Blues
NO TEARS TONIGHT

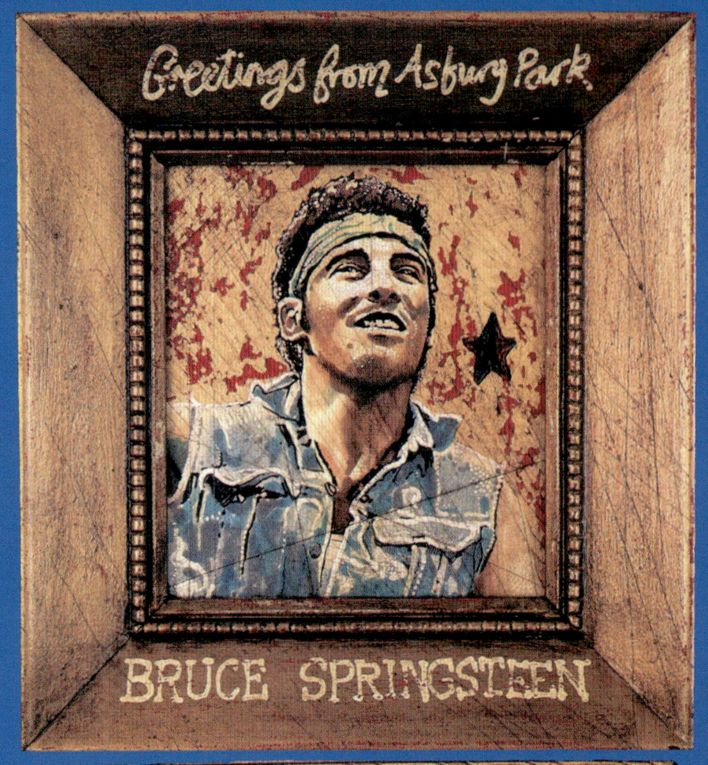

Greetings from Asbury Park
BRUCE SPRINGSTEEN

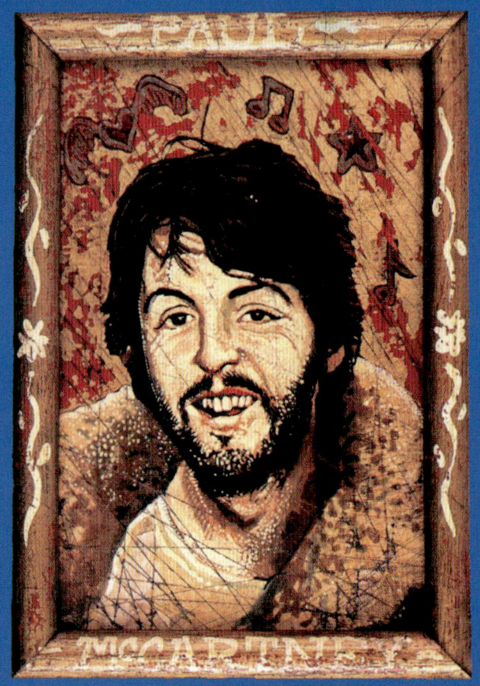

PAUL
McCARTNEY

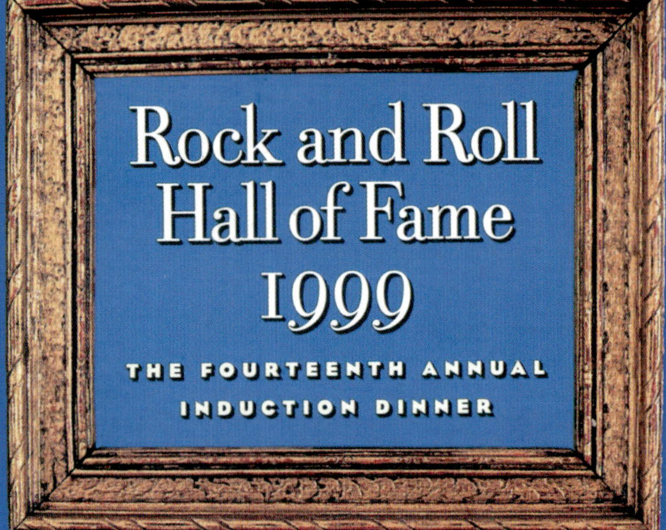

Rock and Roll
Hall of Fame
1999
THE FOURTEENTH ANNUAL
INDUCTION DINNER

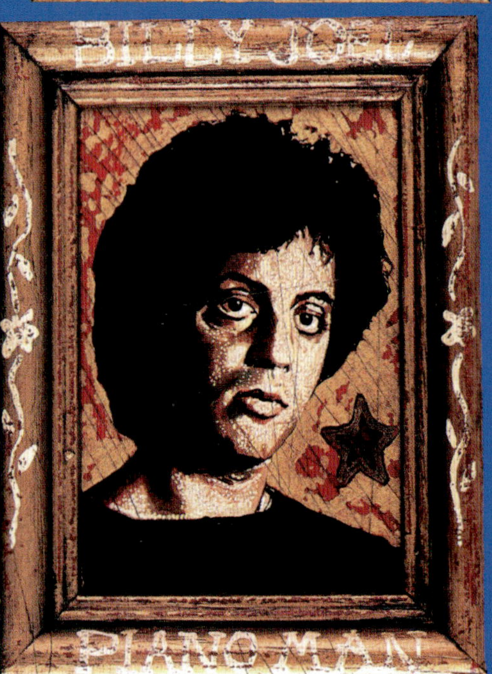

BILLY JOEL
PIANO MAN

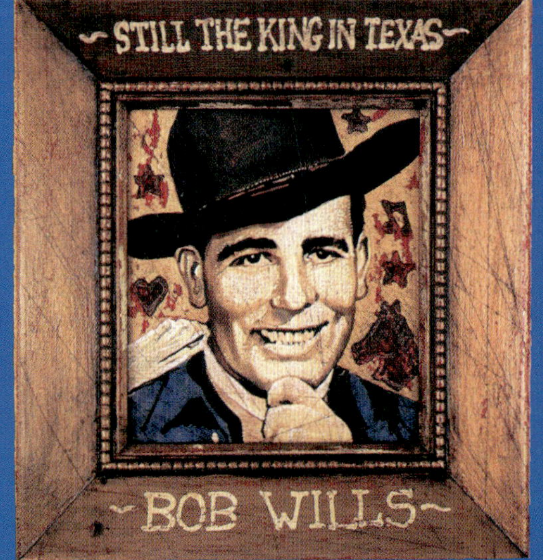

~ STILL THE KING IN TEXAS ~
~ BOB WILLS ~

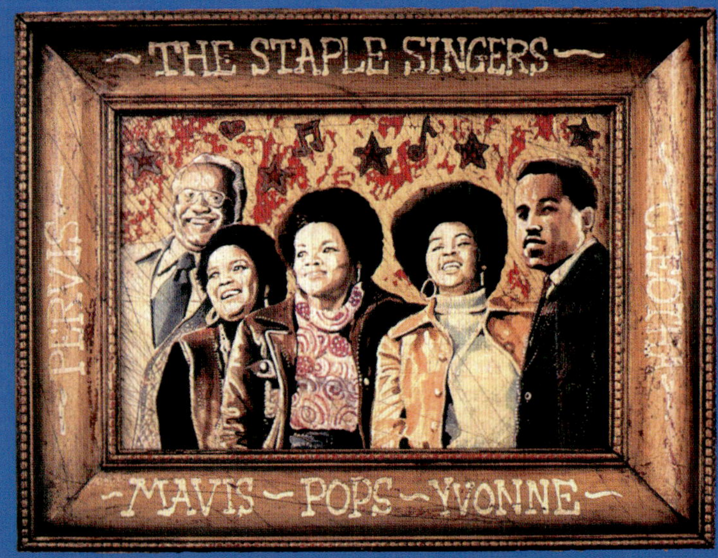

~ THE STAPLE SINGERS ~
PERVIS
CLEOTHA
~ MAVIS ~ POPS ~ YVONNE ~

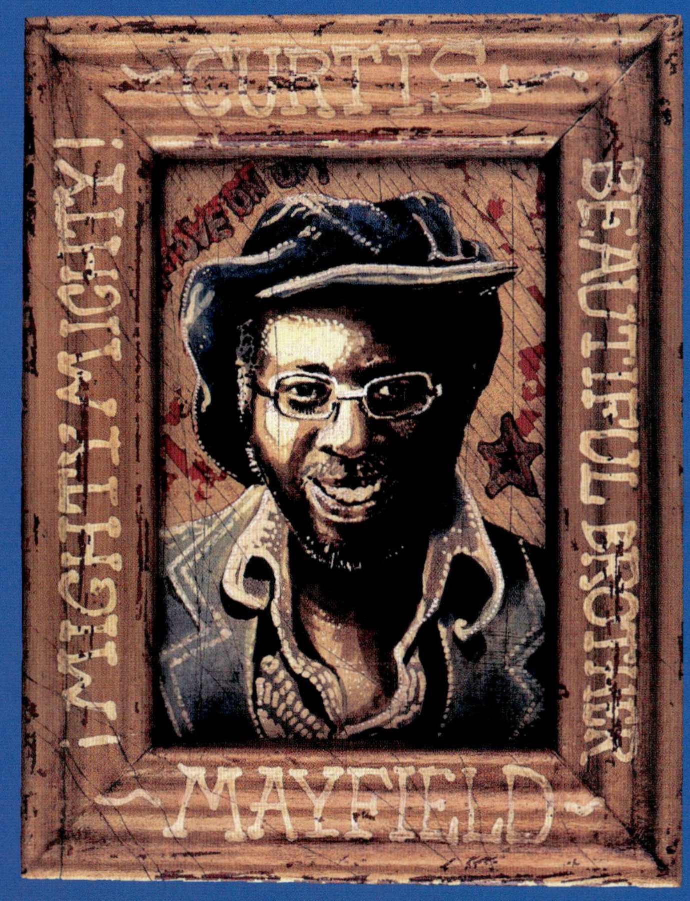

CURTIS
MIGHTY, MIGHTY!
BEAUTIFUL BROTHER
MAYFIELD

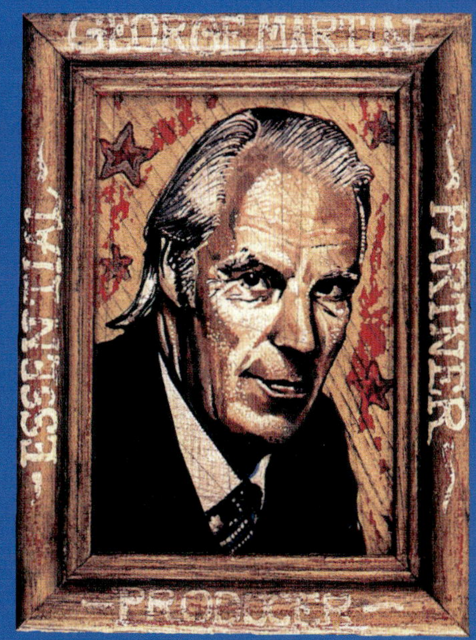

GEORGE MARTIN
PRODUCER
PARTNER

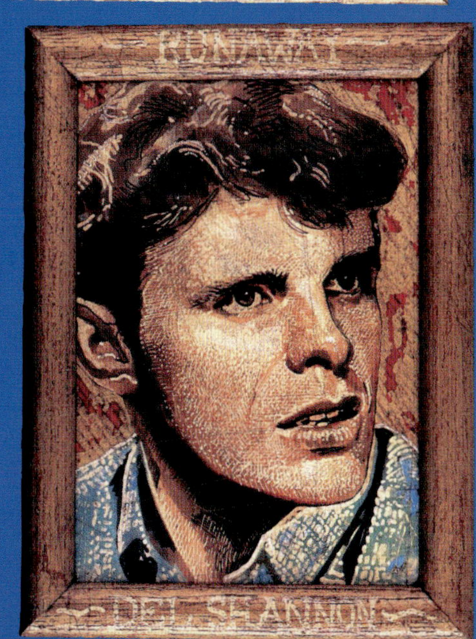

RUNAWAY
DEL SHANNON

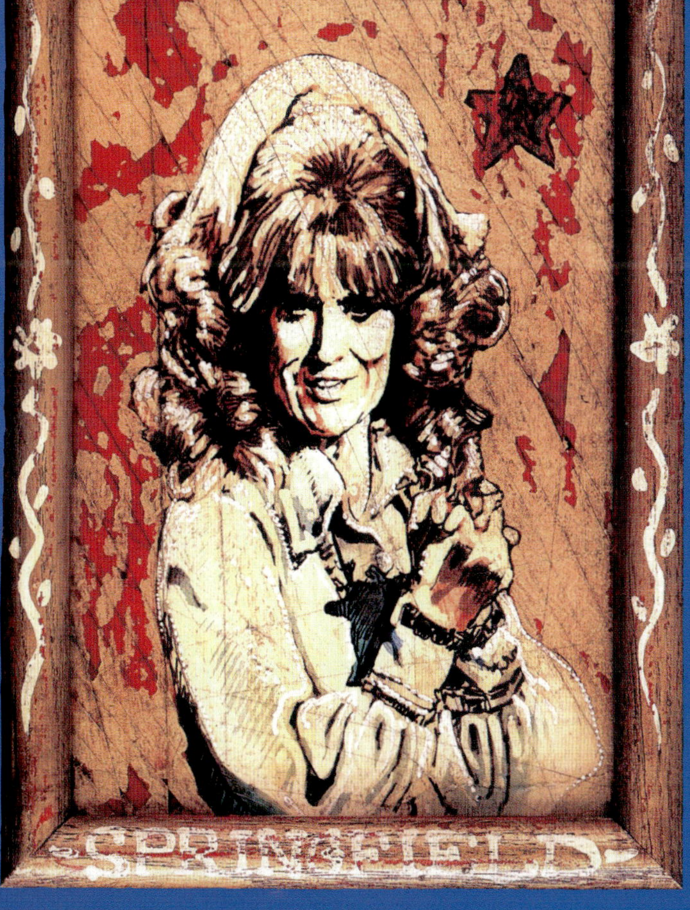

~DUSTY~
SPRINGFIELD

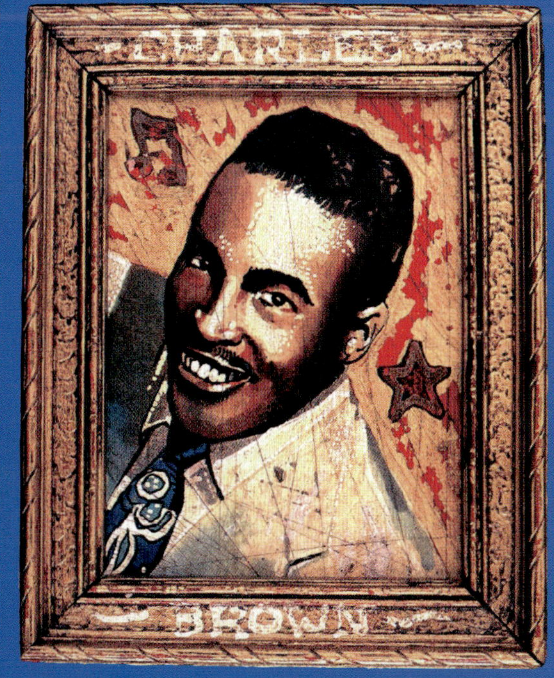

~CHARLES~
~BROWN~

I Picked Up the Pieces

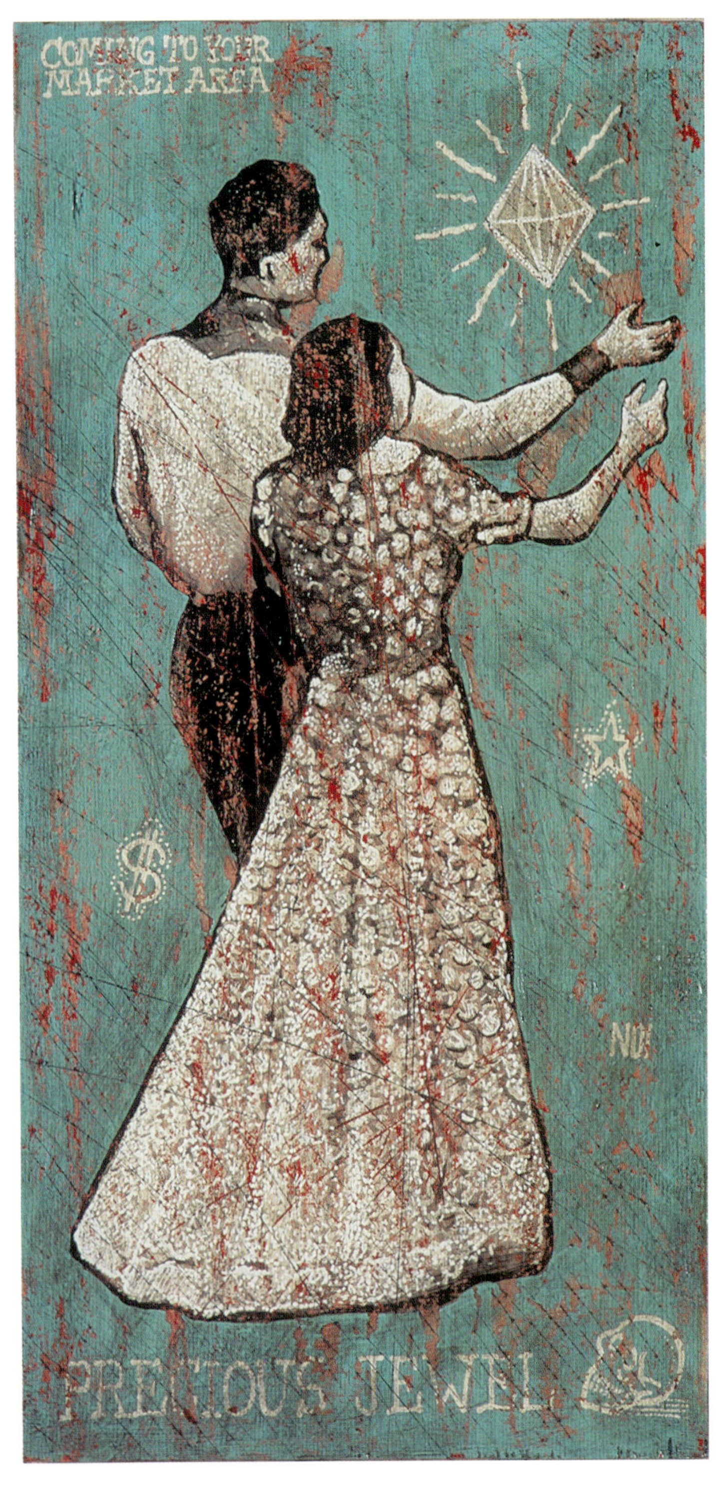

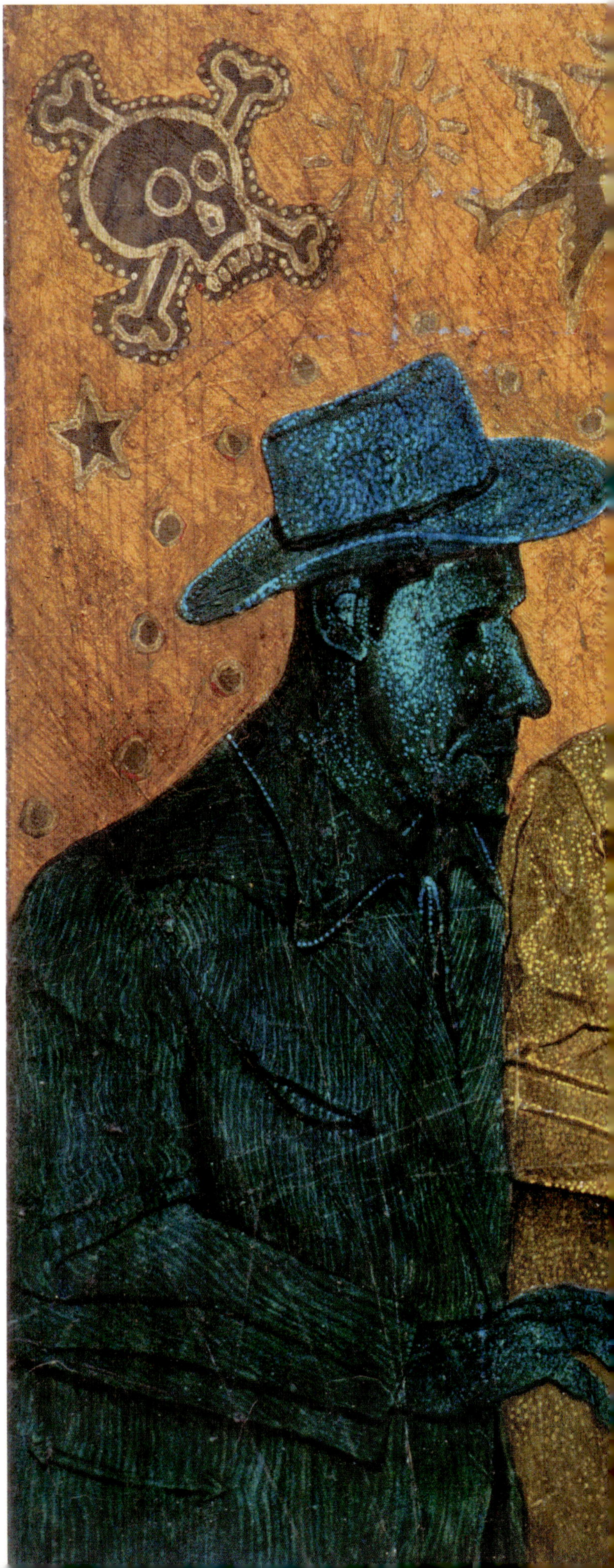

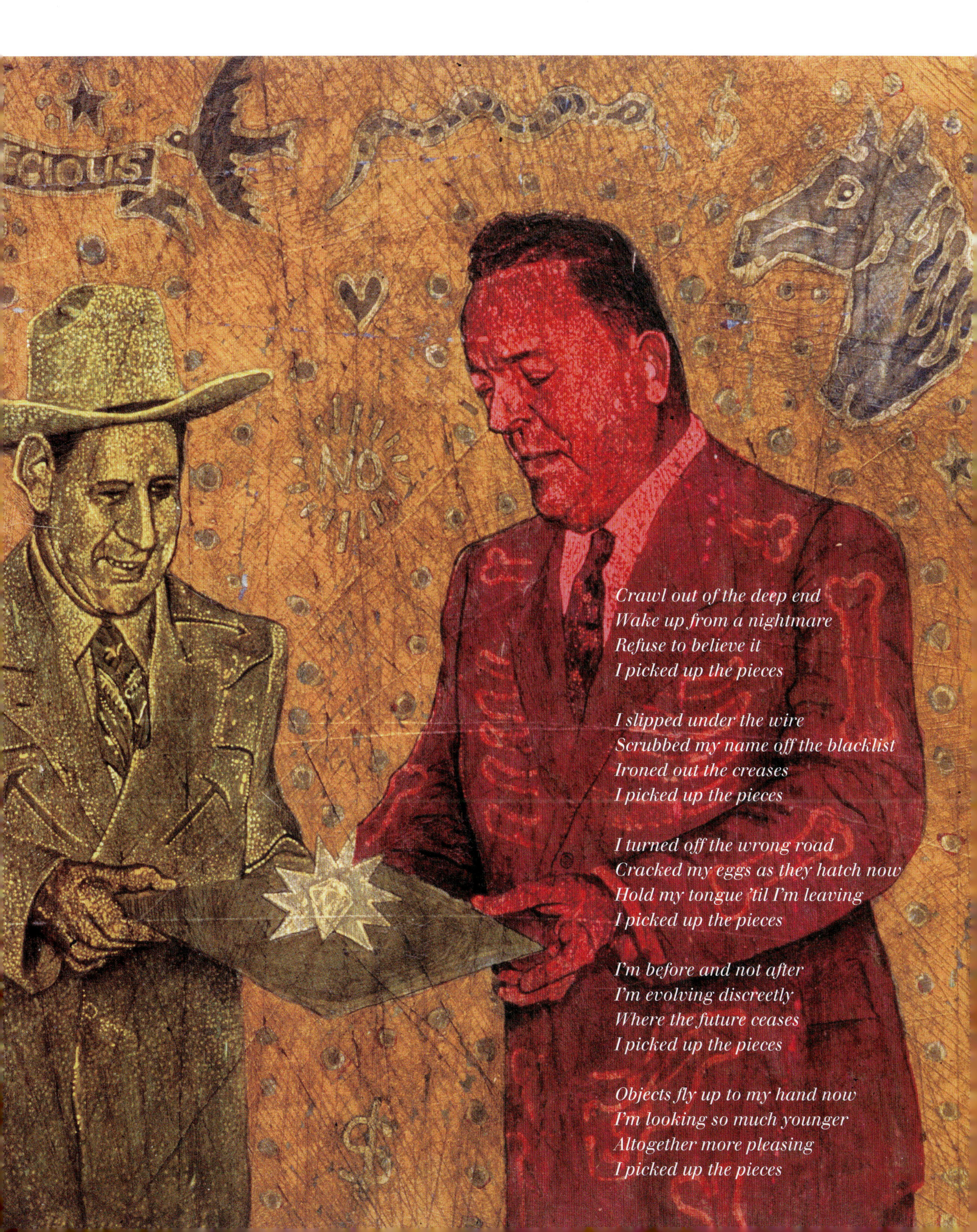

Crawl out of the deep end
Wake up from a nightmare
Refuse to believe it
I picked up the pieces

I slipped under the wire
Scrubbed my name off the blacklist
Ironed out the creases
I picked up the pieces

I turned off the wrong road
Cracked my eggs as they hatch now
Hold my tongue 'til I'm leaving
I picked up the pieces

I'm before and not after
I'm evolving discreetly
Where the future ceases
I picked up the pieces

Objects fly up to my hand now
I'm looking so much younger
Altogether more pleasing
I picked up the pieces

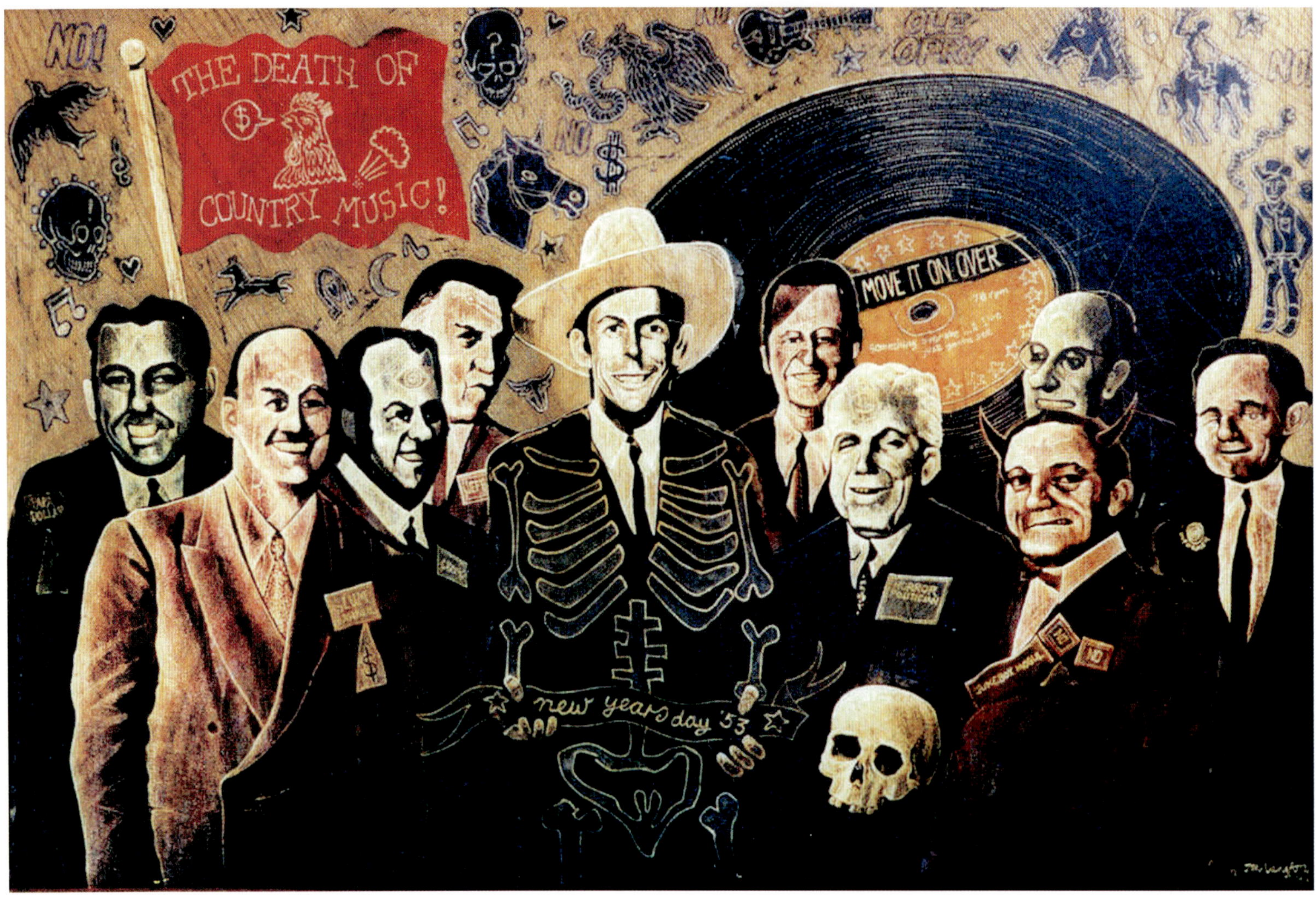

Not long ago I decided the Country Music I loved was pretty much dead so I made some gravestones and took them to Nashville hoping to piss people off. We got loads of press and the gallery pestered all the Music Row types to come on down and attend their own wake. One big label delighted us by asking to be removed from the mailing list, but the opening of THE DEATH OF COUNTRY MUSIC art show was a bit of a disappointment—it was packed!

Packed with industry insiders who guzzled the free wine and perused the stones approvingly, anxious to know that I knew that they knew what I was on about. There I was calling them murderers and they just whipped out their checkbooks. The following Monday Mercury Records called and asked me to do the cover for a compilation of unreleased Hank Williams tracks. Zap! They Herbert Marcusered me again! Every man has his price and that day mine was 6 grand.

The Death of Country Music

Well my body is a temple, safer than a prison
I've done some demolition
And in a world gone wrong
The bones of Country Music rattle round the planet
So we light the flame and fan it
Deep into the night
Where the city casts its shadow
We leave the straight and narrow
And tomorrow and forever seems so far away
Where the dance floor's overcrowded
And the music's getting louder
People do some breathing while they're cheatin' death
Tonight the West is sleeping
And the desert will be creeping
Inch by inch, across the continent
And the bones of Country Music
Lie there in their casket
Beneath the towers of Nashville
In a deep black pool of neglect ➡

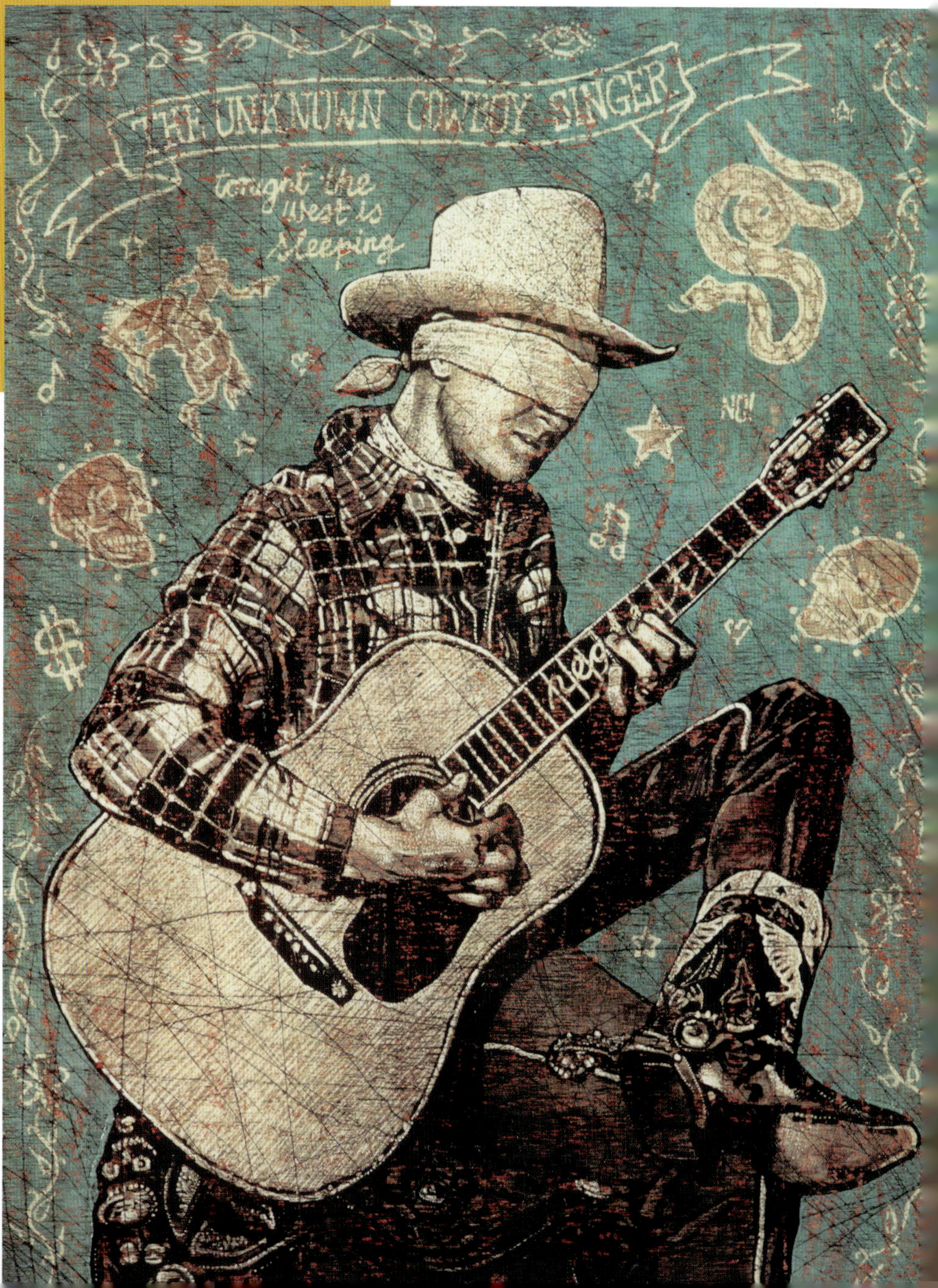

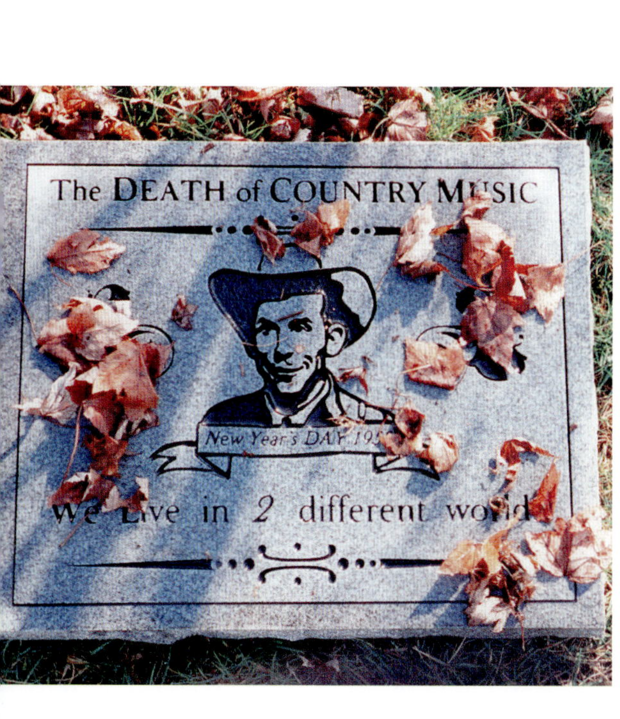

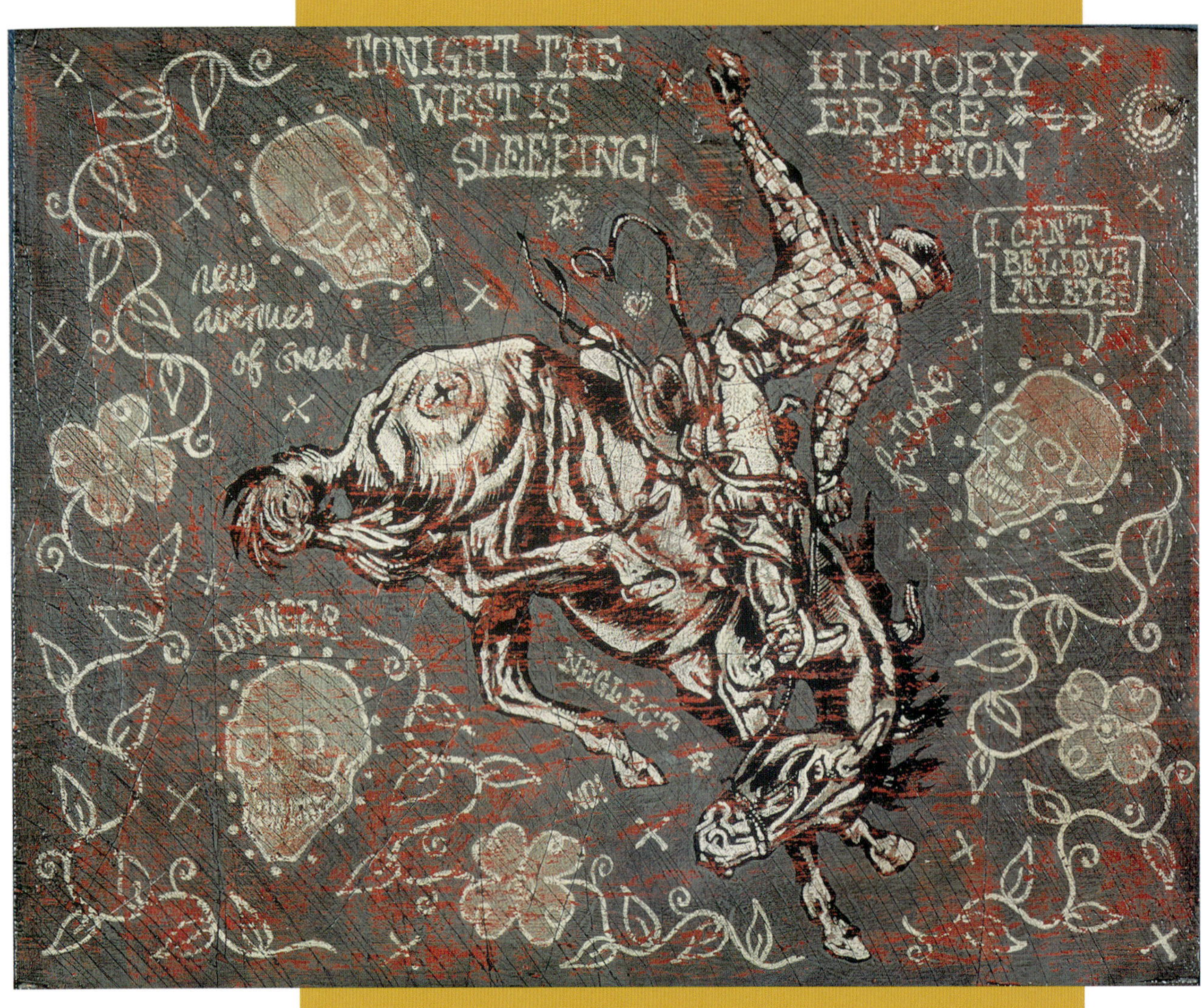

AND WE SPILL SOME BLOOD ON THE ASHES

So we cast our nets in the water
We drag the pool and we caught 'em
Grind 'em up and snort 'em, deep into the night
And we spill some blood on the ashes
Of the bones of the Jones and Cashes
Skulls in false eyelashes
Ghost-riders in the sky
Well the Hank bone's connected to the Buck bone
And the George bone's connected to the Hag bone
And the Willie bone's connected to the Billy Bones
Pickin' the flesh off the bones
The Death Of Country Music!

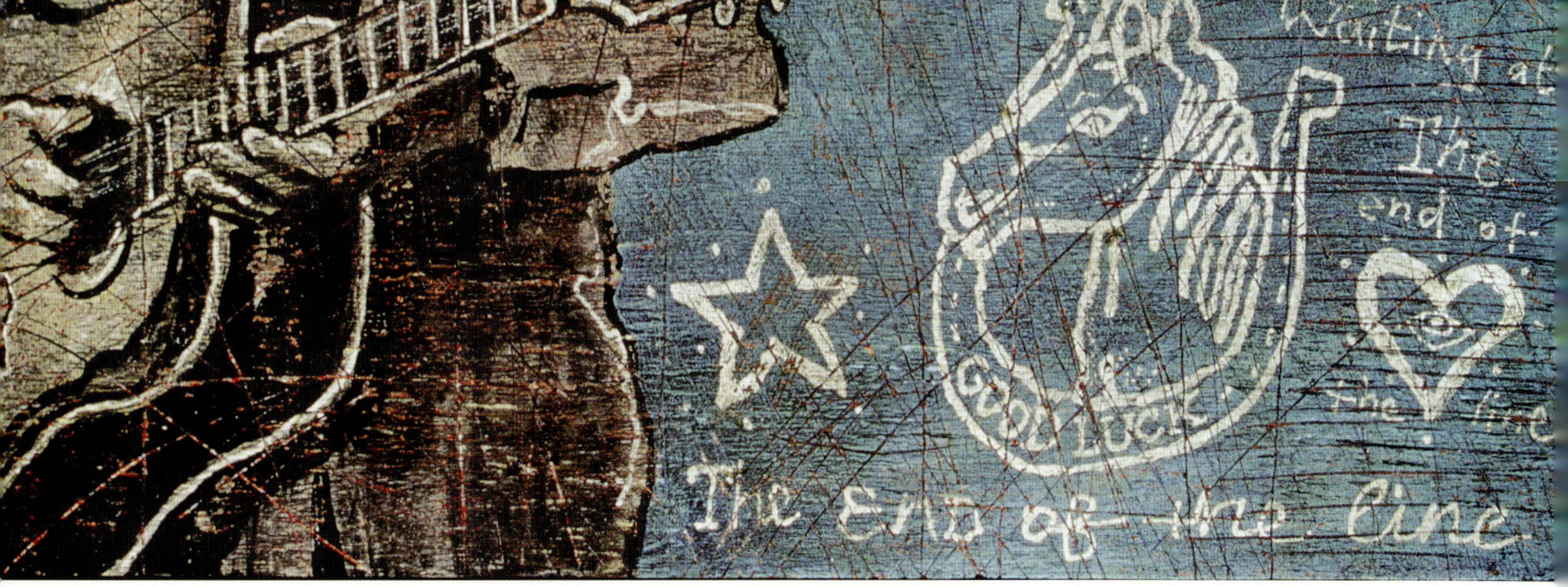
ath the towers of
NASHVILLE
OF THE BONES OF THE JONES AND CASHES
waiting at
The
end of
GOOD LUCK
The end of the line

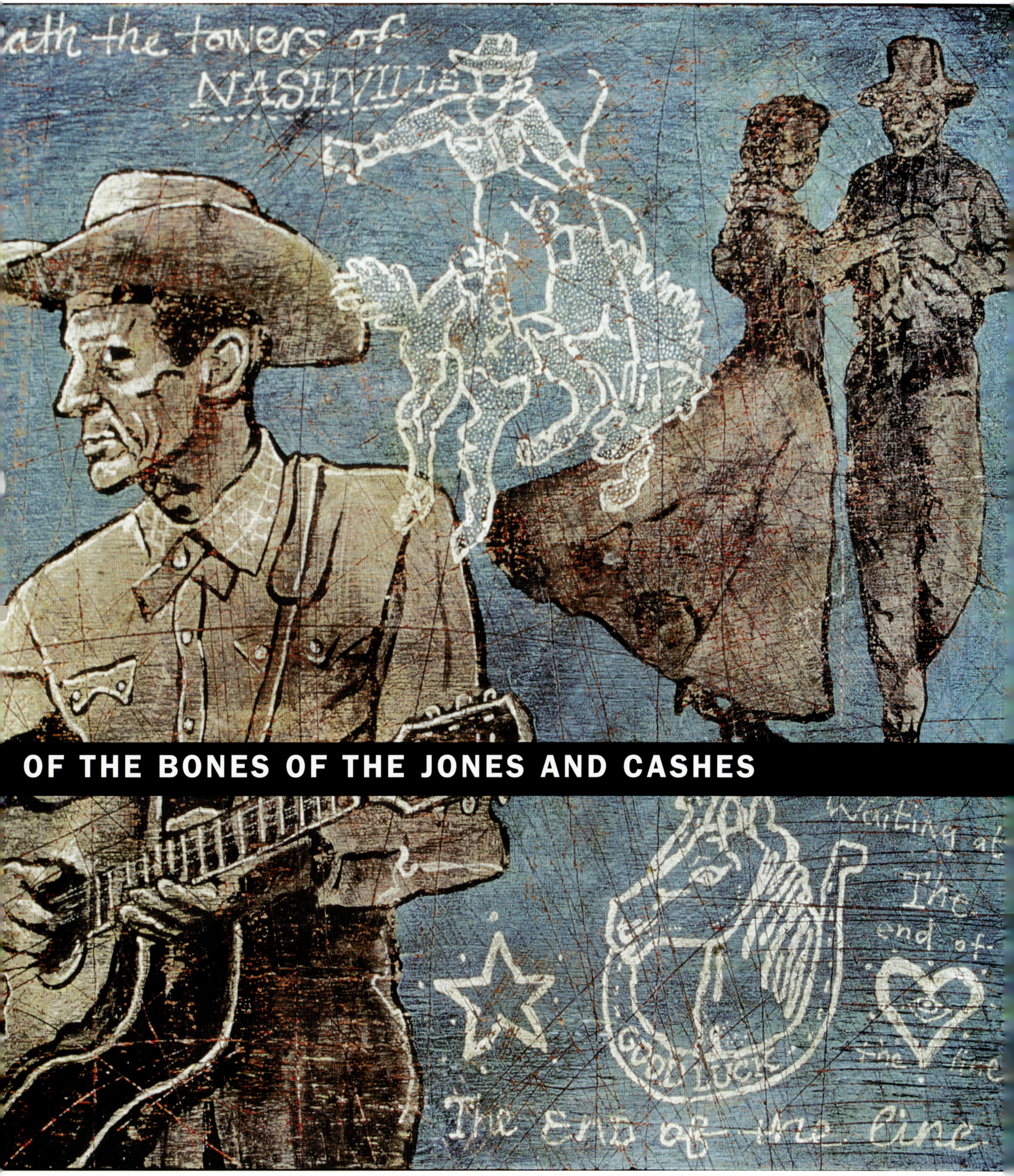

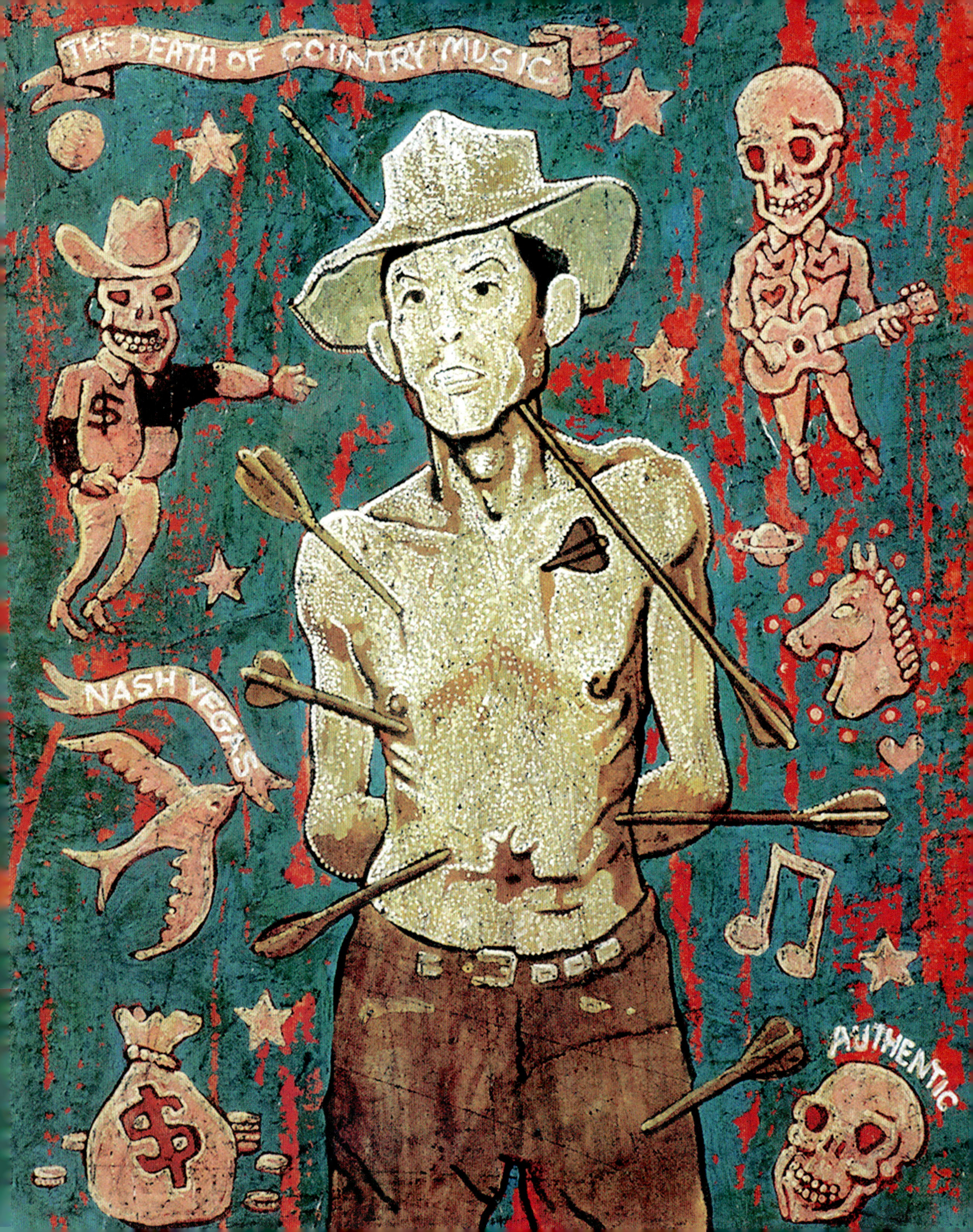

THE DEATH OF COUNTRY MUSIC
NASH VEGAS
AUTHENTIC
$
$

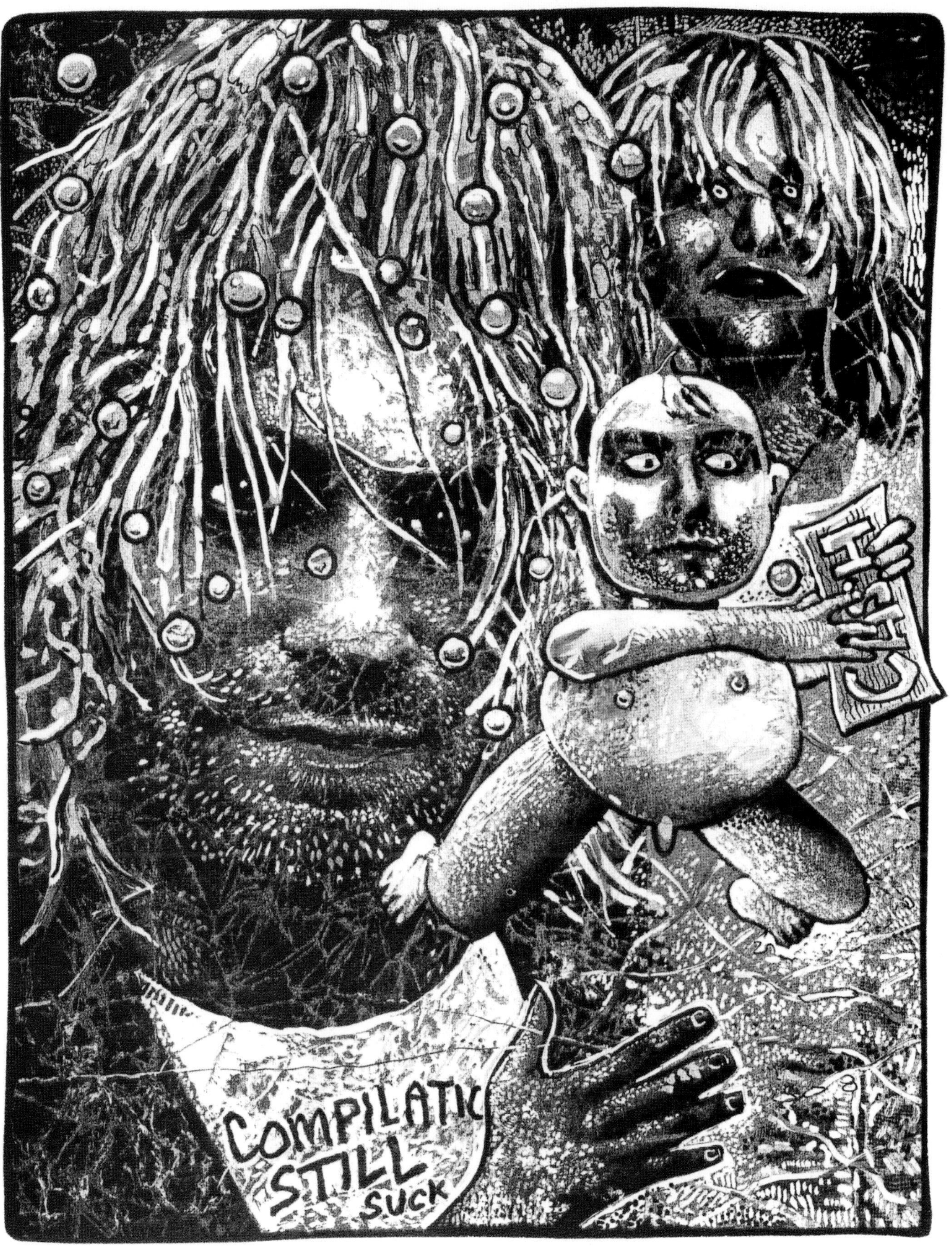
Hi.std
COMPILATI
STILL
SUCK

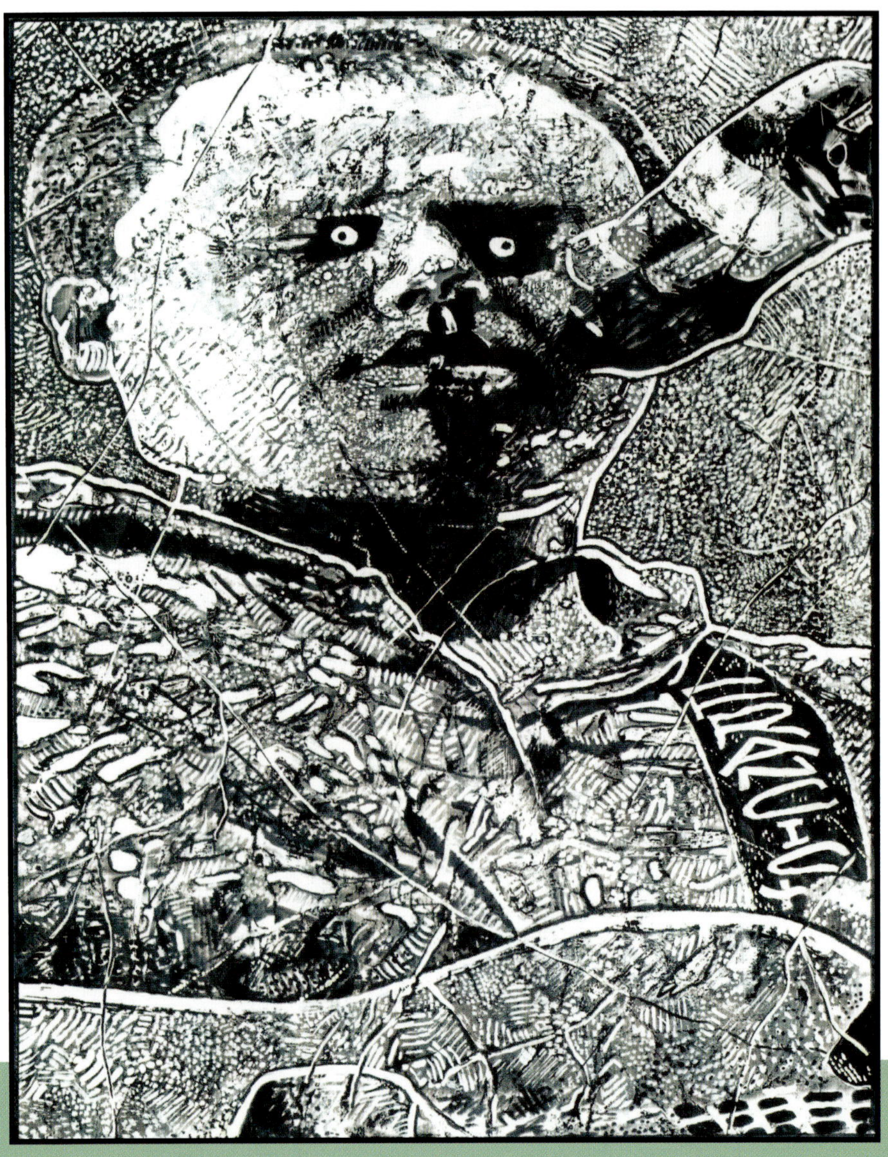

Are You an Entertainer?

Are you an entertainer?
We grope in the gloom of this stale Hyatt room
Yeah, I'm a real performer
I'll swallow this rum and blow coke up your bum

Get the money, don't leave anything behind
Just some pieces of your heart and fragments of your mind

With something less than a whisper
& Just a flicker of her eye
She could hold the whole room in her one dry palm
Have 'em eating out of her mouth
& Leave 'em hanging out to dry

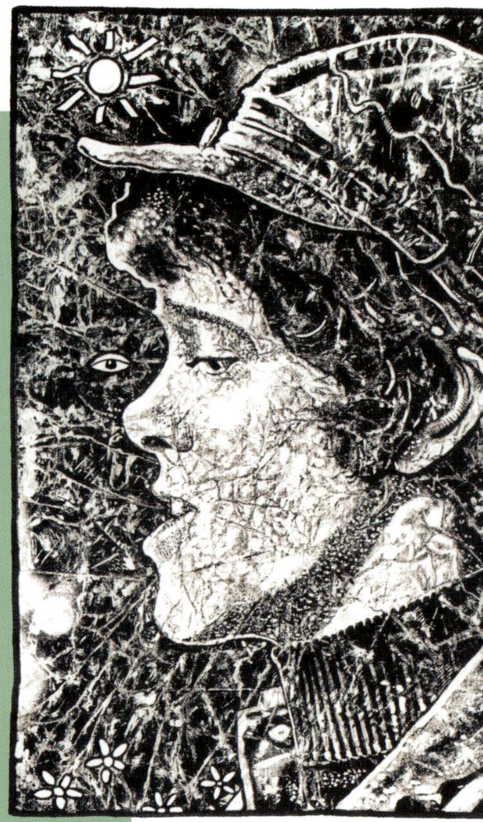

We leave tonight. Yeah, straight offer the show
Drive for a while & get 2 cheap rooms
Get up early & go man go!

I'm on the road to Damascus again at 30,000 feet
I'm crying but I can't find a reason
Missing all my new friends that Ill never meet again
I'm in a little trough today
Is this Lawrence or Columbus? I just can't tell
It's my midweek crisis
Locked in my cell in the Ritz-job Motel

He went down with the curtain
To laughter and applause
He was certainly dead
Before he hit the floor
The only way to go man go
That's what he always said
After all those hours of waiting
All the bottles & the beds

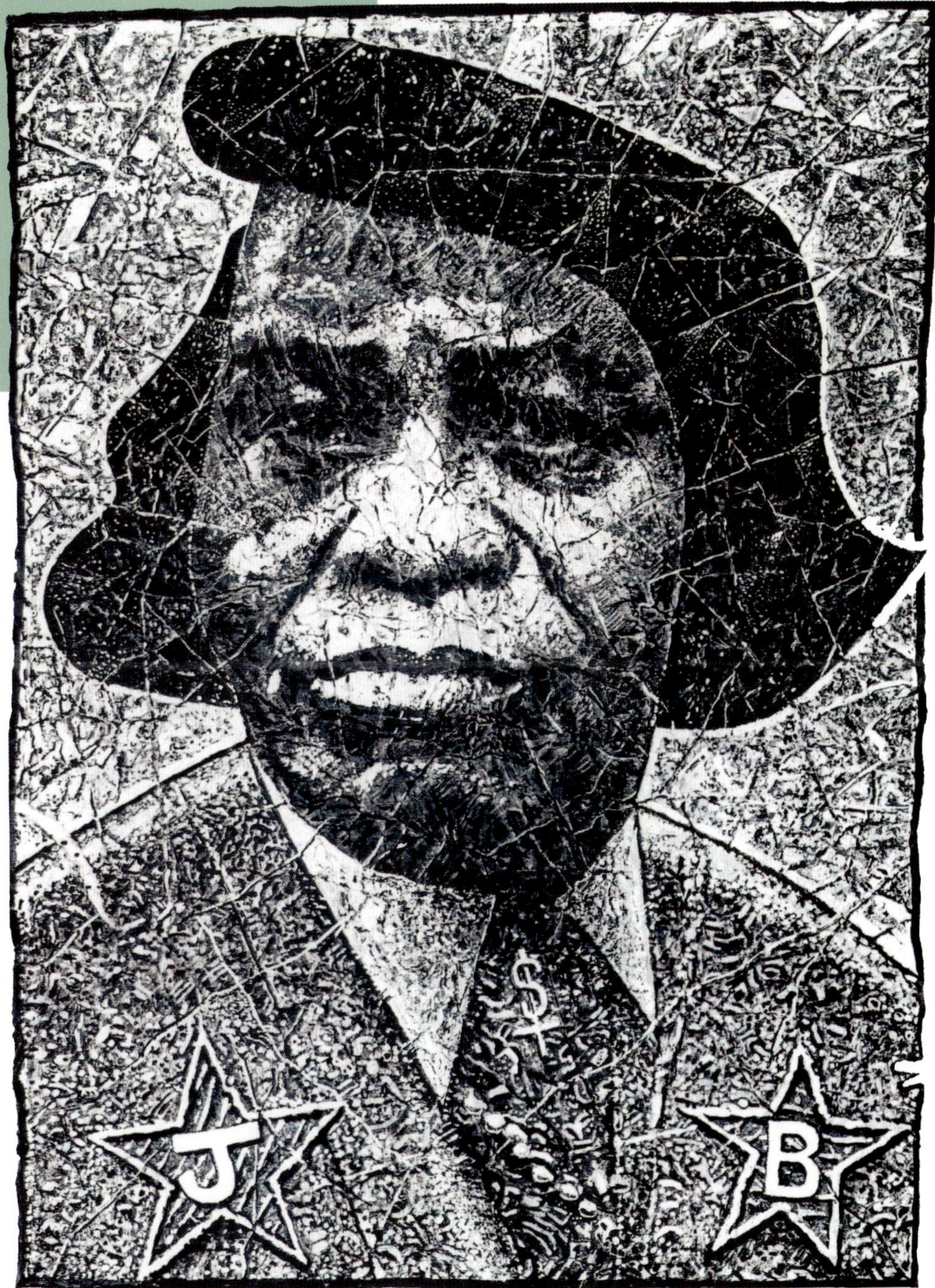

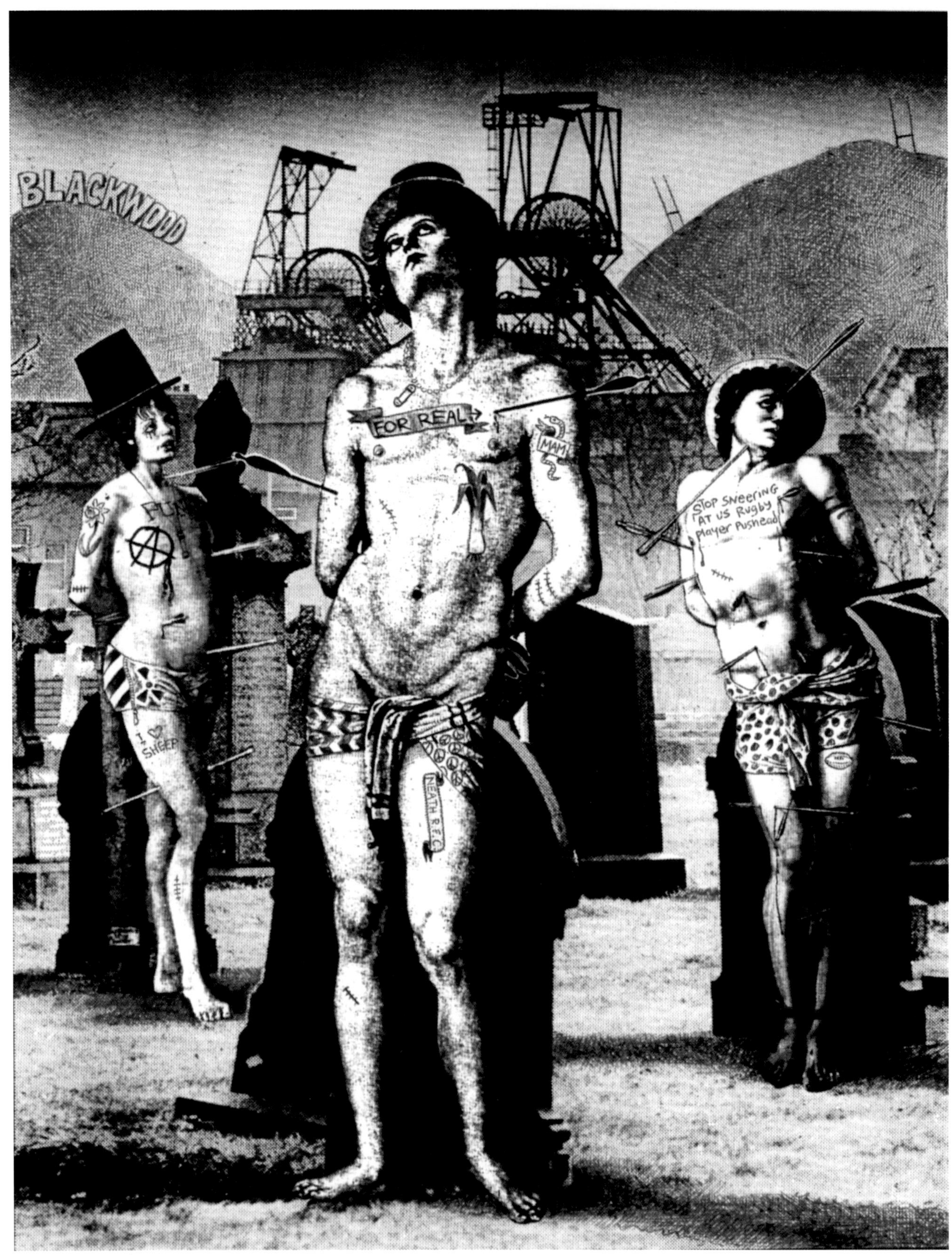

BLACKWOOD
FOR REAL
MAM
NEATH R.F.C.
FUK
I ♥ SHEEP
Stop Sneering
at us Rugby
Player Pushead

It's Not Enough

You can be the last one standing
While the surface of the earth melts
Like a chocolate bar
Throw me out with the garbage
I'll never get that far
Bury me in the street
Scatter me like beads of mercury
Have me stuffed just like Trigger
Or pickled for a souvenir
My paint is peeling
My nails all rust
At the peak of my popularity
I'm crumbling into dust
It's not enough . . .

I'm entertaining, I'm mesmerizing
Collapsing as we speak
I left my clothes all neatly folded
Now I'm heading on up the creek
Past the university of boredom
The shrunken-head bar and grill
The death-wish casino
The paradise garage sale
On the deck of the wreck of the Marie Celeste
Where Rock 'n' Roll came to die
I'll still be trying to change the channels
As my life goes flashing by
It's not enough . . .

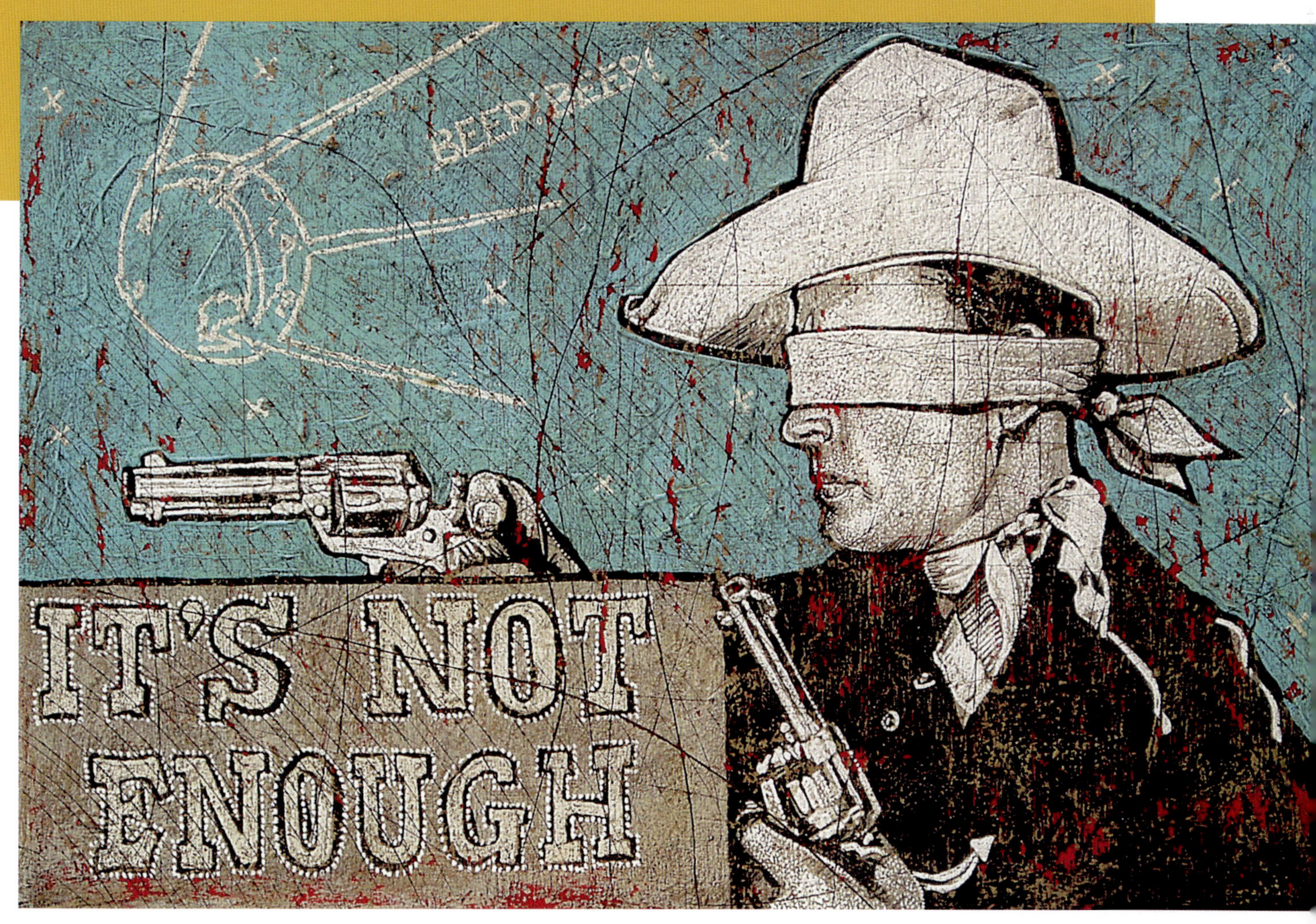

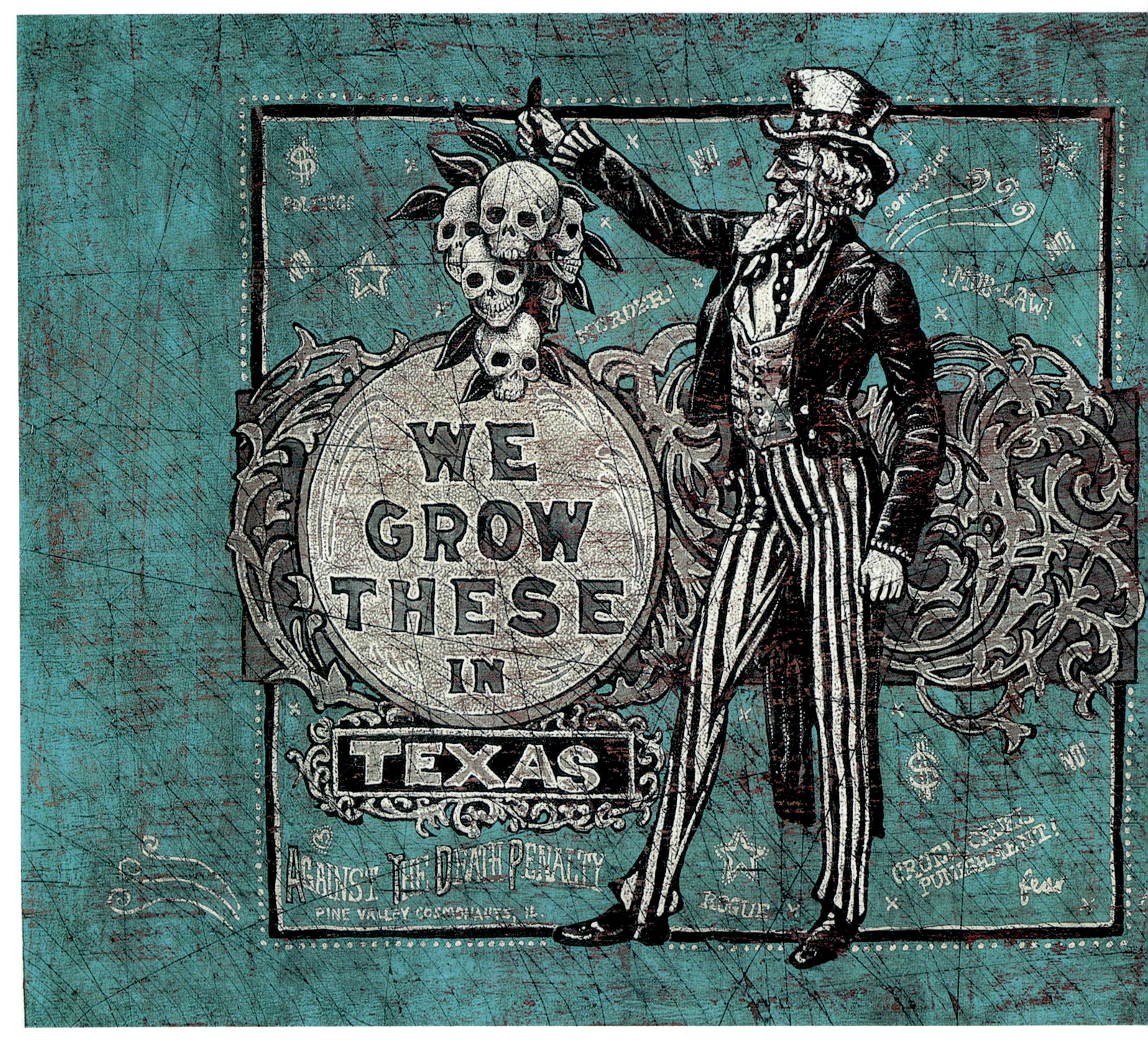
WE GROW THESE IN
TEXAS
AGAINST THE DEATH PENALTY
PINE VALLEY COSMONAUTS IL

THE EXECUTIONER'S LAST SONGS

Most benefit albums are crappy, tossed-together, artistic botch-jobs that guilt you into coughing up for causes no one could really disagree with anyway—a feel-good rush of righteous concern that quickly fades to complacency and amnesia.

So we decided to make a record to support the Illinois Coalition Against The Death Penalty. No fear of fluffiness there!

Activist and death-row lawyer Dick Cunningham told me that support for capital punishment in the United States is a mile wide but only an inch thick. I wanted to make a really good CD as an extra little chisel to get modest but useful amounts of cash into the hands of an organization that needed it and knew what to do with it. These people had rolled up their sleeves & for years had fought a contentious, glamour-free battle in the courts—case by case, out in the cold & on death row, where no one's supposed to care. Things were moving. Even the Republican governor of Illinois recognized the system was broken. There was a moratorium in place.

We called the albums THE EXECUTIONER'S LAST SONGS and they were packed with murder ballads—old, very old, & brand spanking new. "The Pine Valley Cosmonauts consign songs of murder, mob law & cruel, cruel punishment to the realm of myth, memory & history"—or so it says on the cover. Meaning: wouldn't it be nicer if we could just sing about all this mayhem without actually having to do it . . . wishful thinking on my part.

Initially the death songs vs. the death idea was a sort of one-liner, no more than the conceptual glue to hold these records together. Later I realized that many of the songs we'd chosen had in fact been big hits during Country's golden age, despite their morbid subject matter—but none of them could be played

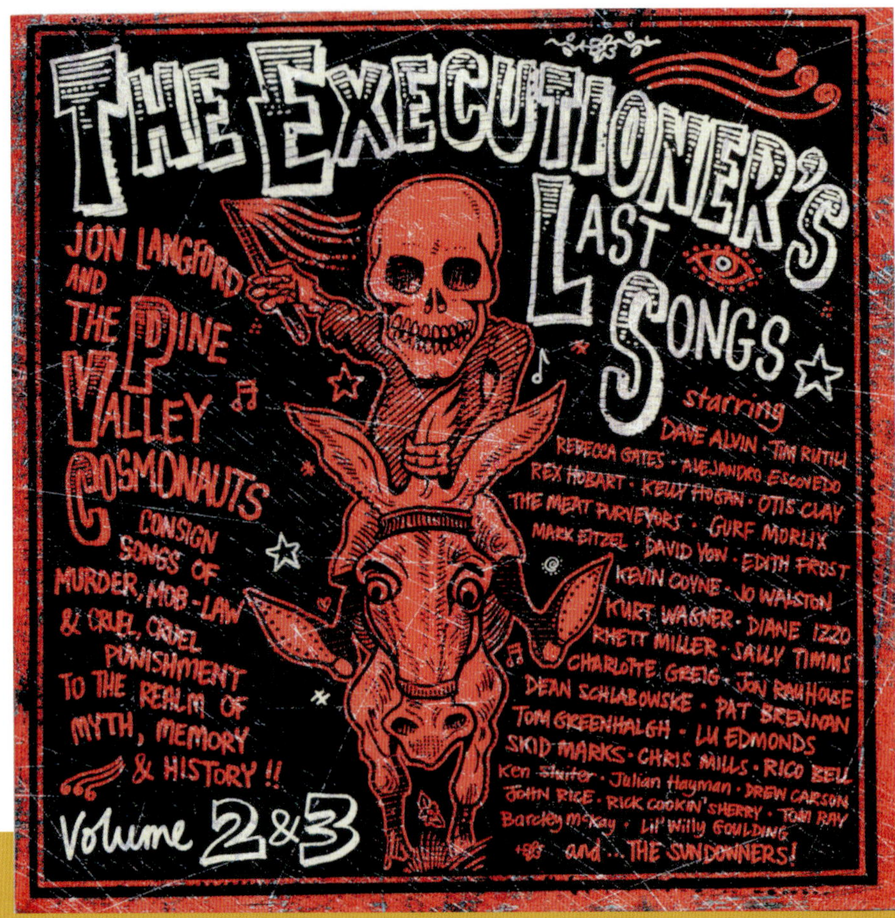

Idiot Whistle

"This disc is dedicated to Richard Cunningham, an attorney for condemned men his whole legal career. He used to tell me that when politicians came to talk about the Death Penalty to get out my idiot whistle. Politicians love the Death Penalty because it makes a bunch of candy-asses look like tough guys. Kind of like the war on drugs or terror or poverty. Well, they want you to know that they are the warring-est little soldiers on God's green earth. They especially love executions, there's nothing like putting a black man or a brown man or some good ole hillbilly white trash to death. Kind of makes their shoes shine a little brighter, makes 'em feel downright up-righty. Politicians know better than you and me, hell they'll tell you that themselves. An Eye for an Eye? Meaning when one spills blood we should spill more blood to make things right? That makes perfect political sense. Just remember, here in Illinois 17 men just walked off Death Row after being exonerated by DNA testing. An Eye for an Eye. Know that when the state executes someone they do it in our name. They're doing it for you and me. Know that execution does not bring back a loved one to life, that execution degrades us and dehumanizes us, that revenge and justice are not the same thing and killing anyone for any reason furthers the cycle of violence. The President has just signed off on another execution. Get out your idiot whistle."

—Tony Fitzpatrick (from *The Executioner's Last Songs*. Volume 1) on Country radio today. Death songs, cheating songs, drinking songs—the stock currency of classic Country—have been banished from the airwaves in favor of a weird sanitized fantasy vision of small-town, bible-belt America, where the only D.I.V.O.R.C.E. is from reality.

5 minutes of field research on Chicago's US99 is all you need to confirm my prejudices. "Let them cry, let them giggle / Let them sleep in the middle / Oh, just let them be little," followed by "If Heaven was a pie it would be cherry"—which did at least mention death, but only as a cozy conduit between earthly abstinence and an afterlife where we eat pie and watch fireflies at twilight for all eternity. If Loretta Lynn had released "The Pill" in 2005, her cheeky feminist salute to chemically empowered redneck homemakers would never have been heard, since recreational sex and contraception currently don't play too well up the towers of Nashville. Tranquilizers are the preferred prescription. Meanwhile, on the streets of urban America, down on death row and far away in ruined Iraqi cities, revenge killing is the growth industry.

So far from consigning anything to myth and history, we were just doing what good art (and proper Country music) had always done—confronting the realities of our time and posing a question: Why is this material so unsuitable for the ears of contemporary Americans, when their grandparents used to eat it up?

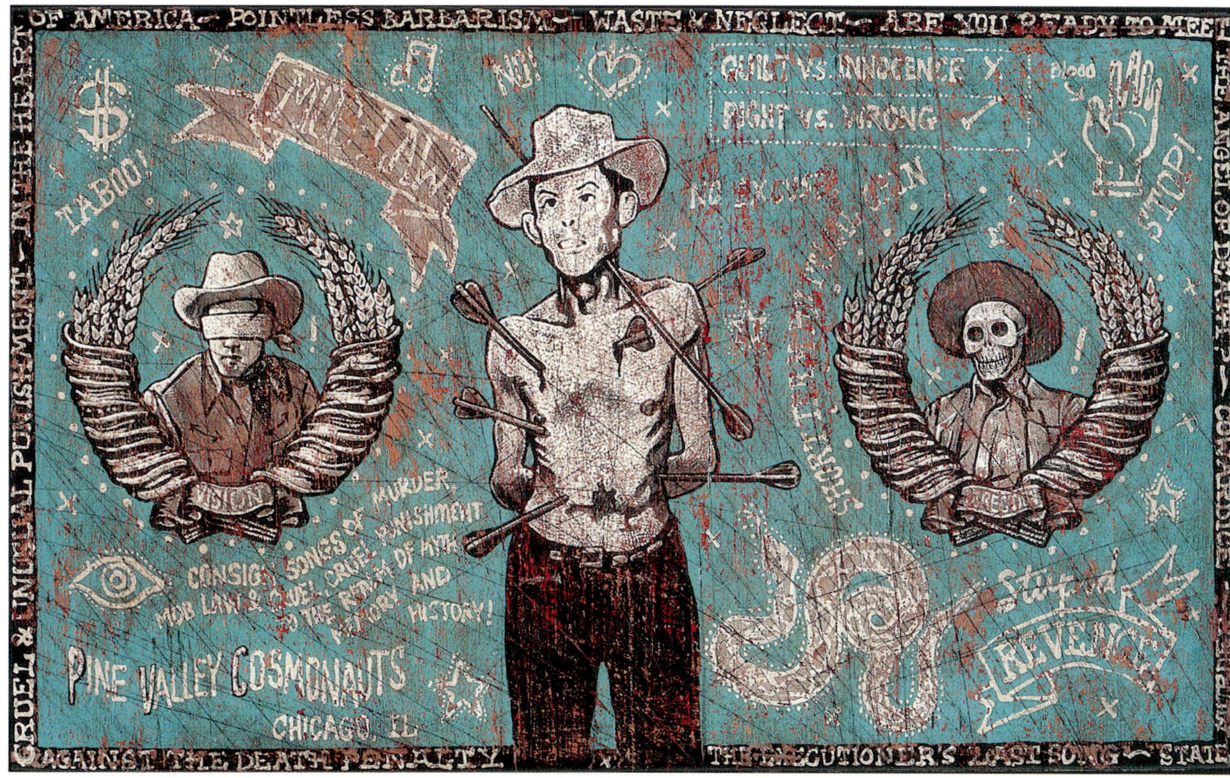

Charlton Heston comes down from the mountain and plants the stone tablets in the courthouse yard. On the Top Ten rundown "Thou Shalt Not Kill" is number 6 with a bullet! But the hanging judge still dons the black cap & hands down the sentence. "Thou shalt not kill" . . . but who exactly art Thou? And who decides who isn't?

The State kills the killer, in my name, in your name. Cleanly and neatly, ropes are measured, the condemned is weighed, the gurney is sterilized, the chemicals measured out, some guns hold blank bullets, and the executioner's face is always well hidden.

No forgiveness, no redemption—only CONTROL, as the wild and the random, the hot blood and the passion are fed their last supper before eradication.

The Special Forces move into the insurgent-held city and the first thing they do is secure the hospital. Because if they control the hospital they control the flow of information, the numbers of the dead. They decide how many died. And our dead are flown home at night, under cover of darkness, to unknown locations. No photographs, no ceremony, no honor guard, no dead soldiers in this screenplay—body bags slip in thru the back door like coy celebs.

Control the body, control the mind. Control the songs and control our dreams, and those dreams like our deaths won't belong to us anymore.

No death songs on the Nashville radio. No songs that might inflame our base killer instincts or fuel our wildest dreams. Too much reality might go to our heads, so contemporary country music becomes just another way to hide from an evil frightening world, like golf and extreme makeovers. So what? It's just entertainment. It's not doing anyone any harm. But Country Radio's shrinking playlists and continuing retreat from its own history mirror a deeper malaise that's eating this country alive—a consolidation of power and money that's forced America's own retreat from democracy and the continuing disenfranchisement of its people.

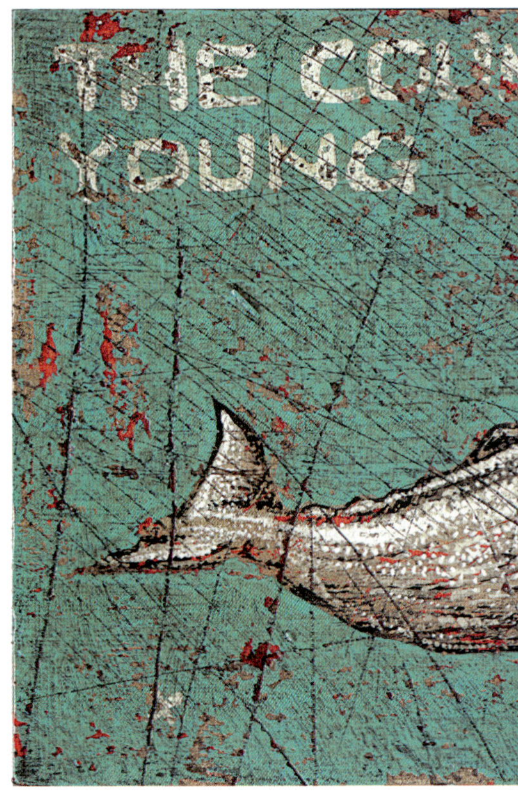

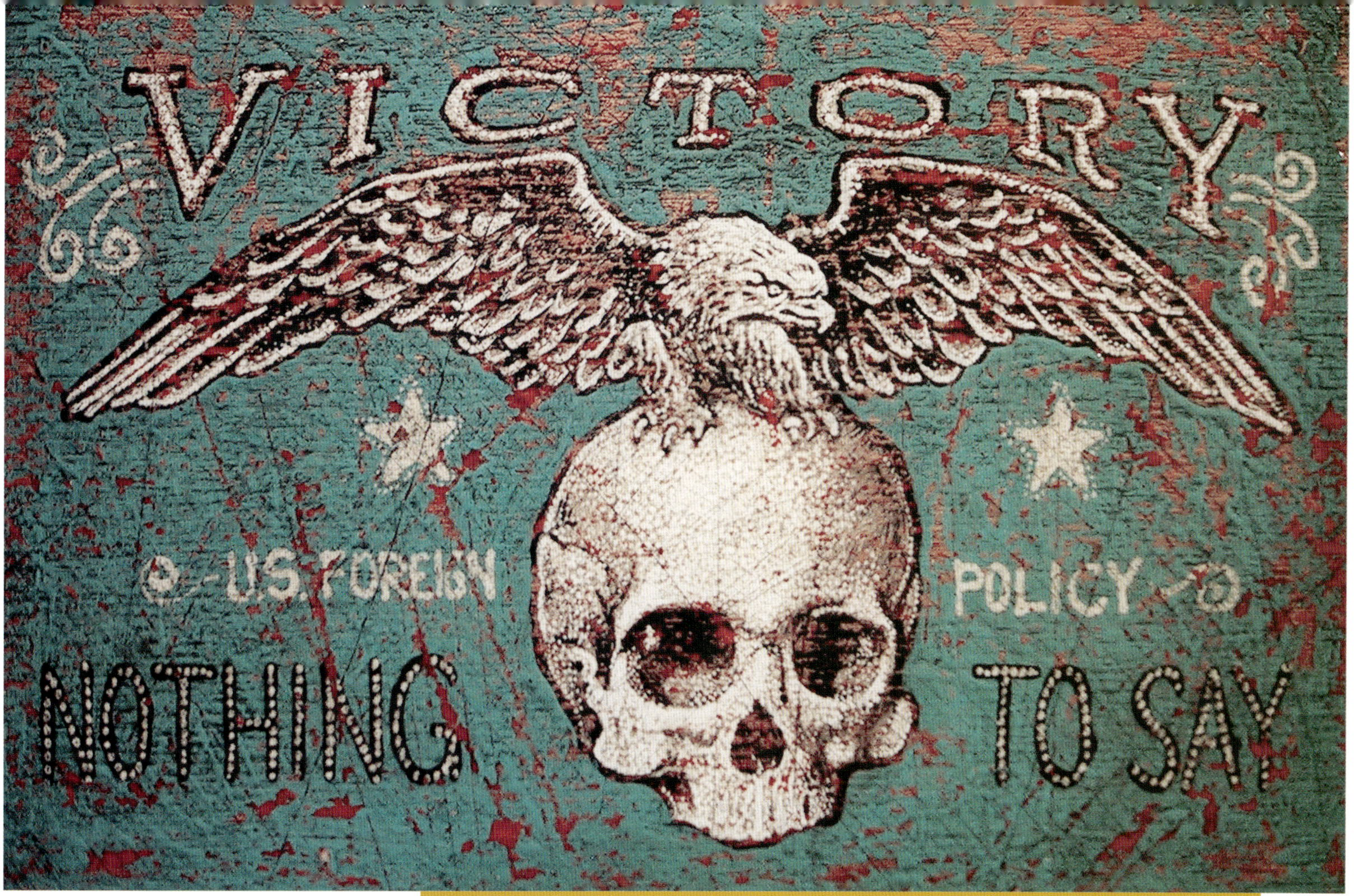

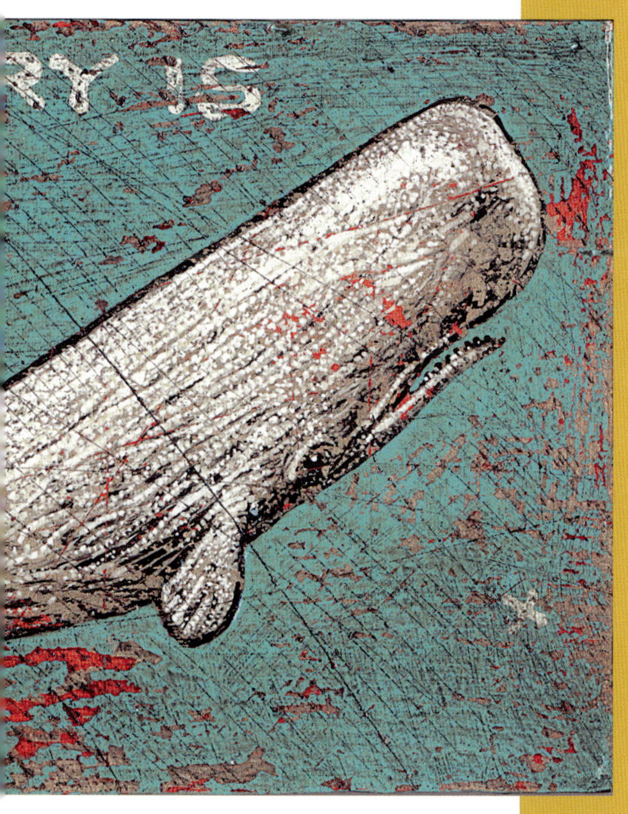

The Country Is Young

The country is young, just crawled to its feet
Takes a step and collapses in a heap
Resist the temptation to slap the child down
Try to remember its age
Realize the potential, deflect all its rage
Not too big on the sharing, the gentle or the caring
The country is young, the country is young

Lost like an orphan, on the day it was found
Taken down to the river, but it just wouldn't drown
So big and so clumsy, never knew it was born
Suddenly torn in bright lights & loud noise
You'd better wipe its fat ass & buy it some toys
Not too big on the sharing, the gentle or the caring
The country is young, the country is young ➡➡

The country is young, it's got bad growing pains
Growing out of its clothes, stretching out on the plains
& One day, I know, before it's much older
It's gonna pick up the phone and call the cops on me
Feed on itself to set us all free
Not too big on the caring, the gentle or the sharing
But still so much fun – the country is young

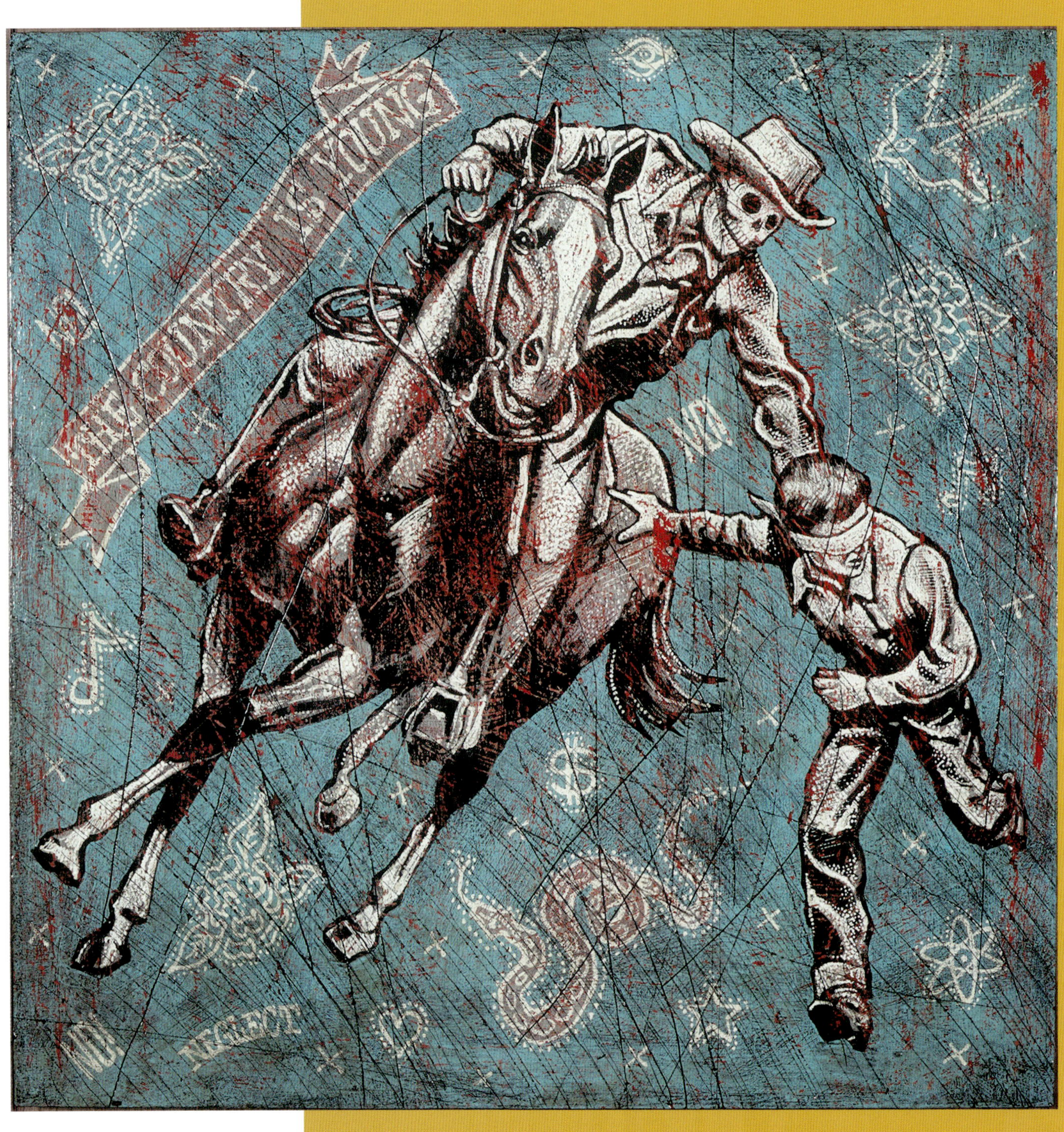

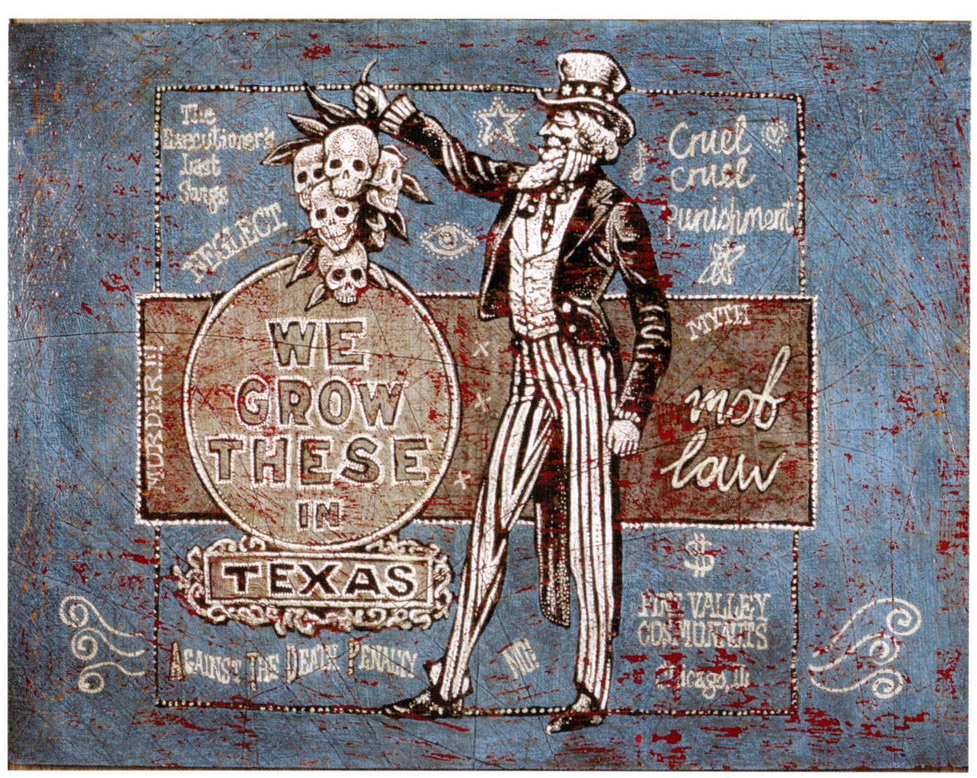

If, as Rennie Sparks says, songs are like dreams, powerful and non-literal, a place where we process and make sense of the information, symbols, moral choices, taboos, and unspeakable urges that bombard us everyday, then to remove or censor them—to deny their existence—borders on a form of mind control. But what do they have to gain by force feeding us dross and turning us into zombies? Well, quite a lot. I could be charitable and assume this isn't a deliberate policy but rather the unfortunate by-product of a greedy obsession with increased advertising revenue, maximum profits, and blissfully fellated stockholders. But it's mind control, all the same.

I worried that a CD of death, murder, and execution songs aimed at opposing the death penalty might be seen as a contradiction—but aren't the forces that demand and uphold capital punishment the same as those that suppress and deny the legacy of these songs? Songs so powerful and scary they just don't trust us with them. Songs that remind us that we have a history and there might be something to learn from it.

Mussolini described Fascism as the perfect marriage of State and Corporate interests: toss in a smoke grenade of fundamentalist fervor and you've got the current blinkered, virulent, incompetent, and self-serving elite, moving surely to control our lives and deaths, our songs and our dreams. They recognize no contradictions, mouthing THOU SHALT NOT KILL as they pull the switch and wave the bombers off over the horizon.

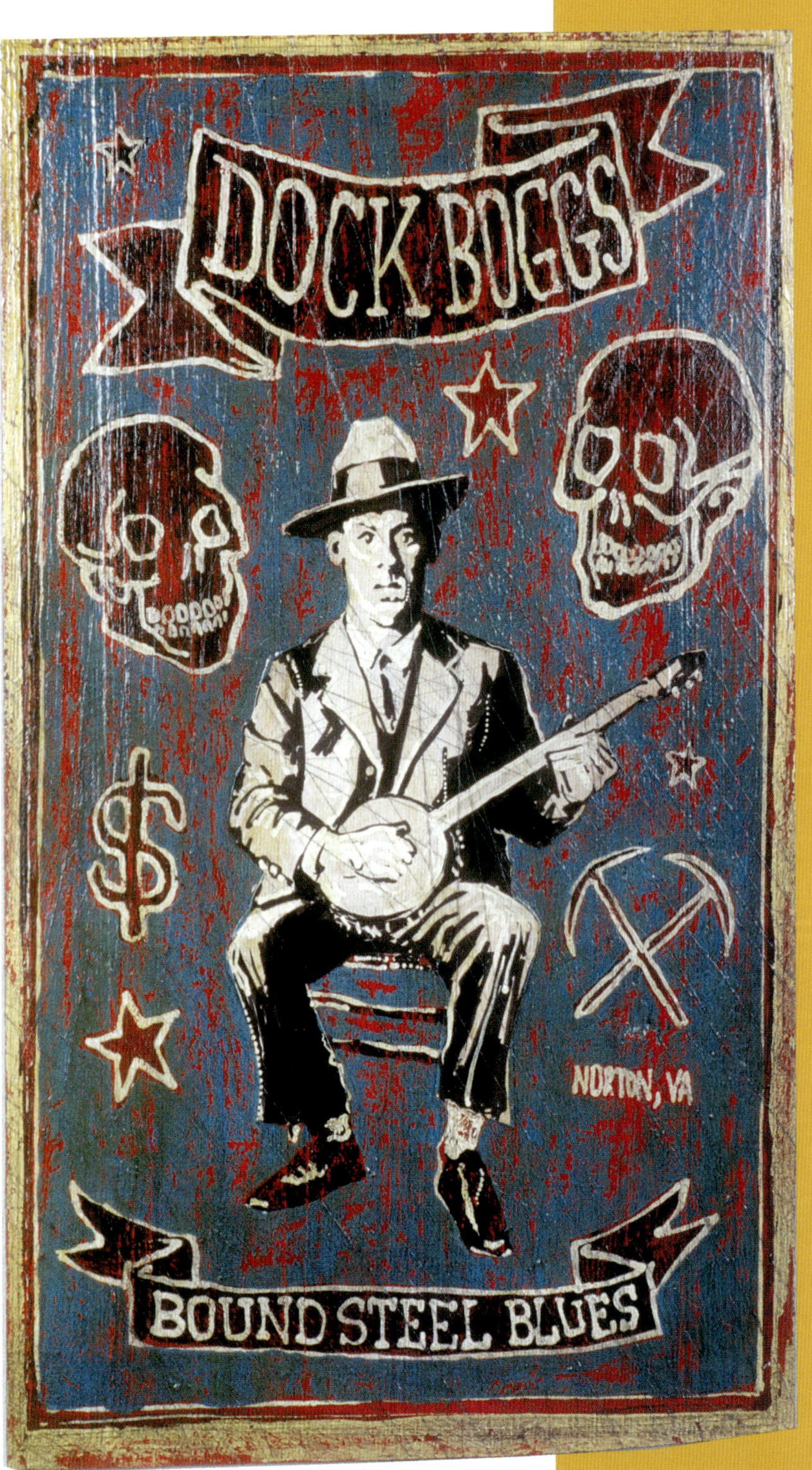

Hell's Roof

History is written by the winner
This is a loser's song
I took this job in the summer
Never saw the winter rolling on
Never thought it would end in a second
A burn out smoking wreck
Expectations and ambitions
Were just a rope around my neck

Broke my back to earn a crust
Saw my dreams die in the dust
Now I'm walking on hell's roof
Looking at the flowers
Walking on hell's roof
Looking at the flowers

Oh all in bloom – Red yellow and blue
So sweet and true – There's nothing better to do

Well I'm not hiding
Come and find me
What am I doing?
There's no need to remind me
Walking on hell's roof
Looking at the flowers
In the A to B and the miles per hour
Keeping out of reach of that higher power
Where the bees are buzzing in the April showers

The spoils belong to the victor
This is a consolation song
Your life is science fiction
In a flash then you'll be gone
No more trials and no more trouble
Bad luck or bursting bubbles
Walking on hell's roof
Looking at the flowers

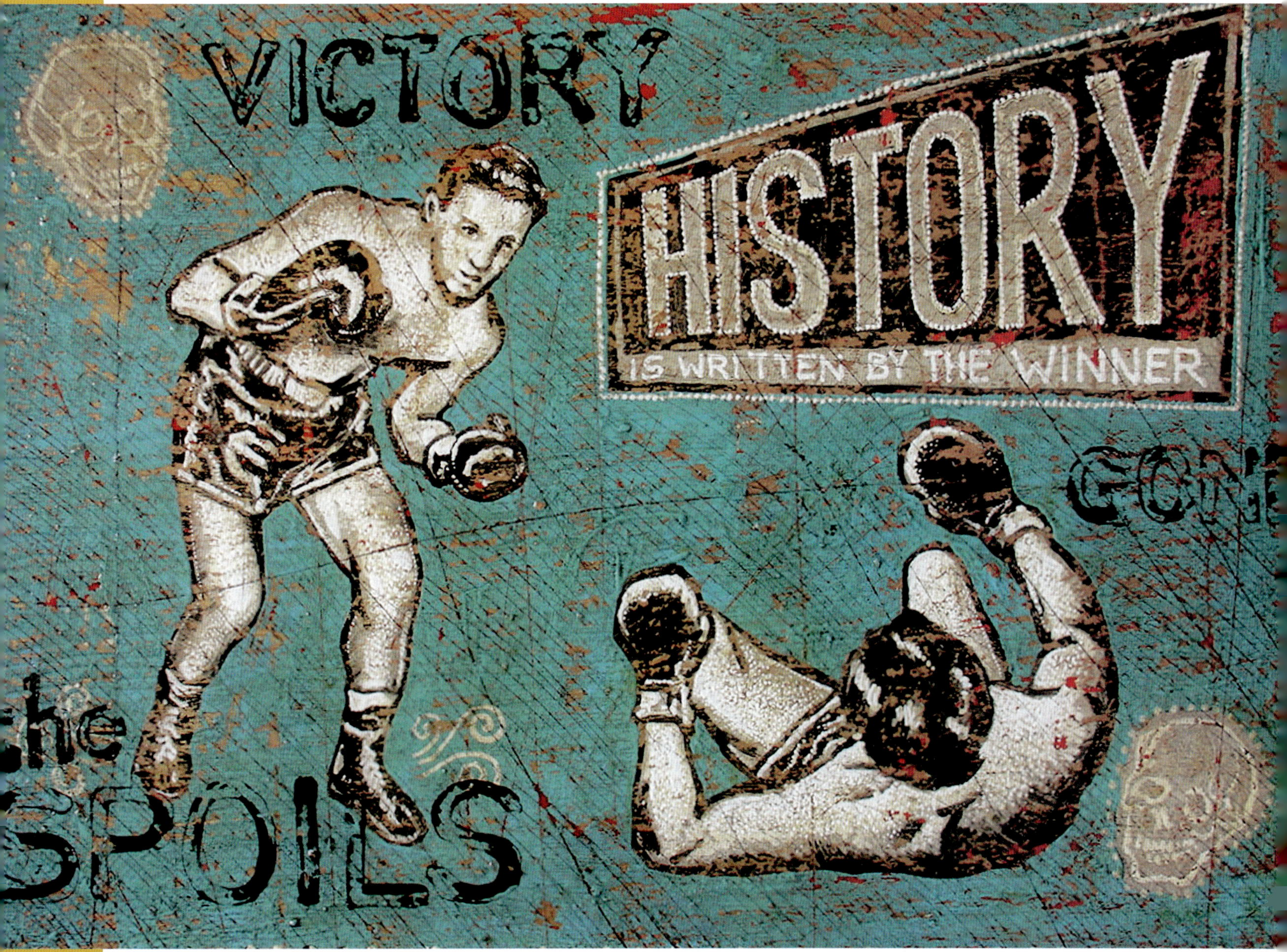

VICTORY

HISTORY
IS WRITTEN BY THE WINNER

GONE

the
SPOILS

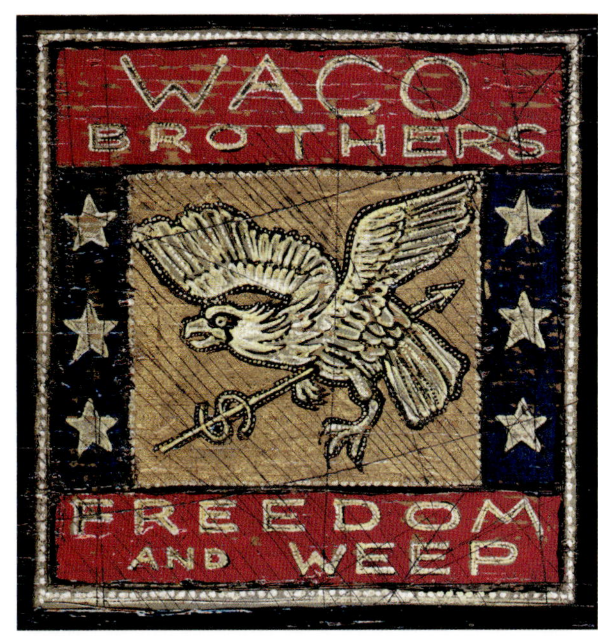

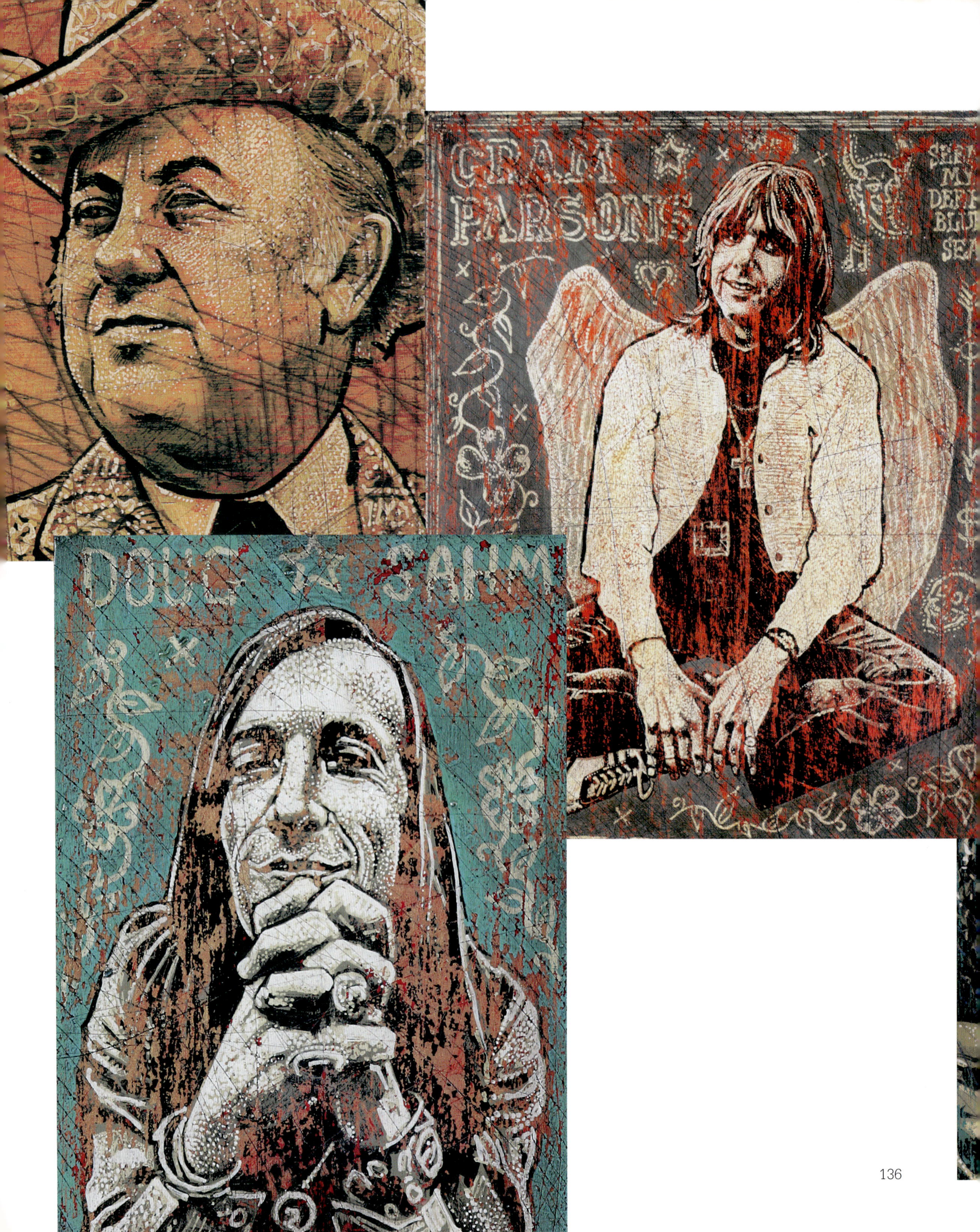
GRAM
PARSONS
SELL
MY
DEEP
BLUE
SEA
DOUG SAHM

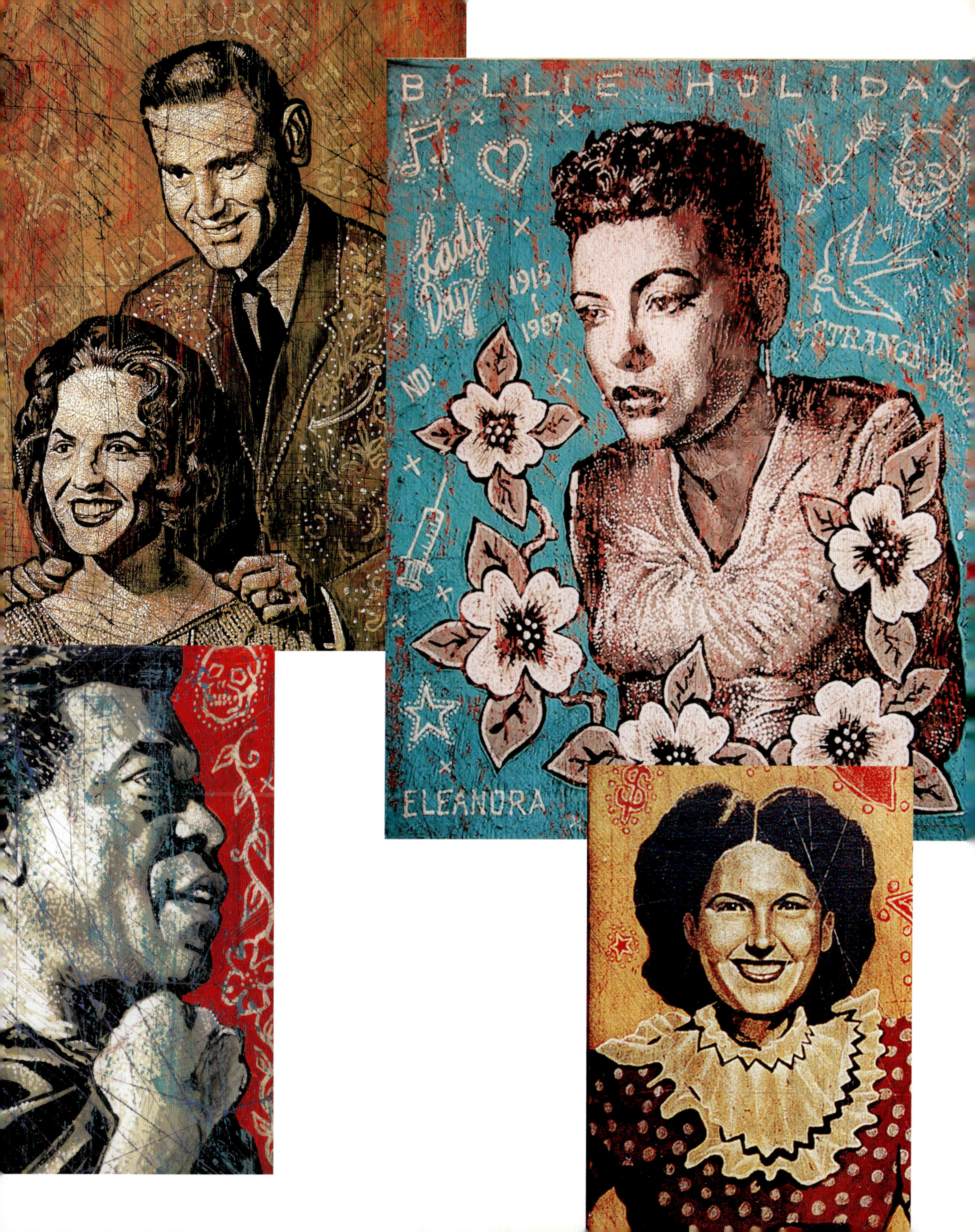

BILLIE HOLIDAY
Lady Day
1915
1959
ELEANORA

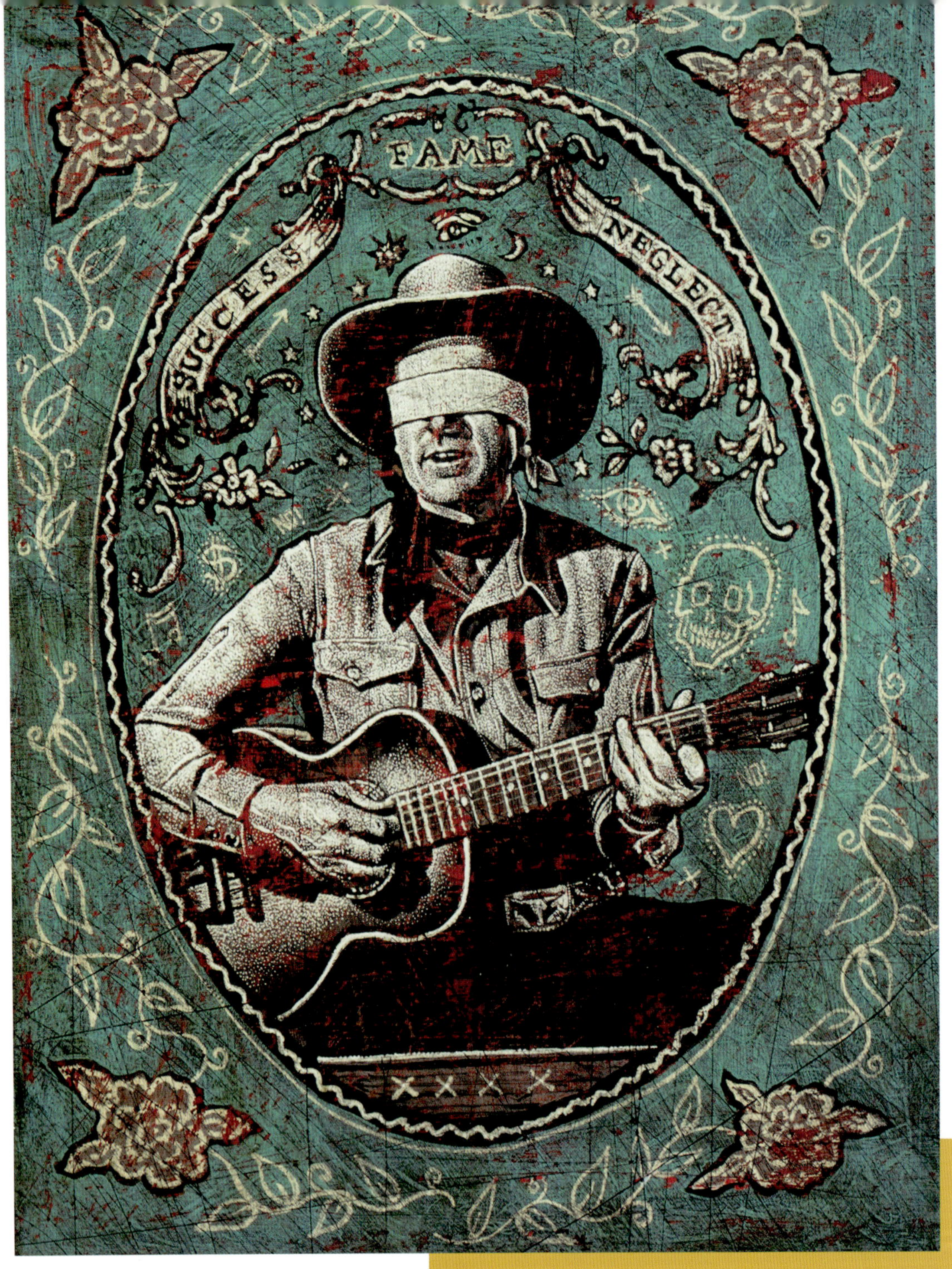

Chosen One

The winner shall win and keep winning
The last will again be least
Alarm bells ringing, turn back the clock
You're invited – you're the feast?
What a way to celebrate
Born this day my only son
God & nature having fun
Daddy says you are the chosen one
Chosen, chosen one

And he's the master of disaster
Treating wounds with sticking plaster
Kill or cure, whichever's faster

Gotta get some heel in here
Somebody'll have to pay
Armageddon out of here
Dragged out by another wave

Loaves & fishes, drugs & guns
One for all and all for one
Dumb Boy the patriot
One day you'll run out of luck
Krakatoa, east of Java
Smother me with molten lava
Call the master of disaster
Treat your wounds with sticking plaster
Kill or cure, kill or cure, kill or cure
Whichever's faster

This mayhem so seductive
This destruction is instructive
Pop-a-top for mass production
Learn to follow new instructions
Cruel New Jerusalem
Population minus one
Leave a message, got to run
Daddy says I was the chosen one
The chosen, chosen one
He's the master of disaster
Treating wounds with sticking plaster
Kill or cure, kill or cure, kill or cure
Whichever's faster

Now God is weeping
Took the day off, drunk or sleeping
Your faith is shaken, there's no mistaking
We're only as strong as the drugs we're taking
Flesh and blood and opium
Daddy says I was the chosen one
Slay the dragon, make a buck
One day, one day, one day you'll run out of luck

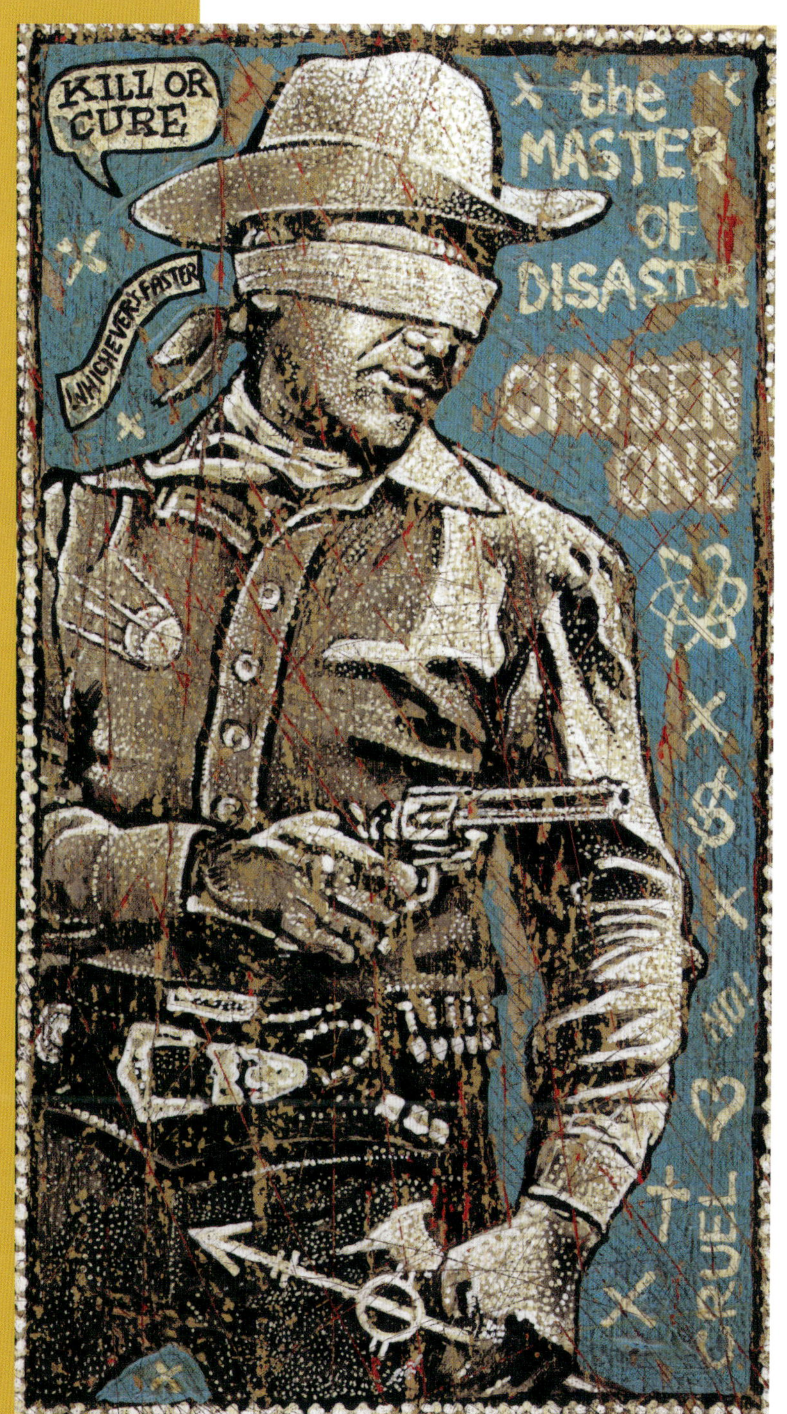

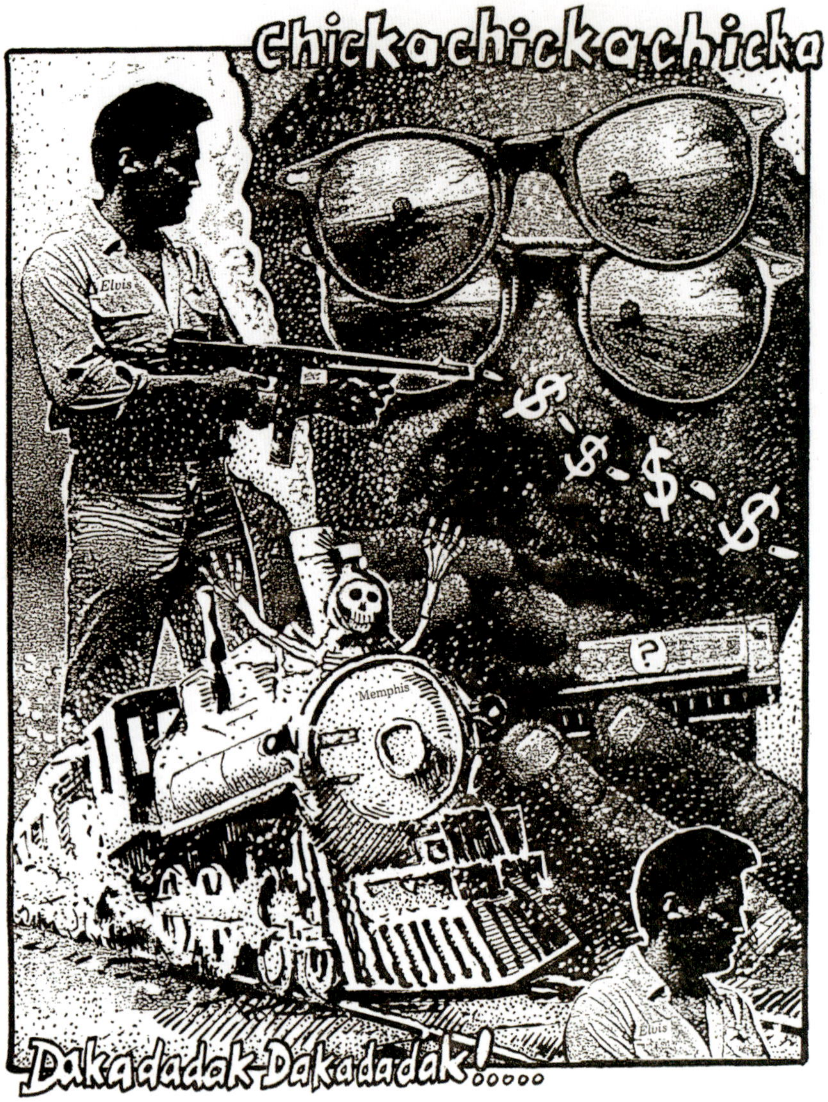
Chickachickachicka
Elvis
Memphis
Elvis
Dakadadak Dakadadak!.....

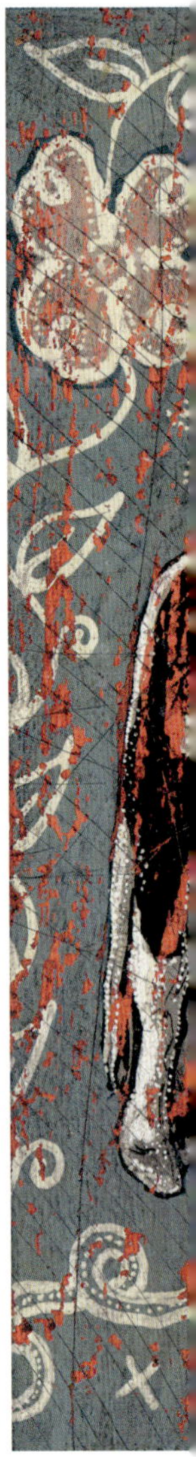

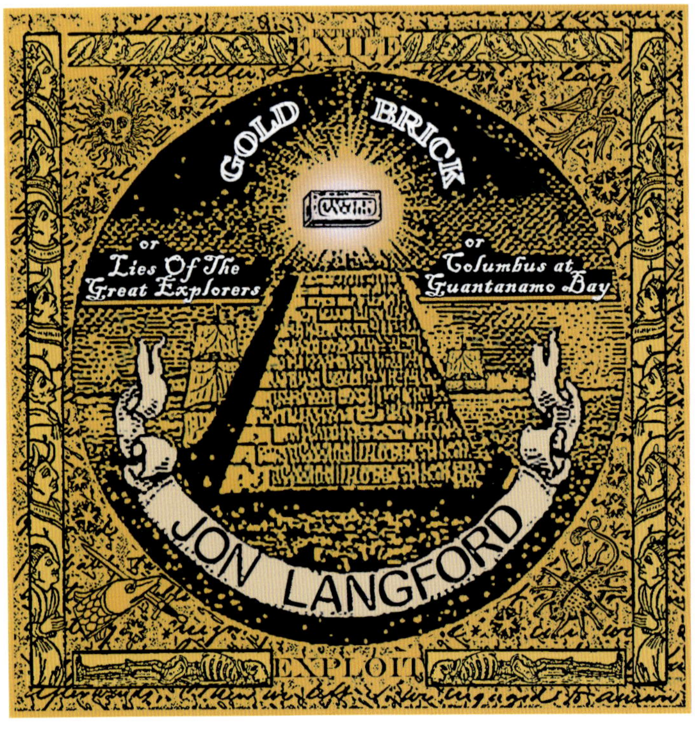
EXILE
GOLD BRICK
or Lies Of The Great Explorers
or Columbus at Guantanamo Bay
JON LANGFORD
EXPLOIT

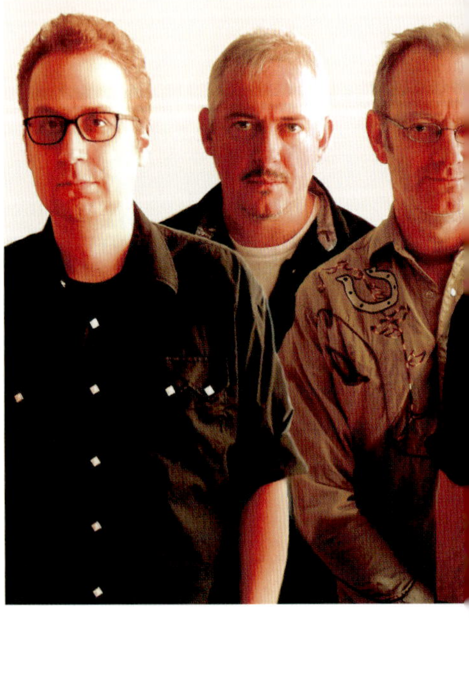

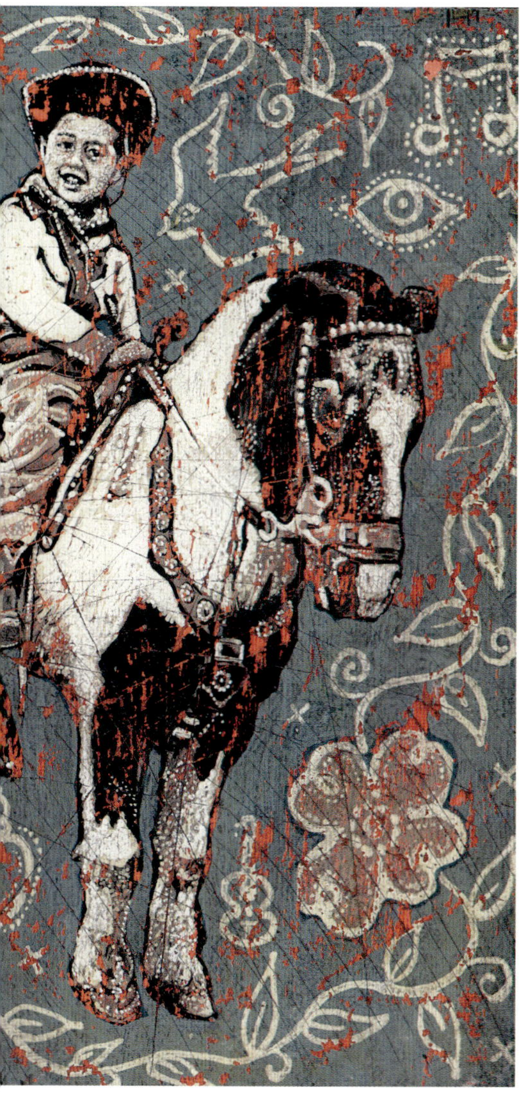

INDEX OF ART

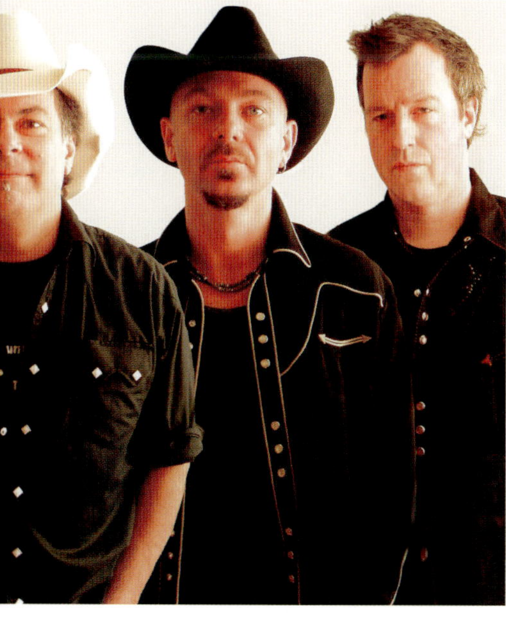

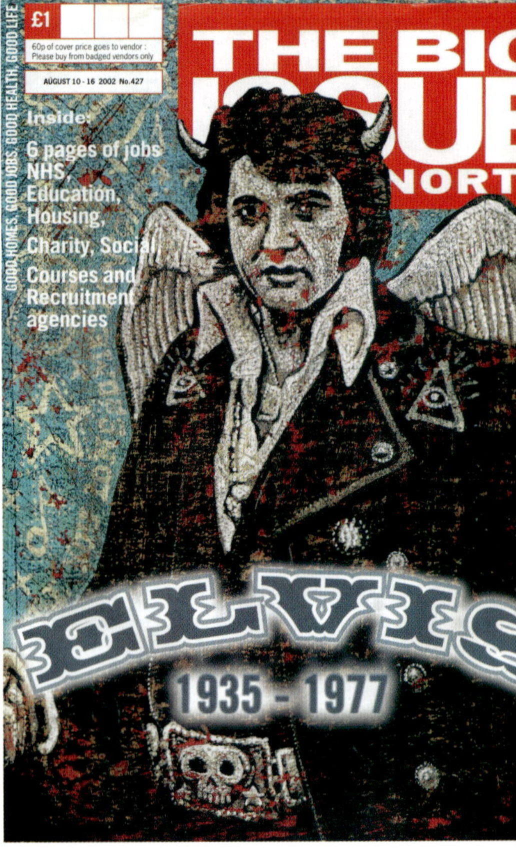

£1
60p of cover price goes to vendor :
Please buy from badged vendors only
AUGUST 10 - 16 2002 No.427
THE BIG
ISSUE
NORTH
Inside:
6 pages of jobs
NHS
Education,
Housing,
Charity, Social
Courses and
Recruitment
agencies
ELVIS
1935 - 1977

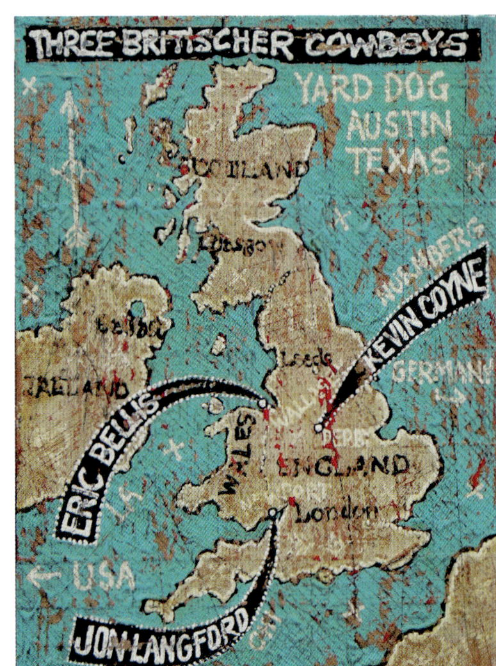

THREE BRITISCHER COWBOYS
YARD DOG
AUSTIN
TEXAS
SCOTLAND
KEVIN COYNE
GERMANY
IRELAND
Leeds
ERIC BELLIS
WALES
ENGLAND
London
USA
JON LANGFORD

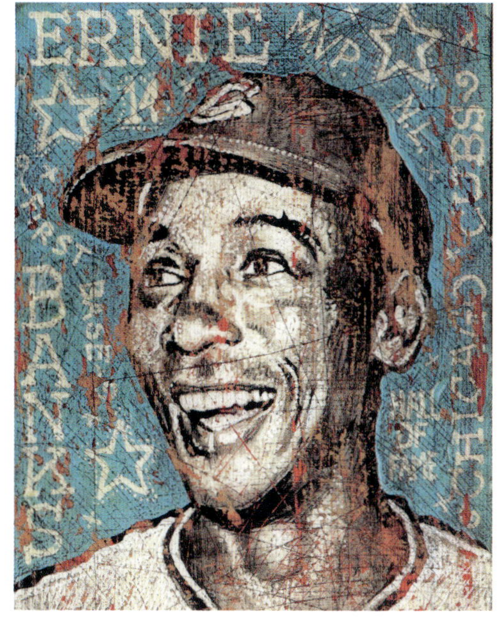

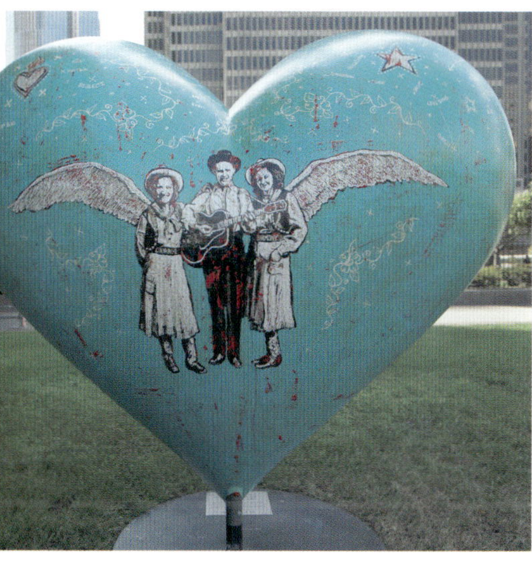

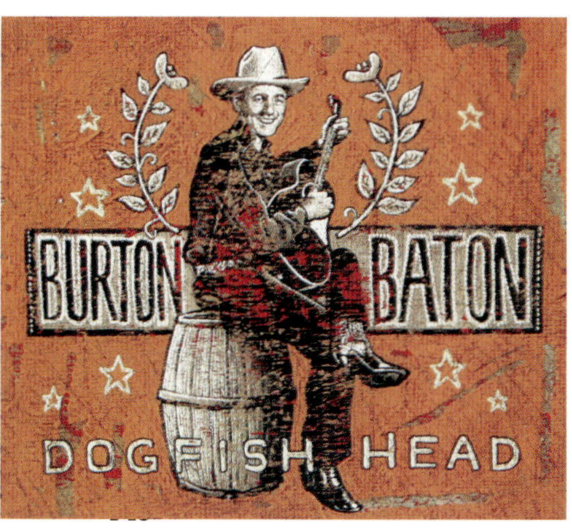

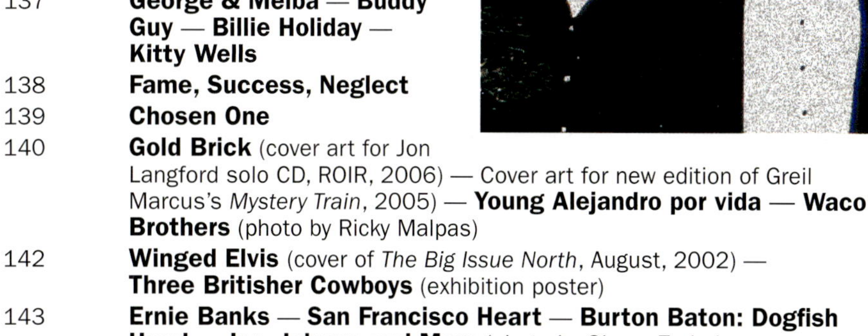

ACKNOWLEDGMENTS

Thanks to all Mekons, deputy Mekons, Waco Brothers, Pine Valley Cosmonauts, and Three Johns, Ron & Wendy Weiss and everyone at Shirts Our Business for their unwavering generosity, David O. Cornelius back in Bettws for making me look, T.J. Clark for calling my Mum, Terry Atkinson for the historical snot, David Ravel at Alverno Presents and Tom Crawford (WMSE) for instigating the *Executioner's Last Songs* performance, Tony Fitzpatrick for a mighty shove in the right direction (and again for introducing me to Dick Cunningham), Theresa Mucha and Steve Campbell for the skills they shared at Big Cat & White Wings, Rico Bell for his wicked craftiness and inspiring lunchtime trips to the printers, Sally Timms for the brutal editing & finely tuned pomposity radar, Jean & John, Dylan Thomas, Maria Cunningham, LL, Wendy Frith, New Arcadian Press, Carlton B. Morgan for the little brown envelopes full of great pop speech bubbles, The Ship & Pilot, Anne Lehman, Charlotte Greig & John Williams in alt. Cardiff, Marc Riley, The Man Band, Bet Jones, Bob DePugh, Jane Bowman, Billions, Lester Bangs, John Rice, Helmi Coyne, Chris Mills, Greil & Jenny Marcus, Johnny Cash, Tony Baker, Mr. Ash, Pat Brennan, Randy Franklin (& Jan & Chuckles) at Yard Dog, John Peel, Peter Wright at Buried Treasure & Low Noise, Frank Swider, the Ex, TAG in Nashville, Lucky Star in Milwaukee, Vito Acconci, Maxwell's, Dan Ferrara, Other Music, the Garofalos, Johnny Frigo, Thomas Masters, Morlen Sinoway, Mike Bordanero, Peter Taub at the MCA, Phillip Bither at the Walker, Dan Zanes, Kathy Acker, Hogan, Buckner, Burch, Loney, Dowd, Rosetta & Cindy Wills, John & Val Richards, Hywel at Llantarnam Grange, The Globe in St. Pete's, Roq La Rue in Seattle, La Luz de Jesus in Hollywood, Ralph and Finbar, Terry Nelson, Jenny Toomey, Amy Lombardi, Edith Frost, Hebe Joy, Rob Lentz, Augen Gallery in Portland, David Lusenhop (the Cincinnati Gravestone Kid), Mike & Colleen Miller, The Old Town School Of Folk Music, David Yow, Rosie Flores, Cousin Fred security, the Redskins, Mitch Flaco, Mark Terrill, Alejandro Escovedo, Steve Earle, Bill Leader, the Handsome Family, Sheila Sachs, Lounge Ax, Whirlaway, Bob Roth, Adrian Collins, Chris & Heather, Fred Armisen, Carmen & Imi Knoebel, Barbara Manning, Pete & Debbie, Julie & Rob, Irvine & Marjorie Young, The Rauhouses of Lilliwaup, Unca Dave, Graham Parker, Titch Jones, Slim's, Doug & Randy Simmons, the Sexy, Minus 5, the Hideout, WXRT for their eclectic leanings and opening day mayhem, Bloodshot, Kengineer, Touch & Go, Neil & Lucas Cooper, Schuba's, Brenda & Glen, Chip Taylor, Delilah's, Jean Cook, Xgau, Fitzgerald's, Tony Maimone, Ellie Hollinshead, Kevin Titzer, Legendary TJ's, Barry Mills, Louise & Dave Talbott, Gang Of Four, Dan Massey, Dr. George and Aphrodite Tsatsos, Big Len, Big Den, my Mum and my famous older brother Dave, Helen, Jimmy & Tommy, Chicago, Wales, and Steve Connell & Kathryn Juergens at VCP for somehow managing to put this book together...

Artwork photographed by Frank Swider, Marty Perez, James Crump, Randy Franklin, David Lusenhop, and Jon Langford.

www.mekons.com — www.bloodshotrecords.com — www.quarterstickrecords.com — www.roir-usa.com — www.buriedtreasurerecords.com — www.yarddog.com (permanent online art show at Yard Dog Folk Art, Austin, TX) — www.billions.com (Langford, Timms, Waco Brothers, Mekons booking) — www.icadp.org (Illinois Campaign against the Death Penalty)

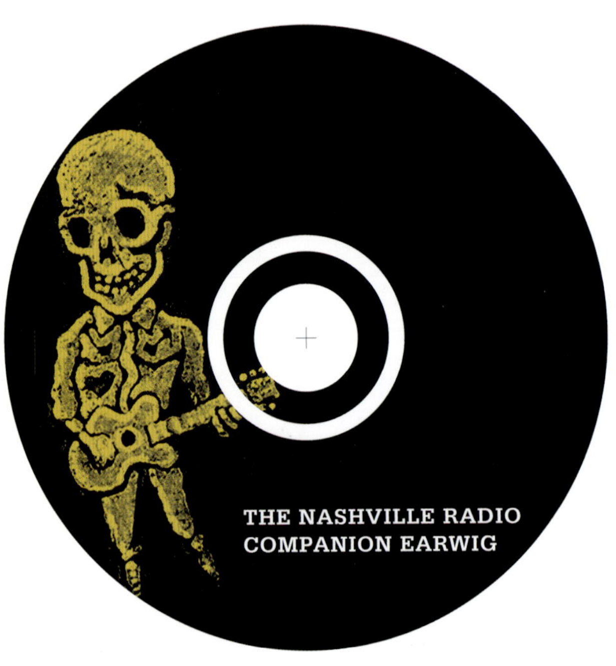

THE NASHVILLE RADIO COMPANION EARWIG

1. The Death of Country Music
2. Slightly South of The Border
3. Oh No, Hank!
4. Dollar Dress
5. Tubby Brothers
6. Now We Have the Bomb
7. Hell's Roof
8. The Return of the Golden Guitarist
9. Pill Sailor
10. Hank Signs His Contract
11. Insignificance
12. It's Not Enough
13. Ugly Band
14. Blink of an Eye
15. Tom Jones Levitation
16. I Picked Up the Pieces
17. Nashville Radio
18. The Country Is Young